A Photographic History of
AMPHIBIOUS WARFARE
1939-1945

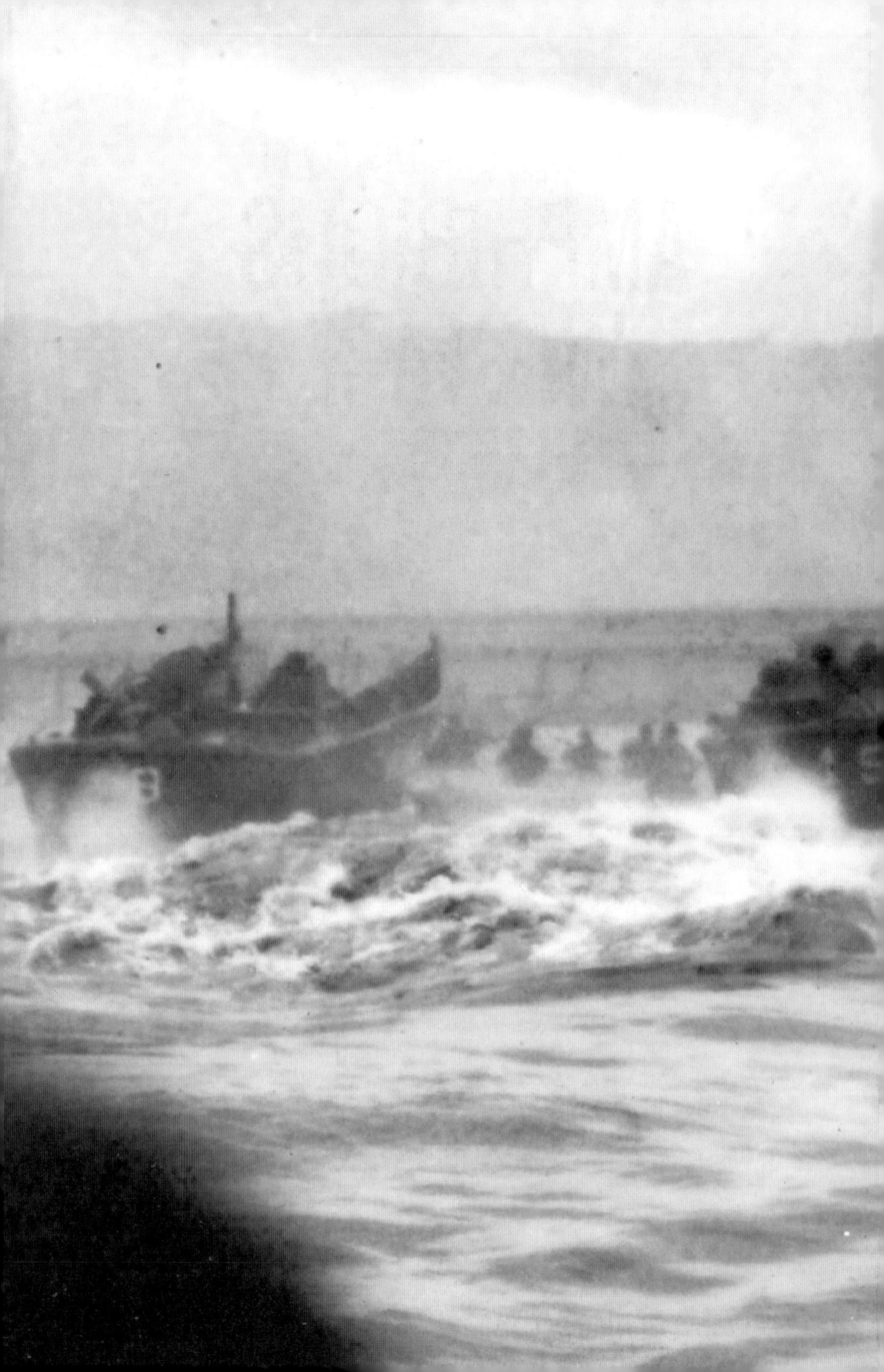

A Photographic History of
AMPHIBIOUS WARFARE
1939-1945

SIMON & JONATHAN FORTY

Pen & Sword
MILITARY

First published in Great Britain in 2023 by
PEN & SWORD MILITARY
an imprint of
Pen & Sword Books Ltd,
47 Church Street,
Barnsley,
South Yorkshire.
S70 2AS

Copyright © Pen & Sword 2023

A CIP record for this book is available from the British Library.

ISBN 9-781-39908-265-5

The right of Simon and Jonathan Forty to be identified as Authors of this Work has been asserted by him in accordance with the Copyright, Designs and Patents Act 1988.

All rights reserved. No part of this book may be reproduced or transmitted in any form or by any means, electronic or mechanical including photocopying, recording or by any information storage and retrieval system, without permission from the Publisher in writing.

Printed and bound by CPI UK

Pen & Sword Books Ltd incorporates the Imprints of Pen & Sword Aviation, Pen & Sword Maritime, Pen & Sword Military, Wharncliffe Local History, Pen & Sword Select, Pen & Sword Military Classics and Leo Cooper.

For a complete list of Pen & Sword titles please contact
Pen & Sword Books Limited
47 Church Street, Barnsley, South Yorkshire, S70 2AS, England
E-mail: enquiries@pen-and-sword.co.uk
Website: www.pen-and-sword.co.uk

Previous page: The ultimate amphibious operation of World War II—D-Day, 6 June 1944, Omaha Beach.

This page: A busy scene in the Pacific as USSs *LST-204*, *LSM-23* and landing craft landing cargo at Leyte, 20 October 1944.

Contents

Introduction 6

Chapter One **Raids** 32

Chapter Two **Landings** 54

Chapter Three **Evacuations** 176

Chapter Four **What Might Have Been** 190

Appendices 198
   1. Landing Craft 198
   2. Resupply 214
   3. Waterproofing 218
   4. Medical 224
   5. Intelligence 228
   6. Beaches: control and construction 230

Abbreviations 237
Acknowledgements and Credits 238
Bibliography 239
Index of Operations 240

Kwajalein—waves of LVTs and landing craft head for the beach in a well-organised, carefully planned attack. By 1944, the Allies had the tools, tactics and training necessary to conduct successful amphibious warfare.

Introduction

Amphibious warfare—sending a force by sea to assault a hostile shore by landing troops—had been practiced for centuries before World War II. Examples abound: from antiquity, the Trojan war and the Roman invasion of Britain, the Viking attacks on many European shores, the Mongol invasions of Japan in the 13th century and the Japanese of Korea in the 16th century—and in the 19th century the British campaign on Walcheren, the assault of the Allies against Russia in the Crimean War or the Union assault on Fort Fisher during the American Civil War.

World War I also saw large-scale amphibious attacks. The Gallipoli landings of April 1915 showed the problems inherent in such operations. Some half a million men became casualties as the Turkish Army held off an Allied force intent on knocking Turkey out of the war it had recently joined. This attack, promoted by British First Sea Lord Winston Churchill, highlighted many of the factors that would need to be considered carefully—and handled rather better—in future operations. From the start, the specifics of the mission were unclear and the location of the landings were indicative of overconfidence and bad planning. Poor logistics; faulty maps and intelligence; lack of artillery and other equipment; insanitary conditions—all contributed to the Allied failure and high casualty figures. Gallipoli showed how it shouldn't be done.

In 1917, the Germans launched an amphibious operation on a smaller scale than Gallipoli. Operation Albion landed 24,500 men in the west Estonian archipelago and saw the Germans successfully push the Russians out. All three services played their part, with a strong accent on minesweeping. This operation pointed the way for the future.

In 1940 it was the Germans again who showed modern inter-Service cooperation when it invaded Norway. Amphibious warfare now incorporated an important aerial component in a combined operation that saw paratroops join ship-borne troops in an attack that was heavily supported by bomber aircraft. The German success—although they lost the cruiser *Blücher* and missed the opportunity to capture the Norwegian king, parliament and gold reserves—saw Norway fall, but with significant naval losses, particularly destroyers. This would prove a major disadvantage later in 1940 when they started to plan for Operation *Seelöwe*: the sea-borne invasion of Britain.

Perhaps more important to the story of amphibious warfare was the little-known landing operation at Bjerkvik on 13 May 1940, when landing craft followed a

Continued on p. 13.

Above: The Seven Years' War pitted Britain against France and, from 1761, Spain. The response to Spain's declaration of war were the 1762 expeditions to Cuba and the Philippines, where they assaulted and took Havana and Manila. This etching shows the unopposed landings and the attack on Fort Cojimar, Havana, on 7 June 1762.

Below: The landings of the British expeditionary force at Aboukir on 8 March 1801 were opposed by General Louis Friant, 2,000 men and 10 guns. The landing boats carried 50 men each who attacked the defenders with bayonets and routed them—although some 730 were lost in the process.

Above: During the Crimean war, a British Division was landed off Eupatoria, north of Sevastopol on 13 September 1854. The lithograph shows the men on landing barges pulled by whaleboats manned by sailors. The soldiers carried heavy loads: rifle, bayonet, 50 rounds of ammunition; blanket and greatcoat; extra boots, spare clothes; water and three days' rations (meat and biscuits).

Below: Another Crimean war landing, near Kerch on 22 May 1855. This was the second expedition (the French one had failed) which opened up the way into the Sea of Azov allowing the destruction of the Russian naval squadron there.

The Gallipoli landings proved unsuccessful and are remembered in particular by the Australian and New Zealand Army Corps—the ANZACs—who landed on 25 April 1915. The battles ended 10 months later on 9 January 1916 when the allied force was evacuated. The casualties were significant: 34,000 British dead, 9,800 French, 8,700 Australian, 2,700 New Zealand, 1,300 Indian and 49 Newfoundlanders—along with nearly 57,000 Turks. Many military strategists felt that it showed that amphibious warfare was only something for raiding.

Opposite, Above: ANZAC soldiers lined up on deck, carrying heavy backpacks, ready for the landing.

Opposite, Below: Landing troops at Anzac Beach on the day after the first landing. Note the shrapnel bursting over the boats and British battleship in the distance.

Above: Australian 4th Battalion and mules for the 26th (Jacob's) Indian Mountain Battery landing on 25 April.

Below: The beaches at Cape Hellas were under the guns of the Turkish fort at Sedd-el-Bahr. 300 men of the 700 first wave on V beach died.

Right: In September 1917, the Germans attacked the Baltic islands in the Gulf of Riga—Operation Albion. Strategically important to both sides, taking them would threaten St Petersburg and pressurise the Russians to surrender. This would allow men to transfer to the Western Front. The Russian defenses included thousands of mines and some British submarines.

Below: The landing force—mainly the German 42nd Division plus a cycle brigade—consisted of 23,000 men, 5,000 horses, 1,400 vehicles, 150 machine guns, 54 guns, 12 mortars and munitions and provisions for 30 days, all transported in 19 steamers. It assaulted at Tagga Bay on 12 October. Protected by a substantial naval force and air support provided by bombers and zeppelins, in spite of the defenses, the German minesweepers cleared a passage and the army disposed of the Russian garrisons, taking 20,000 prisoners.

bombardment and disgorged French tanks and men of the Foreign Legion onto a beach above Narvik. It was a small beginning, but showed the potential of specialised craft.

Operation *Seelöwe* would have been the first major amphibious operation of modern times and the German preparations saw large numbers of barges and transports collected together and many innovations in tactics and new equipment—German landing craft ramps for vehicles, major AA defences, the use of airscrew engines and hydrofoils, submersible tanks, mobile landing bridges and pontoons. The strategic moment was right. The Luftwaffe could have dominated aerial battles over the south of England. Details of the planned invasion show that the *Kriegsmarine* pulled together sufficient vessels to carry 13 divisions. All seemed ready for the operation.

As we know, it didn't take place. To Hitler and the high command the threat of the Royal Navy was too great. On top of this, the Luftwaffe wasn't able to knock out the RAF to ensure air superiority. The high command of the *Kriegsmarine* had looked closely at the likely outcomes and decided that the Royal Navy was just too strong to allow slow-moving troopships to land their cargoes. This, along with the successes of the RAF in bombing the barges and transport fleet assembling in northern France in September, led to *Seelöwe*'s postponement.

As German eyes moved eastwards, so a period of raiding began. After Dunkirk, Churchill had pushed for a 'reign of terror' on the German-held coasts and so the Commandos were formed. The first raid—Operation Collar on 24/25 June 1940—was unsuccessful but others, after suitable training and planning had taken place, were more useful both for morale-building purposes as well as some real benefits, such as the raid on the radar station at Bruneval, Operation Biting. The commandos went on to play an important role during the war although raiding proved less effective than Churchill had hoped. It also led to the infamous 'Commando order' whereby commandos and other special forces were executed by the Germans rather than taken as prisoners of war.

One thing the fall of France did make clear was that a significant amphibious operation would be needed at some point to free western Europe of the jackboot. The Germans knew it and began to strengthen their shore defences expending huge amounts of reinforced concrete and tying down large numbers of men. It also led to arguments between the British and Americans, once the latter had joined the war. Having agreed that Europe would take precedence over the Pacific, the Americans pressed for an immediate invasion. The British, with greater experience of the pitfalls of amphibious operations and the extraordinary prowess of the German war machine, suggested a less direct strategy. While American suspicion of British intentions may have dominated these early discussions, there is no doubt that the Allied amphibious operations in North Africa (Torch) and the Mediterranean (Husky, Avalanche and Baytown) informed the eventual assault on the beaches of Normandy. Additionally, the development of specialist equipment—from landing craft to amphibious tanks—during 1942 and 1943 added impetus to the eventual assault.

However, while the size of the amphibious operations in the Mediterranean and Normandy was larger than most of those in the Pacific until Okinawa (Operation Iceberg), the nature of the war in Europe was essentially land-locked. Neither the Germans nor the Soviet Union developed significant amphibious capabilities because most of the fighting in Europe was on the Eastern Front where the ability to cross rivers was more important. While the Germans had been innovative and creative in their consideration of the invasion of Britain, they didn't pursue the ideas. In the Pacific, however, the invasion of territories taken by the Japanese—particularly the islands that could be used for airfields—was predicated on amphibious warfare, just as the Japanese successes in the Pacific in 1941 and 1942 had also been as a result of amphibious operations—the 'Bicycle Blitzkrieg' in Malaya was initiated by an amphibious assault. Using night attacks, surprise, speed and aggression—and a sophisticated range of landing craft—the Japanese were able to subjugate a vast tract of territory in a short space of time (see also pp. 16–17.)

The tide turned and the next three years of fighting in the Pacific saw amphibious warfare reach a high level of operational development—and much of this was learnt on the job. However, it's not accurate to think that the US armed forces were completely unprepared for this sort of warfare. *Field Manual 31-5* of 2 June 1941 *Landing Operations on Hostile Shores* gives the state of the art from an American perspective. Comparison with the version of 1944 shows how much changed over the intervening period. For example, in 1941 the section 'Standard Army and Navy Boats' identified US Army Higgins 36ft boats, navy launches and tank lighters; the USN had motor boats, launches and whaleboats and sail/oar-driven craft: whaleboat, dinghy, wherry and punt. In 1944, the appendix says: 'Several types of ships and craft have been developed for particular uses in connection with amphibious operations. The landing craft may be further classified as personnel landing craft, vehicle and tank landing craft, and amphibian vehicles'. It goes on to detail the main types of craft: LST, LSD, LSM, LCVP, LCI(L), LCM Mks 3 and 6, LVTs and DUKWs—in less than three years the face of amphibious warfare had changed forever.

FM 31-5 identified the phases of an amphibious operation as:

'**a. Planning.** *Preparation and coordination of plans for the expedition.*
'**b. Concentration and specialized training.** *Concentration of forces selected for the operation, their organization into an integrated task force, and their joint training.*
'**c. Embarkation.** *Assembly of troops, equipment, supplies, and vessels at places of embarkation, and actual combat loading of the landing force in assault vessels.*
'**d. Voyage.** *Sea journey from points of embarkation to the landing area.*
'**e. Landing.** *Assault against the hostile shore.*
f. Consolidation. *Tactical organization and consolidation of beachheads, establishment of 'major supply points ashore, and unloading of adequate supplies and reinforcements.'*

ARMY	NAVY
a. Deploy into boats used for landing	a. Provide, man, equip and operate landing ships and craft required for landing operations. All or part of the landing boats may be furnished occasionally by army engineer amphibian boat units.
b. Man naval weapons on ships and landing boats when requested by proper naval authority. When requested, set up and operate army weapons on vessels in which army troops are carried.	b. Provide defense against enemy naval forces.
c. Deploy from landing boats and gain a foothold on shore.	c. Land army forces in accordance with the army plan of operation (unless prohibited by uncontrollable circumstances) and support the landing with all available forces.
d. Remove obstacles from normal grounding point of assault landing craft inland.	d. Remove underwater obstacles up to the normal grounding point of assault craft. (Joint teams are frequently employed.)
e. Provide such details as are required to expedite loading and unloading. Normally, these details are elements of the supporting shore party.	e. Unload vessels in accordance with army debarkation plans and requirements. Operate ship and boat equipment necessary to accomplish army requirements.
f. Organize, operate and control shore installations used primarily for debarkation of army personnel, equipment and supplies.	f. Provide, in outlying ports, means for embarkation or debarkation of army troops, equipment and supplies when such means cannot be provided or obtained by the Army.
g. Organize and conduct operations to extend the beachhead, Conduct operations beyond the beachhead for accomplishment of the mission.	g. Organize and operate necessary sea lanes of supply for forces on shore.
h. Evacuate casualties to the beach and care for casualties on the beach (aided by naval medical personnel).	h. Evacuate casualties to ships and assist in care of casualties on the beach.

'It identified the army and navy responsibilities and functions during landing operations on a hostile shore as shown in the table opposite.

'The ground, naval, and air components are organized into a Joint Task Force under a designated commander. A joint task force may operate as one force or be divided into subtask forces, each of which may be termed a Joint Attack Force. ... A joint attack force is an organization capable of conducting a landing operation. The components of a joint attack force are:
a. The Landing Force, which includes all ground elements, both combat and service, participating in the landing operation. In this manual, the landing force is considered to be one reinforced infantry division. Smaller landing forces may be organized.
b. The Naval Force, which includes all naval elements (except air) involved in the landing operation.
c. The Air Force, which includes all naval aviation allotted to the joint attack force, and such Army Air Force aviation as may be allotted by the Joint Task Force commander. ...'

FM 31-5 gives the timetabling of the operation:

Continued on p. 18.

JAPANESE AMPHIBIOUS TACTICS BASED ON EXPERIENCES AT WAKE
Edited information from *Intelligence Bulletin* Vol. I, No 8: April 1943

The Japanese had shown the world the power of amphibious warfare with its conquest of Malaya and the Pacific islands. The first attack on Wake Island was foiled, but a subsequent attack on 23 December 1941 was successful and the garrison surrendered the same day. Lessons learned by the Japanese in the attack on Wake Island are contained in a recent enemy document.

'GENERAL PROCEDURE
You must not use a plan of attack that has been used previously, because the enemy can anticipate our actions. And don't forget to take the enemy by surprise. This is absolutely essential.
  '*Our method of operation must be determined only by the progress of the battle.*
  '*There are many cases where the soldier must value speed more than finesse.*
  '*The issue of victory lies in the constant maintenance of the offensive spirit. The great success of this operation [capture of Wake Island] was due, in the final analysis, to the constant display of this spirit by all personnel, without regard for their own lives.*
  '*It is necessary to train especially picked troops for the landing force.*
  '*In landing in the face of the enemy, it is necessary to utilize timely diversions and deceptive movements. If the diversion does not succeed in its purpose, it will hinder rather than help the subsequent operations. Because the diversion effort at Wake was carried out before the invasion force landed, the result was rather to alert the enemy than to deceive him. In view of this, similar operations in the future should be thoroughly prepared beforehand in regard to time, place, and method of attack. It also is essential to have thorough communication arrangements so that all units can be advised of any last-minute changes in our landing plans.*
  '*In case the landing is restricted to a very narrow front and there is no room for a diversion, you must either carry out a thorough bombardment before and after the landing, or make the landing in overwhelming force. If the attempt is made to land secretly (that is, using only motor boats and landing only small numbers at one time) on a place like Wake Island where landing is limited to a small area, it is evident that great losses will be incurred.*
  '*In the invasion of a strategic island, the command must be unified. The invasion forces consist of the Occupation Force, the Covering Force (naval and air), and also a force we may call "Cooperation." [Comment: This force is believed to be composed of reserves and unloading units.] The power of these forces cannot be developed fully if there is a lack of mutual understanding among them.*

'PREPARATIONS FOR LANDING
Because troops easily become scattered at night and control is difficult, execution of the operations must be made simple by detailed preparations. The following factors must be considered in deciding methods of operation, organization, and equipment:
  a. *Troops must be organized and equipped to fight independently during the daytime.*
  b. *Remember that when the enemy's main batteries and other defense areas cannot be captured before daybreak, it is often impossible to get fire support from the ships during the day.* [Comment: This shows a healthy Japanese respect for our shore batteries.]
  c. *At night, hand grenades and grenade throwers are extremely effective in silencing heavy guns. In day fighting, it is necessary to have machine guns and infantry cannon available for use.*

A Japanese Daihatsu type, 14m landing craft. Andrew Higgins studied photos of the bow doors to improve his design.

d. All the first-line fighting strength must be landed at once. Quite often, motor boats used in the first landing become stranded and cannot be used for another trip.

'LANDING PROCEDURE
If the beach is defended, it is absolutely essential to complete the landing before daybreak. In general, it seems that the earlier the landing time, the more effective it will be.

'Although the Wake Island landing was effected 4 hours before sunrise, it turned out that the old saying "The hours of the night are short" was only too true. The landing originally was planned for execution at 2300 hours, but trouble in lowering the motor boats delayed us about 2 hours. It is also necessary to allow extra time for approaching the shore and making the main landing.

'Where there are fringing reefs, low tide is more advantageous for landing than high tide.

'At night the enemy shells pass overhead; so damage is slight, although you receive a fierce shelling.

'It is easy to mistake the landing point at night. The leading boat must approach at half speed or low speed until the island can definitely be seen from the large landing lighters.

'To lead the boats in close formation within range of the enemy's defense guns is extremely dangerous; however, in landing operations in the dark on long swells around an island, and if the boats deploy 4,500 to 5,000 yards from shore, the lighters will find it extremely difficult to hold their course, and almost impossible to reach shore at the designated point. Although four lighters were led within 3,500 yards of the shore at Wake, none of them arrived at the appointed time or place. Two lighters which accompanied patrol boat No 32 lost sight of her on the way because she increased speed. It is necessary for the leading boat to have a low-powered signal light on its stern for signaling to the rest of the boats.

'At the time of landing, the normal speed of the patrol boat should be maintained. When the boats are proceeding shoreward at about normal speed, the enemy has extreme difficulty in aiming.

'It is necessary to unload the boats very quickly after reaching shore, and a great deal of equipment should be made ready in the bow of the boat.

'COOPERATION OF SHIPS AND AIRCRAFT
a. Destruction of land batteries with ship's guns or airplanes is difficult.
b. Direct cooperation between air and land forces is extremely effective, and the cooperation of light airplanes is essential (especially when we are weak in artillery and the enemy has powerful artillery, tanks, and so forth).
c. Detailed reconnaissance of enemy positions by airplanes appears to be extremely difficult.
d. It is sometimes hard to bomb air bases. It was difficult to see and bombard the Wake airfield with ship's guns because it is lower than the road around it.

'COMMUNICATIONS
When landing, it is necessary to devise measures to keep communication equipment from getting wet. In the Wake operation, communication between ships and the shore was impossible because the radios and telephones either got wet or received severe shocks. The rockets and signal pistols also got wet, and, although fired, they were difficult to distinguish from the enemy's machine-gun tracer bullets.

'The methods of communication must be simple. In a landing operation carried out by a number of cooperating units, it is necessary to perfect communications so as to maintain close liaison. It is most important to have several simple, sure means of communications so that they will function regardless of the situation.'

A Japanese Type C landing craft. Note the three MG turrets. The Japanese had developed a range of landing craft in the 1920s and 30s.

TIMETABLE OF A MAJOR OPERATION

S-?	Strategic decisions made, preparation of operational directive ordered. Task commander and commanders of the joint ground, air, and naval components given geographical alert to permit assembly of essential intelligence data.		manders start estimates.
		S-23	Landing force commanders' plans completed. Naval task force commander's attack plans completed. Naval force and air force commanders complete estimates and start plans. Unit transport quartermasters begin unit loading and stowage plans.
S-100	Operational directive issued by Joint Chiefs of Staff or other appropriate headquarters. Ground, naval, and air commanders start estimates.	S-13	Naval force and air force commanders' plans completed. Naval task force commander starts sortie, rendezvous, and cruising plans and orders.
S-95	Joint headquarters established. Joint task force commanders and staffs begin conference.	S-8	Ship loading plans completed. Naval transport commander's plans completed. Transports and other ships made available for loading. Army loading and billeting parties arrive at port.
S-90	Ground task force commander completes estimate and starts army plans. Conference continues.		
S-60	Ground task force commander's plans completed. Landing force commanders start estimates. Naval and air task force commanders complete estimates and start naval and air plans. Staff conferences between landing force, naval force, and air force commanders begins.	S-7	Preparation for loading supplies and ammunition begins.
		S-5	Loading begins.
		S-2	Loading of supplies and ammunition completed. Loading of vehicles begins.
S-35	Landing force commanders complete estimates and start plans. Naval task force commander completes force operation plan. Naval force and air force com-	S-1	Troops embark on assigned ships.
		S	Sailing date.

'A general pattern for a major amphibious operation planning time table follows. It comprises a task force of several joint attack forces. It should be considered only as a reasonable estimate of the average time for completion of various essential plans and preparatory operations in normal sequence. The experience of the different components and variation in the range of the operation will affect the time necessary.'

The organisation of the landings was as follows:

'a. Troop and cargo-carrying capabilities of combat-loaded ships and landing craft are limited, as are numbers of landing craft available to an embarked force and the initial facilities for debarkation and organization of materiel on shore. These and other limitations impose definite restrictions on the organization of a landing force. Requirements for the safety of ships may limit seriously their time in the landing area for unloading. Therefore, special planning is required to reduce ship cargo requirements, assure maximum utilization of space, facilitate rapid debarkation of intact assault, units, provide maximum fire power and essential equipment in assault waves, assure sufficient mobility to initial units, and provide logistic elements for shore supply organizations.

'b. No standard landing force organization can be established except in very general form.

'c. Regimental combat teams, reinforced, constitute normal subdivisions of a division landing force, and naval transport divisions are organized to carry such teams.

'd. An infantry battalion specially reinforced by necessary combat and logistic elements is the basic unit for planning an assault landing. So organized, it is referred to as a Battalion Landing Team (BLT).'

Landing Force

'a. A landing team is a battalion combat team reinforced with the elements required for the operation. The resultant team should contain the means necessary to accomplish its objective and to permit sustained operations ashore until ground operations become normal.

'b. A typical battalion landing team may include the following:
(1) Infantry battalion; (2) Light field artillery battery; (3) Battery of self-propelled anti-aircraft artillery automatic weapons; (4) Combat engineer platoon from organic division engineer battalion; (5) Platoon from infantry cannon company; (6) Platoon from anti-tank company; (7) Detachment from division cavalry reconnaissance troop (amphibious scouts and raiders); (8) Shore party, including special engineer company, naval platoon (beach party), and communication team from joint assault signal company; (9) Shore fire control party from joint assault signal company; (10) Air-liaison party from joint assault signal company; (11) Liaison detail, field artillery battalion; (12) Portable surgical hospital; (13) Other units as required. They may include detachments from such combat units as chemical weapons, field artillery, rangers, tanks, military police, or amphibian tractors or tanks ; or such service units as quartermaster general service, chemical decontamination, and amphibian truck. ...

'e. Based on tactical requirements, and considering economy of loading, the landing force is organized for loading into embarkation groups consisting of all elements which are to embark in one ship or a fixed group of ships. Necessity for accurate organization for embarkation arises from the vital relationship between embarkation and subsequent debarkation for assault. [See pp. 20–21 for a typical loading and attack plan.]

'f. For the movement to shore, the landing force is subdivided into landing groups, each consisting of a battalion landing team, or its equivalent, plus such miscellaneous elements of higher headquarters, liaison groups, or other units as may be embarked with it. The battalion landing team normally is carried to shore by a boat group, plus additional boats attached from one or more ships of the transport division.

'g. Organization of the landing force must be such as to permit employment of battalion landing teams in independent action afloat and ashore, at least during initial phases of the landing assault.'

A key role in later assaults was taken up by amphibious tanks. In northwest Europe, these were mainly Valentine (initially) or Sherman DDs—Duplex Drive—tanks with a flotation screen. In the Pacific, a development of the LVT, the LVT(A)—Amtanks, latterly with the 75mm turret as used on the M8 HMC—led the assaults after Tarawa (see pp. 20–21). They supported the landing by fire on the objective beaches and continued to support the assault by covering the flanks of the beaches, by close-in fire from the water against caves and other prepared positions close to the shore and by furnishing support to troop units holding lines extending to the water. No attempt was made to take them far inland

Continued on p. 24.

AMPHIBIOUS ASSAULT

'(1) The following plan was worked out by the 96th Infantry Division for the loading of all assault-battalions and was completely successful. All concerned were well satisfied with the results obtained. The landing diagram outlined in this section was used as a basis by BLTs in planning their boat assignment tables, and for loading personnel on the assault LSTs.

'(a) 1st Wave The two assault platoons of each of the two assault rifle companies, with one assault platoon of each company reinforced with a section of light machine guns.

'(b) 2nd Wave The balance of the two assault rifle companies, 2 sections of heavy machine guns, artillery FO section, naval gunfire spotter.

'(c) 3rd Wave The balance of the heavy weapons company, shore party reconnaissance personnel, and the anti-tank mine squad.

'(d) 4th Wave Two assault platoons and light machine gun sections of the reserve rifle company, battalion A& P platoon and extra ammunition, advance elements of battalion CP group.

'(e) 5th Wave Balance of reserve rifle company, battalion AT platoon, battalion communication platoon.

'(f) 6th Wave Battalion medical section, regimental troops, equipment or supplies, advance elements shore party, combat engineers.

'(g) Call Wave One line mortar company per assault regiment (12 DUKWs).

'Boat teams were numbered from right to left within each battalion exactly as shown on the diagram.

'(2) Loading of LSTs.
Three LSTs were available to embark the assault elements of each assault BLT and one LST was assigned to the Amphibious tank company supporting each assault BLT. These four LSTs were loaded in accordance with their LST loading plan which is based on the following principles:

'(a) The two assault rifle companies of each BLT are completely loaded on one LST along with the battalion commanders party so that:

1. Last minute briefing could be accomplished.
2. Liaison parties with the underwater demolition teams need return to only one ship.
3. Latest intelligence information and pictures need be dispatched to only one ship to reach all the assault forces in the BLT.
4. The 1st and 2nd waves all come out of one LST thereby reducing the control necessary at the target in forming the assault waves in the right order.

'Battalion personnel loading chart as used in diagrams on next page.

'(3) There is a distinct time interval between naval gunfire support and the infantry artillery supporting fires. True, the amphibious

UNIT	LST A	LST B	LST C	LST D
1 BLT		(416)	(199)	(311)
1st Wave		184		
2nd Wave		212		
3rd Wave			124	
4th Wave				143
5th Wave				123
6th Wave			55	
Unload Det			20	20
Free LVTs		20		25
2 Shore Party			49	
3 Am Tractor		75	95	85
4 AM Tank	180			
5 Cml Co	150			
6 DUKW Co	36			
TOTAL	366	491	334	396

tanks do provide immediate fire support, but their vulnerability and lack of training in good indirect fire makes their value doubtful. The 4.2 mortars usually can give support by H+2 hours while the artillery in several instances came in with unit supporting fires by H+4 or 5 hours.'

Right: Sketch showing LST loadings of the 96th Infantry assault battalions. First a wave of amphibious tanks, followed by as many as six LVT waves.

Below: Amtanks first saw action in the Marshall Islands campaign, the LVT(A)-4 with a 75mm gun arriving in time for the battle for Saipan.

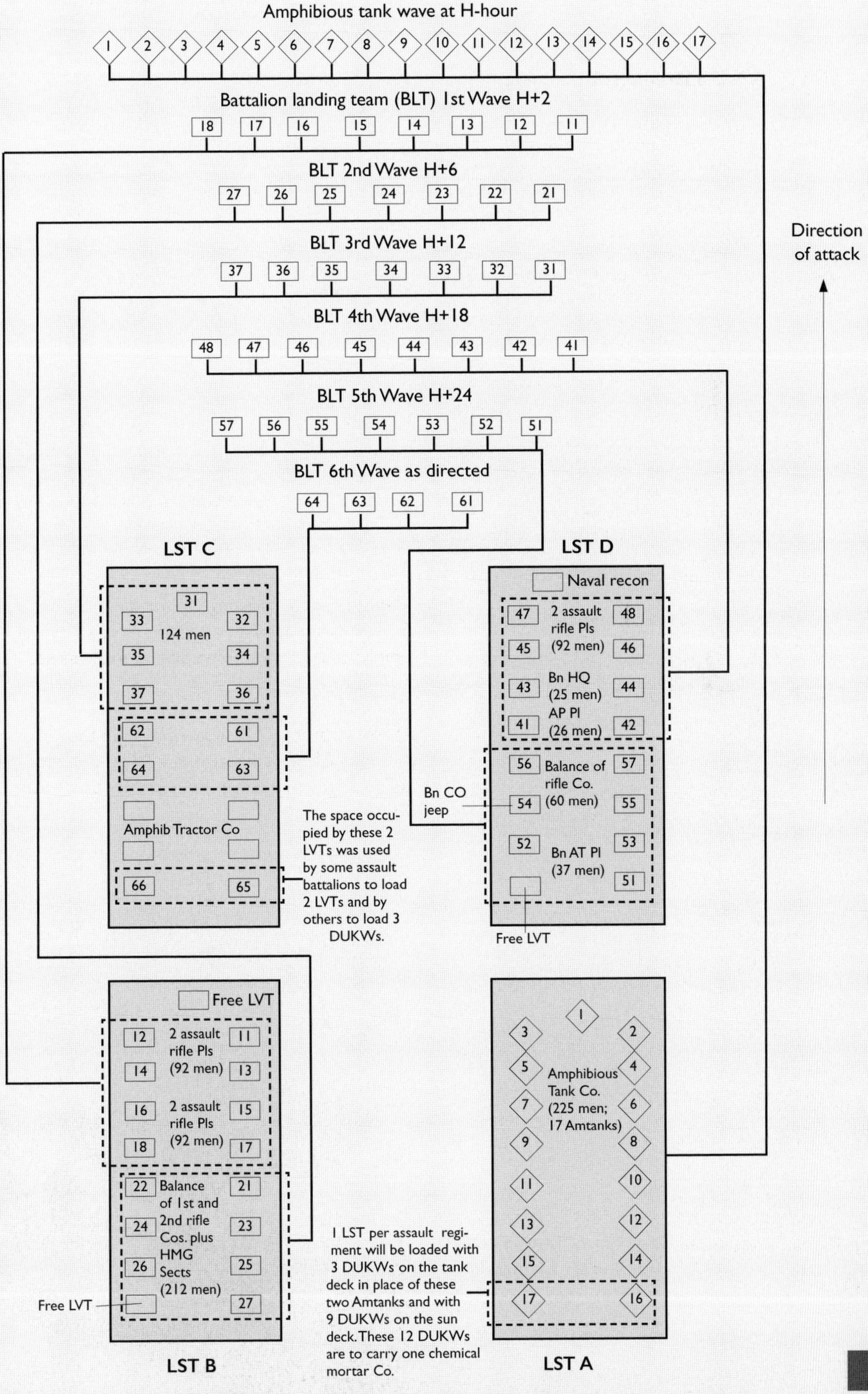

Amphibious tank wave at H-hour
1 2 3 4 5 6 7 8 9 10 11 12 13 14 15 16 17
Battalion landing team (BLT) 1st Wave H+2
18 17 16 15 14 13 12 11
BLT 2nd Wave H+6
27 26 25 24 23 22 21
BLT 3rd Wave H+12
37 36 35 34 33 32 31
BLT 4th Wave H+18
48 47 46 45 44 43 42 41
BLT 5th Wave H+24
57 56 55 54 53 52 51
BLT 6th Wave as directed
64 63 62 61
Direction of attack
LST C
31 33 32 124 men 35 34 37 36
62 61 64 63
Amphib Tractor Co
66 65
The space occupied by these 2 LVTs was used by some assault battalions to load 2 LVTs and by others to load 3 DUKWs.
LST D
Naval recon
47 2 assault rifle Pls (92 men) 48
45 46
43 Bn HQ (25 men) 44
41 AP Pl (26 men) 42
56 Balance of rifle Co. (60 men) 57
Bn CO jeep
54 55
52 Bn AT Pl (37 men) 53
51
Free LVT
LST B
Free LVT
12 2 assault rifle Pls (92 men) 11
14 13
16 2 assault rifle Pls (92 men) 15
18 17
22 Balance of 1st and 2nd rifle Cos. plus HMG Sects (212 men) 21
24 23
26 25
Free LVT
27
LST A
1 3 2 5 4
Amphibious Tank Co. (225 men; 17 Amtanks)
7 6 9 8 11 10 13 12 15 14 17 16
1 LST per assault regiment will be loaded with 3 DUKWs on the tank deck in place of these two Amtanks and with 9 DUKWs on the sun deck. These 12 DUKWs are to carry one chemical mortar Co.

776 Amtank Bn Operation Report Ryukyu Campaign, 16 July 1945

'This report [excerpts are edited] may be of special interest in that it describes the first large-scale employment of amphibian tanks as supporting artillery. During the Ryukyus Campaign the 776th Amphibian Tank Battalion fired a total of 41,297 rounds of 75mm ammunition in support of infantry operations.

'Methods of employment in both primary and secondary missions differ greatly from those prescribed in current training manuals and directives. Our methods are the result of practical experience in the field, and have been proven sound. ...

'That the landing on Okinawa was unopposed tends to obscure the importance of the secondary mission (supporting fires) of the unit. It is significant, however, that this unit placed ashore in the first wave the equivalent of four well-trained battalions of artillery hours before the landing of the division artillery itself. Subsequent action proved the unit's capabilities as artillery; had artillery support been needed immediately following the landing, it was available.

'Most of the firing done by this unit followed displacement from positions initially occupied upon landing. Two line companies displaced forward five times while the other two changed battery position six times. The unit was finally relieved from attachment to Division Artillery when extended lines of communication created a greater need for defending the coast against envelopments. Thereafter the line companies maintained the equivalent of two platoons (batteries) each for fire support, while the remaining platoons maintained a beach cordon some five miles in length in which an estimated 80 Japanese infiltrators were killed.

'Although six vehicles were struck by enemy shell fire only one, which struck a landmine, was damaged beyond repair. Casualties totaled 2 officers WIA and evacuated, 5 EM KIA; 14 EM WIA and evacuated; 1 EM DOA. Concurrent training and second echelon maintenance were such that the unit could, upon completion of the Ryukyus Campaign, have staged another operation upon ten days' notice.

'Planning for the Okinawa operation was based upon the Battalion's mission and was strongly influenced by its experience on Leyte.

'Prior to Leyte the Battalion had received artillery training under the 7th Div Arty. Having benefitted by combat experience, the Battalion resumed this training during the rehabilitation period in preparation for the operation against Okinawa. Officers were detailed from the 7th Div Arty as instructors in Battalion schools, and a course of instruction was established for officers, gun crews, and fire direction center personnel. The objects of this course of instruction were to accomplish further refinements in fire direction center procedures, train company fire direction center, give necessary training to commissioned enlisted replacement personnel, and provide refresher courses for all personnel concerned.

'Upon completion of the Leyte operation the Battalion was reorganized for combat employment:

'**Bn HQ, HQ &Serv Co**
CO and 1/2 Bn staff in Mk IV LVT(4)(A) (amtrac)
Bn Ex O and 1/2 Bn staff in Mk IV LVT(4)(A) (amtrac)
Bn Maint Sect & shops in 3 Mk IV LVT(4) (amtrac)
Med Det, initially in 2 Mk IV LVT(4) (amtrac) (revert to S–4 after evacuation of casualties to LSTs ceases)
Bn Com Sec & Msg Cen in Mk IV LVT(4) (amtrac)

'**Line Companies:**
Co CO & FDC in Mk I LVT(A)1 (amtank)
Com & Rcn Sec in Mk I LVT(A)1 (amtank)
Each Plat in 4 Mk IV LVTs (A)4 (amtank)
FDC personnel were distributed among the platoons' 4 amtanks.
Each platoon amtank carried 8 men, or 1 in excess of normal crew
Co Maint Sect in Mk IV LVT(4) (amtank)

'Twenty LVTs (A)1 thus made surplus were left on Leyte with the rear echelon. These would have been turned in if this been possible.

'Two dry runs of the landing were conducted at Leyte in which the Battalion simulated its primary mission of beach assault and its secondary mission of providing artillery support from positions ashore. Communications, formation and control of landing waves, and simulated fire missions from artillery observers were practiced during each dry run.

'The combat elements of the Battalion were transported to the target in eight LSTs ... and impedimenta and wheeled vehicles accompanying the forward echelons were loaded on a ninth LST. This LST carried the Bn S–4 section and all company supply sergeants. Tactical integrity of platoons was preserved in the loading of combat units. Company impedimenta carried with the platoons and companies was held to a minimum and arrangements were made for one member of each company supply section to remain aboard Co HQ LSTs until this equipment was unloaded at the Battalion's beach supply dump. Subsequently, this personnel manned the Battalion dump.

'Launching was accomplished in the LST assembly area approximately 5,000yd offshore and the landing waves of LVTs were formed with the assistance of naval wave guide officers in small boats. The line of departure was 4,000yd offshore and was crossed by the first wave at 0800. Continuation of shelling of beaches by LCI rocket boats slowed movement of first wave making the landing 12 minutes late. Howitzers in the first wave fired approximately 16 rounds per gun each during the assault of the beaches; more rounds would have been fired if fire had been received by the landing waves from the beach areas. A few enemy shells of heavy caliber struck in the water as the assault waves came ashore, but they were observed to do little damage and no damage whatsoever to this Battalion. The reef offered no serious obstacle to the landing and a sufficient number of openings were found in the seawall to permit the Battalion to reach its objective line approximately 200yd inland. Landing was simultaneous at 0842, H-Hour+12 minutes.

'Companies A, B, C, and D landed on beaches Purple I, Purple II, Orange I, and Orange II, respectively. The first wave consisted of the LVT(A)4s. Immediately in rear of these and ahead of the first wave of infantry in amtracs the fire direction center and pioneer vehicles moved ashore. The two medical vehicles landed on Beaches Purple I and Orange II respectively, in the 6th wave, at 0915. (Medical vehicles of the amtrac battalions landed on the other beaches of the 7th Div zone.) … During the assault, control was exercised by the Battalion Commander by radio.'

Example Fire Missions

1 April 'The Battalion moved rapidly inland 200yd according to plan and was prepared to deliver supporting fires for the infantry within 30 minutes of landing. Forward observers of the Div Arty landed with the assault battalions and controlled the fire of their supporting amtank companies after reaching the shore. No enemy small arms fire was encountered and only sporadic hostile shells fell in the area. An enemy mortar shell struck an amtank of the 3d Plat of Co C, wounded five members of its crew, and temporarily put the vehicle out of action.

'By the end of the first day the assault infantry regiments had advanced almost to the L+3 line, or about 4,700yd inland. Because of this rapid advance it was necessary to begin early forward displacement of the Battalion in order to insure that efficient fire support could be delivered.'

4 April Cos A and B fired a preparation for the infantry advance, marking the first time this type of fire was delivered by any element of the Battalion on this operation. Subsequently, because of the nature of enemy resistance, many such fire missions were accomplished.'

10 April 'Firing by Co A during night of 9/10 April was credited by the forward observer with breaking up a local enemy counter-attack against of 184th Inf.' [Cos. A and B reinforcing 57th FA Bn; Cos C and D were in support of 17th Inf Regt.]

19 April 'The attack against strong enemy positions on commanding terrain jumped off at 0640, after one of the greatest artillery preparations of the entire Pacific war. Naval warships and aircraft took part in the bombardment. Cos A, B, and C fired approx 2,000 rounds each during the preparation.'

20 April 'Because of enemy small boat activity at night, the G–3 of the 7th Inf Div assigned sectors of responsibility for the defense of the beach.'

27 April 'Effective at 1800 the Battalion was relieved from attachment to Div Arty, and attached directly to the Division with a mission of defending the beach area in its sector against enemy infiltration. …'

29 April 'At 2245 an outguard of Co B observed and fired MG on rowboat … sole occupant was killed … the dead Jap was dressed as a woman.'

30 April 'At 0130 an outguard of Co B detected activity on the reef, and opened fire with MG … two Japs killed … At 0500 an outguard of Co B killed a Jap sergeant carrying a satchel charge.'

Further attacks took place through May.

DATE	CO.	H.F.	N.B.	CONC.	REG & S.M.	AMMO
Apr 1	A	1			1	105
	B	1			2	120
	C	2	1		2	109
	D	2			2	357
Apr 4	A	6	1		2	744
	B	5	1		5	642
	C				4	23
	D		2		3	68
Apr 10	A		1	2	1	665
	B	10	2			272
Apr 19	A	1	3	22	1	2,026
	C		15			1,171
Apr 20	A	1	3	15		647
	B	3		17	10	3,770
	C		1		2	21

CO. = company; H.F. = harassing fire; N.B. = normal barrage; Conc = concentration; Reg &SM. = registration and special missions.

or to use them as tanks due to their vulnerability when not waterborne—but see pp. 22–23 for their use as artillery.

LVTs were particularly useful in the attack on Iwo Jima due to the difficulties encountered in operating wheeled vehicles in the soft sand of the beaches. They were used in unloading from LSTs during the early stages of the assault and moved their loads to inland dumps or to provide direct troop support.

While the Pacific required amphibious warfare for almost every step, in Europe there was much use of amphibious assets in smaller operations but the main Allied usage centred around six major set-piece invasions: 'Torch', 'Husky', 'Avalanche', 'Anvil', 'Dragoon' and 'Neptune'. (See also sections in Chapter 2 Landings.) In many ways the most remarkable was 'Torch', for which some troops were ferried all the way across the Atlantic. However, the hostile but little defended shores of North Africa cannot be compared to those the Allies faced in Sicily, Italy and Normandy. It was on these beaches that the hard details of large-scale amphibious warfare were ironed out.

In Europe, as part of the all-arms battle, airborne troops were used to capture key locations in coup de main missions, to seal flanks and reinforce when things got tight. The development of landing vessels and an armada of support craft went hand in hand with specialised vehicles for use at the beach head, the most important of which was probably the humble DUKW, but also includes the British AVRE and ARK. Also developed were the surveying of landing areas, beach control units and all the equipment used to allow heavy vehicles to exit soft, sandy beaches. These topics will be discussed further in the pages that follow.

Opposite, Above: The LVT (landing vehicles tracked) series first came into use for ship-to-shore haulage using the unarmoured LVT-1 and -2s in 1941–43. After Tarawa an armoured version—the LVT(A)-1 with a turret-mounted 37mm—was hurried into service in 1944. Here 7th Infantry head towards the beach at Okinawa.

Opposite, Centre: The LVTs were improved with rear ramps introduced on the LVT-4 (up till then troops mounted/dismounted over the sides) and heavier armour and weapons. However, the 37mm of the LVT(A)-1 proved too small and so the 75mm howitzer that had armed the M8 HMC was used to create the LVT(A)-4. These carried 100 rounds of 75mm ammo and had an open top. In total 1,890 of these were built, seeing action first at Saipan. The turreted versions were known as Amtanks, the unturreted as Amtracs/Amtracks or Alligators. Here, LVT(A)-4s head towards Peleliu in September 1944.

Opposite, Below: The LVTs were used in Europe by both US and British troops, particularly in the major river crossings such as the Po in Italy or Rhine and Elbe in Germany, and in the fighting around the Scheldt. The British called them Buffaloes and 200 had been delivered by the end of 1943. By the time of the Rhine crossing 600 were available. This photo shows men of the Canadian North Shore Regiment mounting a 79th Armoured Division Buffalo during Operation Veritable, 8 February 1945. Note the barrel and shield of the 20mm Polsten cannon.

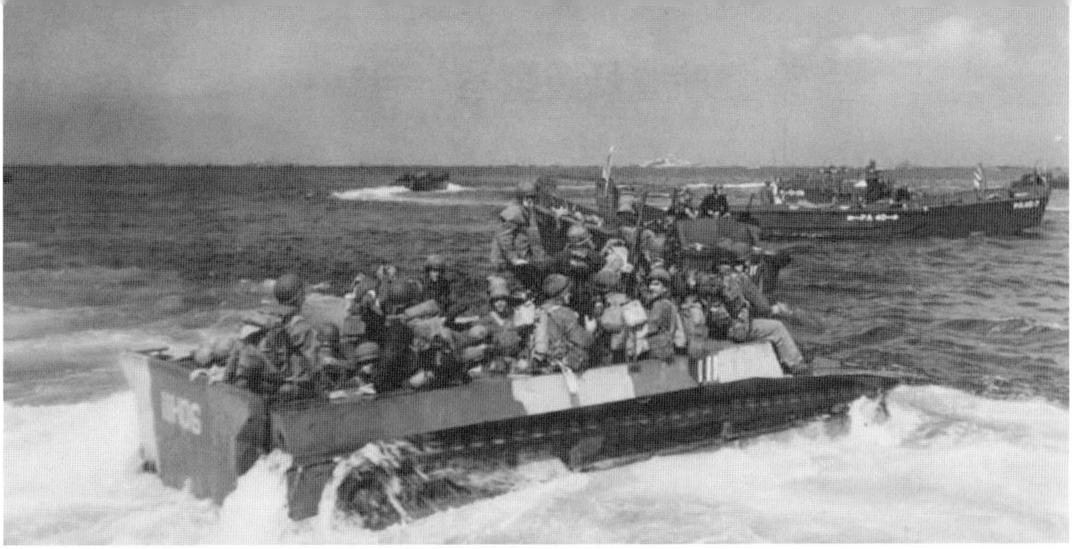

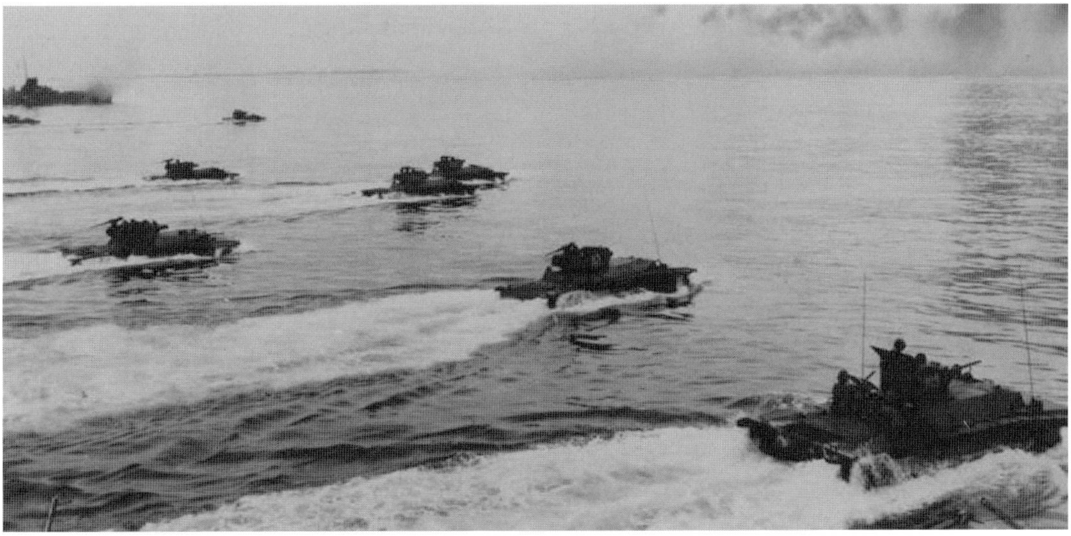

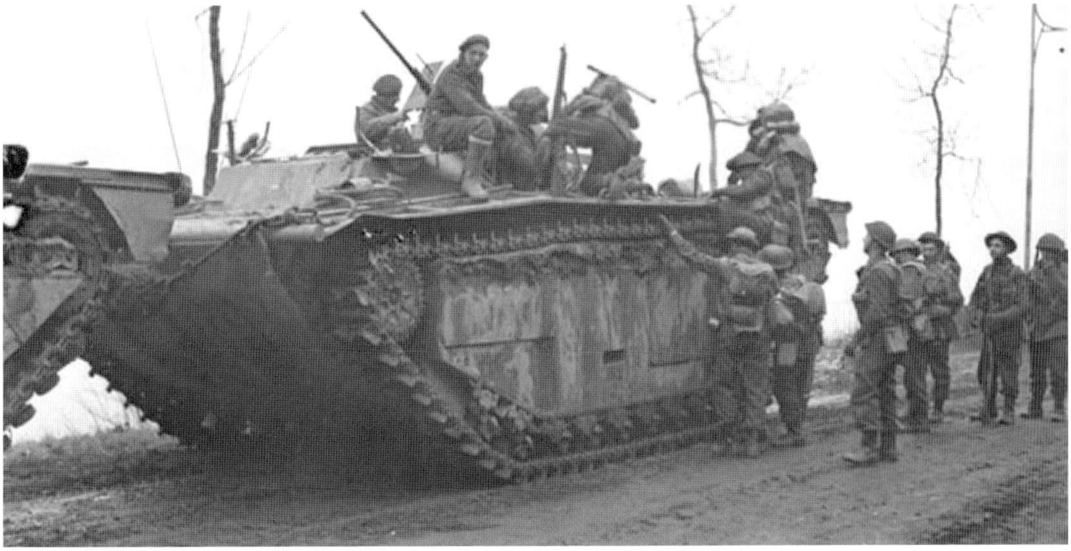

AIR AND NAVAL FORCES

The support of the naval and airborne forces were key elements of amphibious warfare. They are not dealt with in any detail in this book, other than the craft that were used to deliver troops to shore (see Appendix 1). FM 31-5 said of air and naval forces:

'a. The aviation elements of a joint attack force, operating separately or at such distance from the other attack forces that central control of air operations is impracticable, includes both army and naval aviation. When the Army Air Force elements available can cooperate with all of the Joint Attack Forces taking part in the operation, these air elements are held under command of the air commander of the Joint Task Force, and the aviation directly under the Joint Attack Force commander is limited to naval and marine aviation, either land-based or ship-based, or both.

'b. Heavy bombardment aviation normally will not be assigned directly to a Joint Task Force. The theater air force commander should plan for the diversion of any necessary heavy bombardment aviation from its normal mission for the purpose of augmenting the air forces of the Joint Task Force or assisting in the accomplishment of the mission of the air commander of the Joint Task Force.

'Primary missions are to attain and maintain air superiority by destruction of the enemy air forces and air bases within operating range of the proposed area of landing, to isolate the battle area by destroying communications and enemy reserves and reinforcements, and to conduct air missions against targets on the immediate front of the landing forces. Appropriate types and quantities of planes and armament for air attack missions must be provided.

Aircraft carriers ensured that assaulting forces had on-call ground support, as well as fighting for air superiority over the battlefield. Many of the islands provided airfields to further the long-range bombing campaign against Japan. Warming up at a Majuro Atoll Airfield, August 1944, F4U-1A/D Corsair fighters are about to depart on a strike on a nearby Japanese-held island, carrying 500lb bombs.

'a. A naval force assigned to a joint attack force usually consists of combat ships, transports, cargo ships, landing ships and craft, and essential supporting naval vessels. It is subdivided into such naval task groups as are appropriate to the various operations involved and the scheme of maneuver adopted.
'b. Normal naval tasks during a landing operation include:
(1) Reconnaissance; (2) Protection against enemy naval and air forces; (3) Furnishing, manning, equipping, and operating ships and craft required for the landing force; (4) Mine sweeping; (5) Gunfire support [an example of the intense shore bombardments provided by naval forces is shown on pp. 28–29. See also p. 129]; *(6) Screening operations; (7) Fire from boat guns; (8) Removing underwater obstacles; (9) Signal communication between ships and shore.'*

In the ETO, the Allied naval forces in the Mediterranean were less worried by enemy naval than air forces. As they gained air superiority, that threat receded—there was little Luftwaffe activity over the D-Day beaches—but mines were a continuous problem The D-Day plan was built around a significant minesweeping operation to ensure mine-free lanes for the huge naval force—over 5,000 vessels took part in the invasion. During the three-month battle of Normandy at least 20 vessels were damaged or sunk by mine damage, but only four between 5 and 7 June.

In the Pacific, however, the aerial threat was always present—especially after the Japanese introduced the kamikaze. These suicide missions killed nearly 4,000 Japanese pilots but posed a significant threat, as the report on battle damage on pp. 28–29 highlights.

USS *Ward* burns in Ormoc Bay, Leyte, after being struck by a kamikaze, 7 December 1944. There had been suicide attacks before Leyte—most notably on the cruiser HMAS *Australia*—but the Kamikaze Special Attack Force carried out its first mission at Leyte Gulf, sinking the aircraft carrier USS *St. Lo*. In all, kamikazes sank at least 47 ships and rendered unserviceable many of the other 190–200 hit.

Battle Damage
Edited excerpts from Commander Lingayen Attack Force Report (Mike I).

This appendix to Lingayen Attack Force Report, examines the incidence of suicide attacks at the start of the kamikaze campaign. In August 1945 the Anti-Suicide Action Report estimated that 1,100 enemy aircraft 'sortied with suicidal intent to attack our surface forces.' Of these, '500 were splashed or turned back by CAP; 420 missed ships as a result of AA fire; 180 hit ships. Of the 600 which were taken under fire by ships c. 180 hit ships; 78 missed ships but damaged them; 342, missed ships and caused no damage. The Lingayen report said:

'2. Damage may be classified as (1) Above Water and (2) Below Water. In general the above water damage results from gunfire, suicide dives and bombs. Below water damage results from attack by torpedoes, bombs, hand placed charges and mines.

'3. Battle damage sustained by ships under operational control of CTF79 during this operation was as follows:

'ABOVE WATER:

Vessel name	Jan	Time	Attack
KITKUN DAY (CVE71)	8	18:10	SD
LeRAY WILSON (DE414)	10	07:10	SD
ALLEN M. SUMNER (DD692)	10	07:12	SD
DUPAGE (APA41)	10	19:15	SD
GILLIGAN (DE508)	12	c. 08:0	SD
RICHARD J. SUESENS (D11342)	12	c. 08:00	SD
BELKNAP (APD34)	12	c. 08:00	SD
WARHAWK (AP168) missed	12	09:15	SD miss
LST 700	12	09:15	SD near miss
LST 700	13	07:55	SD
ZEILIN (APA3)	13	08:22	SD

'BELOW WATER DAMAGE

LST 925	10	03:10	Hand
WARHAWK (AP168)	10	03:20	EB
LST 610	10	c. 03:25	Hand
LST 1028	10	c. 03:30	Hand
ROBINSON (DD 562)	10	c. 03:50	Hand
LCI(G) 365	10	c. 04:00	EB
LCI(M) 974 boat sunk	10	c. 04:00	Hand
PHILIP (DD 498)	10	04:15	EB

exploded at 25 yards by gunfire

[SD = suicide dive; Hand = hand-placed explosive; EB = explosive boat]

'DAMAGE BY FRIENDLY FIRE

DICKERSON (APD21)	11	Dusk	20mm gasoline fire
STAFFORD (DE411)	12	09:15	20mm 13 wounded
WARREN (APA53)	13	08:22	20mm 1 killed 23 wounded

'SUICIDE DIVE ATTACK

'4. The newest form of attack and that of primary importance was the Suicide Dive. Although far from new the second most evident form of attack was by hand placed charges. Coupled with the increase in the number of automatic weapons comes an increase in the most regrettable type of damage, that caused by friendly fire. Although a few bombs were dropped, no damage was sustained therefrom by this force. No known torpedo attacks were made either from aircraft, submarines or surface craft.

'5. The CAP liquidates many potential Suiciders but there will always be some who will reach the AA gunfire area into which the CAP cannot advantageously enter. It remains for the gunfire from the ships to disintegrate the diving plane before it can strike. In this event it may be useful to consider a typical Suicide attack. Once inside the reach of the CAP the plane first encounters the fire of the 5 inch battery. This can be highly accurate provided the plane flies a steady course at constant speed.. However, the attacking plane in its approach weaves, dives or climbs continuously. In such an event success by the gunners can be attained only through an error in the solution. In this part of the defense less attention must be paid to an accurate solution and more attention to earliest and greatest volume of fire.

'6. The Suicider is quite deliberate in his approach, remaining outside of range of the automatic weapons until he has looked the situation over and obtained the desired position from which to strike. The dive is frequently initiated by a wing-over or diving turn from which the pilot straightens out and without any attempt at evasive measures dives at full throttle toward his selected target.

'7. Observations of recent target practices show clearly that the automatic weapons gunner still suffers from an inability to lead the target. The very large majority of fire is still placed behind the target. If this be so when firing at a 100 knot target then the error will be correspondingly magnified when firing at a 400 knot target.

'8. From his attack position, outside of automatic weapons range, the Suicider can be expected to reach his target, if not stopped, in about 20 seconds. At the initiation of the attack the gunner may be expected to be following the target. Thus, the reversal a large change of course at the outset requires the _utomatic sight to completely reverse its generated lead. This takes an appreciable time during which the directed fire will be considerably off the target. The fatal defect in this type of sight becomes evident when the plane accelerates rapidly in the dive. As long as acceleration continues, and it will to the target, the lead generated will never be enough to bring the fire up to the target. The immense volume of fire normally thrown behind a diving Suicider can do nothing but give hlim more enthusiasm for the job in hand.

'Fifty percent of that fire must be placed ahead of the plane. To obtain this result lead generating sights should be fitted with a control that when used will cause the sight to rapidly over-compensate for the speed of the target. The defect in generated lead also exists when a plane approaches and passes a ship close aboard. An acute angle at first, the angle between the line of sight and the path of the target increases until it becomes a right angle and then decreases. The angular rate of traverse of the guns is accelerating up until the plane passes with the result that the generated lead will lag the most when the target is within most effective range. Under this condition in order to hit the target the gunners must shift from sight to tracer control at some point in the planes approach.

'ATTACK BY HAND PLACED CHARGES
'9. In attacks by hand placed charges miscellaneous small boats were used. These boats depended upon stealth rather than speed in their approach. They have been described as about 18 feet long and "looked like an ordinary rowboat with an outboard motor" or "like a wherry with an outboard motor". One observer stated that the approach was discovered by hearing the exhaust of the "two cycle motor" before the boat could be seen. One boat was reported to be in the form of a small catamaran with an outboard motor. In this case the resulting explosion was of such in tensity that it was evident that the charge must have been of such size that it could not have been carried by the catamaran but must have been suspended beneath. In two instances the Japs were seen to roll a spherical mine-like object about two feet in diameter over the gunwale as the boat reached the ship's side. In two other cases observers stated the explosion occurred when the boat touched the ship's side. These latter two may have been explosive boats but in each case the resulting damage indicated the charge had exploded ten to fifteen feet below the surface. In one attack a Jap was seen to throw a charge as the boat passed close aboard.

'10. The success of these attacks by small boats can be attributed mainly to the lack of alertness and readiness for action by the ships at anchor. Attack by PT boats was anticipated but infiltration by small, quiet, low powered boats caught those on watch unprepared. Lights and portable automatic weapons which could be instantly trained on a boat under the counter or close alongside were not at hand. Most boats when first seen were so close that machine guns mounted on the ship could not be brought to bear. Corrective measures are obvious, in special watches, portable machine-guns, hand grenades.

'11. As this attack depends entirely upon surprise for success it was not to be expected that a repetition would soon be attempted. However, as we approach the Japanese mainland the territory becomes more and more favorable for such sneak attacks. The suicidal nature of the Jap is ideally suited, so we must be prepared for unexpected variations in this stealthy, sabotage-like form of attack.

'RECOMMENDATIONS
• AGAINST SUICIDE ATTACKS
1. For action against a diving attack, install on all automatic weapons equipped with lead generating sights, a control which when used will cause the sight to rapidly over-compensate for the speed of the target.

2. In the 5 inch AA fire put less emphasis on an accurate solution and put more stress on opening fire as soon as within range and maintaining the maximum volume of fire.

• AGAINST ATTACK BY SMALL BOATS
3. Take increased precautions to detect and counter sabotage like forms of attack.
4. At night when at anchor equip the deck sentries with portable searchlights and portable automatic weapons, and hand grenades.
5. Continue to man 20mm and 40mm guns in anticipation of high speed PT boat attacks.

• AGAINST DAMAGE BY FRIENDLY FIRE
6. Insist that personnel seek the maximum cover compatible with their duties.

7. Use safety observers at automatic weapons.

8. Use blindfold drill to train automatic weapons gunners to recognize dangerously low angles of fire by the feel of the gun's position rather than by what is seen in the sight.

'Elsewhere the report also said that: 'Immediate and drastic action within the individual ships and landing craft is necessary. In particular, all gunnery personnel must be impressed with the fact that the 20mm projectile does not have a self-destructive element, and that it is an inanimate but explosive object which possesses neither discretion or discrimination.'

USS *New Mexico* is hit by a kamikaze on 12 May 1945, while off Okinawa during Operation Iceberg.

Preliminary Bombardments
Edited excerpts from Observers' and 96th Infantry Reports on the Okinawa Operation, 3 March–9 April 1945.

'All landing operations in the Nansei Shoto were to be preceded by shore-based air, naval air, and surface bombardments of objectives in Formosa, the Nansei Shoto, and the Kyushu-Western Honshu area.

'a. The Naval Gunfire Support Plan was, of necessity, a very detailed one providing for effective support of the Expeditionary Force regardless of whether the Preferred or Alternate Plan was ordered executed. The fact that fast carriers, minesweepers, underwater demolition craft, transports, and other combat ships, a total of some 1,400 ships, would be operating in waters adjacent to the target area made it imperative that careful and coordinated plans be made so as to insure maximum efficiency.

'b. Okinawa was to be bombed by shore-based planes prior to the arrival of the Amphibious Support Group. On L-8 it was to be bombarded by carrier-based planes and fast battleships of Task Force 58. Other bombardments by this Task Force were to be designated by the Commander, Task Force 52.

'c. Underwater demolition teams were to undertake reconnaissance and demolition on the main and demonstration beaches concurrent with the bombardment, commencing on L-4.

'd. The plan called for supporting the capture of Okinawa by sustained neutralization, destruction, counter-battery, and harassing bombardments commencing on L-7: by intensive close support of the landings on Kerama Retto, Keise Shima, and Okinawa; by bombardments for supporting the diversionary feint at the landing near Sakibaru Saki; and thereafter by delivering call, deep supporting, counter-battery, illumination, and harassing fires. The plan also provided for the destruction of shore installations for firing torpedoes. Finally, it aimed to prevent the movement by sea of enemy troops for support or evacuation of the position.

'e. For this purpose the Amphibious Support Force under the command of Rear Admiral Blandy (until 06:00 on L Day when Vice-Admiral Turner was to assume command) was divided into five fire support groups:

Fire Support Units

Unit One (Rear Admiral Fischler)
BB #1 *Texas*
BB #10 *Arkansas*
CA #1 *Chester*
CA #2 *Tuscaloosa*
DD #1 *Laws* (F Des Div 110)
DD #2 *Longshaw*
DD #3 *Morrison*
DD #4 *Pritchett* (FD)

Unit Two (Rear Admiral Joy)
BB #2 *Maryland*
BB #3 *Colorado*
CA #4 *San Francisco*
CA #5 *Minneapolis* (F)
DD #5 *Hall* (F Des Div. 101)
DD #6 *Halligan* (FD)
DD #7 *P.-Hamilton*
DD #8 *Laffey*
DD #9 *Twiggs*

Unit Three (Rear Admiral Deyo)
BB #4 *Tennessee* (FTF 54)
BB #5 *Nevada*
CA #6 *Wichita* (F Cru Div 4)
CL #1 *Birmingham* (F)
CL #2 *Mobile*
DD #10 *M. L. Abele* (FD)
DD #11 *Zellars*
DD #12 *Bryant* (FD)
DD #13 *Barton* (F Des Div 119)
DD #14 *O'Brien*

Unit Four (Rear Admiral Rodgers).
BB #6 *West Virginia* (F Bat Div 4)
BB #7 *Idaho* (F)
CA #7 *Portland*
CA #8 *Pensacola*
CL #3 *Biloxi*
DD #15 *Porterfield* (F Des Div 109)
DD #16 *Callaghan*

DD #17 *C. Young* (FD)
DD #18 *Irwin*
DD #19 *Preston*

Unit Five (Rear Admiral Smith)
BB #8 *New Mexico*
BB #9 *New York*
CA #9 *Indianapolis*
CA #10 *Salt Lake City* (F)
DD #20 *H. L. Edwards*
DD #21 *Newcomb* (F Des Div 111)
DD #22 *Leutze*
DD #23 *R. P. Leary*
DD #24 *Bennion* (FD)

'f. The Target Priority Schedule was broken down into four priorities:

'(1) *First Priority* Installations which threaten ships, aircraft, and underwater demolition team operations. Specific targets, in order of importance, were to be: any battery, including torpedo tubes and rocket projectors, which opens fire on our ships or planes; coast defense guns; dual purpose guns; heavy AA; automatic AA; covered artillery emplacements within effective range of ships on landing beaches; open artillery emplacements where the presence of guns is confirmed by observation, if within effective range of ships or landing beaches; AT guns on or near the landing beaches; ships, barges, or boats.

'(2) *Second Priority* Installations which threaten assault forces in the ship-to-shore; movement and landing, Specific examples of these targets, in order of importance were to be: blockhouses and substantial buildings; pillboxes; seawalls fronting on the landing beaches with the stipulation that at least two breaches were to be made per beach; command posts; unidentified installations; earth-covered structures; areas of heavy growth.

'(3) *Third Priority* Installations which threaten or oppose landing force operations after the landing, or which affect the ability of the enemy to continue resistance. These, in order of importance, were to be: ammunition storage; storage areas; fuel dumps; camps or bivouac areas; communication centers and facilities; traffic which is of sufficient quantity and type to insure probable damages; urban areas; railroad centers and inland road junctions.

'(4) *Fourth Priority* Installations which should not be fired at prior to L Day, In order of importance they were to be: unoccupied rifle pits, foxholes, and fire trenches; open artillery enplacements when presence of guns is not established by observation; empty revetments; antitank trenches or sections of trenches; barbed wire.

'(5) Bridges were not to be fired upon except with the specific approval of Commander, Task Force 52:
    g. The Schedule of Fire was written up in table form.
(1) Tables were drawn up for each day commencing with L-7 to include L+1 day.
(2) They listed the number of Fire Support Unit, the ship number, the major caliber to be used; what the ship was to fire at (or to do) and at what time (as the table divided each day into hours from 0700 to 1900).
(3) Separate tables were computed for the schedule of fires on L-6 day for Yakaba Shima, Kuba Shima, Aka Shima, Geruna Shima, Hokaji Shima and Zamani Shima; on L-5 for Amuro Shima and Tokashiki Shima.
(4) A sketch showing the positions of DDs, LCIs, LSMs; the routes to be taken by LVTs and LCVPs on L-6 and L-5 around the smaller islands was attached to the plan.
(5) Separate tables were made for the Northern Attack Force and the Southern Attack Force for L Day with sketches showing the positions to be taken by combat ships of the fire support groups.

'h. Although they were not included in the Schedule of Fire Plan, it must be borne in mind that a sizeable number of gunboat support craft, landing craft support; mortar support craft, RCMs and rocket craft, landing ship medium (rocket) were to add to the planned fires described above.'

The 96th Infantry Division report said:

'The naval bombardment exerted a profound effect on the morale of our troops. In such terrain as exists in Okinawa it probably produced but few casualties in proportion to the vast amount of ammunition expended. Many of the caves in which the island abounds, and in which the enemy took shelter, were constructed into the steep hills and bordering the rivers and streams which run east and west. Consequently the cave openings faced north and south and naval gunfire, delivered from the west, could never achieve a direct hit within the cave. To effect any casualties in such a cave would require a burst at the exact height of the cave entrance and just in front of it. These apertures were about three feet wide and five feet high. Not all caves are so ideally situated, but they all present a small target area, affording utmost protection except where a direct hit or very near miss is secured.

'Naval bombardment was delivered on a scheduled basis until after the shore fire control parties had established themselves ashore. Thereafter, fire was delivered on call. The control of fire, and its coordination with air strikes, was very effective. The operation of air control parties followed established procedure,

'Communications functioned well in initiating, and adjusting fire missions. Naval gunfire remained available on call throughout the period covered by this report. It was used repeatedly by the 96th Infantry Division on enemy targets in the Naha Area with great effect, particularly in restricting Japanese counter measures. The slowness of the Japanese reaction to the landing on L-day, and the following day when the operation was at the critical stage, with troops ashore and supplies afloat, is attributed to the destruction of communication facilities by scheduled fires. Called fires on assembly areas and traffic centers prevented enemy interference with the consolidation of front line positions. Such fire also inhibited the disruption of unloading until all assault shipping had been cleared,

'From reports of other operations I have studied, I believe that naval gunfire was more accurately delivered in this operation than heretofore. I believe that naval gunfire achieved its maximum technical efficiency in the Okinawa expedition.'

USS *Colorado* during the pre-invasion bombardment of Okinawa, 29 March 1945.

THE COMMANDOS

Churchill wanted to set Europe alight after France fell, and the commandos were the result. They were under the control of Combined Operations Command, directed by Admiral of the Fleet Roger Keyes (17 July 1940–27 October 1941), then Lord Louis Mountbatten, (till October 1942) and then Maj-Gen Robert Laycock. Trained in clandestine warfare, usually inserted by sea, there were various types of commando. First, the Army Commandos. Set up as raiders, by 1944 they had conducted over 60 raids on the coasts of northwest Europe, as well as conducting operations in the Mediterranean, North Africa and Burma. In early 1944 they were organised into Special Service brigades and spearheaded landing operations. On D-Day, for example, commandos captured Port-en-Bessin from Gold Beach, and linked up with 6th Airborne to help protect the bridges over the Orne and adjacent canal. Then there were the Royal Marine Commandos, who fought alongside the Army Commandos: Nos 1 and 4 Bdes in northwest Europe; No 2 Bde in Italy, Yugoslavia and the Mediterranean area; and No 3 Bde in Burma. In late 1944 the Special Service title was dropped—the SS initials having bad associations! Also created were RN Beach Commandos, whose job was to control beachheads, and RAF Servicing Commandos.

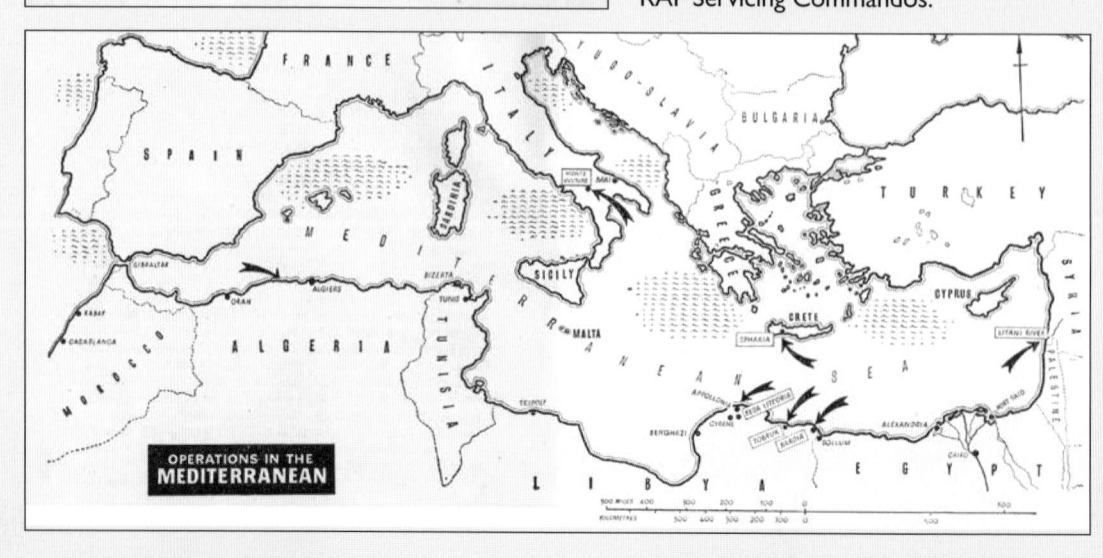

1 Raids

The Allies made a great deal of use of special forces. Most of their missions were small-scale operations that forced the Germans to tie up men and materiel to protect their conquests. Initially, these were undertaken by the newly formed Small Scale Raiding Force, made up mainly of officers and foreign national recruits from the SBS and the SOE using MTBs from Coastal Command. The SSRF was in turn absorbed by the newly formed Commandos.

There were hundreds of operations, such as the 'Cockleshell Heroes' attack on German shipping in the Gironde (see Operation Frankton) in December 1942. The Germans' response to raids and their fear of an Allied invasion meant that by D-Day the Atlantic Wall stretched from Norway to Spain, thousands of miles of reinforced concrete bunkers housing big guns and men that could have been better used elsewhere. Additionally, so angered by these attacks were the Germans that Hitler put out the *Kommandobefehl*—Commando order—on 18 October 1942. This ordered that anyone who took part in 'so-called Commando raids in Europe or in Africa, are to be annihilated to the last man ... Even if on discovery they make obvious their intention of giving themselves up as prisoners, no pardon is to be given on any account.' Six of the 'Frankton' force captured by the Germans were executed.

'Frankton', for all its morale-building on the Allied side, pointed out a number of flaws in the way it was organised—a parallel operation by SOE was taking place in the same location unbeknown to the Royal Marines Boom Patrol Detachment, which could have enhanced its effectiveness. While this was easy enough to sort out, other raids were also less than successful: for example another late 1942 operation, 'Agreement', in North Africa showed how speed of movement, surprise and bravery couldn't make up for faulty intelligence and lack of heavy weapons.

Nevertheless, raiding continued—in the Aegean and Adriatic especially, to the end of the war.

In the Pacific, the short-lived Marine Raiders unit was given few chances to perform as it had been trained, used instead as conventional infantry. Disbanded on 8 January 1944 after a lifespan of less than two years, they had had to fight the USMC's dislike of an elite grouping within an elite unit that was desperate for more men—so the Raider units became part of 6th Marine Division (1st Raider Battalion) and 4th Marines (2nd, 3rd and 4th). The Raider Training Battalion at Camp Pendleton joined 5th Marines.

Operation Claymore (Allied) 4 March 1941 Lofoten Islands, Norway

This was the first of a dozen British commando raids on German-occupied Norway. After defeat and retreat from the continent, these attacks were a reflection of Churchill's determination to strike back and take the fight to the enemy once more to boost British morale. 100 miles from the Arctic Circle, the Lofotens were an important centre for the processing of fish and the production of fish oil from which glycerine could be made. Glycerine was vital for the German war effort because it was a major ingredient in explosives such as nitroglycerine and in propellants such as cordite. This made the islands an important target and a good place to begin raiding.

This first attacking force left from Orkney and consisted of Nos 3 and 4 Cdo, a Royal Engineers section and some 50 Norwegian volunteers who would become the core of the future Norwegian Independent Company 1. They were supported by the Royal Navy's 6th Destroyer Flotilla and two troop transports.

Surprise was complete. Four ports were attacked, the landings were unopposed and the unfolding mission met little resistance. In an operation lasting only about six hours, using naval gunfire and demolition parties, the boiling plants and factories were destroyed along with hundreds of thousands of gallons of stored fish oil. Ten ships were also sunk and over 200 German prisoners and Norwegian Quisling regime collaborators were taken, as well as 300 new volunteers for the Free Norwegian Forces in Britain.

The most significant aspect of the raid, however, was the capture of a set of rotor wheels for an Enigma encoding machine along with its naval code books from the German armed trawler *Krebs*. The machine itself was thrown overboard but the rotors and books helped the British crack the Nazi battle codes at Bletchley Park, thus enabling Allied shipping to avoid the *Kriegsmarine*'s submarine wolf packs in the North Atlantic.

Operations Archery and Anklet (Allied) 26/27 December 1941 Lofoten Islands and Vågsøy, Norway

Simultaneous raids 300 miles apart, the smaller Operation Anklet was a diversion to distract from the main 'Archery' attack. The target of 'Anklet' target was, once again, the Lofoten Islands and it was carried out by 300 troops from No 12 Cdo and the Norwegian Independent Company 1, supported by a cruiser and eight destroyers.

Again the landing and raid was unopposed and the invaders suffered no casualties. At 06:00 on Boxing Day two harbours (Reine and Moskeneson) on the east side of the island of Moskenesoy were occupied, the wireless station and transmitters at Glaapen destroyed with its operators among the German prisoners taken along with the crews of several small boats.

Meanwhile the larger Operation Archery was taking place against German positions on the island of Vågsøy, 300 miles off the Norwegian coast. Commandos from Nos 2, 3, 4 and 6 companies took part, along with soldiers from Norwegian Independent Company 1, supported by a cruiser, four destroyers, a submarine and two troop transports as well as RAF bombers and fighter-bombers.

Following a successful naval bombardment the dawn landing objectives were all achieved except at the town of Måløy on southeastern side of the island, where a unit of experienced *Gebirgsjäger* (mountain troops) ensured the fighting descended into a bitter house-to-house battle. Four factories, fish oil tanks, ammunition and fuel stores, the telephone exchange and various military installations were all destroyed, 10 ships were sunk, 100 prisoners taken (along with still more Norwegian volunteers) and a complete copy of the *Kriegsmarine*'s code seized.

On the negative side, German coastal artillery hit the cruiser, killing four men and the commandos had 17 killed and 53 wounded. The commander of the Norwegian Armed Forces in exile, Captain Martin Linge, was killed in an attack on the local German headquarters and eight Royal Air Force aircraft were shot down. These raids achieved what Churchill had been aiming for, as it convinced Hitler to build more coastal and inland defences in the country, bolstered with an additional 30,000 troops.

Above: Burning fish oil tanks at Stansund, 4 March 1941.

Below: A souvenir of the mission.

Operation Biting (Allied) 27/28 February 1942 Bruneval, France

This British Combined Operations raid on a German coastal radar station at Bruneval, near Le Havre in northern France, took place on the night of 27/28 February 1942. British curiosity had been aroused after the construction of several of this type of installation, their coastal locations hinting at their true purpose. Thick German defences around them precluded a seaborne attack alone, as it would leave ample time for the target to be destroyed by its handlers, so an airborne assault with a seaborne evacuation of the captured equipment was conceived as the best way to sufficiently surprise and overwhelm the garrison. After a period of intense training a company of airborne troops (C Company, 2nd Parachute Battalion) landed at night a few miles from the target, then successfully attacked and seized the Bruneval installation. The Würzburg radar array was dismantled and the attacking force then withdrew to the prearranged evacuation beach, overwhelming any German opposition and also taking with them two German radar technicians. They and their prize were then taken by landing craft to waiting fast MGBs and whisked back home across the Channel. Casualties were light for the whole operation and the equipment enabled the British to understand the state of German radar capability and begin creating countermeasures. The Bruneval Raid later became The Parachute Regiment's first Battle Honour.

Left: The Würzburg gun-laying radar was an important element in the German defence against Allied aircraft. Operation Biting allowed British scientists to get their hands on a Type D (illustrated is a Type D on a Type A mount) which led to the creation of a jamming system.

THE LIE OF THE LAND. A scale-model, built up in exact detail from the reconnaissance photograph (*inset*), and used in the instruction of the men who went to Bruneval. The radiolocation apparatus can be seen "standing in a shallow pit between the cliffs and an isolated house." On the cliff's edge is a German machine-gun post.

Above and Opposite, Below: The combined operation was a complete success.

Below: Today, a memorial marks the location of the raid. Two Allied and five German soldiers were killed during the raid.

37

Force Viper (UK) 20 March 1942 Padaung, Burma (today, Myanmar)

Volunteers from the 1st RM Coast Regiment and MNBDO 1 (Mobile Naval Base Defence Organisation) along with some Burma Naval Volunteer Reserves and civilian engineers formed Force Viper in Rangoon in February 1942. They patrolled the waterways around the port with Irrawaddy Flotilla Company boats until the British were forced to leave Burma (General William Slim left Rangoon on 6 March). Thereafter, Force Viper protected the British left flank as they retreated along the Irrawaddy and Chindwin rivers. They impeded Japanese advances, ambushing Japanese river patrols. Lt Col G.R. Musgrave took over command of 'Viper' and Burma II Cdo. Reinforced by the commandos, Viper Force attacked Japanese positions at Henzada on 17 March. A few days later, further reinforced by a company-sized detachment of the Burma Military Police, they tried to ambush the Japanese further up the Irrawaddy. The commandos, with an RM MG section, No 2 Platoon Royal Marines and the Burma Military Police, set up their positions, but the enemy did not fall into the trap. On 31 March the Japanese—who had been hiding in Padaung village—attacked Force Viper which lost an officer and 35 men missing.

Left: This map shows Force Viper's main encounters with the Japanese.

Above Right: Force Viper included 106 marines who had volunteered in Columbo for special service in Burma. Two bearded marines are seen on the *Chittagong* with the captain and a native crewman on *Doris*.

Centre Right: Force Viper fought from an improvised flotilla of touring launches and motor boats, seen here on the Irrawaddy.

Below Right: Yenanyaung's oil is destroyed so the Japanese cannot use it.

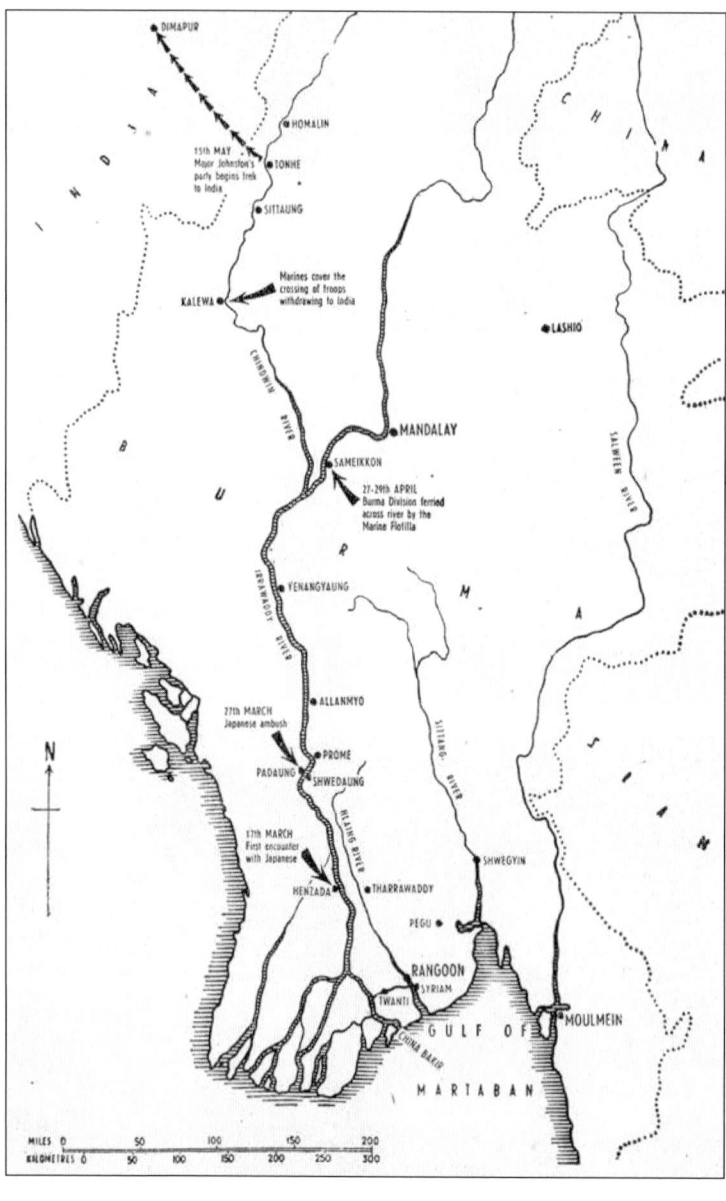

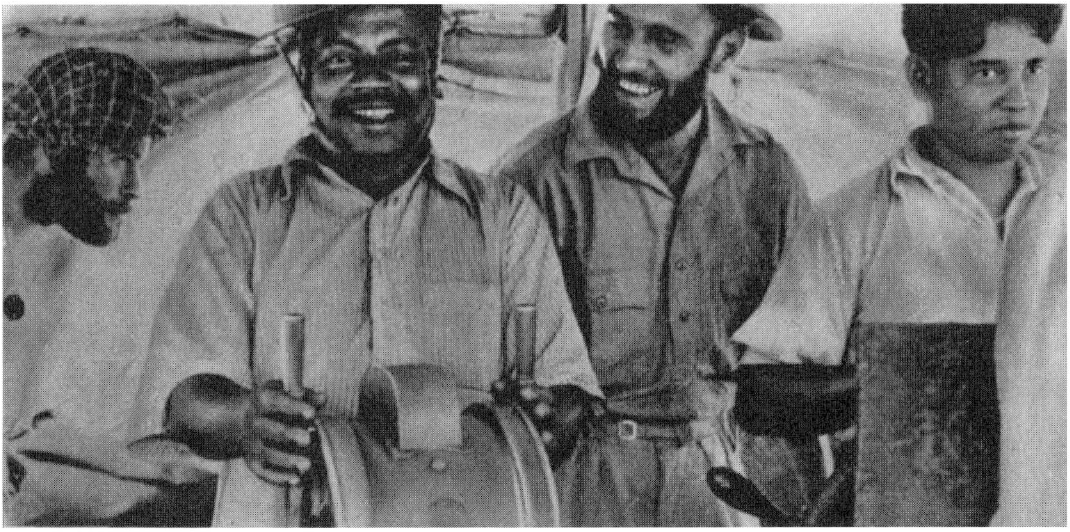

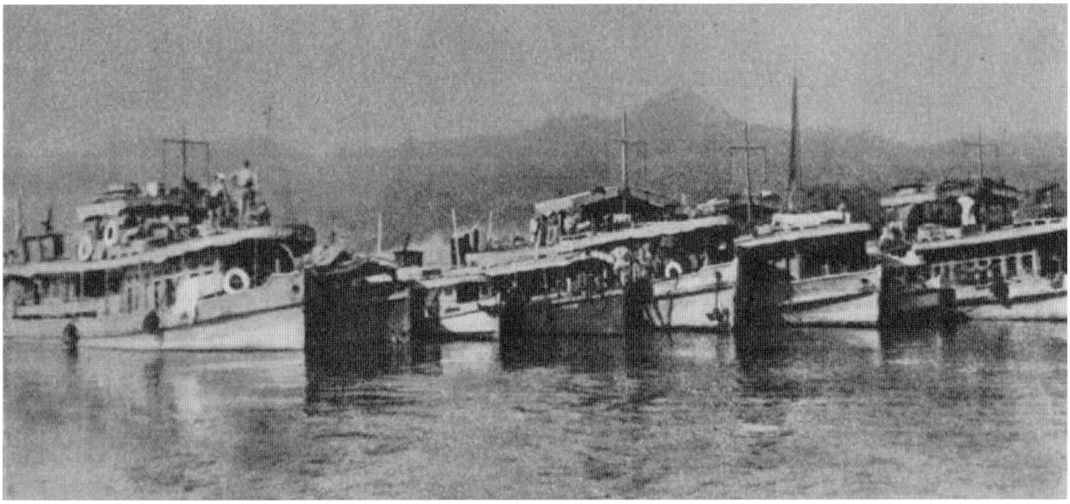

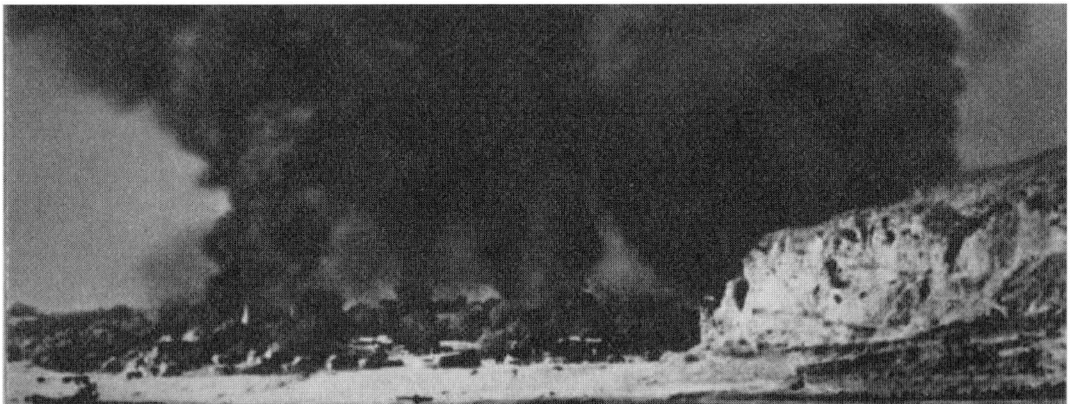

Operation Chariot (UK) 27/28 March 1942 St Nazaire, France

Possibly the greatest raid of the war, Operation Chariot's audacious assault deservedly won 89 medals, including five Victoria Crosses. It also put the largest dock facilities on the French Atlantic coastline out of action for the rest of the war, thereby preventing the deadly German battleship *Tirpitz* from disrupting Atlantic convoys, leaving her instead confined to Norwegian waters.

Set five miles inland up the Loire estuary, the *Normandie* dry dock facilities at St Nazaire had a well-protected access channel that passed close to a shoreline bristling with blockhouses and gun emplacements, so the raiding force had to consist of boats light enough to cross the sandbanks farther out. To achieve this 18 MTBs, MGBs and MLs were used, along with a specially lightened and adapted obsolete destroyer, the *Campbeltown*, packed with explosives.

The raiding force consisted of the Royal Navy along with men from Nos 1, 2, 3, 4, 5, 9 and 12 Cdo. Under low cloud, an ineffective RAF bombing raid began the operation at around midnight on 27/28 March. This merely served to warn the defenders. The attacking boats initially flew German flags and transmitted German signals to confuse the enemy until they were two miles from the target, when the swastikas were replaced with the Royal Navy's White Ensign. In the ensuing maelstrom of fire, half the men aboard the smaller ships were either killed or wounded and only two succeeded in unloading their commandos. Fierce close-quarter fighting ensued.

At 01:34 the *Campbeltown* was successfully driven into the dock gates and scuttled. At noon on the 28th its delayed explosives destroyed the lock gates and over 400 German soldiers on the ship itself and its vicinity. British casualties were severe: only 228 of the 622 who left Falmouth returned. Casualties included 169 dead and 215 captured. Of the 18 craft which set out from Falmouth, only four returned. Despite the heavy losses the operation was an outstanding success—it took until 1948 for the dry dock to reopen.

Right: *Campbeltown* wedged in the dock gates before it exploded.

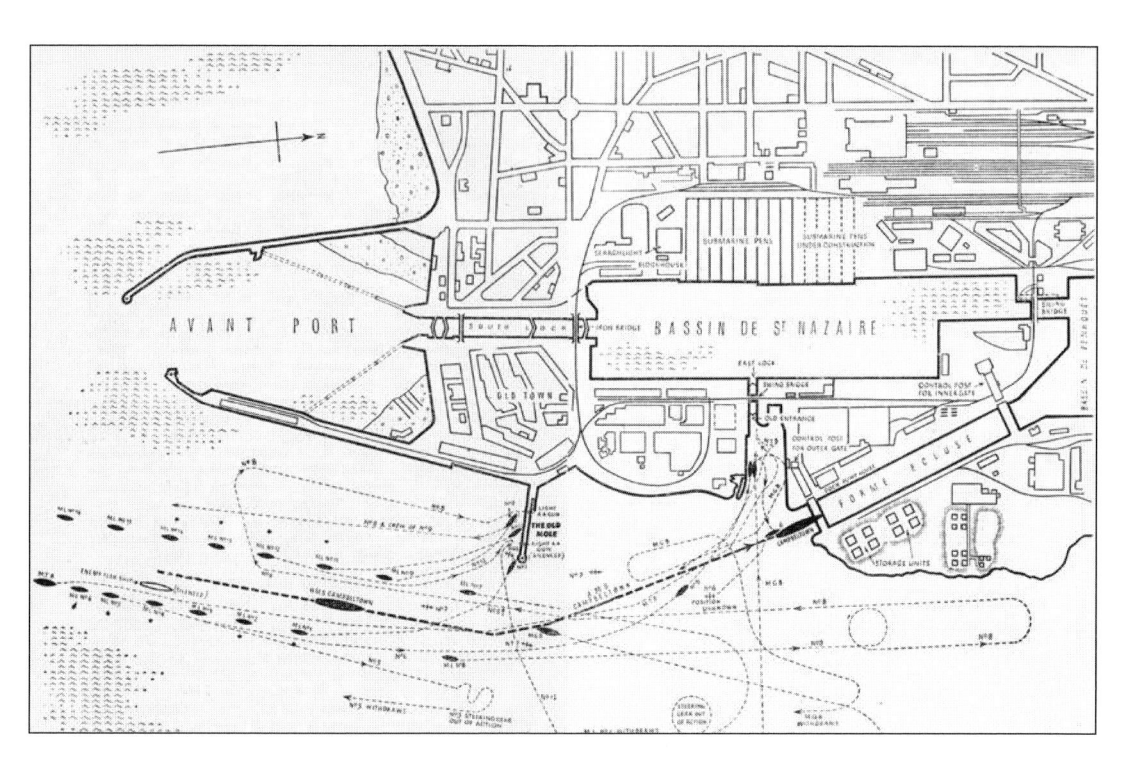

Left: Some of the lucky few to return from St Nazaire.

Below Left: An artist's view of the fighting.

Above: The action at St Nazaire.

Below: Tulagi's Blue Beach on 7 August.

Operation Watchtower (US) 7-8 August 1942 Tulagi Island, Solomon Islands

Tulagi Island lies north of Guadalcanal and the raid was part of the battle for that island (see p. 74). Tulagi was the scene of the first action by the Marine Raiders, a counterpart of the British commandos. On the morning of 7 August 1st Raider Battalion (under Lt Col Merritt A. Edson) embarked onto Higgins boats. After a preliminary bombardment the first wave, Companies B and D, headed for shore. As they waded the last 100 yards, it became obvious there was no enemy opposition. Companies A and C followed quickly. They advanced southeast and ran into heavy Japanese resistance about noon. Well entrenched, refusing to surrender, the Japanese in caves and bunkers had to be winkled out with explosives. On the

Above: Tulagi from the air on 7 August.

Below Right: Map showing the island.

Opposite, Above: Raiders return to Pearl Harbor, Hawaii on board *Argonaut* on August 26 following the Makin Island raid.

Opposite, Below: Lt Col Evans F. Carlson, USMCR, and Maj James Roosevelt hold a Japanese flag taken from the Japanese HQ after the raid on Makin Island.

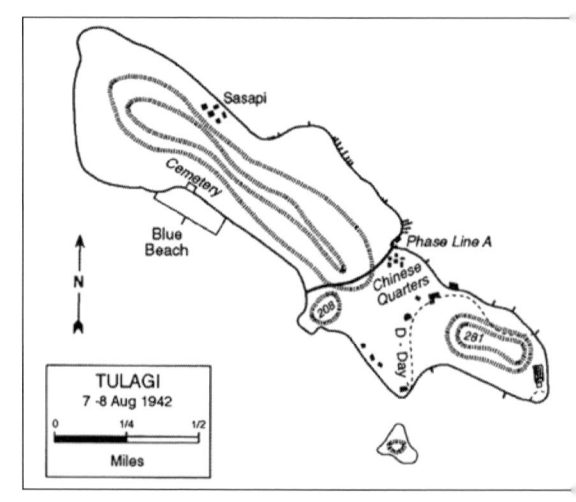

8th, at 09:00 two companies of 5th Marines joined the Raiders and fought the final enemy concentrations. At 15:00 Edson declared the island secured. The raiders lost 38 DIA and 55 WIA. All but three of the 350 Japanese defenders had died.

However, on the night of 8 August Japanese surface forces surprised the Allied units guarding the transports. Four Allied cruisers and a destroyer were sunk, and 1,200 sailors died, making the operation a costly victory.

Other actions took place at neighbouring islands: the 1st Parachute Battalion, USMC, assaulted (by sea) and took Gavutu Island while 3rd Battalion 2nd Marines took Tanambogo. Both islands were in US hands by 9 August.

Raider Operations
Edited excerpts from FM 31-5 of November 1944,

'GENERAL.
'a. Amphibious operations may include landings of especially trained and transported raider forces, lightly armed and equipped, on shores not suitable for usual landing forces because of natural underwater barriers, difficult shore terrain, or adverse sea conditions.
'b. Infantry rifle troops are well suited to operate as raiders. With basic organization and equipment, they may be trained sufficiently in a few weeks to accomplish missions of average difficulty. Cavalry reconnaissance troops of infantry divisions, or other similar units, also may be adapted quickly to this type of operation.
c. Raider forces are assigned missions within their capabilities to accomplish within the time available before scheduled withdrawal.

'LANDING CAPABILITIES
'a. Raider troops are trained to land at places where usual methods are impracticable, by use of rubber or other light boats or by swimming.
'b. The special training and equipment of raider troops gives them additional capabilities of swift movement and surprise in landings from destroyers, LCI (L), submarines, flying boats, or other craft.
'c. Raiders should be trained to operate individually and in small groups so that wider deployment in landing and greater mobility ashore are possible than for a normal landing force.
d. In very cold weather, raider troops with special watertight rubber clothing and protective devices may land when other troops cannot. To reduce loss from drowning, troops landing from rubber or other small boats must carry only minimum equipment—weapons, ammunition, water, and rations.

'LIMITATIONS
'a. Raider operations are characterized by lack of sustained fighting power due to difficulties of supply and transportation.
'b. Operations are limited largely to night landings because of the vulnerability of rubber landing craft.
'c. Strong offshore winds or currents delay or prevent landings.'

Makin Island Raid (US) 17 August 1942 Gilbert Islands

Companies A and B of 2nd Raider Battalion (under Lt Col Evans F. Carlson) were delivered to Makin (today, Butaritari) Island in Makin Atoll by two minelaying submarines, the *Nautilus* and *Argonaut*. The raid achieved its purpose in as much as it killed the Japanese garrison for the apparent loss of 30 men, but it didn't divert Japanese attention from Guadalcanal as had been hoped. The raid highlighted the problems that raiders faced from adverse weather, heavy surf on small boats and poor equipment. After the event there were doubts, too, about the commander, Carlson, who was awarded a second Navy Star but who had actually sent a surrender document to the Japanese after having failed to extract his men through the surf. (It was delivered after the raid had finished.) Nevertheless, the raid was a huge propaganda victory for the Americans at a difficult time. What they didn't know was that nine raiders had been left on the island. When they finally surrendered, they were taken by the Japanese to Kwajalein Island and beheaded on the orders of Admiral Koso Abe who was hanged postwar for war crimes.

Tasimboko Raid (US) 8 September 1942 Guadalcanal, Solomon Islands

The American landings on Guadalcanal (see p. 74) on 7 September 1942 were the starting point in their strategic intent of liquidating the Japanese base at Rabaul and cutting the 'Tokyo Express': the Japanese night-time resupply of New Guinea and the Solomons. The landings succeeded in gaining a firm foothold at Lunga Point around an airfield (it became Henderson Field on 12 August). The immediate Japanese response was to send 35th Infantry Brigade under Maj Gen Kiyotake Kawaguchi to retake the island.

By 7 August a sizeable Japanese unit had been landed east of Lunga Point at Taivu and had started to move towards the American perimeter, planning to attack from the south. Alerted to the Japanese arrival by coastwatchers, a raid against the Japanese at Taivu Point and the nearby village of Tasimboko was planned. 1st Raider Battalion rifle companies embarked on two APDs and two converted tuna boats for the operation—the weapons company and Parachute Battalion, under Raider command, would follow later.

When they landed they realised that the Japanese force was larger than they expected—but that it had moved inland and hadn't left a large rearguard. This defended stubbornly but once the second raider contingent arrived, they were able to get on top of the opposition and entered the village around noon. They destroyed the Japanese brigade's stores of food, ammunition and weapons, and damaged Japanese logistics, fire support and communications for the loss of two dead and six wounded.

The raiders were extracted and moved to what would become known as 'Edson's Ridge'. There they endured two nights (12/13 and 13/14 September) of heavy action as Kawaguchi's central unit of around 3,000 men bore down on the five companies of Raiders and the Parachute Battalion.

The Japanese attacks were held and 'Red Mike' Edson was awarded the Congressional Medal of Honor for his inspired leadership.

Operation Jubilee (UK/CAN) 19 August 1942 Dieppe, France

Dieppe was the largest raid of the war up to that time, planned in an attempt to coordinate combined Allied forces, test German defences, seize a port and maul the Luftwaffe. It also saw the first Canadian action of the war and the first use of the American Rangers, the American equivalent of the British commandos. From beginning to end it was an unmitigated disaster, resulting in almost the entire force of 6,000 men, mostly Canadians, including an armoured regiment, being killed, wounded or captured within ten hours as the unpreparedness and inexperience of the Allies was driven painfully home.

Originally scheduled for July and known as Operation Rutter, bad weather saw it postponed. Montgomery thought it should be called off altogether, but when he was sent to command Eighth Army, Mountbatten—then Chief of Combined Operations—pushed hard for its reinstatement.

So it was that, early on the morning of 19 August, commandos and Canadian troops attacked the gun batteries to the east and west of the port before the main assault went in. However, the element of surprise had been lost when the invading fleet encountered a German convoy and only one battery was taken. The main attack on the port was led by the Essex Scottish Regiment and Royal Hamilton Light Infantry and was to have been supported by the 14th Canadian Armoured Regiment. However, the armour turned up late, leaving the infantry regiments without support and exposed to such heavy fire that they were unable to overcome the seawall. When it arrived, the armour had problems with the shingle beach and the seawall and other obstacles. Very few of the attackers—and only 15 tanks which were stopped by concrete blocks—managed to get off the beaches, becoming instead sitting ducks. To compound the disaster, the two reserve units were thrown in. The Fusiliers Mont-Royal were immediately pinned down under the cliffs and the Royal Marines sent in to support them had most of their landing craft destroyed by enemy fire.

The mission was aborted by 11:00 and fewer than 2,500 of the 6,000 attackers made their way back to England.

The fallout from the raid was considerable and as might be expected from such a costly mistake, there was a lot of blame-shifting and whitewashing. In fact, the failure of the raid did much to highlight issues that needing fixing before a second front could be opened. It laid bare the problems of attacking a defended port which led to the development of the portable Mulberry harbours. It inspired the specialised armoured vehicles required to break through beach defences, including swimming, bunker busting, bridgelaying, anti-mine and flamethrowing tanks. It highlighted the need for proper intelligence about the beaches and their defences, and the imperative for the involvement of heavy-gun bombardments and heavy bombers. Two years later, Operation Overlord showed that the Allies had learnt their hard lesson.

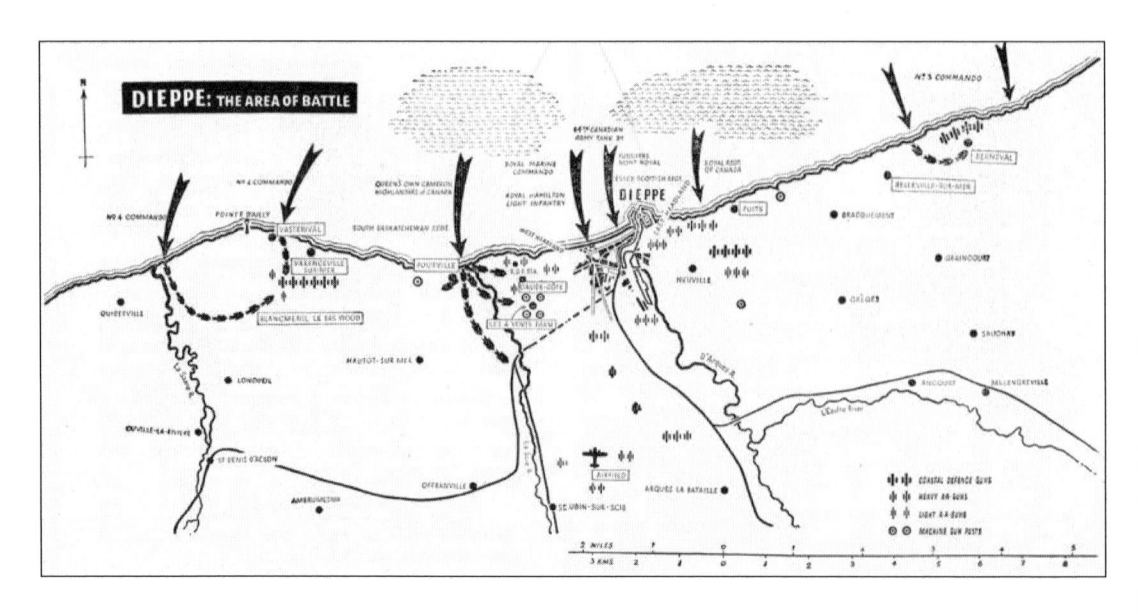

Above: The attacking craft prepare for action. Landing craft losses were 33 of 179: 17 LCA, 8 LCP(L), 5 LCT, I LCM, I LCS, I LCF. In autumn 1942 Combined Operation HQ reported on the lessons to be learnt from Operation Jubilee (see summary on p. 44). One of the main lessons concerned support of the landings—not just in a bigger pre-assault bombardment, nor stronger bombing, although both were mentioned, but in 'overwhelming fire support during the initial stages of the attack. It is during these vital minutes while troops are disembarking, cutting or blasting their way through wire, clearing beach mines and finding routes over obstacles that the need for close support is at its greatest ... It is quite certain that the "Support Craft" which are now available do not meet the requirement envisaged ... They are too lightly armed and too lightly armoured.' What was needed was 'an entirely new type of support vessel ... which might be described as a shallow-draught armoured gun-boat.' These comments related to craft in action for the first time: a Beach Patrol Craft with twin 4-inch DP guns; LCFs, with four Oerlikons and eight 2-pdr Pom-Poms and two LCG(L)s, each with two 4.7-inch guns in open gun houses. These had come into service during 1942. One of the LCFs got close to shore and gave 'close support until she was disabled, her captain killed, her guns put out of action one by one until she finally sank'.

Below: The only successful part of the operation was Lord Lovat's No 4 Cdo, which knocked out its target, the battery at Varengeville.

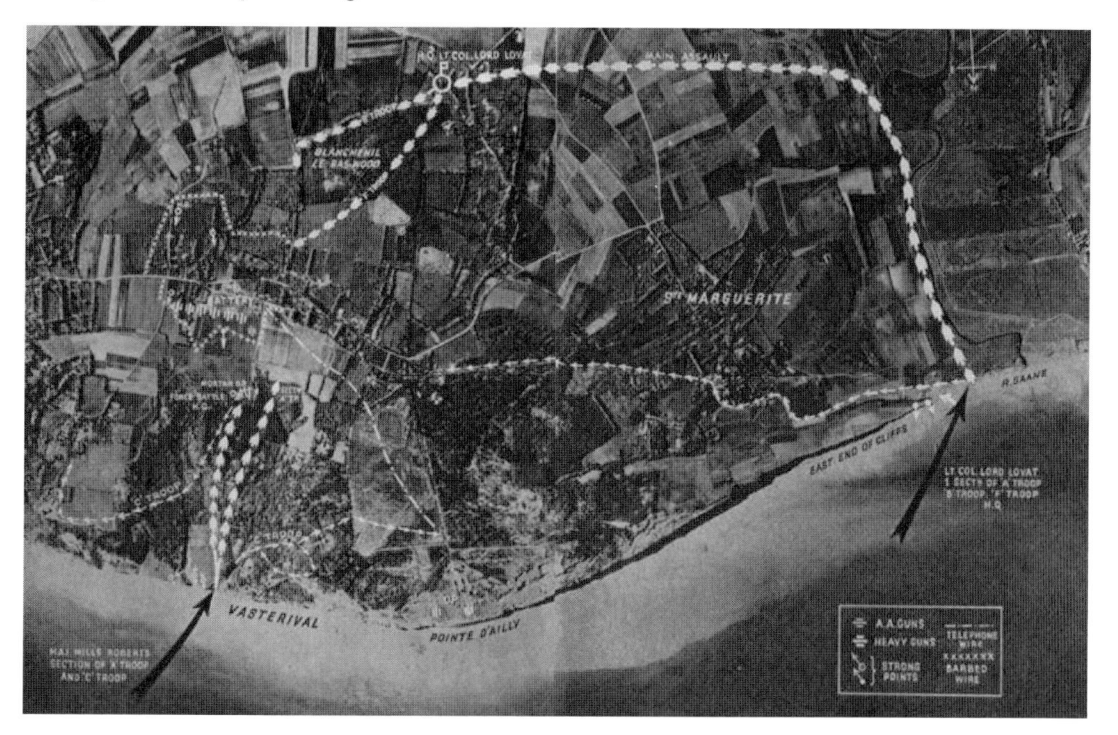

The Raid on Dieppe Lessons Learnt
THE LESSONS IN SUMMARISED FORM

'324. The need for overwhelming fire support, including close support during the initial stages of the attack.

325. The necessity for the formation of permanent naval assault forces with a coherence comparable to that of any other first line fighting formations. Army formations intended for amphibious assaults must without question be trained in close co-operation with such naval assault forces.

326. The necessity for planning combined operation at a Combined HQ where the Force Commanders and their staff can work and live together.

327. The necessity to plan a raid so as to be independent of weather conditions in the greatest possible degree. A plan based on the assumption that weather conditions will be uniform is very likely to fail; therefore a plan which can be carried out even when they are indifferent or bad is essential.

328. The necessity for flexibility in the military plan and its execution. To achieve this, the assault must be on the widest possible front limited only by the possibilities of control and the amount of naval and air support available.

329. The allocation to the assault of the minimum force required for success and the retention of the maximum force as a reserve to exploit success where it is achieved.

330. The necessity for as accurate and comprehensive a system of control and communications as it is possible to establish.

331. The dissemination of knowledge to officers and other ranks, each of whom should know the intention of his superior, the outline of the operation and the details of the task of his own unit and those on the flanks.

332. The value of special training, particularly in amphibious night operations. Such training must include rehearsals and the testing of inter-communication arrangements.

333. The necessity for fire support in any operation where it has not been possible to rely on the element of surprise. This fire support must be provided by heavy and medium Naval bombardment, by air action, by special vessels or craft working close inshore, and by using the fire power of the assaulting troops while still seaborne. Special close-support craft, which should be gun-boats or some form of mobile fort, do not exist and must be designed and constructed.

Support by the Royal Air Force is effective within the limits imposed by time and space.

334. Assaults must be carefully timed. Whether to assault in darkness, at dawn or dusk or in daylight, must depend on the nature of the raid, and on certain conditions, such as tide and distance, which will vary in every case.

335. Tanks should not be landed until the anti-tank defences have been destroyed or cleared.

L.C.T. carrying tanks must not linger on the beaches beyond the time required to disembark their loads.

336. Great and continuous attention must be paid to security problems and greater use made of subordinate officers who should be put partly into the picture, so that they can control the men under them. Only important extracts from Operation Orders should be taken ashore, be kept in manuscript form and have their official headings removed.

337. Briefing of the troops should take place as late as possible.

If airborne troops are used, arrangements must be made to increase the number available so as to cut down the time needed for briefing.

Airborne troops provide means of achieving surprise and should be used as often as possible subject to the limitations of the weather. It should be regarded, however, as exceptional for a plan to depend for success entirely on their use.

338. Unless means for the provision of overwhelming close support are available, assaults should be planned to develop round the flanks of a strongly defended locality rather than frontally against it.

339. A far higher standard of aircraft recognition is essential both in the Royal Navy and the Army. This should be achieved by means of lectures, photographs and silhouettes, personnel of the Royal Observer Corps should be carried in ships.

340. Beach Signal parties should not land complete with the first wave, but only when the beach has been secured.

341. The importance and necessity of using smoke cannot be over emphasized and quantities of smoke must be carried in any operation of the size of the assault on Dieppe.

342. Some form of light or SP artillery must be provided once an assault has got across the landing place and is making progress inland.'

Right: The beach at Dieppe. In the background, the cliffs overlook the vehicles stranded below: a Dingo in the distance and a Churchill in the foreground. With waterproofed hulls and air intake and exhaust trunking (the Y-shaped trunking at rear) they were able to make their way through the shallows.

Operation Agreement (UK) 13–14 September 1942 Tobruk, Libya

An ambitious plan, Operation Agreement was an attempt to wreak havoc in North Africa, using Royal Marines, the Long-Range Desert Group, the SAS and men of the Argyle & Sutherland Highlanders and Royal Northumberland Fusiliers. Its focus was Tobruk; subsidiary operations targeted Benghazi ('Bigamy'), Jalo Oasis ('Nicety') and Barce ('Caravan').

The amphibious element of the operation aimed at disrupting Axis supply lines in the buildup to the battle of El Alamein which would open on 23 October. The key harbour at Tobruk was the main target but the British planners had either not realised how effective the defenders were or had assumed that surprise would give them more of an edge. In fact, the Italian marines of the 3rd Battalion, 'San Marco' Regiment and the 88mm guns of the German defenders under Generalmajor Otto Deindl were extremely effective.

The operation was a complete failure. The Allies—British, New Zealand and Rhodesians—lost 800 killed and 576 captured as well as umpteen vehicles destroyed. At sea, a cruiser, two destroyers, four MTBs, two MLs and a number of landing craft were lost to the gunfire of Italian *motozattere* and other light craft.

The key elements were the German and Italian air assets: command of the skies was evidenced by the loss of HMSs *Coventry* and *Zulu* to dive-bomber attacks; the destroyer HMS *Sikh* was struck by Italian 152mm shore batteries and German 88mm anti-tank guns, while picking up troops.

Below: Italian torpedo boats *Castore* and *Montanari* (top right) firing upon British MTBs and MLs at Tobruk harbour, 14 September 1942.

Operation Frankton (UK) 7-12 December 1942 Gironde, France

A limpet mine attack on shipping in Bordeaux carried out by the RMBPD, 'Frankton' took place in December 1942. Six two-man folding Cockle Mk 2 kayaks were transported to the Gironde estuary by submarine HMS *Tuna*, one was damaged during assembly, leaving only five and ten men to complete the mission. Of these only two survived and escaped through the French underground network, two died of hypothermia and the rest were captured and executed.

Of the five kayaks launched from the *Tuna* on 7 December, three became separated with their crews eventually caught or betrayed over the next days. It took five nights for the remaining two to reach Bordeaux through heavy seas and enemy patrols, one placed eight limpet mines on four vessels including a fast patrol boat, the other placed eight limpet mines on two vessels, five on a large cargo ship and three on a small liner. The two crews then separated and set out on foot for the Spanish border. One pair were captured and shot by the Germans, joining in death the six others also captured. The final pair eventually made it back home. In 1955 a heavily fictionalised version of the story was depicted in the film *The Cockleshell Heroes*.

Above: The two-man teams head off to the Gironde in Cockles Mk II canoes.

Below: 'Frankton' memorial in Saint-Georges-de-Didonne, near Royan.

Operation Jaywick (Allied) 26 September 1943 Singapore, Straits Settlements

'Jaywick' was the first operation carried out by the Z Special Unit, a sabotage and raiding group made up predominantly of Australians, with several British SOE officers who had escaped from Singapore (then Straits Settlements, today a republic). 'Jaywick' targeted shipping in the Japanese-occupied Singapore Harbour and for transport used a captured Japanese coastal fishing boat, the *Kofuku Maru*, renamed the *Krait*. The crew went to great lengths to appear as native Indonesian fishermen, dyeing their skin and wearing sarongs. Arriving off Singapore on 24 September six men using folboats (folding kayaks) paddled 30 miles to hide in a cave on a small island near the harbour. On the night of 26 September they used limpet mines to sink or damage six Japanese ships, totalling almost 40,000 tons, and then slipped away without being discovered. The Japanese presumed it to be a case of local sabotage and issued severe punishments to the local population, while the *Krait* arrived safely back in Australia.

Operation Rimau (Allied) 10-16 October 1944 Singapore, Straits Settlements

Operation Rimau was the second attack on Japanese-held Singapore Harbour, to be carried out by the Z Special Unit, again under the command of Lt Col Ivan Lyon, following the successful Operation Jaywick. Again folboats and limpet mines were to be used for the actual assault. The mother ship was a junk named *Mustika*. It had no engine and had been captured in late September off the coast of Borneo by the submarine *Porpoise*. Just an hour before the raid was due to start disaster struck when a coastal Malay Police boat discovered and challenged the *Mustika*. After a firefight in which some of the enemy crew escaped, Lyon decided to abort the mission and scuttled the ship, splitting the men into four groups to make their escape using the folboats. There then followed a series of battles with the Japanese on different islands as the men from Z Special Unit were hunted down. Those that weren't killed in the fighting either died of their wounds in captivity or were tried and executed by the Japanese for espionage.

Below: The *Krait*.

1944
Operation Rimau

11 September 1944
Lt. Col. Ivan Lyon & 22 men of Z Special Unit boarded the HMS Porpoise for the takeoff of Merapas, nr Singapore, in a follow on mission to the successful Operation Jaywick.

Operation Gauntlet (BR) 25 August–3 September 1941 Spitzbergen, Norway

The island of Spitzbergen in the Svalbard Archipelago, warmed by the North Atlantic Current, may be inside the Arctic Circle but is usually less cold than equivalent locations on the same latitude. In the 1940s it had profitable coalmines and was also the location of a number of weather stations.

Because of this, a plan was proposed to land two Canadian infantry battalions and other troops to take possession of the island. However, this changed during August 1941. Rather than occupy the island, it was decided to leave them unusable by the enemy. The mines were owned by Norway and Russia and both governments agreed that the infrastructure should be destroyed to stop the Germans from making use of them.

This was effected by Operation Gauntlet: the landing of Canadian, British and Free Norwegian troops on Spitzbergen. They destroyed stores and equipment and burnt 450,000 tons of coal at the mines before reembarking the troops and taking with them the civilian population and some French PoWs who had been interned by the Soviets. The weather station wireless transmissions ceased and the Allied armada left along with its prizes: three colliers and five other vessels.

Operation Citronella (GER) 8 September 1943 Spitzbergen, Norway

'Citronella' was an eight-hour German raid on Spitzbergen in the Svalbard Archipelago. It was carried out by the battleships *Tirpitz* and *Scharnhorst* along with nine 'Narvik' class destroyers from the 4th, 5th and 6th Flotillas and a battalion fortress infantry from 349th Grenadier Regiment. It was carried out primarily to encourage Hitler to keep the surface ships he possessed in action.

The ships set off on 6 September; early on the 8th the *Scharnhorst* and the 5th and 6th Destroyer Flotillas landed troops in Advent Bay, while *Tirpitz* and the 4th Flotilla sailed to Barentsburg, where they began a bombardment then landed the battalion of fortress troops. Coal heaps, ammunition and fuel dumps, food and water supplies and electricity generators were all destroyed in the ensuing assault and bombardments. The Norwegian defenders valiantly shelled the destroyers with their Bofors guns, inflicting some damage until silenced by the *Tirpitz*, the survivors then fled inland.

Nervous of the British Home Fleet being tipped off by the Norwegians, the Germans didn't linger long before they returned home with some 30 Norwegian prisoners.

Canadian and Norwegian troops boarding the boats after their successful operation on Spitzbergen.

Operation Endowment (BR) 22 March 1944 Hvar, Yugoslavia (today, Croatia)

The German invasion of Yugoslavia took place between 6 and 17 April 1941. The resulting guerrilla warfare by Chetniks (royalists) and Partisans (Tito's communists) led to large numbers of German and other troops—mainly Bulgarians—tied down in the area. There were numerous anti-guerrilla sweeps through the country—and an attempt to capture or kill Tito at his Drvar HQ in May 1944 (Operation *Rösselsprung*). These operations left all but the island of Vis in German hands. Tito moved there after the attempt on his life. The Germans planned an invasion of Vis (Operation *Freischütz*) but it never happened. British air and other assets (including over 1,000 British troops—Land Forces Adriatic) protected Tito. Among the troops were Nos 40 and 43 RM Cdo, 2nd Highland Light Infantry, batteries of artillery, a COPP and numerous partisans.

From this base there were a number of raids and landings on nearby islands in 1944 before and after Operation *Rösselsprung*. The map (**Right**) shows: Brac (Operation Flounced, 31 May–5 June), Hvar (Operation Endowment, 22–26 March), Korcula (various operations including Shoot III, 21 April; Decomposed II, 31 July–2 August; and Grandfather, 25–27 August), Mljet (Operation Farrier, 22–24 May) and Šolta (Operation Detained, 8–10 May).

'Endowment' took place after Second *Panzerarmee* withdrew troops from Hvar. No 43 Cdo and men of the 1st and 4th Battalions, 1st Dalmatian Brigade, NOVJ (the Yugoslav Partisan National Liberation Army) landed on the 22nd and swept the island. The fighting continued after the commandos were withdrawn on the 24th; the partisans left on the 28th/29th when there were reports of major German reinforcements. The butcher's bill was 32 DIA and 152 PoW for the Germans; 3 DIA and 23 WIA on the Allied side.

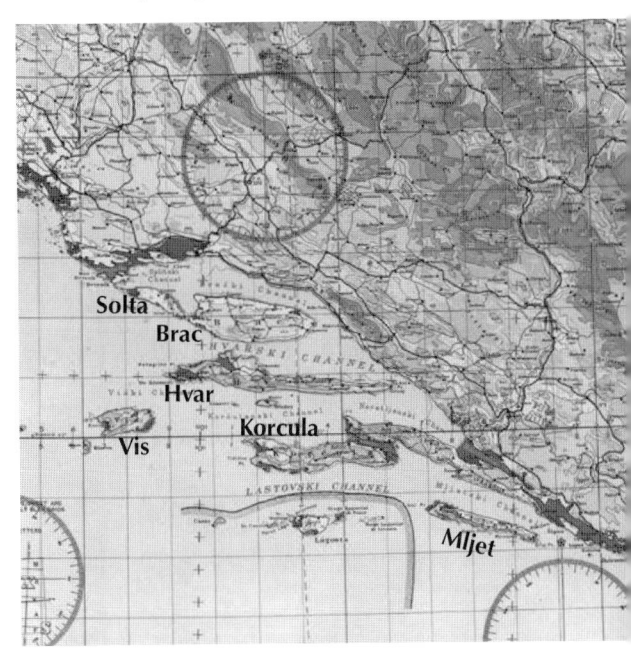

The Dalmatian shoreline and profusion of islands provided a perfect environment for clandestine operations, and 1944 and 1945 saw many take place: commandos, SAS/SBS, LRDG, SIS/SOE/OSS and guerrillas all fought the Germans and ran away, forcing them to spread their troops around the Balkans. Many of the operations were into Italy to rescue PoWs who had escaped—or evaders—such as Operation Darlington II on 24 May 1944 that saw 100 PoWs picked up by a No 9 Cdo LCI.

Operation Sunbeam (BR) 17/18 June 1944 Portolago Bay, Leros, Greece

The islands nearer Greece had become important targets with the surrender of Italy on 8 September 1943. However, with the Americans implacably opposed, as was CIGS Gen. Sir Alan Brooke, Churchill's baby—the grabbing of Rhodes and islands in the Dodecanese—Operation Accolade—failed horribly (see p. 100).

Raiding was more successful. Raiding Forces Middle East was in charge of operations nearer Greece, and the SBS (originally the Special Boat Squadron, it became the Special Boat Service in early 1945) played an important role in the overall plan—codenamed 'Fireater'. The Levant Schooner Flotilla and its successor, the Anglo-Hellenic Schooner Force, provided the caiques to transport clandestine forces using harbours in Turkish waters. Many of the operations included significant Greek involvement. Laki Harbour in Portolago Bay was the Italian navy's main base in the eastern Mediterranean, and on 17 June was being used by two German destroyers as well.

Just before midnight on 17 June a Fairmile motor launch delivered three canoes each containing two members of the Royal Marines Boom Patrol Detachment, the same unit that had provided the crews for Operation Frankton (see p. 48). Indeed, one of the marines attacking Portolago Bay was

Eric Fisher, whose canoe had been damaged before 'Frankton' forcing him to pull out.

The three canoes were commanded by Lt J. F. Richards (paired with Marine W. S. Stevens) in *Shark*; Sgt J. M. King and Marine R. N. Ruff were in *Salmon* and Cpl Johnny Horner and Marine Eric Fisher were in *Shrimp*.

They entered the harbour at 01:10 on the 18th and began to attach limpet mines to the ships' sides. The limpets had powerful magnets and were set off by timer. They also had anti-handling devices; unfortunately, they didn't carry much explosive.

They mined three escorts and two destroyers. Remarkably, even though they were sighted a number of times, none of the canoes was stopped and all of them reached the island of Kalymnos where they hid up. From about 04:45 they started to hear explosions

Above: A caique of the Levant Schooner Flotilla.

as the mines went off. A resounding success, the operation had neutralised German naval forces in the Aegean.

Operation Tenement (BR/GR) 17/18 June 1944 Island of Symi, Greece

On 12 October 1943, following the Italian surrender, the island of Symi was occupied by German troops. Once Operation Accolade was over, the British increased the raiding in the Aegean.

Operation Tenement was the last time the SBS operated in the Dodecanese. After this the area was passed to the Greeks. They had been heavily involved and more than shown their worth—and the operation against Symi more than proved the point. The force breakdown for the attack was split between SBS led by Maj 'Jock' Lapraik and Greeks.

Their mission was to eliminate the garrison, to destroy enemy installations, capture or destroy enemy shipping and evacuate quickly.

Operation Tenement was completely successful and over 100 Germans were taken prisoner.

Operation Floxo (UK) 29 October 1944 Dubrovnik, Yugoslavia (today, Croatia)

The British Government's policy of supporting Tito and supplying the partisans had started in September 1943 when SOE arranged the Maclean Mission. A conservative MP, Brig Fitzroy Maclean spent some time with Tito and reported back to Churchill that the partisans (rather than the Chetniks) were the forces to assist. Churchill gained Stalin and Roosevelt's approval and from December 1943 aid began to be siphoned towards the partisans.

In October 1944 the British Floydforce was in Yugoslavia to help partisans stop the German withdrawal of *Heeresgruppe* E from Greece and Albania via Montenegro. Floydforce was to provide artillery support. The force, commanded by Brig J. P. O'Brien-Twohig, consisted of batteries from 111 Field Regiment, RA, No 43 Cdo and 479th Army Field Coy, RE. It sailed in four LCTs and three LCIs from Bari to Dubrovnik on 27 October 1944 and arrived the following day.

Their first target was to block the German breakout at Risan, along the coastal route of the Bay of Kotor, headed by units of XXI *Gebirgskorps*. They did so with Finney Force: 211 Field Battery with eight field guns and C Troop of No 43 Cdo. The RA battery commander, Maj Pat Turner, was in overall command. They were in action by 30 October, when they became the first British Army unit to fight directly alongside communists. Accurate shelling saw the Germans hole up in Ledenice barracks in Risan. When it eventually surrendered on 17 December, the Germans had sustained 43 dead; over 70 wounded and 197 unhurt German soldiers entered captivity.

The Raiding Support Regiment, a troop of No 43 Cdo and 479th Field Coy, RE went to Nikšić where it found the route had been blocked by partisans. They were then sent to Podgorica, fighting until Floydforce was pulled out and returned to Italy on 22 December.

Operation Roast (UK) 1-3 April 1945 Lake Comacchio, Italy

This was primarily a diversionary raid to clear the spit of land between Lake Comacchio and the Adriatic, to convince the Germans that the British spring offensive would begin on the coast, and take their eyes away from the Senio River. It would also provide a platform for an attack on the Argenta Gap. Operation Roast was commanded by Brig Ron Tod and also involved Italian partisan fighters of 28th Garibaldi Brigade. Tod's force consisted of the whole of 2 Commando Brigade, with elements of Nos 9, 40 RM and 43 RM Cdo and the Special Boat Section, equipped with LVTs and storm and assault boats, supported by tanks of the North Irish Horse.

The plan was for a four-pronged assault: across the lake and from the west, the southwest and the east, capturing bridges across the three canals that punctuated the spit. However, the low level of the lake and its thick muddy bottom rendered the LVTs useless and the crossing was both exhausting and took much longer than anticipated. Despite this, some five hours late, the commandos completed their insertion and began their attacks.

The opposition was from German 98th Division and, apart from one bridge that was blown by the Germans, over the next 48 hours all the objectives and the spit were taken after some heavy fighting, including bayonet charges to finish off the opposition and almost 1,000 prisoners taken. Corporal Tom Hunter of No 43 RM Cdo and Anders Lassen, a Danish soldier of the SBS, both earned posthumous VCs for individual heroic actions.

Below: A map of the Lake Comacchio area.

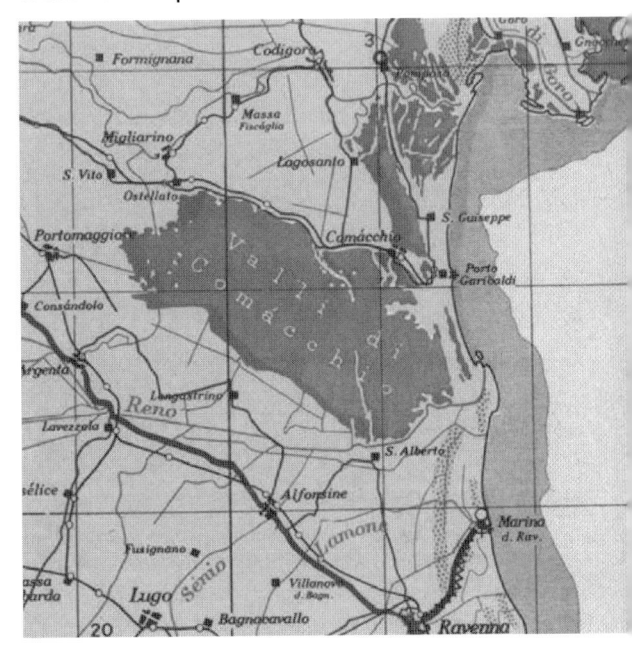

Operation Opossum (AUS) 8-11 April 1945 Ternate Island, Borneo

Z Special Unit unit carried out covert operations in the South West Pacific theatre (see Operations Jaywick and Rimau, p. 47). The unit had trained in schools in Australia, such as Camp Z in Refuge Bay, Z Experimental Station near Cairns, and the Fraser Commando School on Fraser Island. On 11 April two operations involving the unit were reaching a climax: 'Copper' in New Guinea was a recce that ended in disaster when the eight-man patrol was hunted down with only one survivor; 'Opossum' in the Moluccas was more successful.

The force that took part in 'Opossum' consisted of Dutch Capt Kroll and a Timorese corporal from the NEIA and 10 Australians from Z Special Unit. The party left Morotai, some 200 miles from Ternate, on 8 April aboard two Australian-crewed US Navy patrol boats. They landed in the north of Hiri Island and eight of them made their way round the island towards the narrow strait between them and Ternate.

Their mission had originally been planned to rescue an Australian airman on Ternate, but it became clear he had been moved, just as Sultan Iskander Mohammed Jabir Shah, who had been helpful to the Allies, sent men to Morotai by prahu (native boats) to say that he, his two wives and children who were under Japanese detention on the island, feared for their lives.

The mission became a rescue, approved by MacArthur from his HQ on Morotai. Word was sent to the sultan, and on the 10th he, his family and retinue made their way over to Hiri where they were greeted rapturously by the locals. They were chased the next day by the Japanese. In the resulting firefight two Australians, Lt George Bosworth and Pte Higginbotham, were killed, as were most of their attackers. PT boats picked up Z Force, the sultan and his family who were taken to Morotai where he spoke with MacArthur before being flown to Australia. They settled in Wacol, Queensland until the end of the war.

The LCT(R)s were converted British Mk 3 LCTs. A British 970 Radar with a maximum range of 25 miles provided targeting information. Ranging was by salvoes of three rockets. A number were given to the USN by reverse Lend-Lease and saw action in Normandy and Operation Dragoon. They could fire 1,000 3-inch rockets but reloading took some hours. The US Navy introduced the Landing Ship Medium (Rocket)—a class of 12—in April 1945.

2 Landings

Although the failure of Operation Jubilee, the raid on Dieppe, was a bitter blow much was learnt about what was required for a major landing operation. First and foremost, it was obvious that every aspect of such a mission required training, careful planning and resources and suitable equipment. Less than three months after Dieppe, on 8 November, the Anglo-American landings in North Africa—Operation Torch—were considerably more successful, although they too provided lessons (see pp. 84–87), as did each further operation. By the time of D-Day, 6 June 1944, training in every aspect of amphibious warfare ensured that most of those taking part had been suitably trained.

The operational methods, organisation and equipment had also changed. DUKWs, LVTs, LSTs—the hardware was there, if not in quite the numbers that commanders would have liked: lack of landing craft saw delays, for example, in Operation Dragoon, the landings in the south of France. In the Pacific, a new operational language had been learned with all three services forging a combined arms approach that would have been unthinkable in the 1930s. In particular, logistics and resupply had reached high levels of efficiency.

Of course, these developments weren't one-sided. While amphibious attack had developed, so had defences. The Axis powers had had long enough to build up their defences. In Europe this took the form of the Atlantic Wall. The concept of attempting to defend everything may have been flawed, but had the invasion been delayed and every beach been as well-prepared as Omaha, the results may have been different.

A major role in the success of the Normandy landings was the deception operation—'Fortitude' part of the overall Operation Bodyguard—that kept German eyes fixed on the Pas de Calais. Other deception operations included 'Mincemeat' before Sicily (the 'Man Who Never Was') and the projected Operation Pastel that was going to suggest to the Japanese that Formosa was the target and not the south of Japan.

The operations are listed in this chapter in date order, but it's important to recognise the strategy behind these operations and the choice of targets: for example, MacArthur's strategic Operation Cartwheel (see p. 89) in the SW Pacific area. The decision to bypass Japanese troop concentrations and isolate them, to 'island-hop' to gain airfields that could provide support and attack anywhere, and the harrying of Japanese transport and logistics formed a brilliant overall strategy that led to victory.

Operation *Weserübung* (GER) 9 April–10 June 1940 Denmark and Norway

'*Weserübung*' was the name given to the German invasions of Denmark and Norway that began on 9 April 1940. It started with the swift occupation of Denmark ('*Weserübung Süd*'), where, by threatening the terror bombing of Copenhagen, the Germans coerced the Danes into surrendering without much fighting within six hours. It included airborne assaults (the first of their kind) to secure the Storstrøm Bridge and the Aalborg airfields, a surprise landing of infantry at Copenhagen and a ground assault across the Jutland peninsula. In all these places there were brief skirmishes before the German troops called in air support and the Danish troops were ordered to fall back. Some German armoured cars and guns were knocked out and the Danish air force was virtually destroyed on the ground. The king was defended more fiercely and German attacks at Amalienborg were repulsed but the threat of the Luftwaffe bombing Copenhagen's civilian population effectively ended any further resistance.

Norway had more strategic significance for Germany, since it was from its ports that the critical Swedish iron ore was exported to the Fatherland. It too was unprepared for the German invasion as its main ports north of Oslo to Narvik were quickly seized by German troops transported on destroyers. Only in Oslofjord were they held up by the big guns of the Oscarsborg Fortress, which managed to sink the German flagship *Blücher* and severely damage other German ships. German air superiority however was overwhelming and when a parachute battalion took the Oslo and Stavanger airfields, the captial's resistance ended, although it had given time for the king and his government to escape. The German ground offensive inland moved heavy armour and artillery to link up and reinforce the forward elements, encountering sporadic stiff resistance as the Norwegians fought a tactical retreat, waiting for British reinforcements.

The British and French began to land troops at Narvik on 14 April, and at Namsos and Åndalsnes to attack Trondheim, but the Germans landed fresh troops to thwart them there and reinforced Narvik by air. Over the next weeks the battle for Narvik was fought bitterly to a final conclusion as the Allies finally retook the port on 28 May, but events in France were now changing the situation in Norway and 25,000 Britons and Frenchmen were evacuated from Narvik only 10 days after their victory. Norwegian resistance continued in the north until 10 June, when the 6th Division surrendered after all Allied forces had been evacuated.

Oscarsborg Fortress in Oslofjord (circled **Below** and **Above Right**) was under the command of Oberst Birger Eriksen. On 9 April 1940, the German heavy cruiser *Blücher* was engaged by three Norwegian batteries: Rauøy, Bolærne and Oscarsborg whose 280mm guns (**Centre Right**) hit the *Blücher* twice before 533mm torpedoes launched from North Kaholmen Island finished the job. 700 died when the ship sank (**Below Right**).

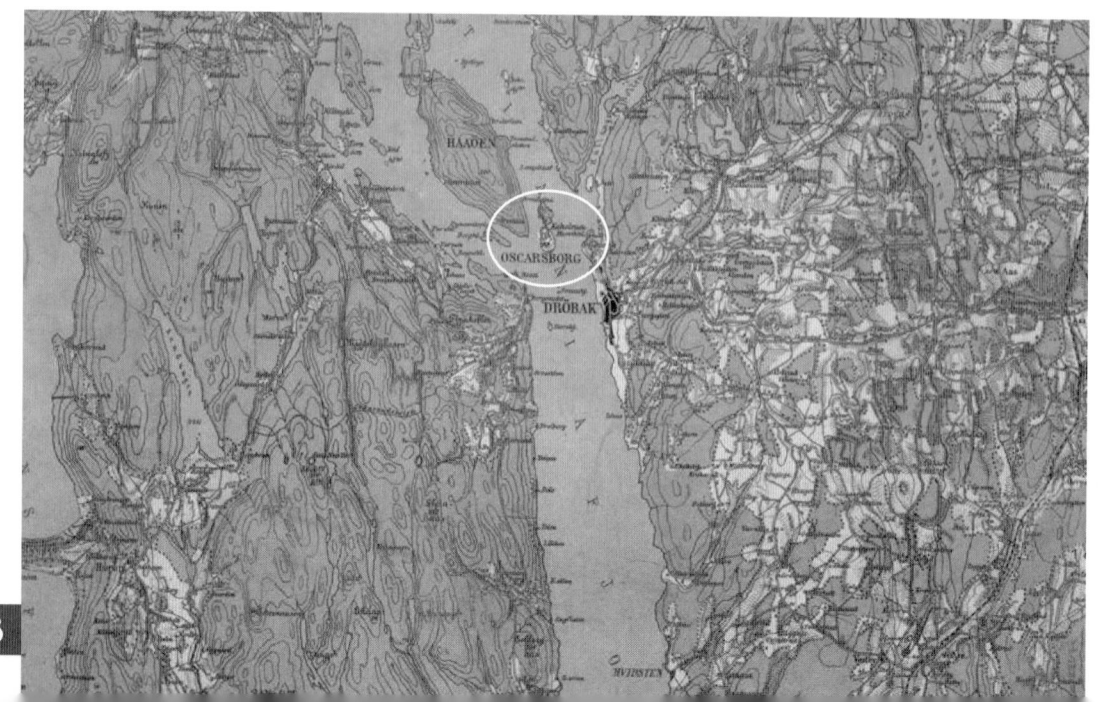

57

The main Allied operations in Norway against Trondheim were 'Sickle'—the landing at Åndalsnes to the south of Trondheim—and 'Maurice'—the northern half of the pincer operation designed to close on the lodgement of the 138th *Gebirgsjägerregiment* of Generalleutnant Eduard Dietl's 3rd *Gebirgsdivision* at Trondheim (operations started on 16 April and 3 May 1940 respectively).

Above left: German destroyers at Narvik.

Left: French troops during the battle of Narvik.

Below: Germans unload equipment during the campaign.

Opposite, Above: The end of an inept and costly campaign—the swastika flies over a Norwegian town.

Opposite, Below: Map of the campaign showing landings.

Operations Maurice and Sickle (Allied) 14 April–5 May 1940 Norway

The Allies response to the German invasion of Norway was late, rushed, ill-conceived, under-resourced and ultimately a complete failure, but given what was happening at the same time further south along the coast of Europe, entirely predictable too. Perhaps the only positives to come out of it were the first defeat of the German *Wehrmacht*, expelled (briefly) from Narvik and the safe extraction of the Norwegian king and government.

British and French troops were landed at Narvik, Namsos and Åndalsnes with the intention of retaking Trondheim. At Namsos some 6,000 inexperienced and ill-equipped Allied troops were put ashore, the French without half their equipment. Air superiority enabled the Germans to resupply and make short work of both these incursions.

In the north things went a little better: the Royal Navy had scored some success against the *Kriegsmarine* and a British, French and Polish expeditionary force of 38,000 was landed over the period 14 April–15 May in various locations. On 28 May Narvik finally fell, but the Allies had already decided to evacuate their forces from the country.

However, during the battle for Narvik the first British use of landing craft took place on 13 May when two MLCs and a LCM(1) landed Hotchkiss tanks and LCAs landed men of 13e DBLE at Bjerkvik after an initial bombardment. A tactical success, as the official history puts it: 'So ended, with only 36 casualties, the first of the opposed landings on which Allied fortunes in the later war years were so largely to depend and our first experiment in war with the landing craft which proved to be one of the main instruments of victory.'

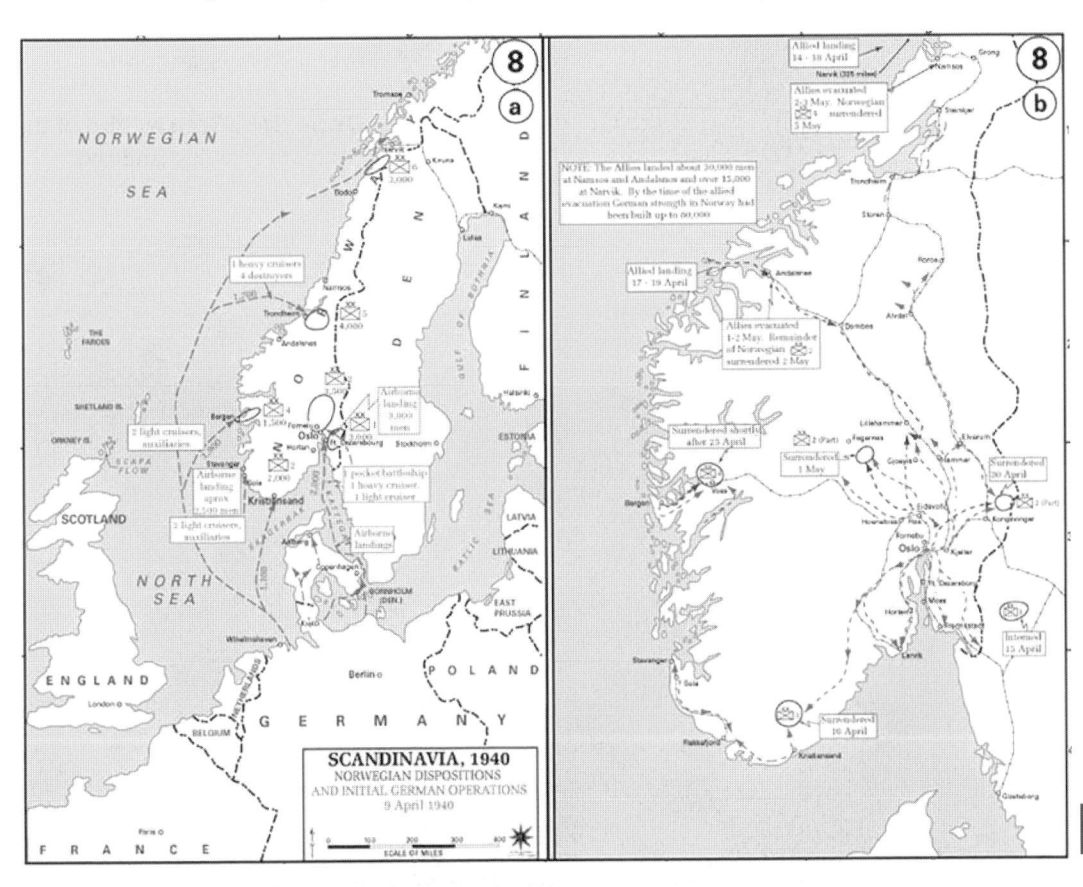

Operations Valentine and Fork (BR) 13 April and 10 May 1940 Faroe Islands and Iceland

To deny the Germans the use of Iceland and the Faroe Islands, both of great strategic importance to the forthcoming battles in the North Atlantic, the British invaded them. The Faroe Islands were occupied on 13 April by 250 Royal Marines who were replaced in May by the Lovat Scouts. In turn in 1942, they were replaced by the Cameronians (Scottish Rifles).

Iceland, hitherto also linked to Denmark—which had been overrun by the Nazis on 9 April—attempted neutrality and wouldn't join the Allies, so the British, in the form of some 750 Royal Marines, landed at Reykjavik. The British troops were replaced on 17 May when Canadian troops—2nd and 3rd Infantry Divisions—arrived to take over the occupation. In turn, up to 30,000 American troops were stationed in the country later in the war.

In fact, the Germans had no intention to invade either location immediately, but after the British took the plunge the Germans did prepare Operation *Ikarus* to attack Iceland. It never happened.

Operation Menace (Allied) 23-25 September 1940 Dakar, French West Africa (today Senegal)

Operation Menace was an Allied attempt inspired by Gen de Gaulle to take the Vichy-held port city of Dakar. In late September 1940 a task force—made up of the aircraft carrier HMS *Ark Royal*, two battleships, five cruisers, ten destroyers and several transports carrying 8,000 troops—was sent to negotiate a peaceful handover or else take Dakar by force. On 23 September, following a propaganda leaflet drop, Free French aircraft from the *Ark Royal* landed at the city's airport but were promptly arrested and an Allied ship trying to enter the harbour was fired upon. This led to various exchanges between the shore batteries, Vichy ships and the Allied force, with casualties on both sides. An attempted landing was defeated and abandoned, with the Allies eventually withdrawing, leaving Dakar and French West Africa in Vichy hands and de Gaulle's reputation consequently suffering a substantial knock.

Above: HMS *Ark Royal* at the beginning of the war. Overhead, a flight of Fairey Swordfish.

Below: Royal Marines en route to Dakar.

Operation Appearance (UK)
16 March 1941 Somaliland

Operation Appearance was a landing by British and Commonwealth forces, on beaches to the east and west of Berbera, in order to retake the British Somaliland Protectorate from the Italian army, which had conquered it just seven months previously in August 1940. The troops used were a proper British Empire force, made up of 3,000 men assembled from the Aden Striking Force. This comprised the 1st, 2nd and 15th Punjab Regiments, 11th (South) African Division, a Somali commando detachment, the 1401/1402 (Aden) Companies, an Auxiliary Military Pioneer Corps Group and a motor transport (MT) troop. They were conveyed by the suitably conglomerate Force D consisting of two cruisers (HMSs *Glasgow* and *Caledon*), two auxiliary cruisers (HMSs *Chakdina* and *Chantala*), two destroyers (HMSs *Kandahar* and *Kipling*), two Indian trawlers (*Netavati* and *Parvati*), *ML109* and various transports, tugs and lighters in which the troops were to be towed. The night landings themselves were late due to the difficulty of finding the few gaps through the offshore reefs. All of the troops were ashore before dawn, meeting little real opposition, and the town was captured by 09:20 that morning. The Italians retreated quickly to Eritrea.

Above Right: Nigerian soldiers of the West African Frontier Force remove monumental stones placed by the Italians to mark the boundary of their new empire on the Kenya–Italian Somaliland border 1941.

Centre and Below Right: Men of the King's African Rifles. They fought the French in Madagascar, the Italians in East Africa (Sgt Nigel Leakey won a posthumous Victoria Cross) and then went to Burma to fight the Japanese.

Operations *Marita* and *Merkur* (GER) 6 April and 20 May 1941 Greece and Crete

Italy invaded Greece from Albania in October 1940. The Greeks—with British assistance—first held the Italians and then counter-attacked. By April 1941 the Italians needed help so the Germans, in spite of their impending assault on the Soviet Union, attacked Greece from Bulgaria—Operation *Marita*. In a lightning swift campaign the Germans rolled back the Greeks and the Allied forces—British, Australian and New Zealand—who had come to assist them. The Allies were able to hold off the final debacle at Thermopylae while an evacuation was organised (see pp. 179–183), but by 30 April the Germans had taken the whole of the country along with 7,000 Allied PoWs.

A month later, the Germans initiated Operation *Merkur*, attacking Crete which was where Greek King George II and many of the troops from the Greek

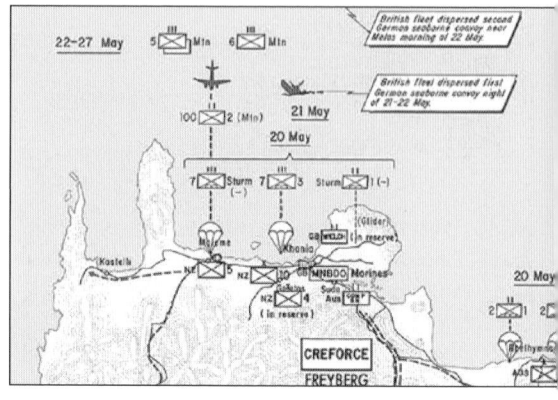

Above: The Royal Navy twice stopped the *Gebirgsjäger* from being delivered by sea; most were flown into airfields captured during the *Fallschirmjäger* assault (**Below**).

Above: The British and Commonwealth forces lost over 3,500 KIA, 1,918 WIA and over 12,000 made PoW—some of the latter seen here.

Below Left: A German submarine chaser in the Aegean.

Right: German troops in the Aegean—note the ribbed life jackets.

mainland had been evacuated. The battle started with an airborne invasion by paratroops and gliders, and the Germans suffered heavy casualties.

There were a number of attempts to land German and Italian forces by sea to help the paratroopers. On the night of 20/21 May, a convoy of fishing boats was intercepted and turned away, with over half lost. On 22/23 May another attempt was aborted after interception by the Royal Navy, although it lost two cruisers and a destroyer in the process.

The Germans had more luck on 28 May when two Panzer PzKpfw IIs were successfully landed as were 3,000 men from the Italian 50th Infantry Division 'Regina'. By this time the British had decided that they had lost the island and began to retreat south. On the night of 26/27 May the British landed part of Layforce, around 800 men from Nos 7, 50 (ME) and 52 (ME) Cdo, at Suda Bay. They were to provide assistance to the rearguard as the Allied troops retreated for evacuation.

Operation Beowulf II (GER)
9 September–21 October 1941
Estonian Islands

'Beowulf' was a German and Finnish assault on the Soviet-held islands of Saaremaa, Hiiumaa, Muhu and Vormsi, off the eastern coast of Estonia in the mouth of the Gulf of Riga. The islands were defended by 23,700 Soviet troops of 3rd Rifle Brigade and attacked by the German 61st Infantry Division, with the addition of assault pioneers and artillery. A joint German and Finnish task force consisting of light cruisers and coastal defence ships provided protection for over 250 barges, ferries and assault boats which transported the attacking troops. Also involved were 12 MFPs (see p. 212). The smaller island of Vormsi was taken first on 9 September, with the main assault beginning on the 14th with a landing on Muhu. By the 17th the causeway linking Muhu to the island of Saaremaa was breached and the Soviet garrison was slowly pushed back to Sorve Peninsula by the 23rd. With their defences steadily destroyed by naval gunfire and the assault pioneers, the Soviets on Saaremaa surrendered on 5 October. The assault on the final island, Hiiumaa, had begun on 12 September, with the Soviets steadily pushed back to the Takhuna Peninsula. By 21 October it was all over, with a combination of German air and sea superiority any hope of escape or rescue had been cut off. The Soviets lost almost 5,000 men with a further 19,000 captured. German casualties were almost 3,000 killed, missing, or wounded.

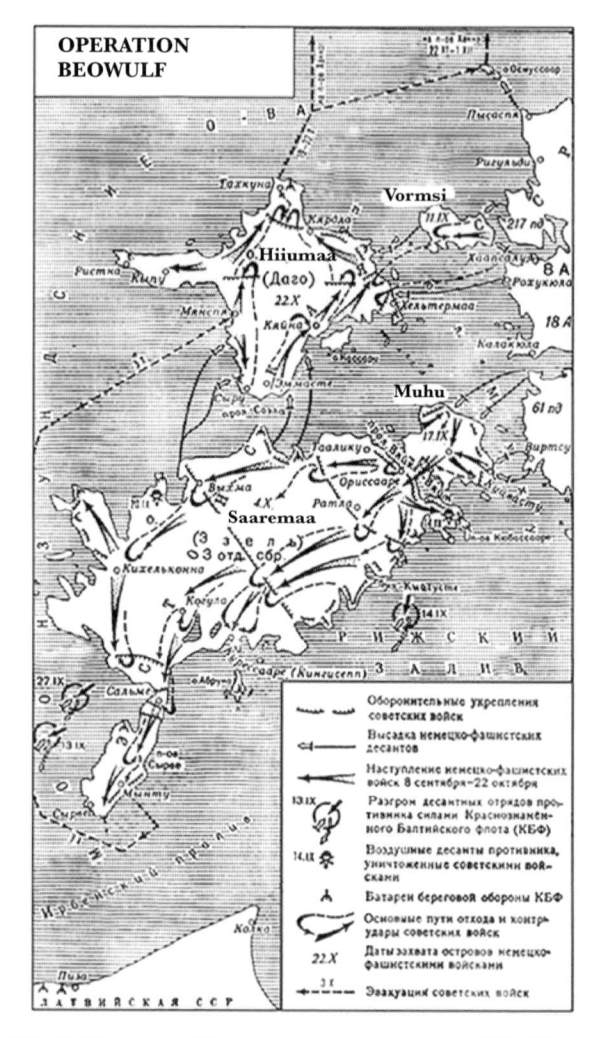

The aftermath of the fighting at Feodosia in the Crimea.

Kerch-Feodosian Landing Operation (SOV) 26 December 1941 Kerch Peninsula, Ukraine

The Germans had started the siege of Sevastopol on 30 October 1941, having landed troops in the Crimea, as part of Operation Barbarossa. The Soviets reacted in December 1941 with two amphibious landings by the 44th and 51st Armies at Kerch and at Feodosia planning to advance west and relieve the siege. The Germans extracted their forces—46th Infantry Division—from the peninsula and set up strong defensive positions—although the XLII *Armeekorps* commander, Lt-Gen Hans Graf von Sponeck, was court-martialled for doing so. The German defensive line held in the face of a number of attacks during spring 1942, thanks to its artillery and the incessant Luftwaffe attacks interdicting resupply of the Kerch peninsula, concentrating on Soviet shipping. Between February and March the Luftwaffe sank over 15,000 tons of the Black Sea Transport Fleet forcing the Soviets onto the defensive. They had lost over 350,000 men in their offensives; the Germans around 24,000. Finally, Operation *Trappenjagd* (Bustard Hunt) opened on 8 May, and saw Erich von Manstein's German and Romanian Eleventh Army clear the peninsula of Soviet troops. The Soviet evacuation from Kerch saved some 116,000 men but left behind over 162,000 dead or captured.

Below and Bottom: The Kerch–Feodosian Operation failed in its attempt to relieve Sevastopol.

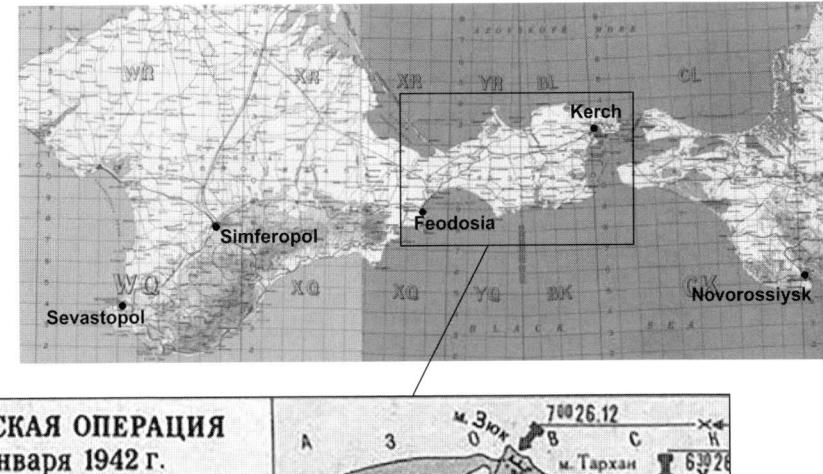

Southern Operation (JAP) 7 December 1941 Malaya (today, Malaysia)

The Japanese invasion of Malaya began just before midnight on 8 December, an hour and a half before their attack on Pearl Harbor (across the Pacific and a date day behind). The British knew what was coming but had dithered and it cost them dearly. The invasion force, in three troop transports escorted by cruisers and destroyers, used the 56th Infantry Regiment reinforced with artillery, landing on Badang and Sabak beaches just to the east of the port of Kota Bharu, the capital of North Malaya and a main British airbase. They were opposed by the 8th Indian Infantry Brigade, supported by artillery, who had mined the beaches and fortified them with barbed wire and pillbox machine gun emplacements. They were thus able to pin down the first and second waves of the Japanese attack, with support from the RAF and RAAF, who managed to sink one of the troop transports. Despite this and the heavy losses incurred, the determined Japanese were finally able to break through some of the critical defences and take the port. British counterattacks were unsuccessful and the airport was abandoned. The Japanese then divided their forces in two, one column moving east down the coast towards Kuantan and the other south towards the Perak River. Two hours after the Kota Bharu attack, an even larger Japanese force landed 100 miles further north, in the Kra Isthmus of neutral Thailand. The British defences crumbled and Singapore fell on 15 February 1942.

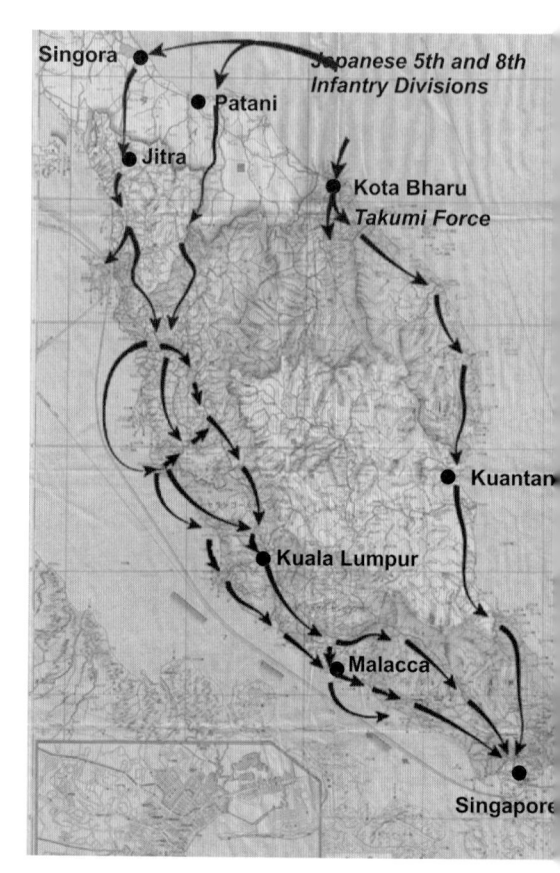

Philippines (JAP) 8 December 1941-8 May 1942

The Japanese invasion of the Philippines was timed to coincide with their other operations in the Far East and also across the Pacific in Hawaii. It began on 8 December with air strikes launched from Formosa which destroyed more than half the USAAF planes in the country on the ground (despite the attack being anticipated). It was followed on 10 December by air raids on Manila and three simultaneous, virtually unopposed, landings on Luzon, launched to capture US air bases and complete the destruction of American air capability. The main force came ashore at Lingayen Gulf on 22 December and quickly overran the inexperienced Filipino troops deployed around the Luzon coastline. Despite being outnumbered on paper, the Japanese force of some 57,000 made short work of the defending US and Filipino forces mostly deployed on the two main islands of Luzon and Mindanao. On 24 December, 7,000 troops from the Japanese 16th Division landed at Mauban, Atimonan and Siain in the east of Luzon. The remaining Allied forces were soon in full retreat towards the Bataan Peninsula and the island of Corregidor, where they somehow managed to hold out until April 1942, despite receiving almost no support from the US government. Eventually 76,000 men surrendered, many of whom would die on the Bataan Death March or in the prison camp to where it led. The last US troops in the Philippine Islands surrendered on Mindanao on 12 May.

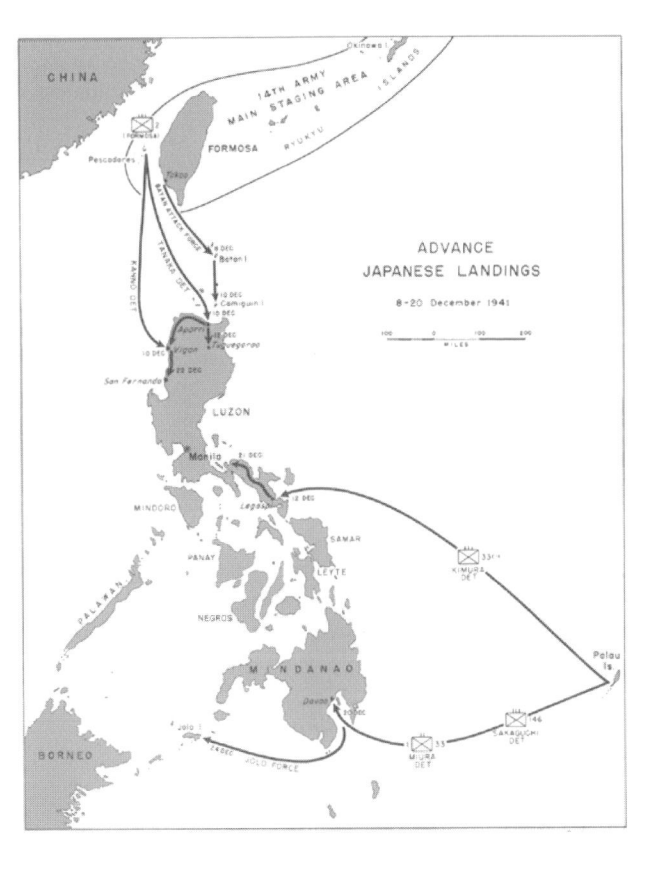

Opposite, Above: Japanese 1940 map showing the landing at Kota Bharu and in Thailand on 7 December and advance to Singapore—including amphibious hops down the western coastline. The Japanese assaulted Sarimbun Beach on Singapore Island on 8 February.

Opposite, Below: The Japanese attack on Malaya is often called the bicycle Blitzkrieg.

Left: US troops surrender at Corregidor.

Above and Below: Japanese troops landing at Lingayen Gulf, 22 December 1941.

Opposite, Above: Japanese small craft underway off Corregidor Island, at the time of its capture in May 1942.

Opposite, Centre: The Japanese advance through Corregidor.

Opposite, Below: The Japanese showed they were a long way ahead of the opposition in the field of amphibious warfare in 1942, advancing deep into the Philippines and Netherlands Indies and threatened Australia. A mixture of good equipment, speed and savagery allowed them to brush their opponents out of the way. Their troops proved to have great endurance and the ability to advance great distances with very little sustenance. As an example a captured Japanese document reported in *Intelligence Bulletin* looked at 'Conveniences for Personnel' and how to preserve food for the advance: 'The best method for carrying and preserving rice is to put it in a rice basket and add 3 or 4 pickled plums. [The plums are preserved by a salt solution.] Rice kept in this manner will not spoil for 17 hours or more. If it is carried in a rice box, without pickles, it is liable to spoil after 11 hours. In any case, rice must be cooked hard and its container must be dried thoroughly. Rice carried in mess kit, without pickles, will keep for 13 hours.' It's interesting to contrast this with the rations carried by the Allied soldiers.

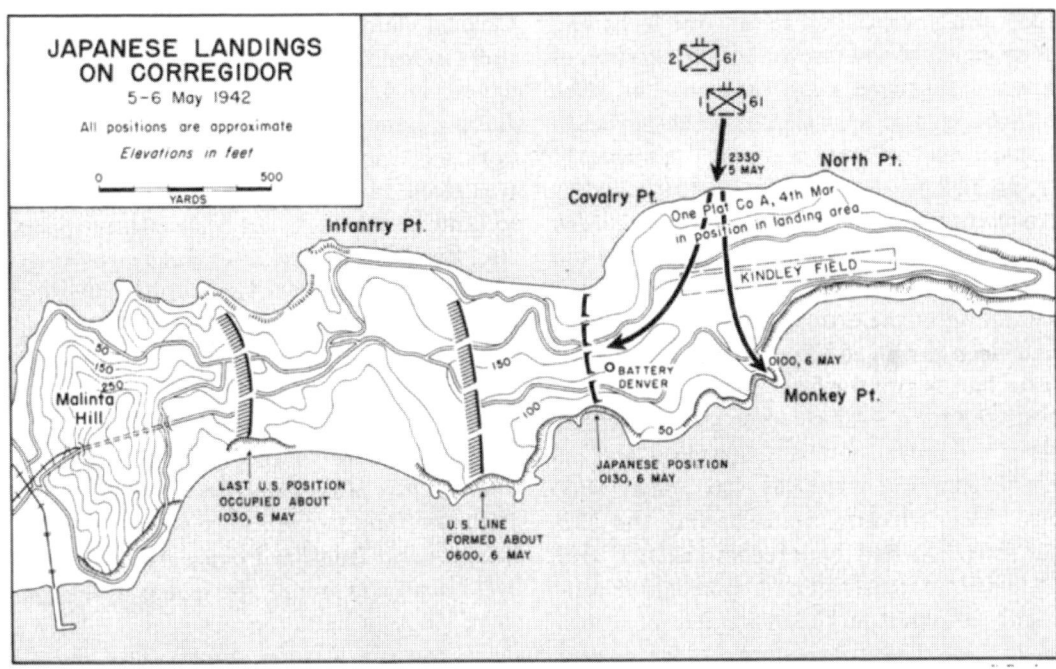

JAPANESE LANDINGS ON CORREGIDOR
5–6 May 1942

All positions are approximate

Elevations in feet

0 — 500 YARDS

Malinta Hill · Infantry Pt. · Cavalry Pt. · North Pt. · KINDLEY FIELD · Monkey Pt. · BATTERY DENVER

2330 5 MAY
One Plat Co A, 4th Mar in position in landing area
0100, 6 MAY
JAPANESE POSITION 0130, 6 MAY
U.S. LINE FORMED ABOUT 0600, 6 MAY
LAST U.S. POSITION OCCUPIED ABOUT 1030, 6 MAY

Operation R (JAP) 23 January–9 February 1942 Rabaul, New Britain

Rabaul was the capital of the Australian Territory of New Guinea and an important harbour—although prone to seismic activity (the town was destroyed by a volcanic eruption in 1937 and the new town by one in 1994). The Allies hadn't built up its defences or garrison which numbered around 1,400 when the Japanese attacked with a 15,000-strong brigade group and a large naval presence. The Australians fought gamely, but it was an unequal struggle and 1,000 were forced to surrender. Some of these were murdered by the Japanese; others—as many as 800 PoWs and 200 civilians died when their transport was sunk by an American submarine.

The Japanese turned Rabaul into a major defence hub—their largest base in the New Guinea area and both a key element in their defence and a key target for the Allies. MacArthur's Operation Cartwheel (see p. 89) was designed to neutralise Rabaul. It did so effectively, bottling up the forces: there were still nearly 70,000 Japanese troops in the area at the end of the war.

RAAF reconnaissance photograph of Truk on 9 January 1942, showed a concentration of enemy shipping giving warning of the Japanese thrust south to New Britain and New Ireland in the next two weeks. Unfortunately, the warning didn't change the outcome.

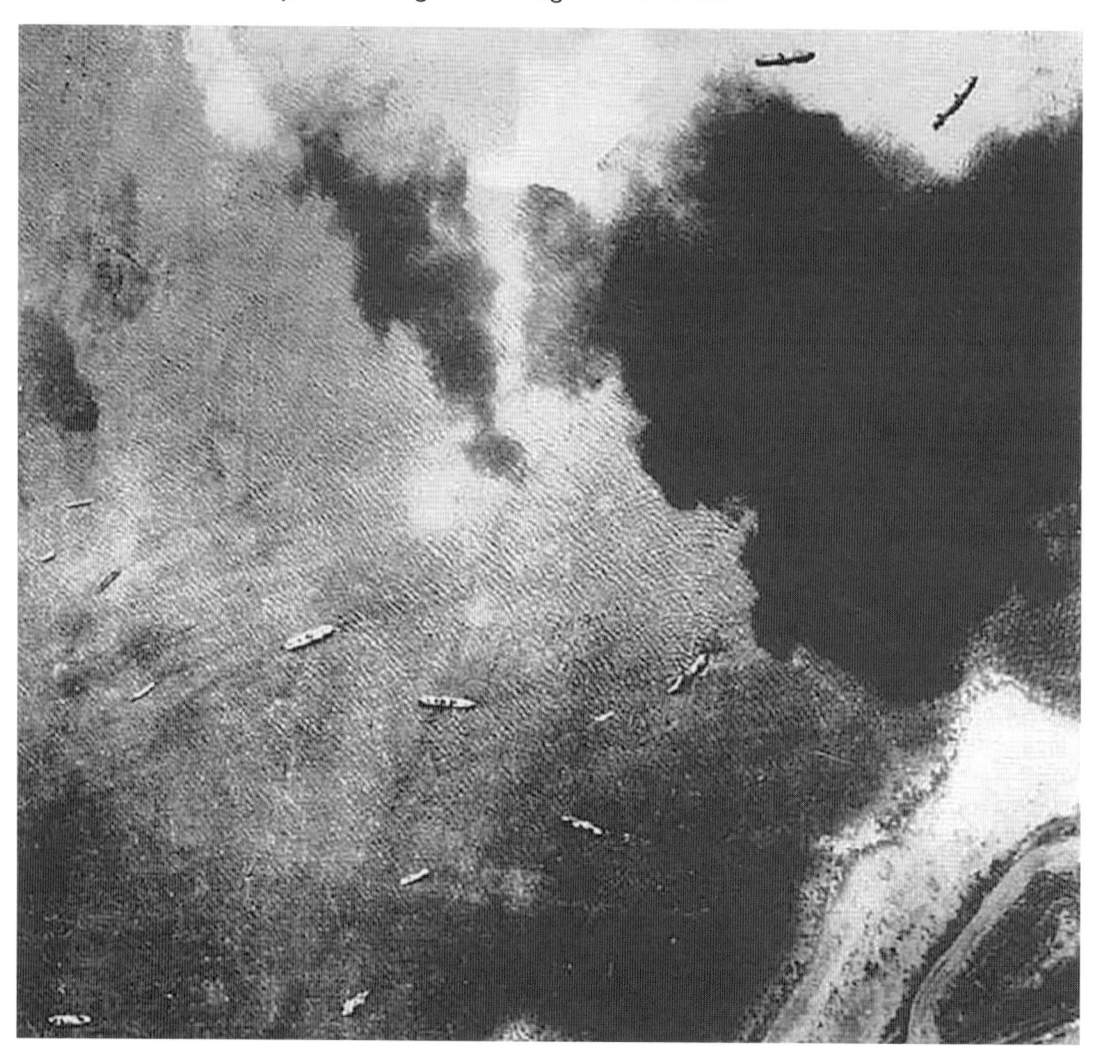

Netherlands Indies (JAP) 23 December 1941-21 February 1942

Prior to the Japanese invasion, the 1,400-strong Sparrow Force arrived to defend the island. It consisted mainly of Australian troops, but with some British, US and Dutch East Indian units too. The Japanese launched two simultaneous attacks on the two parts of Timor (Portuguese East and Dutch West) on the night of 19/20 February 1942.

In the east 1,500 troops from 228th Regimental Group landed at Dili, in the face of which an orderly withdrawal was conducted. It was covered by the very small but very capable 18-strong Australian Commando No 2 Section, stationed at the airfield, who held up the Japanese for a considerable time before withdrawing into the mountainous interior.

In the west an air attack was followed by the main landing on the undefended southwest side of the island by the remainder of 228th Regimental Group—two battalions totalling around 4,000 men along with five tankettes. After three days of intense fighting the Japanese forced the surrender of the bulk of the Allied troops, but several hundred Australian commandos remained at large in the mountains fighting a guerrilla war, resupplied by aircraft and ships based in Australia some 400 miles away. The commandos inflicted heavy casualties on the Japanese and tied down an entire division sent in reinforcement, however eventually the weight of numbers told and the Australians had to evacuate.

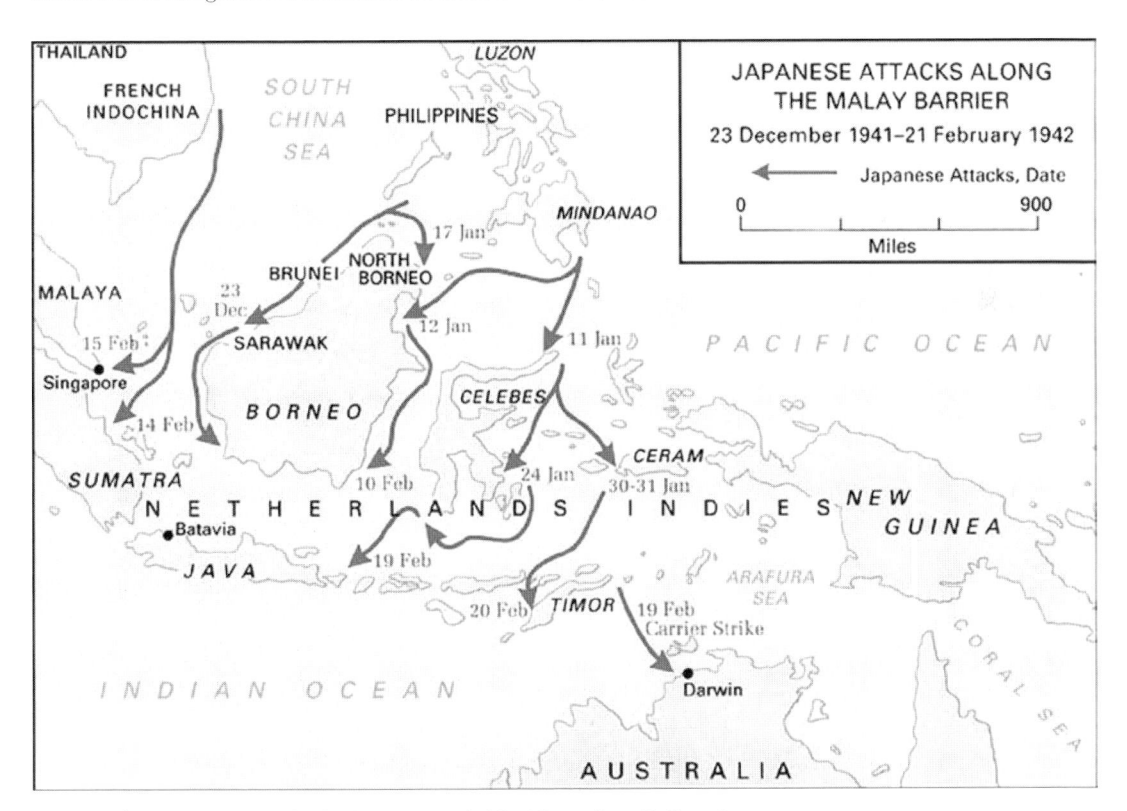

Operation AL (JAP) 6-7 June 1942 Aleutian Islands

The only invasion of the Continental United States was in the Aleutians where first Kiska (6 June) and then Attu (the 7th) were invaded by a small Japanese force numbering 1,000 (Imperial Army, Attu) and 500 (Imperial Navy, Kiska). The landings were unopposed and the surviving inhabitants of both islands were sent to prison camps—three Americans died during the invasions. Once taken, a mixed force of soldiers and civilian labourers moved in to build an airfield. The American response was to blockade the islands—a number of attempts to resupply the Japanese forces came to nothing—bomb them repeatedly and, eventually, to invade and liberate them (see p. 98).

Operation Ironclad (Allied) 5 May–6 November 1942 Madagascar

The Allies recognised the potential risk to their shipping in the Indian Ocean if the Japanese were given the use of Vichy-held Madagascar with the excellent harbour and port of Diego-Suarez on its northern tip, so they resolved to take it first. Substantial assets were assembled for the operation, named 'Ironclad', consisting of Force 121—some 10,000 men made up of British infantry battalions, commandos, marines, light artillery and one Special Service squadron with six Valentine infantry tanks and six Tetrarch light tanks. They were transported by Force H, made up of 50 ships including two aircraft carriers, a battleship, cruisers, corvettes, destroyers, troopships and minesweepers. Opposing them were some 3,000 Vichy troops, for the most part Madagascan and Senegalese native troops with French officers, eight coastal batteries, warships, submarines and aircraft.

On 5 May 1942 British 29th Infantry Brigade and No 5 Cdo landed at Courrier Bay and at Ambararata Bay, and were then reinforced with 5th Infantry Division and Royal Marines. The landings met with virtually no resistance, although the Courrier Bay force had to get through mangrove swamps and thick bush before storming the port. The Ambararata Bay force progressed well until it reached the Vichy Naval Base at Antisarane, which was more heavily defended.

The first frontal assault on the morning of 6 May was unsuccessful and most of the tanks were lost. Another successful attack infiltrated through the swamps and a daring dash to the harbour using an old destroyer, HMS *Anthony*, landed 50 Royal Marines in the Vichy defenders' rear, where they caused mayhem.

Antisarane surrendered that evening and 'Ironclad' had succeeded. A subsequent campaign to secure the entire island, Operation Stream Line Jane, began some four months later on 10 September. The Allies broke into the interior, mopped up the remaining Vichy and secured the whole island by the end of October.

Below: The landings and course of HMS *Anthony*.

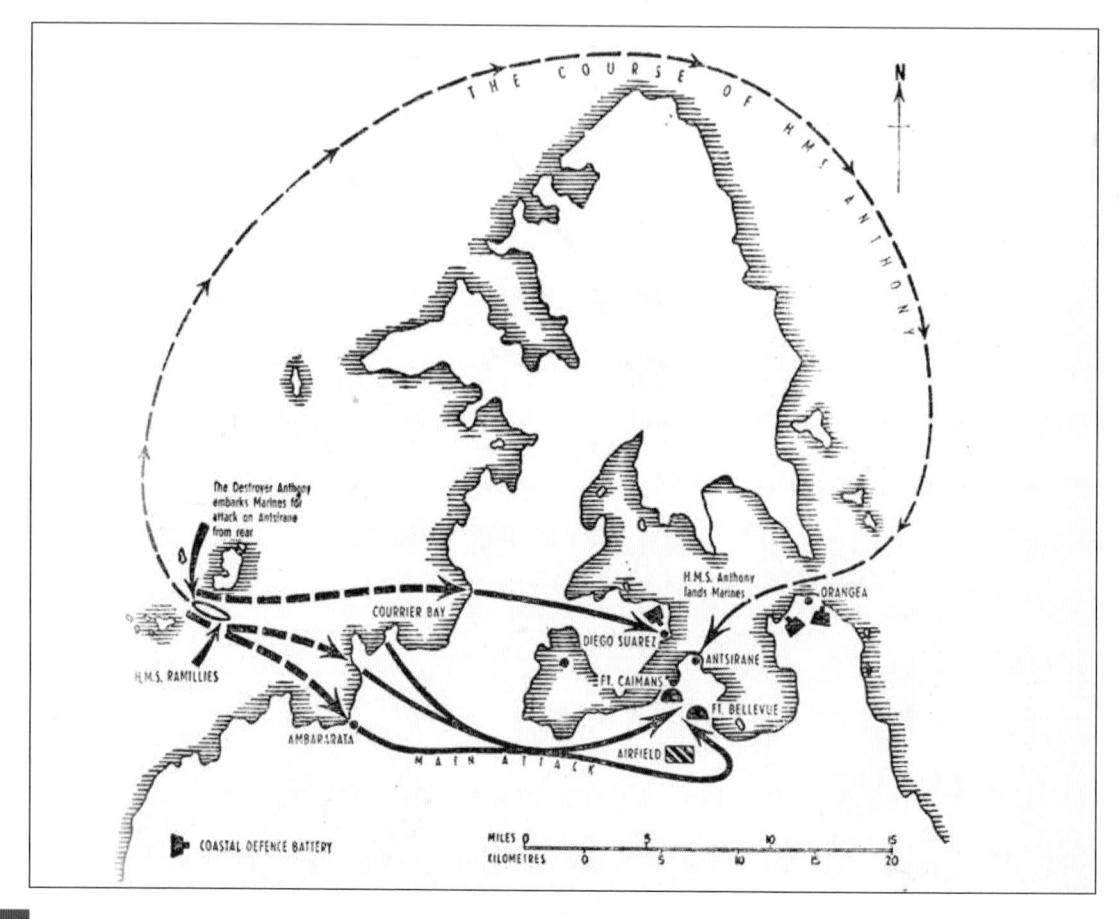

Above: The landings were by LCA and were unopposed.

Above Right: HMS *Ramillies* provided the 50 Royal Marines who were with HMS *Anthony*.

Below: On 23 March 1942 No 5 Cdo left Britain from Glasgow aboard *Winchester Castle*. They landed at Courrier Bay on 5 May, took the battery of 6-inch guns on the cliffs above and then marched towards Diego Suarez. Having taken their objectives, their next landing was on 10 September on the west coast of the island at Majunga, which they took after street-fighting. They were preparing to attack Tamatave on the east coast on the 18th, but it surrendered after a bombardment.

Landing craft clustered offshore during reinforcing landing operations at Lunga Point, Guadalcanal, in November 1942. The airfield was renamed after Maj Lofton Henderson, USMC who died in the battle of Midway.

Operation Watchtower (US) 7 August 1942 Guadalcanal, Solomon Islands

On 7 August 1942 Operation Watchtower began with assaults on Guadalcanal (largest of the Solomon Islands) and the smaller isles of Tulagi, Gavutu and Tanambogo. These were the first major amphibious landings undertaken by US forces in the war and marked a critical turning point in the Pacific war. Guadalcanal and its vicinity became the centre of continuous naval, aerial and land combat, a titanic struggle that cost both sides heavily in men and matériel—especially surface fleet ships.

Ironically, the battle for Guadalcanal began quietly with an unopposed landing, for the Japanese were taken by surprise. Thinking it was just a raid, they had instructed the 3,000 men who had been building an airfield to flee inland—unlike the battles on Tulagi, Gavutu and Tanambogo where the Americans got a taste of the ferocious Japanese no-surrender defence and the number of casualties that could result.

The marines occupied the Guadalcanal airfield, but then Japanese naval forces defeated the US fleet in the vicinity, forcing it to flee, leaving the 1,000 or so marines isolated, although they managed to get the airfield working and land some fighter and bomber aircraft. The Japanese then landed more troops onto the island on 18 August—the 2nd Battalion of the 28th Infantry Regiment led by a Colonel Ichiki and a special naval landing force, who were assigned the task of defeating the marines.

Ichiki underestimated US numbers, firepower and resolve and without waiting for the 35th Infantry Brigade who were set to reinforce him, charged the well dug-in marines who were armed with machine guns with mortar and artillery support. The attack was heavily defeated and the Ichiki committed suicide for his failure.

By 5 September the Kawaguchi Detachment, consisting of 35th Infantry Brigade and the 124th Infantry Regiment, had arrived on Guadalcanal. It travelled through the jungle to attack Henderson Airfield on 12 September. Despite its ferocity and tenacity, this attack was also defeated with intense and accurate air and ground fire. By the time the Japanese retreated they had lost 3,500 men but the Americans had lost 450—almost half their number.

The Japanese next brought in the 38th Infantry Brigade, their numbers now totalling over 20,000 troops on the island. The US also had replacements and reinforcements totalling 23,000 men (25th Infantry Division and the 2nd Marine Division). The unsuccessful Japanese attacks continued. Finally in mid-November US aircraft from Henderson airfield attacked another Japanese resupply convoy, sinking six troop transports with all their equipment. The emperor then ordered a Japanese withdrawal, which took place between January and February 1943. Some 11,000 Japanese troops were evacuated from Guadalcanal. They had lost somewhere between 20,000 and 30,000 men killed or wounded in their attempts to take the island and the Americans about 7,100 men.

See also p.43 for the Tasimboko Raid.

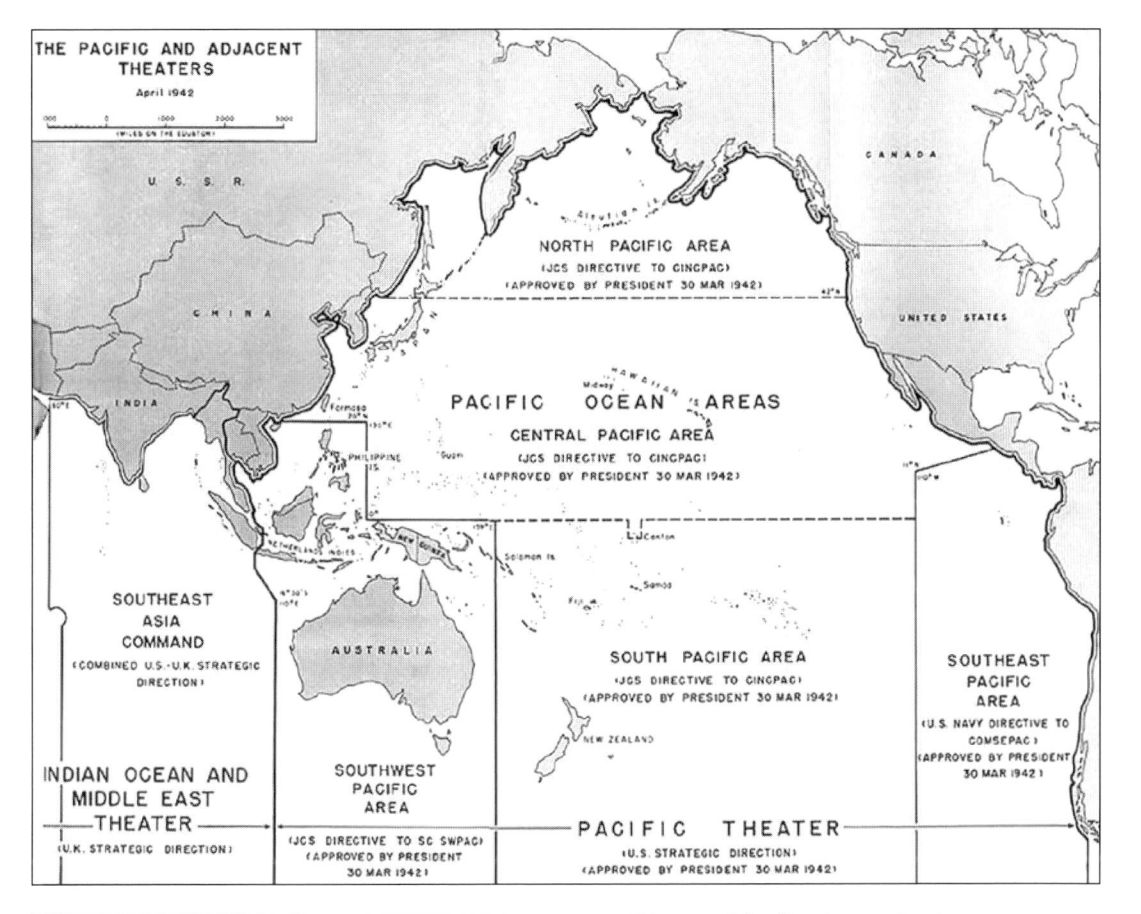

Above: The Pacific was broken up into Allied commands. Gen Douglas MacArthur commanded the Southwest Pacific Area and fought his way to the Philippines. The Pacific Ocean Areas was commanded by Adm Chester W. Nimitz, USN, CiC US Pacific Fleet. The South Pacific Area changed hands during the war. At the time of the Guadalcanal attack it was under Vice Adm Robert L. Ghormley; Vice Adm William Halsey, Jr. took over in October 1942. There was often debate over strategy and timescale between the command areas and particularly between MacArthur and Halsey, exacerbated by their temperaments and that one was army and the other navy.

Left: A Marine Corps M2A4 Stuart light tank is hoisted from USS *Alchiba* into a LCM(2) landing craft, off the Guadalcanal invasion beaches on the first day of landings there, 7 August 1942.

Above: US Marine Corps LVT-1 amphibian tractors on the dock at Wellington, New Zealand, on 20 July 1942, awaiting embarkation on board ships of the Guadalcanal-Tulagi invasion force. The 1st Marine Division was the first unit to make use of the unarmoured LVTs in resupply operations at Guadalcanal during the fall 1942–early 1943.

Right: Maps showing the eastern end of Papua New Guinea, the Japanese landings in Milne Bay and their subsequent retreat and evacuation at the hands of the Australian 7th, 14th and 18th Infantry Brigades. The Japanese sustained around 1,000 casualties with some 625 dead but were able to evacuate 1,318 of the attacking force.

Operation RE (JAP) 25 August–7 September 1942 Papua (today, Papua New Guinea)

Operation RE, also known as the battle of Rabi or Milne Bay, was a Japanese attempt to seize the RAAF airfields on the eastern end of Papua New Guinea for use in a planned assault on the island's capital, Port Moresby. However Japanese Intelligence had seriously underestimated the number of defending troops on the island and as result the invaders were in for a surprise. On the night of 25 August, 2,400 Japanese marines landed with light armour and began to work their way successfully towards the airstrips situated in the lowlands at the head of the bay, opposed by mainly by RAAF fighters. By 31 August they had reached the edge of the fields but then came under ferociously heavy and sustained artillery, mortar and machine gun fire. All flanking attempts proved unsuccessful, for the Allies controlled the high ground.

By 1 September the attack had been defeated and the Japanese forced to retreat, with the invasion force survivors evacuated on 6–7 September. This was one of the first victories against Japanese troops and was an important boost to Allied morale.

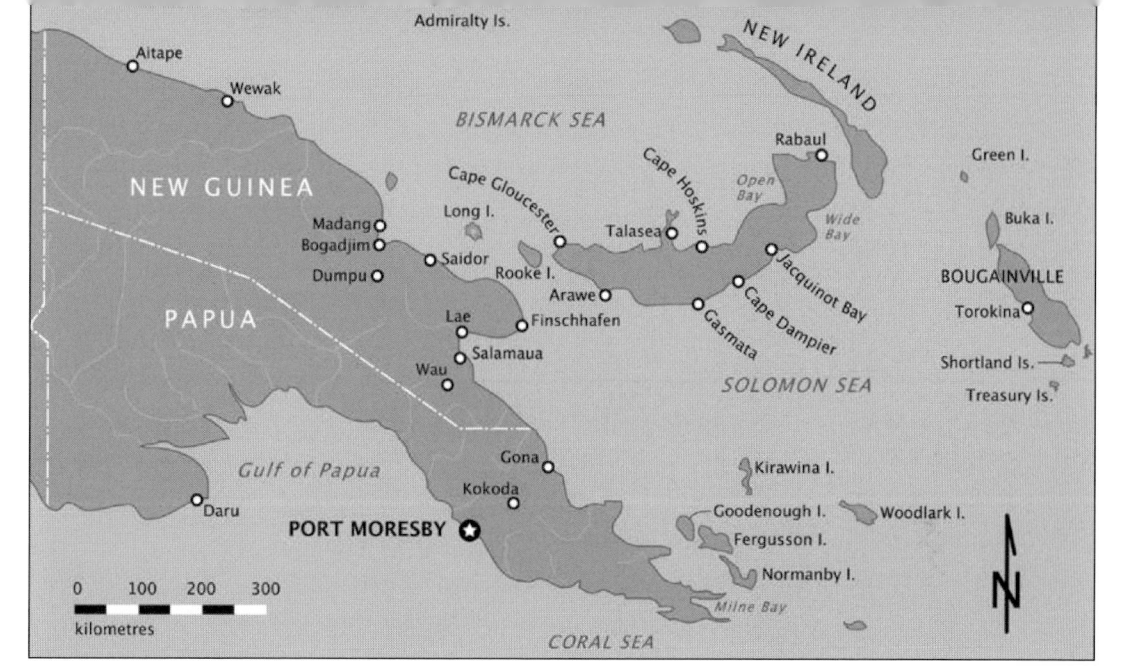

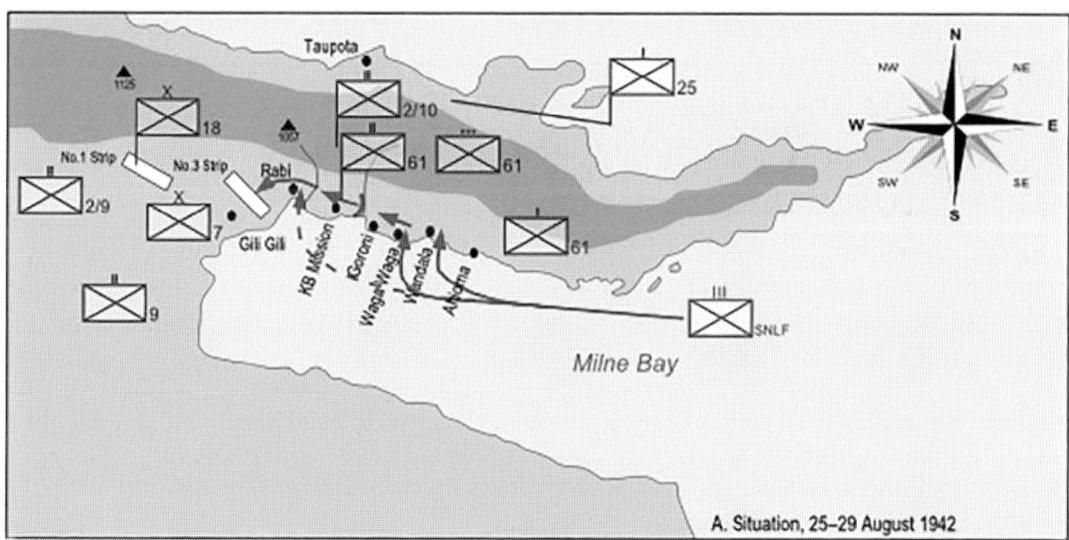

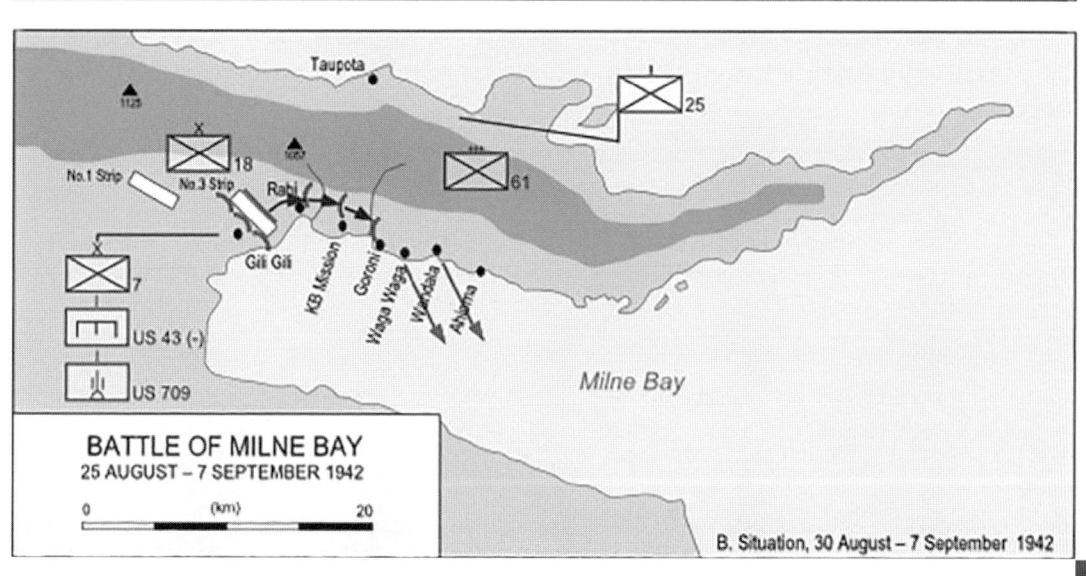

BATTLE OF MILNE BAY
25 AUGUST – 7 SEPTEMBER 1942

A. Situation, 25–29 August 1942

B. Situation, 30 August – 7 September 1942

Operation *Blücher* 1-9 September 1942 Taman Peninsula, USSR

Operation *Blücher* was an Axis assault on the Taman Peninsula in support of Operation *Blau*—the 1942 German summer offensive to capture the oilfields of Baku. '*Blücher*' began on 1 September with an attack by the Romanian 5th and 6th Cavalry Divisions on the Soviet 47th Army from the east, cutting off any potential land escape from the peninsula. This was followed on 2 September with unopposed landings by the German 46th Infantry Division transported by 24 MFPs of 1. *Landungs-Flottille* in the north and XLIX Gebirgskorps in the west, using an ad hoc fleet of ferries, naval ferry barges, engineer ships and assault boats. The attacks had air support and the Romanian 3rd Mountain Division in support, ready to exploit the landings. To avoid encirclement the Soviets evacuated from the south of the peninsula back to Novorossiysk. Soviet naval gunboats initially supported the operation, ensuring it started well. However, after these ships were sunk, the Soviets were increasingly harassed by German 1. *Schnellbootflottille* at their loading points, losing some 20 ships and forcing the surrender of the remaining troops. The Axis secured the Taman peninsula, now controlling the eastern coast and only way to the Sea of Azov.

Below: The Taman peninsula became an important bridgehead for the Germans, protected in 1943 by six lines of defences supplied by MFPs from the Crimea.

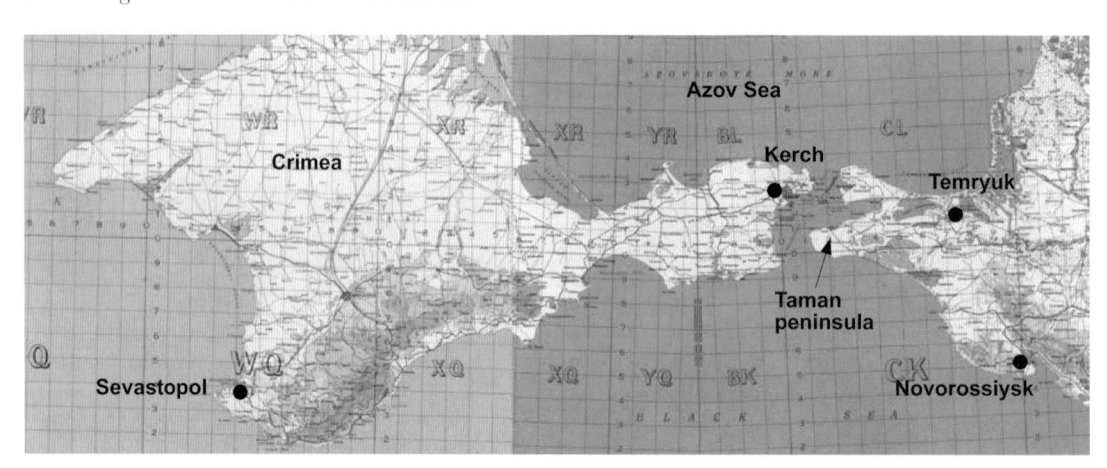

Directive No 43 Continuation of Operations from the Crimea

'1. After clearing the Kerch peninsula and capturing Sevastopol, the first task of Eleventh Armee will be, while ensuring the defence of the Crimea, to make all preparations for the main body of the army to cross the Kerch strait by the middle of August at the latest. The aim of this operation will be to thrust forward on either side of the western foothills of the Caucasus in a southeasterly and easterly direction.

The operation will be known by the cover name "Blücher" (most secret), and the day of the landing will be known as "Bl-Day".

'2. The operation will be executed on the following lines:

'In accordance with the proposals of Eleventh Armee, the crossing is to be planned so that the strongest possible forces are landed in the rear of enemy coast defences. The high ground north of Novorossiysk will then be captured. The ports of Anapa and Novorossiysk will be occupied, thereby eliminating bases for the enemy fleet.

After that, the operation will continue to the north of the Caucasus, its main thrust in a general easterly direction. In this connection it is specially important that the Maykop area be quickly occupied. The decision whether small forces should also be landed on the coast road along the Black Sea in the Tuapse area can only later be taken.

'For this operation Eleventh Armee is to keep the bulk of the medium and field artillery (flat trajectory and howitzer) mortar batteries up to 21cm mortars inclusive, and some of the heavy projector detachments.

'3. The Navy will take immediate steps to secure the necessary shipping for the crossing, in accordance with detailed Army requirements.

'To meet this need, suitable shipping, apart from vessels already available in the Black Sea and the Sea of Azov and those which may be brought in for the operation, will be chartered or bought from the Bulgarians and Romanians.

'During the actual operation, the Navy will support the landing forces during the crossing and protect them with all available means against action by enemy sea forces.

'Naval units detailed to cover the crossing of the landing forces will come under command of Eleventh Armee during the operation.

'4. The task of the Luftwaffe in preparing the operation is the overall elimination of enemy naval forces and harbours in the Black Sea.

'During the operation its task, apart from immediate support of the landing forces, will be to prevent enemy naval forces from interfering with the crossing.

'Preparations are to be made so that the Army forces landed on the Temryuk peninsula may be supplied for several days by air.

'The possibility of using parachute and airborne troops is to be investigated. If possible, 7. Flieger-Division will not be involved in these operations, or at least only in small part. It may be advantageous to employ units of 22. Luftlande-Division as airborne troops.

'5. The enemy is to be deceived into believing that large forces of Eleventh Armee are being moved from the Crimea to the area north of the Sea of Azov. For this purpose a large scale movement by road and rail will be undertaken towards the north, while the actual concentration for Operation Blücher will be concealed by night marches.

'The High Command of the Armed Forces will support this deception by suitable means.

'6. The following special operations (Abwehr II) have been prepared. These special operations are to be examined by the General Staff of the Army with the Office of Foreign Intelligence, Security Section II [Abwehr II], and, if approved, to be included in Operation Blücher.
(a) Parachute drop of a commando detachment in the Maykop area to protect oil installations (Operation Schamil).
(b) Sabotage operations against the triangle of railways Krasnodar-Kropotkin-Tikhoretsk and against the bridges over the Kuban in that area.
(c) Participation of a light engineer company of the Brandenburg Training Regiment, raised for operations of this kind, in attacks on enemy ports and coastal installations.

'7. Details for the preparation and conduct of the operation will be worked out by the Army General Staff in conjunction with the Navy and Luftwaffe.

'I am to be informed daily through High Command of the Armed Forces, Operations Staff, on the state of preparations (provision of shipping) and the forces to be used.

Signed: ADOLF HITLER'

Left: German MFPs in harbour in the Taman peninsula.

Operation *Brazil* (GER) 22 October 1942 Sukho Island, USSR

Lake Ladoga lies to the northeast of Leningrad and was an important part of the supply chain to the beleaguered city. The Axis used various assets to attack these routes and in October 1942 raided an island close to the southern shore. The raiding party was made up of 16 armed Siebel ferries, 7 infantry boats and a 70-man landing group all protected by Italian MAS-526 (*Motoscafo Armato Silurante*, an MTB). The Italian unit (12a *Squadriglia* MAS) had made its way to the lake by way of a long overland journey via the Brenner Pass and Innsbruck to Stettin, and then by ship to Helsinki. The final leg was by road to Sorlanlahti on Lake Ladoga.

Losing surprise when spotted by a minesweeper, the German landing party knocked out two of three land-based 100mm B-24BM naval guns but was unable to dislodge the small Soviet garrison. Retreating, the Germans lost four ferries and an infantry boat, with most of the other vessels damaged, as well as 22 KIA and MIA, and 57 WIA.

Opposite, Above: A *Marinefährprahm* (see p. 212) at sea. Some were converted into use as minelayers.

Opposite, Below, and Above: The Siebel ferries—*Siebelfähre*—were designed for Operation *Seelöwe* by Luftwaffe Col Fritz Siebel. The end result was a flat-bottomed catamaran, square in front with a wide cargo deck that made a perfect weapons' platform—particularly for Flak or artillery (as seen here). Siebel ferries saw wide service.

Below: *Luftwaffen-Fährenflottillen* II and III had been formed in Antwerp but were moved to Lake Ladoga as *Einsatzstab Fähre Ost*. As well as heavy weapons, the Siebel ferries were equipped with dual-purpose machine-gun mounts for use against land or air targets.

Operation Torch (US/UK) 8-16 November 1942 Morocco and Algeria

Operation Torch was an Allied invasion of Vichy North Africa, with three amphibious task forces simultaneously seizing key ports in Morocco and Algeria. Targeting Casablanca was the Western Task Force under Maj Gen Patton, with 35,000 troops carried by a US Navy fleet; targeting Oran, the Centre Task Force consisted of 39,000 US troops under Maj Gen Fredendall escorted by a British naval force; finally Algiers was covered by the Eastern Task Force; its naval element was British, with the Assault Force consisting of 23,000 British and 10,000 American troops under the command of US Maj Gen Ryder.

The Western Task Force did not use a preliminary naval bombardment hoping that French forces would not resist, but a stiff defence caused them some more casualties than they had expected. However, all landing objectives were accomplished by 10 November and the Vichy French surrendered Casablanca before an all-out attack was launched. The Centre Task Force also encountered Vichy resistance from shore batteries, ground forces and an attempted naval sortie from Oran's port which was easily defeated. After an attempt to capture the port facilities failed, a heavy British naval bombardment brought about the city's surrender on 9 November. The Eastern Task Force was aided by an anti-Vichy coup that took place in Algiers on 8 November, so there was no real opposition to the landings, but some serious fighting took place in the port itself. Resistance was overcome by the evening of 10 November, when the city was surrendered to the US and British forces.

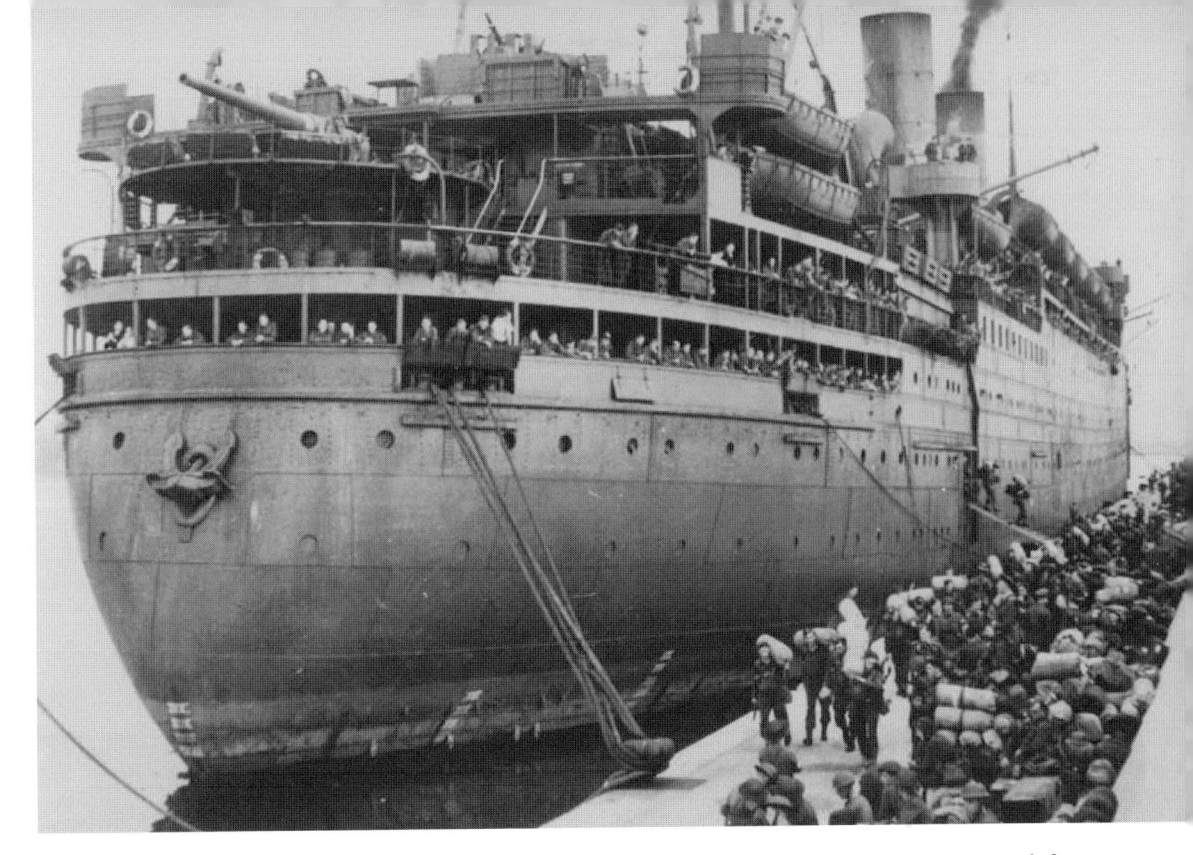

Left: US troops landing on a beach in French Morocco, 8 November. Note tank in water at left and LCVP centre.

Below Left: Invasion convoy en route to Morocco photographed from an SBD off one of the invasion force aircraft carriers.

Above: The merchant ship SS *Duchess of Richmond* disembarking soldiers at Algiers.

Below: The invasion landing points. The Germans were able to reinforce Algeria and Tunisia sufficiently to hold out until 13 May 1943, but the surrender meant 275,000 Axis soldiers became PoWs—a tidy victory, after which the Italian campaign started.

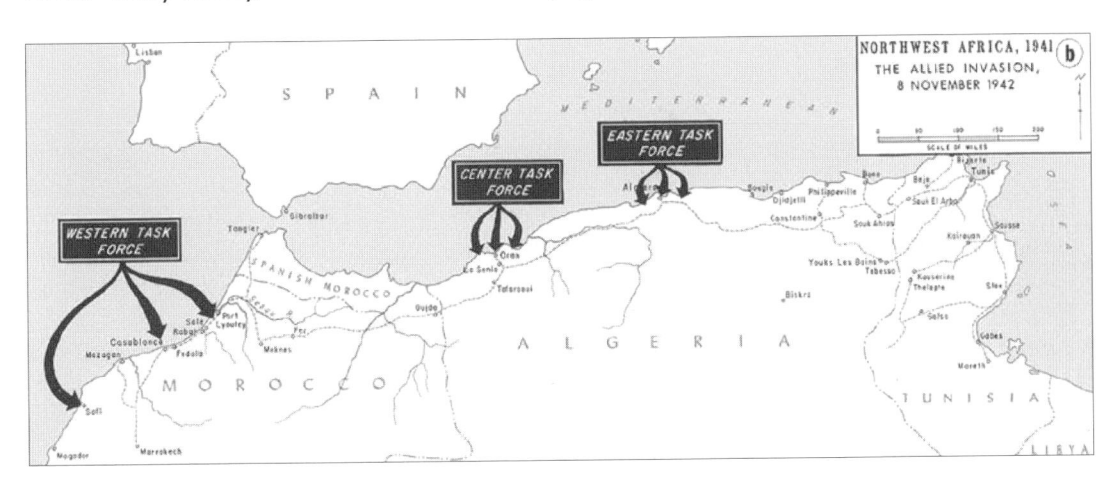

Lessons from Operation Torch

(From official report)

On 19 January 1943, Lt Gen Eisenhower ordered an assimilation of the lessons learnt in the operation to be submitted by 31 January. The reports from the participants had thrown up a range of details from very specific kit issues ('The lensatic compass proved to be too fragile and is susceptible to salt water') to more general issues, for example those supplied by the Eastern Assault Force. These included:

'4. Training:

a. Our great weakness is the lack of adequate doctrine and technique for amphibious operations. This is especially true of the means and methods to be employed by Combat Teams and smaller units. The remedy appears to be to organize a training center employing officers from our Divisions which have had combat amphibious experience, and there develop a technique which is suitable for our organization, for our equipment and for the amphibious missions which our Army may be called upon to perform.

b. Uniformity must be secured as to the method by which rifles, gas masks, and other equipment is carried; in the method of lowering equipment from ship to landing craft; in the methods personnel should use in descending nets; in the method in getting out of landing craft; and finally and most important in the methods in reorganizing ashore.

c. Ship to shore training must include training in rough water as well as quiet water. It must also include training on different types of beaches, that is, on open beaches from which an exit can be made on a broad front, on beaches where there are only one or two exits, and finally on beaches where "scrambled" landings must be made.

d. Another defect in training was that the Battalion landing teams of the U.S. trained Combat Team were trained to land personnel and vehicles in a certain sequence on a single beach. In the "Torch" operation that Combat Team found it necessary to land personnel on two beaches and vehicles on a third beach. This caused considerable confusion.

'5. Equipment:

a. The individual equipment of our soldiers is excellent. The only fault to be found is that there is too much of it. This is especially true of the equipment of the Infantry officer, who is so loaded down with heavy cumbersome equipment so that his mobility is impaired. A careful study should be made of the individual equipment to be carried. This study should be based on the principle that the equipment of both officers and men should be as light as practicable.

b. Weapons and ammunition function satisfactorily. Salt water and salt water spray cause malfunctions in automatic weapons. This can be obviated by giving such weapons a thorough coating of S.A.E.-30 motor oil.

The question of the types of vehicles to be carried is a difficult one. It is recommended, in all future operations, that at least 50% of the T.B.A. 2-ton trucks be taken. All vehicles should be water proofed before landing. A minimum of twelve very lightweight solo motorcycles and twenty four bicycles should be included in the equipment of each battalion landing team.

'6. Communication:

a. Communication troops were generally adequately trained in their individual jobs. There was, however, a number of communication officers who had never had this type of training. Due to the controlled exercises in which our troops had been training, a marked reluctance on the part of communication sections to depart from orthodox book "doctrine" was discovered. It is recommended that our service schools introduce a subcourse in amphibious communications.

b. As this operation involved the use of radio only in the assault phase, the following comments are pertinent to radio:

• The present Infantry Division radio equipment from Division Headquarters to Battalion Headquarters is designed to be used primarily as vehicular sets, consequently little thought is given as to whether portable combination ground and vehicle sets function properly when used as ground stations. The Infantry regiment relies principally on the SCR-284. The weight of this set when dismounted from its vehicle is 110 pounds. This weight added to the individual equipment and arms of the operating personnel is almost prohibitive on long marches. Again, while this set is being carried as a pack it cannot be operated and it is necessary to halt before the set can be placed in operation.
• SCR-195 has proven to be unsatisfactory due to the ease with which it can be masked. It operates satisfactorily from small craft to shore as there are no obstacles to mask the set.
• SCR-536 does not have the necessary range for amphibious operations. A set is needed for use between battalions and companies with a range of approximately five miles. The battery supply of this set is extremely critical since battery drain is high as compared to battery capacity.
• It is recommended that a portable set similar to the British No 46 be developed for this type of operation; that a hand cart in which SCR-284 sets may be mounted with storage batteries as a source of power be issued; that water proof bags be furnished with all radios.

'7. Planning:

a. The biggest defect in planning was that Battalion commanders were not taken into the confidence of the commanders of higher echelons early enough so that they could intelligently make their own plans under the supervision of Division and Combat Team commanders. It is strongly recommended that in future operations Battalion commanders and their staffs be included in the planning of amphibious operations.

b. It is fundamental that Combat Team commanders should be given the task of loading their ships to accomplish the mission which has been prescribed for them. In operation "Torch", the British insisted that the loading plans be made by the Division. It is recommended that in any combined operation, in the future, Combat Team commanders be given the task of loading their ships in order to fulfill their prescribed missions.

'8. Operation:
The actual operations of this force consisted of infantry skirmishes. Field Artillery was not employed due to the fact that high seas prevented its landing in sufficient time to be effectively employed. The infantry 81mm and 60mm mortars were especially efficient in dislodging enemy troops from buildings and prepared defensive works.

'9. General:
The following observation is fundamental. The intermingling of the British and U.S. Army supply systems should be studiously avoided wherever possible. In an operation where the troops participating are partly British and partly American, duplicate parallel channels of supply must be established and maintained. This situation, the constant and never-ending necessity for compromise as to principles and technique of supply make a very difficult task unnecessarily more difficult. In future amphibious operations, the Army element should be exclusively American or British, but not a mixture of the two. Observance of this principle will eliminate many faults in technique which existed in Operation Torch.

'10. Embarkation:
To facilitate the embarkation of troops in an amphibious operations, a "staging area" should be established. This staging area should have a "camp complement" including transportation, cooks, medical officers, and other necessary camp overhead. In an amphibious operation, it is normal that the organic transportation of the unit concerned is loaded a considerable period ahead of the actual embarkation of the troops themselves. During the intervening period the troops are without transportation, and without kitchens (kitchens having been stowed inside the trucks when the trucks were loaded), unless the staging area system is used. In Operation Torch this staging area arrangement was improvised with fairly satisfactory results; it is recommended that it be SOP for all future operations.

'11. Separation of Vehicles and Drivers.
In this operation, in many instances, drivers of vehicles were transported on one ship while their vehicles were transported on another. The bringing together of the driver and his vehicle from different ships, in the dark, and under adverse circumstances presents a very difficult problem of coordination. If landing in the face of active hostile resistance it is believed extremely doubtful whether this could be done effectively. It is recommended, therefore, that in all future operations drivers travel on the same boat with their vehicles.

'12. Rations:
In principle, the British-type 48-hour ration is sound. The American "C" and "K" ration is excellent so far as nutrition is concerned, but the soldier has no place to carry them. The British 48-hour ration is designed to fit into the British type mess tin, but there again that ration will not fit into the American mess tin old or new type. Consequently it is recommended that a ration be developed, following the lines of the British 48-hour mess tin ration in principle and containing the essential items of the U.S. "K" ration, with the containers designed in size and shape to fit inside the U.S. mess tin, new type. The problem of bulk as well as weight is important in landing operations, and such a ration would utilize what is now dead space inside the U.S. mess kit.

'13. Grenades:
At present, the U.S. soldier has no method of carrying hand grenades or M9 AT grenades other than pure improvisation. He now is forced to stick grenades into his trouser pockets or wherever he can. It is therefore recommended that a suitable size haversack, knapsack, or field bag be devised and issued to U.S. troops for this purpose. Among other qualities it should have a wide, firm shoulder strap to avoid a cutting-type pressure over the shoulder or on the neck which is likely to occur when carrying heavy loads.

'14. Life Preservers:
Reports indicate that both the British type "Mae West" and the American self-inflating type life preservers are not completely satisfactory for landing operations. It is recommended, therefore, a type of life preserver capable of sustaining a man with his equipment be developed and issued in all landing operations.

'15. Medical:
a. It is recommended that a lightweight binder be developed and issued to securely immobilize wounded men being carried in litters. This would facilitate the handling of wounded personnel being carried over rough terrain, by air, or when the litter is being taken on or off ships.
b. Individual Venereal Prophylactic Kits: Between the start of our amphibious operation and the ability of units to establish venereal prophylactic stations, a considerable length of time lapses. Experience has shown that immediately after hostilities cease or our mission is accomplished, personnel are prone to expose themselves to venereal disease. It is recommended, therefore, that individual prophylactic kits be issued to each man coming ashore in landing operations to enable him to bridge the gap.
c. Ambulances: The loading of ambulances in the early stages of an amphibious operation is difficult. The use of 1/4-ton, CR Cars, equipped with a frame superstructure to carry litters was found to be practicable in Operation Torch. It is recommended, therefore, that such or similar means be used in the early stages of all landing operations.
d. Morphine Syrette: The use of morphine "syrette" containing compound of morphine tartrate was found in Operation Torch to be necessary and practicable. It is recommended

that in all future landing operations that company aid men and other medical personnel be issued morphine syrettes on the basis of one syrette for every four (4) individuals. In this type of operation against determined opposition, casualties, of course, are likely to be quite high. It is believed that one syrette per four (4) individuals is a practical minimum.

e. It is recommended that a hospital ship accompany an assault task force so that seriously wounded men may be evacuated until adequate hospitals can be established ashore.

f. Battalion and regimental surgeons report that in many cases medical personnel knew nothing of the tactical situation. The medical service, especially in the early stages of the operation, was extremely sketchy. This fact again emphasizes the necessity of having battalion commanders and their staffs taken into the problem early in the planning stage.

'16. Beach Organization:
The beach personnel must be familiar with the troops and types of equipment to be landed. In Operation Torch the beach organization was British on two of the three beaches and was composed of personnel who were not familiar with U.S. equipment and organizations. In many instances they disregarded U.S. priorities and substituted British priorities.

'17. Army and Navy Cooperation:
a. Cooperation between individuals of the Army and Navy, both British and American, was entirely satisfactory. However, it is recommended that the line of demarkation wherein the Navy has full control of the operation until the troops reach the shore, should be changed so that the Army takes control when the troops get into the landing craft. Landing craft personnel should be Army personnel and trained by the Army.

b. Ships of all types and classes were furnished for this operation. From an Army standpoint assault ships should have the following specifications: Tonnage: 10,000 to 15,000; speed; not less than 18m.p.h. cruising speed in order to avoid submarines; sufficient berthing space for seventy five officers and 1,500 men; adequate troop kitchens and dining rooms, adequate bathing facilities; exits from berthing compartments arranged to facilitate the movement of troops to debarkation points; a minimum of five debarkation points on each side of the ship; a minimum of four holds; two forward and two aft; adequate booms so rigged that they can simultaneously handle Army loads; adequate deck space at debarkation points so that troops have sufficient room to disembark; sufficient deck space so that troops can get proper physical exercise.

c. The present landing craft are inadequate in every respect. They are too small to carry tactical units; they broach easily; they break up in moderately heavy seas; their compasses are worthless. It is strongly recommended that a suitable landing craft large enough to carry a platoon of infantry with two units of fire and all platoon weapons be developed.

d. During operations two calls were made on the British naval forces for naval gunfire. In the first case it took one hour to get the gunfire; in the second it took two hours.

e. The only air support of this force during the assault phase, except adequate reconnaissance aviation, was carrier-based naval aviation. One call was made on it—to bomb Fort Lazaret on Cap Matifou. It took two hours to get this support.

f. The time lag for both naval gunfire and air support appears to be excessive. It is suggested that the problem of such support be given careful consideration and study.'

The Central Task Force submission highlighted:

- Need for provision of PoW escort companies.
- Need for Grave Registration Units in assault convoy.
- Earlier establishment of civil administration details. This was emphasised in every report.
- Need for interpreters must be anticipated.
- Loading must place unit and equipment on one ship. Combat loading will be crucial if faced by serious opposition.
- Use of armored units must be stressed.
- Use parachute troops to neutralise important objectives.
- Approach and attack under darkness. Surprise more than makes up for the difficulty of finding the beach.
- All troops selected for assault phase should be experienced troops with the following training: use of compass; Sorting and patrolling; Cutting passage through barbed wire entanglements; Reduction of pill box type fortification; Qualification and combat firing; Pioneer work to include repair of bridges and getting vehicles through mud and sand; CP exercises with particular emphasis on signals communications and reports made to higher headquarters.
- Waterproofed bulldozers needed on beach early ditto service elements of assault units.
- Radio equipment of Air Support Parties must be combat loaded with assault troop vehicles and be mobile.
- AA automatic weapons units should be among the first troops landed.
- Assault divisions light artillery battalions should have at least one 75mm pack howitzer battery and all artillery should arrive asap.
- There was a shortage of suitable artillery officers.
- Need for smoke both to mask convoy and on land.
- Tactically, the ideal formation for landing is combat teams abreast, each in column of battalions. This permits better organization on the beach and simplifies shore logistics.
- Radios must be waterproofed.

Above: A convoy of British troopships, en route to Algeria, seen from the SS *Monarch of Bermuda*. Note 20mm AA gun in the foreground.

Below: The scariest part of the invasion? Undoubtedly climbing over the railings to descend to a waiting landing craft by rope grappling net—generally with an accompaniment of sailors catcalling.

Operation Morsky (SOV) 3/4 February 1943 Novorossiysk, USSR

On the night of 3/4 February 1943 the USSR mounted Operation Morsky—its first amphibious assault of the war—with the objective of retaking the port of Novorossiysk and ultimately destroying the German Kuban Bridgehead. Two landings were planned, the main one at Ozereika Bay to the southwest of the city and a much smaller diversionary attack on Stanichka at Cape Myskhako to the south. Lacking any proper landing craft the Soviets had to use three very old, slow barges to land their tanks and equipment, and as a result the Ozereika operation ended in complete disaster. One of the ships carrying infantry and all the barges was hit and sunk, less than half the 30 tanks making it to the shore. The attack was abandoned and attempts to rescue the stranded troops failed, leaving 1,300 men to death or capture. The smaller diversionary raid at Stanichka was ironically a lot more successful, despite being opposed. Torpedo boats raised a smokescreen, support vessels laid down covering fire and the small number of troops initially landed were swiftly reinforced and thus able to establish then expand their beachhead. By 10 February they were in the outskirts of Novorossiysk and by the 15th over 17,000 men with mortars, artillery and machine guns had been landed. German opposition was intense and for months a stalemate resulted as both sides dug in. Finally, on 10 September 1943 Soviet forces attacked from the northeast and from the Myskhako beachhead, and another seaborne landing was launched from Gelendzhik. After a week of bitter fighting Novorossiysk was liberated. Soviet casualties were high, 21,000 men were killed at the Myskhako beachhead alone.

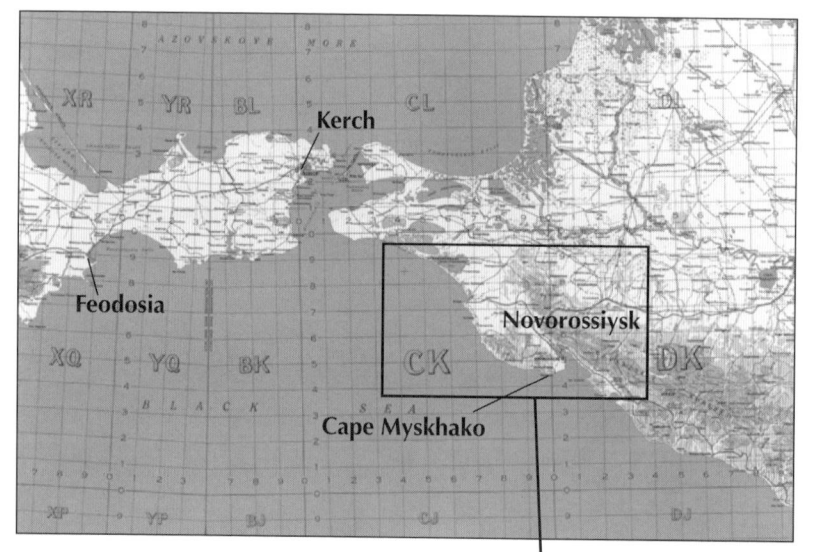

Left and Below: Maps showing the Novorossiysk area. The attack at Stanichka created what became known as Malaya Zemlya—'small land'—originally held by 800 marines, the commander of whom, Maj Caesar Kunikov, received a posthumous award to become a Hero of the Soviet Union.

Operation Cartwheel (Allies) 30 June 1943-20 March 1944 South-West Pacific

Supreme Allied Commander in the South West Pacific Area, General Douglas MacArthur, had approved an envelopment of the Japanese main base of Rabaul through the Elkton plans in 1943. These were agreed in part by the Joint Chiefs, although without the extra seven divisions MacArthur had requested.

Some 13 separate operations were identified in the final 'Cartwheel' plan, of which those listed at right were undertaken (those in bold are examined in detail in forthcoming pages).

Operation Cartwheel initially made heavy use of troops from Australia and New Zealand until Americans became available. MacArthur's strategy was not to strike large concentrations of enemy troops head on, but to bypass them. Amphibious landings—backed up by considerable airpower—proved the ideal way to attack the Japanese where they were weakest, although this did have the disadvantage of requiring blocking forces to keep the bypassed enemy concentrations bottled up, as happened when the time came to attack Rabaul itself. Instead, neutralised, it was bypassed, the troops inside bottled up. Eventually garrisoned by almost 100,000 men, 70,000 were still there at war's end.

Operation Chronicle (previously Coronet) 30 June 1943 Woodlark Island and Kiriwina
Operation Toenails 30 June 1943 New Georgia
 Segi Point, New Georgia 21 June 1943
 Rendova Island 30 June 1943
 Zanana, New Georgia 5 July 1943
 Bairoko, New Georgia 5 July 1943
 Arundel Island 27 August 1943
 Vella Lavella Island 15 August 1943
Operation Postern 5 September 1943 Lae, New Guinea
Operation Goodtime 27 October 1943 Treasury Islands
Operation Blissful 28 October 1943 Choiseul Island
Operation Cherryblossom 1 November 1943 Bougainville Island
Operation Dexterity 15 December 1943
 Arawe, New Britain 15 December 1943
 Cape Gloucester, New Britain 26 December 1943
 Saidor, Papua New Guinea 2 January 1944
Green Islands 15 February 1944
Admiralty Islands 29 February 1944
Emirau Island 20 March 1944

Below: MacArthur's plan for the encirclement and negation of Rabaul.

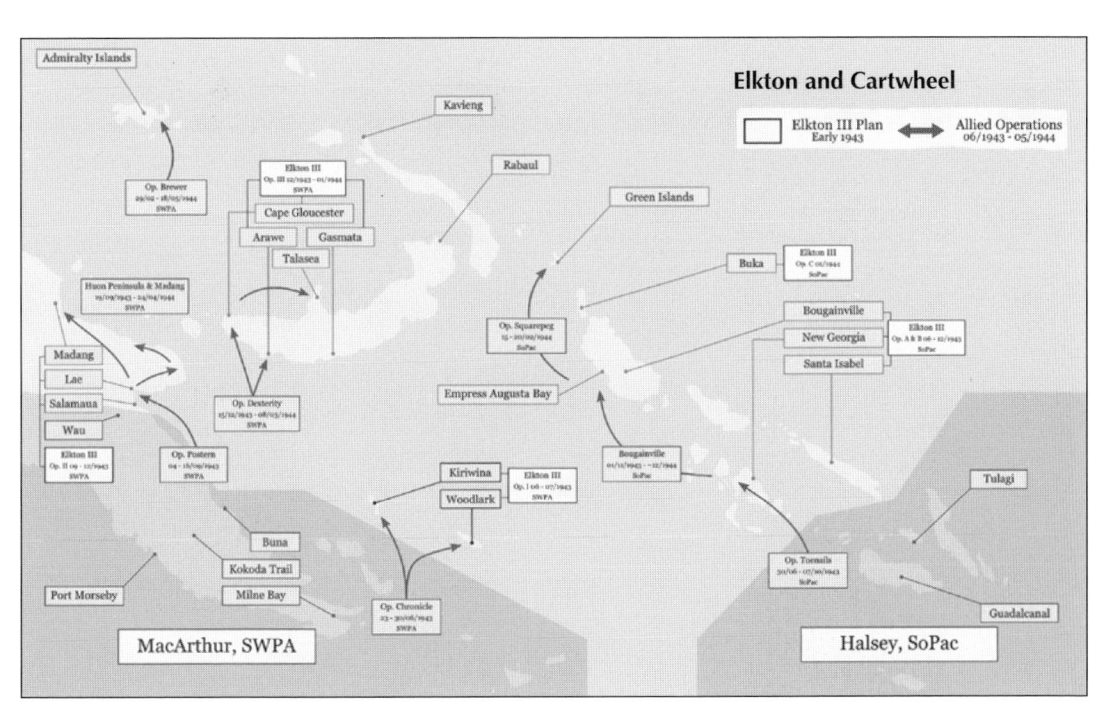

Operation Toenails (US) 30 June–7 October 1943 New Georgia, Solomon Islands

The landings on New Georgia weren't concentrated. After raider patrols had scouted the area, the plan was to attack in three groups. On 30 June, the Eastern Landing Force—the 103rd Infantry Regiment and 4th Raider Battalion—was to land and occupy Viru, Wickham Anchorage and Segi Point, allowing construction units to build a fighter strip at Segi and a torpedo boat base at Viru. The Northern Landing Group (1st Raider Regiment HQ, 1st Raider Battalion and two army battalions) would go ashore at Rice Anchorage and attack Enogai Inlet and Bairoko Harbour overland. The last D-day operation would be the Southern Landing Group's seizure of the northern end of Rendova and its outlying islands. However, the best-laid plans 'gang aft a'gley' and so did these. Increased Japanese presence led Admiral Turner on 20 June to order half the 4th Raiders to move immediately from Guadalcanal to Segi. Two companies loaded on board APDs that day and made an unopposed landing the next morning. On 22 June

Above: Troops climbing down nets hung over USS *McCawley*'s side, to board LCVPs during rehearsals for the New Georgia operation, 14 June 1943.

Below: LCP(R) and other landing craft put infantry and medics ashore on a New Georgia Beach.

two Army infantry companies and the advance party of the airfield construction unit arrived.

The defences of Viru meant a seaborne approach wouldn't work so the raiders were delivered by rubber boat to Segi, from where they trekked to Viru. A difficult march saw them achieve their objective.

The other two companies of the 4th Raider Battalion helped 2nd Battalion, 103rd Infantry to seize Vangunu and the approaches to Wickham Anchorage on 30 June. The raiders' night landing in heavy seas went badly, leaving the two companies thinly scattered along seven miles of coastline. Luckily, there was no opposition and the army units landed unscathed; all the units had concentrated in time to attack Kaeruka which fell on 3 July.

On 5 July, 1st Raider Battalion and the Raider HQ spearheaded the night landing of the Northern Group at Rice Anchorage, from where the battalion was to advance to seize Dragons Peninsula and then Enogai and Bairoko. The former they took losing 54 dead and 91 wounded, killing 350 Japanese and seizing the four 140mm coastal guns.

On 18 July four APDs brought 4th Raider Battalion and fresh supplies to Enogai. From there the raiders headed towards Bairoko. Unfortunately, the defences—four fortified lines on parallel coral ridges just a few hundred yards from the harbour with mutually supporting bunkers protected by coconut logs and coral—were too strong and the enemy was waiting.

The raiders failed to seize the objective and suffered severe casualties. It was only later in August that another attack took place: army troops moved carefully against Bairoko but found the main enemy force had escaped by sea.

The New Georgia campaign saw desperate fighting and each raider battalion had suffered more than 25 percent battle casualties: 1st Raiders had just 245 effectives; the 4th Raiders only 154. In total, US forces sustained over 5,000 dead and wounded with many more disease and psychological casualties. The Japanese, too, lost many men to sickness and some 1,600 dead, 3,800 wounded and over 350 aircraft destroyed. In the end, the Japanese retreated to the outer islands of Arundel (attacked 27 August; Japanese abandoned 20/21 September after heavy fighting), Kolombangara (bypassed and Japanese abandoned by 4 October) and Vella Lavella which was attacked by 6,500 men on 15 August. Fighting continued until 7 October when 3rd New Zealand Division destroying the final pocket, although the Japanese managed to evacuate the final defenders on the night of the 6th/7th.

Marine Raiders head ashore from USS *Sands* on 23 February 1943. They landed without opposition on Pavuvu Island, Russell Islands.

Operation Cleanslate (US) 21 February 1943 Russell Islands, Solomon Islands

The islands were important for their strategic location: they could be used to facilitate the American invasion of New Georgia and the Solomons. The landings involved 10,000 men of the 3rd Raider Battalion, USMC and US Army's 43rd Division. They were unopposed because the Japanese had evacuated at the same time as they left Guadalcanal—only a few weeks after they had occupied the Russell Islands. The successful invasion allowed the construction of two airfields—the first was ready by 15 April—a PT-boat base at Wernham Cove and landing craft bases.

Operation Husky (Allies) 9 July 1943 Sicily

The statistics and logistics of 'Husky' are awesome, for it was the largest amphibious landing of the war in terms of its area and the number of men put ashore on the first day. Over 3,000 ships carrying 180,000 troops, thousands of vehicles and 600 tanks landed at multiple sites supported by 4,000 aircraft, including a massive paratrooper and glider assault group with 137 gliders and 400 transports. From before dawn on 10 July the landings were spread over 100 miles of the southern and eastern coasts. Bad weather caused many mishaps and there were other tragically costly mistakes, as a category 7 gale scattered the air armada, causing various friendly fire incidents, while hundreds of paratroopers in heavy kit jumped too soon and others in gliders were released too early and many were drowned at sea. The rough weather also made most of the sea landings difficult—yet more of a surprise. Some landings were fiercely contested; others not at all, and the fleet lost several ships to air and naval attacks. By the evening the seven Allied assault divisions (three American, three British and one Canadian) had all established themselves ashore and the major port of Syracuse had been captured. There followed a successful five-week campaign to capture the rest of the island.

Axis casualties totalled 37,000 German and 130,000 Italian (mostly prisoners), while the Allies lost some 31,158 killed, wounded or missing. Despite the weather and the escape of a large number of German troops, 'Husky' was a resounding success.

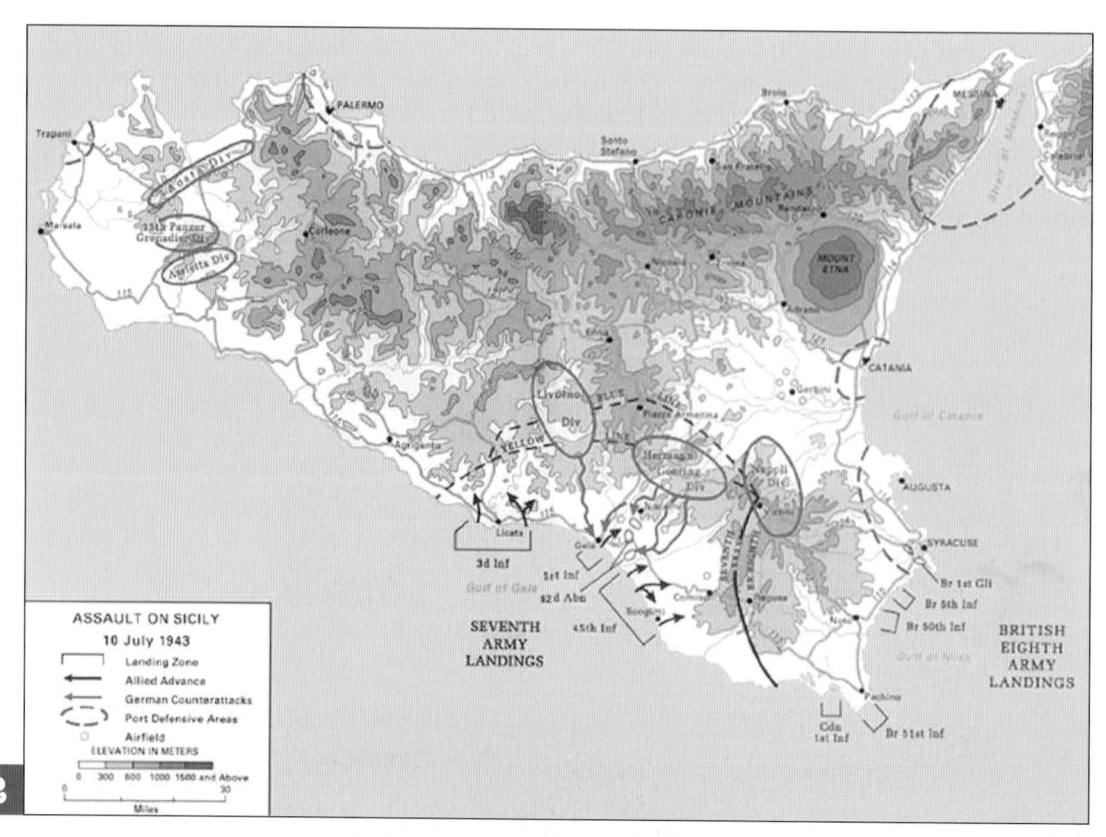

Opposite, Above: troops boarding LCIs at Bizerte, Tunisia, for the Invasion of Sicily. LCIs present include -S-218, -35, -14, -326, -88, -91 and -229 in first row. In second row are -90, -320, -16, -3, -213, -321, -4, -86, -212, -217, -8 and -83.

Above and Below: Both the Luftwaffe and Regia Aeronautica pummelled the US beachhead at Gela, the USAAF unable to provide sufficient air cover to stop them. The immediate consequence of this on D-day was the sinking of USS *Maddox* by an Italian Stuka and damage caused to *LST-345* and *PC-621* as they tried to avoid bombs. However, there were more serious repercussions. Using proximity fuzed anti-aircraft ammunition for the first time in the ETO, the naval gunners let fly at anything in the air with awful consequences for a number of Allied aircraft, in particular on the night of 11 July when Operation Mackall saw 144 C-47s and C-53s of 52nd Troop Carrier Wing take off from Kairouan, Tunisia to carry the 504th PIR to drop over Gela. Of these, 23 aircraft didn't return: 37 did so in spite of heavy damage. Tragically, 318 of the 2,304 paratroops died, some of them shot in the water by gunners raking downed aircraft. In mitigation, an hour before the Luftwaffe had conducted a major raid. Patton called it "an unavoidable incident of combat." The hard lesson was learned, however. When the 504th was dropped at Salerno, there were no losses.

Right: The Action Report of the Western Naval Task Force said of the naval gunfire during 'Husky': 'All sources of information indicated that naval gunfire support was outstanding, more effective and accurate than the military commanders had believed possible. Enemy batteries were silenced, at times by direct hits; searchlights were extinguished and troop concentrations scattered. Most noteworthy is the part played by the cruisers [here one of the 'Brooklyn' class fires its 6-inch guns] and destroyers in turning back the German counter-attack at Gela when the Hermann Goering Division almost succeeded in erasing the narrow 1st Infantry Division beachhead. Fire from cruisers and destroyers was largely responsible for turning the German tanks back. Several tanks were destroyed by direct hits, while others were disabled by near misses.'

Below Right: A famous photograph showing Liberty ship SS *Robert Rowan* exploding after having been bombed on 11 July off Gela. The USN's report on 'Husky' (see pp. 96–97) said, 'Greater attention must be given to the segregated stowage of explosives and inflammables in merchant vessels entering the assault area.'

Above and Below: The British were delivered to the east of the island in three convoys from the Middle East, Tunisia and the River Clyde. Here British troops unload transports. The USN's report on 'Husky' said: 'Unless labor troops are included in the Shore Party organization in greater numbers than now provided, unloading plans should provide for 2 soldiers to be placed in each LCVP and 4 to 6 soldiers in each LCM to unload these boats at the beach ... LSTs should not be employed for unloading transports unless no other types are available. When so employed, special detachments of troops should be assigned LSTs to load stores and unload at beaches.'

Lessons from Operation Husky
(Edited excerpts from Hewitt report—Points were numbered 1–179)

'The Sicilian campaign was unique in many respects, but the most impressive fact was [its] vast scale ... the "lessons learned" should receive close study by those charged with the planning and execution of [future] offensive efforts. In order that maximum benefit maybe derived from the mistakes made and the experience gained, special emphasis is directed to specific items of primary importance recapitulated herewith:

12. The logistic requirements of all military forces should be computed in detail and weighed against the capacity of the beaches selected for maintenance.

13. Where extended beach maintenance is imposed by the absence of suitable ports, the plan should provide for greatly augmented Shore Parties or Beach Groups.

14. Where the assault beaches lack suitable exits, the plan should provide for greatly augmented Road Construction and Transportation units.

15. An advance base, capable of mounting troops, vehicles, and logistic supply, is essential in any shore-to-shore movement.

16. In shore-to-shore assaults, economy of time afloat for troops embarked in landing craft must be considered; staging of craft to other ports may be found desirable.

18. The success of the plan should not be dependent upon the employment of a fair-weather weapon, such as paratroops.

24. A demonstration by naval forces should be planned and executed to confuse the enemy as to the locale of the major landing, and to tax his communications at the outset.

25. If light forces are available, a diversion plan employing deceptive devices should be executed in conjunction with the main assaults. Diversion bombings should be a part of the plan.

26. Where practicable, the initial movement of assault forces should be in conformity with the "cover plan."

27. PTs are suitable for use as flanking offensive screens when used in adequate numbers. When operating against German E-boats, U.S. PTs should be supported by a destroyer.

28. Submarines are eminently suited for pre-D-day reconnaissance of the assault area and for use as navigational beacons to aid the approach of the assault forces to the initial transport area. The ability of submarines to lay various types of buoys to aid the assault boat waves should be exploited where circumstances permit.

30. Preliminary softening of the enemy prior to D-day by heavy scale air bombardment is necessary. This effort should become increasingly heavy with selected targets being land communications, airfields, air forces, and fixed defenses.

31. Naval gunfire plans should provide for engagement, prior to and during the assault, of all enemy defenses that threaten the safe landing of the assault troops on the selected beaches. The control of these fires must be regulated solely by the Naval Commander.

32. The element of "surprise" should be examined with penetrating thoroughness on a realistic and practical basis.

33. The plan should provide for an "assault scale" of weapons and equipment for those military forces making the assault landings.

34. Once Division troop lists have been approved by the Army Commander, changes must be held to a minimum in order that plans of lower echelons may be developed and promulgated to the required forces.

41. The Air Plan should be in detail and show when, where and what fighter cover and air support will be provided the naval and ground forces during the assault phases of the operation.

42. Air plans involving the transport of paratroops over naval forces should be submitted to the Naval Commander for approval.

43. Air forces participating in support of joint operations should be placed under the command of the commander who is responsible for the success or failure of the joint effort.

45. In a theater where maritime traffic is under constant attack by enemy aircraft, it is essential that strong air protection be provided troop-transport movements en route to an amphibious assault.

46. Fighter cover by high and low standing patrols is essential over shipping anchored off the assault beaches; the scale of fighter cover provided for this purpose in this operation was inadequate.

70. Combat-loading plans should limit the materials being loaded to those required by the assault. These plans should have the approval of the Naval Task Force Commander as well as the Army Commander concerned. Once loading has commenced, these plans should not be changed without their specific approval in each case.

71. Greater attention must be given to vertical loading of transports with relation to the Army tactical plan; accessibility of anti-tank weapons must be emphasized in an assault against armored enemy forces.

78 and 79. [See caption on p. 93.] 82. [See caption on p. 92.]

83. Adaptors should be provided to permit interchange of hose, nozzles, and other firefighting equipment when Allied naval and merchant vessels are engaged in the same operation.

84. In combat-loading landing ships and craft particular care must be taken that beaching draft is not exceeded.

85. Landing craft should be used primarily as assault craft and for the immediate follow-up of assault forces. They are not designed for "ferrying service." Army build-up and mainte¬ance should be carried in merchant vessels.

86. Landing craft can transport the necessary logistic maintenance to ground forces by unloading immediately in the rear of our front lines, when our Army flanks reach to the sea. This method is most effective when land motor transport is heavily taxed or when roads are mined and demolished by enemy action.

87. Combat-loading of LSTs require of TQMs a preliminary study of deck arrangements and template loading, in order that vehicles may be properly loaded under their own power. The main deck of LSTs should be loaded to provide increased AA protection to the ship.

88. LSTs are not suitable for carrying stores; if such employment is contemplated, these ships should have installed winches, booms, and other mechanical means for discharging stores to boats and DUKWs alongside.

89. When LSTs cannot be beached, the most effective methods of unloading LSTs, in order of preference, are: (1) over naval pontoon causeways, (2) into LCTs, and (3) into DUKWs.

91. A DUKW, manned by the pontoon crew, should be a part of the equipment of each LST fitted as a pontoon-carrier.

92. LSTs should be altered as follows:
 (1) Strengthen ramp chains and fittings.
 (2) Install 10,000 gallons per day distilling plant. ¬

(3) Install 5-ton boom and winch on main deck in way of hatch.
(4) Install cross-connection between Fire and Bilge pumps and Fresh Water tanks, and discharge piping from Fire and Bilge pumps to bow with 2 1/2" hose connection, to enable discharge of potable water to shore tankage.
(5) Install barrage balloon fittings, winch, etc., provide stowage for barrage balloons, helium gas cylinders, and accessories.
(6) Install 150 portable bunks in after end of tank deck on all 6-davit LSTs.
(7) Install fittings and provide gear on LSTs designated to side-carry pontoon causeways.
(8) Increase diameter of one forward inboard hole on bottom of ramp from 6" to 12" to provide socket for King pin on causeway.

93. LCI(L)s are not suitable for carrying stores; they may be used for transferring personnel from transports to shore, and are particularly well suited for use as salvage vessels on the beaches.

94. One LCI(L), especially fitted out with salvage equipment and trained personnel, should be provided as salvage vessel for each Division beach; each Battalion beach should be provided with one LCM carrying a bulldozer and special salvage gear and trained personnel.

95. The present ramps on LCI(L)s are too heavy and cumbersome. During this operation, ramps were lost due to difficulty in retracting, ramp brakes did not hold, and in heavy seas ramps were thrown back off the rollers. Ramps should be redesigned to provide lighter, longer and wider ramps with suitable power retraction.

96. Assault LCTs should be loaded in such manner that tanks and S.P. guns are able to fire during the approach.

97. LCTs, employed to unload transports, should be provided with double crews to enable continuous operation.

98. LCTs are eminently suitable for side loading from LSTs.

99. LCTs should be altered as follows:
(1) Strengthen ramp chains and fittings.
(2) Render amidship section of bulwark portable on each side to permit side loading and unloading.
(3) Strengthen hull to prevent working and buckling in heavy seas.

100. LCVPs should be altered as follows:
(1) Reduce or eliminate down-by-the-bow trim.
(2) Improve design of rudder and skeg to reduce time required to remove and repair.
(3) Substitute cast steel for brass lifting pads and fittings.
(4) Provide reinforcement in way of cleats, and on Chris-Craft increase size of cleats.
(5) Provide standard ring-type slings for all boats; discard the Chris-Craft curved bar-type sling.

101. There is a definite need for Control Vessels, of the LCC type, having adequate navigational and signalling equipment.

102. Greater emphasis should be given to the training of control vessels in the ship-to-shore movement; these vessels should be an integral part of amphibious forces; attack plans of Naval Task Force Commanders should provide in detail for the full employment of Control Vessels.

103. Greater attention should be given to the selection, training, equipping and briefing of Amphibious Scouts.

104. Scout boats should be fully employed as smokers to cover assault craft under favorable wind conditions.

105. Scout boats should be employed to assist in the hydrographic surveys off the assault beaches.

Sections 106–122 on Shore Parties and 123–136 on Beach Parties, see p. 233.

138. In shore-to-shore movements, LSTs should be used as hospital ships if regular hospital ships are not available. Such LSTs, as designated for this use, should be provided with standee bunks, and the medical complement should include one officer and four enlisted men.

139. Combat-loaded transports carrying wounded should not be used for the evacuation of Prisoners of War.

140. The Army should provide guards for Prisoners of War embarked in naval ships; this should be set up in the Army-Navy plans; the unexpected withdrawal of combat troops for this purpose is not desirable.

143. Lethal Barrage Balloons Units ["lethal" because an explosive charge was attached] of trained naval personnel should be provided for each APA, XAP, AKA, LST and merchant vessel included in the assault forces.

144. Army balloon units should not be eliminated from Troop Lists on the pretext that such units are not "fighting troops"; lethal balloons are essential in amphibious operations.

146. Barrage balloons should be erected every 200 yards on the beach, over gasoline and ammunition dumps, and at the seaward and shoreward ends of each pontoon causeway.

148. Transports, merchant vessels and LSTs must give greater attention to the laying of smoke screens during an air alert; the plans of Naval Task Force Commanders should cover the details of the smoking plan.

152. Neutralization of assault beach defences by full employment of naval gunfire is a prerequisite to a successful landing against opposition.

153. The training of Naval Gunfire Liaison officers should include some of the elements of Ranger training, particularly overhead fire, battle courses, and physical conditioning courses.

157. When naval gunfire compels the enemy to evacuate an area, the Army ground forces should advance promptly to exploit the enemy's retirement.

158. The rocket armament of LCS(S)s is most effective in neutralizing beach areas.

159. Destroyers are superior to British LCGs in rendering close supporting fire, particularly when target is obscured.

160. AA fire discipline in our ships requires improvement. Graduates of aircraft identification schools should be assigned to all destroyers and larger ships.

161. There is a vital need for the development of our radar installations to enable the detection of enemy aircraft approaching ships from landward.

162. Enemy bombers frequently direct bombs at night against targets which disclose their importance by the volume of their fire.

163. The use of tracer ammunition at night is a controversial subject. A heavy barrage at night usually keeps enemy bombers at heights where they must resort to area bombing yet, on occasion, enemy bombers have sought shelter in our flak when pursued by our night fighters.

164. Non-tracer 40mm projectiles should be developed for use of these batteries at night when controlled by radar.

165. A self-destroyer 20mm projectile should be developed.

166. High-capacity ammunition employed by our 6" cruisers was very satisfactory.'

Operation Landcrab (Attu) and Operations Cottage (Kiska) (Allies) 11 May and 15 August 1943 Aleutian Islands

When the Japanese No 3 Special Landing Party and 500 marines landed at Kiska on 6 June 1942 they inflicted a psychological blow upon the Americans for the first loss of US soil to the enemy. Operation Cottage was launched to rectify this and 15 May 1943 saw an amphibious force of 34,426 American and Canadian troops land on Kiska, an island in the Rat Islands group of the Aleutian Islands of Alaska.

The bulk of these troops came from the US 7th Infantry Division, with 5,300 Canadians mainly from 13th Canadian Infantry Brigade. There was also a 2,000-strong mixed group of Canadian and American commandos formed into the 1st Special Service Force made up of three 600-man regiments. They were supported by US and Royal Canadian Air Force fighters and three Canadian armed merchant cruisers and two corvettes, who softened up the enemy position with bombing raids and bombardments.

When the landings went in to Kiska on 15 August they were entirely unopposed and the invaders found that the island had been abandoned by the Japanese, who had in fact secretly left a fortnight earlier. Despite this there were casualties as result of friendly fire incidents, Japanese booby traps left behind and a US destroyer hitting a mine.

The battle of Attu that had taken place in May 1943 couldn't have been more different. The Americans had landed in two areas, north and south on 11 May. The northern landings went well. The southern at Massacre Bay were hampered by fog and the cloud cover negated air support. The vehicles and artillery bogged down so the infantry had to slog it out in the cold, suffering from frostbite, trench foot as well as the Japanese, whose final banzai charges were only just held. Their failure led to mass suicide by the survivors.

By 30 May it was all over: the Allies had lost 549 KIA, 1,148 WIA and of the 1,814 who had fallen sick over 600 had died. Of the Japanese garrison of 2,900, only 28 survived.

Above: Japanese Daihatsu abandoned on Kiska.

Below: *LST-451* broke her mooring lines in gale force winds in February 1944 and ended up beached at Lash Bay, Tanaga Island. Saved by Seabees she lived to fight again and saw action at Saipan, Tinian, Leyte, the Philippines and Okinawa.

Above: Holtz Bay, Attu. The conditions saw vehicles and artillery bog down and the fighting fall to the infantry.

Below Left and Right: Landing craft are swung out and then head for the landings on Attu.

Operation Accolade (UK) September–November 1943 Aegean Sea

Pushed hard by Churchill, in the face of opposition from his own commanders and flat refusal of involvement from the Americans, Operation Accolade was designed to take advantage of the Italian capitulation and take control of the Aegean Islands thus giving a measure of control of the eastern Mediterranean. The operation was a complete failure that would ultimately see some 4,600 British servicemen captured, 357 killed and nearly two-thirds of the LRDG committed to 'Accolade' captured or killed. British forces also included 150 men of the SBS and No 3 Cdo and nearly 3,000 regular troops of 234th Brigade.

The main trouble was that the Germans reacted faster than the Allies, who argued and dithered. The British—in the form of a small team of SBS—tried to persuade the Italians on Rhodes to surrender. This failed as the Germans had been building up their forces on the island and seized it themselves.

'Accolade' had allowed one of the last major German victories in the war. Fortunately it was also one of the last British defeats.

Opposite: The Italians controlled the Dodecanese islands and so when the armistice of 8 September 1943 took place, the British tried to get the garrison of Rhodes to hand the island over to the Allies. The Germans forestalled them, here and elsewhere in the Aegean, and were able to maintain their control over the islands almost till war's end. They did so on Rhodes by establishing a powerful presence in July 1943, *Sturm-Division-Rhodos* with four *Panzergrenadier* battalions and 150 tanks and AFVs—here PzKpfw IV Ausf Gs. The garrison finally surrendered to the British in May 1945.

Opposite, Below: German troops landing on Leros.

Below: An MFP lands German troops on Kos.

Operation *Eisbär* (GER) 3–4 October 1943 Kos, Greece

Following the capitulation of Italy in September 1943 the Germans moved swiftly to take over all Italian assets. On Kos British SBS teams took over the port and, near Antimachia, the only airfield on the Aegean islands they controlled. Some 1,500 men from 1st Durham Light Infantry, 11th Parachute Battalion and RAF personnel were landed. They were aided by some 3,500 Italian soldiers who had decided to join them. Leros and some other smaller islands were also occupied with light numbers of troops.

In response, the Germans launched Operation *Eisbär* to recover Kos. Early on 3 October preceded by multiple airborne landings of 1,500 paratroopers, a German fleet of ten vessels transported a battlegroup made up of 22. *Infanterie-Division (Luftlande)* and Brandenburg special forces—a mixture of marine troops, 1./*Küstenjägerabteilung* and the 5th *Fallschirmjäger* Battalion, along with light artillery and armoured cars. They landed in multiple locations: Marmari and Tingachi in the north, Camare Bay in the southwest, Forbici in the northeast and Capo Foco in the southeast.

Enjoying full air superiority, they quickly overwhelmed the Italians and British and forced them to surrender. Over 3,000 Italians and 1,400 Brits were captured, with over 100 Italian officers then executed on Hitler's orders.

Operation *Leopard* (GER) 12-16 November 1943 Leros, Greece

Another German operation in the Dodecanese, '*Leopard*' was launched to recover the island of Leros. The British had reinforced the sympathetic Italian garrison of approximately 9,000 with another 3,000 men, using elements from the Royal Irish Fusiliers, the Royal East Kent, the King's Own Royal Lancaster and the Queen's Own Royal West Kent Regiments. The original plan had been to hold the high ground inland, but the new British commander, Brig Robert Tilney, insisted on a forward defence of the coastline and spread his forces out accordingly. They were supported by air assets based in Africa which on paper seemed substantial—260 aircraft all told—but their German adversaries had their assets at much closer quarters and were able to attack Leros almost continuously.

The German invasion force consisted of III./ *Infanterie-Regiment* 440, II./IR 16 and II./IR 65 of the 22. *Infanterie-Division (Luftlande)*, parachutists from I./ FJR 2, and 1./*Küstenjägerabteilung* of the Brandenburg Division. After a 50-day air bombardment, the landings began on 12 November at Palma Bay, Pasta di Sopra and Pandeli Bay. The British, spread too thinly, were outnumbered in situ and easily overwhelmed. Both sides landed more men but the German reinforcements were more substantial and their air superiority was critical. By 16 November the British position had become untenable and Tilney surrendered, along with 3,200 British and 5,350 Italian soldiers.

Operations Baytown and Avalanche (Allies) 3 and 9 September 1943 Calabria and Salerno, Italy

It took 40 days between success in Sicily and the invasion of Italy, during which time the Germans rushed 13 divisions to Italy and took over from the Italians in Rome and Naples.

It was obvious where the Allies would land, so when the three-pronged invasion of mainland Italy began on 3 September with XIII Corps of Montgomery's Eighth Army landing at various points on the eastern coast of Calabria (Operation Baytown)—with the idea of drawing German forces away from the main invasion at Salerno—the Germans stayed put, exercising in the Salerno area, leaving the Eighth isolated and a long 300-mile march away from the action along roads whose infrastructure had been compromised.

'Avalanche' began on 9 September. Another opportunistic operation ('Slapstick') was launched simultaneously 130 miles away, following an offer by the Italian government to open the ports of Taranto and Brindisi. 'Slapstick' was accomplished by British 1st Airborne Division unopposed, with two infantry divisions soon disembarking behind it.

In the main operation, US Fifth Army, comprising US VI Corps and British X Corps, landed on a 35-mile front to the south of Salerno using the British 46th and 56th Infantry Divisions in the north and the US 36th Infantry in the south, with the Sele River in between their positions.

In an unsuccessful attempt at surprise there was no preparatory naval or aerial bombardment. The landings were violently opposed by the Germans, whose fierce counterattacks over the coming days almost succeeded in overwhelming the beachhead.

Intense naval bombardments, heavy air support and the arrival of 504th PIR saved the operation, and the Allies were further helped when Hitler decided that Italy south of Rome was no longer a strategic priority and forbade any further reinforcements. After a 10-day knife-edge battle the Allies finally succeeded, but it had been a close run thing.

Below: Supplies for Fifth Army are loaded in a Sicilian port.

Right: German coastal defence batteries in the area of the 'Avalanche' landings.

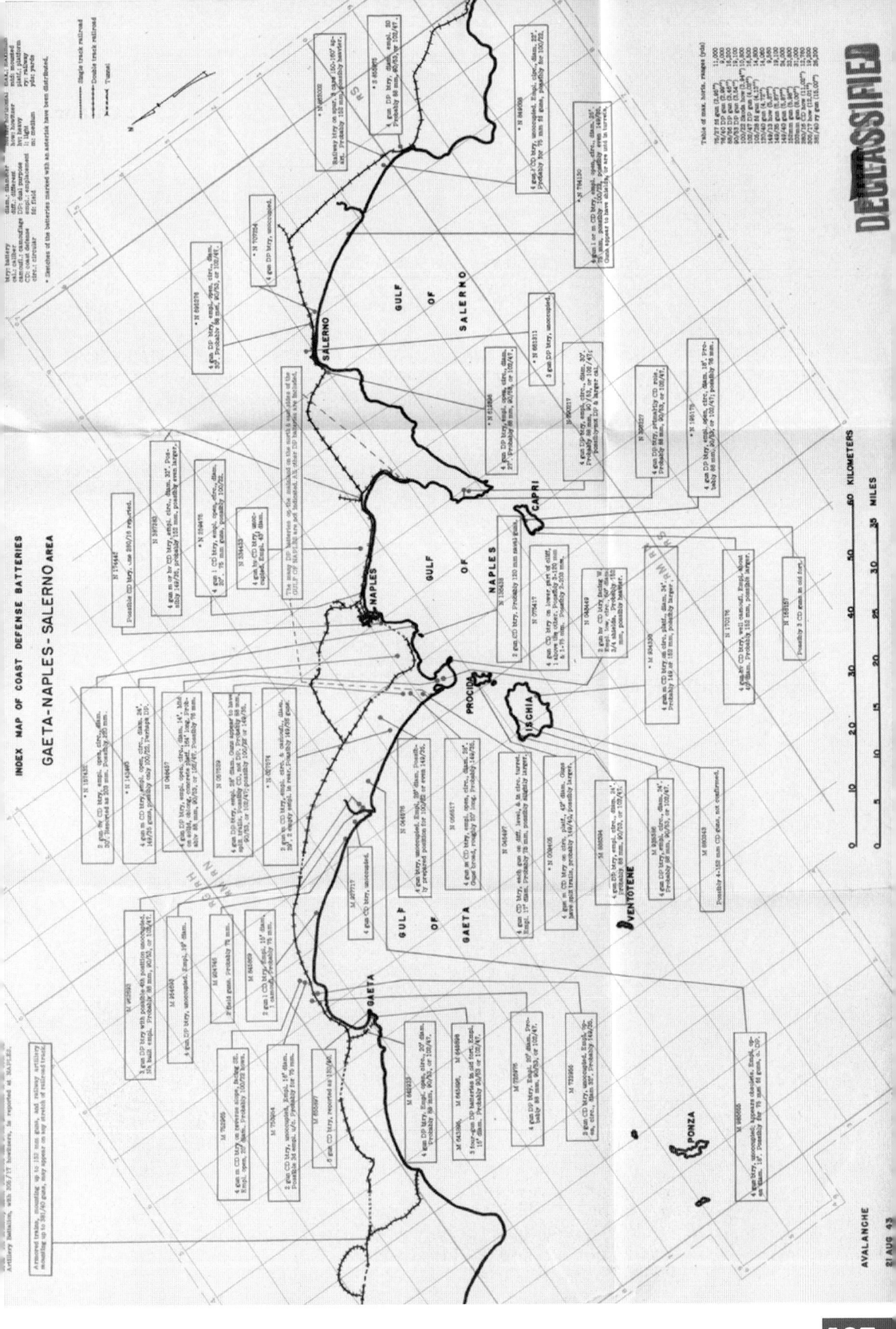

INDEX MAP OF COAST DEFENSE BATTERIES
GAETA-NAPLES-SALERNO AREA

AVALANCHE
21 AUG 43

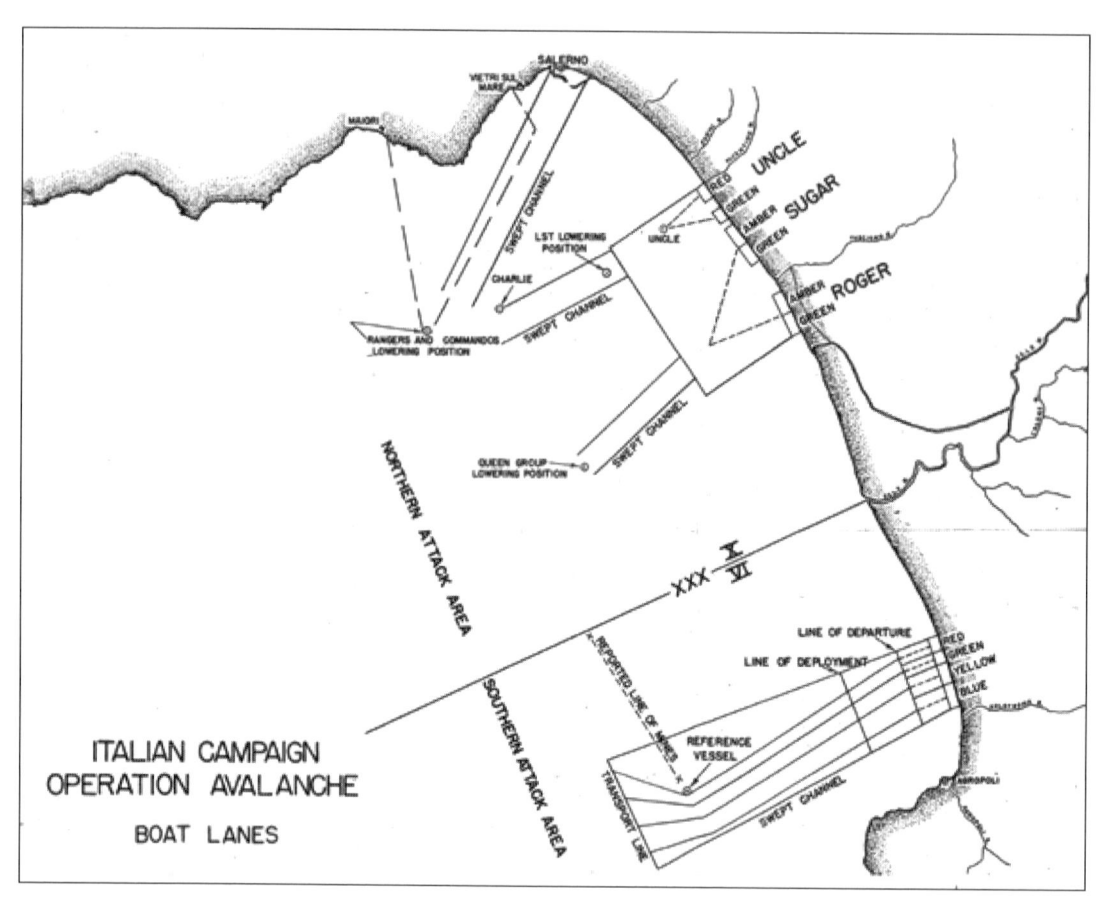

Above: The 'Avalanche' landing beaches. The Rangers went for Maiori, the commandos for Salerno itself; British 46th and 56th Infantry Divisions the Northern Attack Area; 36th (US) Infantry Division the Southern Attack Area.

Below: Concerned US reinforcements watch a German bomb explode as they head for the beaches.

Salerno scenes: *LCT(5)-30* off the American sector's Yellow Beach. The tower is the medieval Torre de Vedetta di Paestum. It was used as an observation post (**Above**); USS *LST-379* unloading tanks of C Company, 191st Tank Battalion across a pontoon causeway (**Below**); USS *Savannah* is hit by a German radio-controlled bomb on 11 September 1943. The bomb hit the top of the ship's number three gun turret and penetrated deep into her hull before exploding. The photograph shows the explosion venting through the top of the turret and also through Savannah's hull below the waterline. A motor torpedo boat (PT) is passing by in the foreground. (**Bottom**).

Operation Cherryblossom (US) 1 November 1943–21 August 1945 Bougainville Island, Solomon Islands

The fighting on Bougainville may have started at the end of 1943, but it didn't end until Japan surrendered in 1945. Part of this was planned: the objective in landing at Cape Torokina was to build airfields that would help reduce Rabaul. The landings were made by 3rd Marine Division, commanded by Marine General A. H. Turnage, USMC. Some 14,300 troops landed initially, with little opposition as they had achieved complete surprise. As the perimeter expanded, so the Japanese were able to land reinforcements. The heavy jungle and the tenacious Japanese defence meant that fighting on the island dragged on into 1944. In March the Americans had to withstand a major counterattack. Having done so, the Japanese were effectively beaten. They lost 5,400 killed in that attack alone out of a total of 8,200 KIA and 16,600 dead of disease or malnutrition up till October 1944 when the Australian Army replaced the Americans. The fighting continued until the Japanese surrendered in August 1945.

Opposite, Above: A Marine Corps LVT-1 churns toward the shore at Cape Torokina on the first day of landings.

Opposite, Below: LCP (right) landing craft take men and supplies ashore in Empress Augusta Bay to reinforce the Cape Torokina Beachhead, 6 November 1943. In the centre of the photo is USS *Kilty*, a 'Wickes' class destroyer turned APD that landed New Zealand troops on Stirling Island on 27 October and marines on Bougainville 5 November.

Above: Reinforcements wade ashore from 'LST-1' class *LST-353* on the shores of Empress Augusta Bay, on 6 November 1943. Also present are USS *LST-488* and *LST-70*. Note barrage balloon overhead. It was probably the detonation of a mortar round on *LST-353* that caused the West Loch disaster at Pearl Harbor on 21 May 1944 when six LSTs sank and 163 USN personnel died.

Below: Army troops land on Bougainville on 5 January 1944, to reinforce US marines on the Island. Landing craft have had parent ship hull numbers blacked out for security purposes. Note members of marine machine gun unit watching the soldiers come ashore.

Operation Galvanic (US) 20-23 November 1943 Gilbert Islands

During 1943 the focus of American attacks on the Japanese had been in the southwest and south Pacific where General Douglas A. MacArthur commanded. To open up a second front, the Commander-in-Chief, US Pacific Fleet and Pacific Ocean Areas, Admiral Chester W. Nimitz, USN, ordered two amphibious operations: the invasion of the Gilbert Islands in November 1943 and the Marshalls in late January 1944 (see p. 118). In the Gilberts the main fighting was on Makin (which had already seen action—see p. 43), Betio and Tarawa. The assault task force (Rear Admiral Richmond K. Turner, USN) landed USMC and US Army troops on the islands. The land invasion was commanded by Major General Holland M. Smith, USMC

There was a pre-invasion bombardment from sea and air and then two attack forces went in—Northern against Makin, Southern against Tarawa Atoll. The Northern Attack Force (Task Force 52) was commanded by Rear Admiral Richmond K. Turner, USN, and landed 27th Division on two beaches. On Red Beach, all went as planned, but as the landing craft neared Yellow Beach the Japanese engaged. Most went aground and the troops were forced to walk to the beach in low water. Nevertheless, despite the determined resistance, the island fell on November 23.

Betio Island, the largest part of the Tarawa Atoll is only two miles long and 800 yards at its widest point, surrounded by 550-yard wide shallow reef with a long pier jutting out beyond it where ships could unload and an airfield located in its southwest corner. Yet on this tiny island nearly 6,500 men lost their lives within 76 hours of intense combat.

Tasked with its capture and supported by the Southern Carrier Group, the Southern Attack Force included three battleships, five escort carriers, five cruisers, 21 destroyers, an LSD and 16 transports containing the 2nd Marine Division—some 18,600 assault troops. Despite heavy pre-landing air strikes and naval bombardments, it took three days of the most bitter fighting to subdue the fanatical 4,500 Japanese (especially the Sasebo 7th Special Naval Landing Force and 3rd Special Base Force), who were well dug-in, having had the time to prepare the ground with interlocking machine gun pillboxes and bunkers. Lack of proper charts and tide tables also affected the fortunes of the assault as a low neap tide prevented landing craft from getting over the reef, leaving many stuck and open targets and forcing marines to wade several hundred yards to reach the shore under intense Japanese fire.

By the end of the first day, of the 5,000 marines who had landed, 1,500 were dead or wounded and the issue was very much in doubt. But the marines held the tiny beachhead and the next days saw it slowly expanded using tanks, flamethrowers, artillery and ships' gunfire. Each pillbox and bunker had to be taken individually. In the end only one Japanese officer, 16 enlisted personnel and 129 Koreans surrendered alive.

Opposite, Below: Operation Fetlock saw the occupation of Funafuti Atoll (2 October 1942) in the Ellice Islands. By April 1943 it had an airbase just within range of the Gilbert Islands, but other islands in Nanomea and Nukufetu Atolls were closer, so they were occupied by Marine 7th Defense Battalion in August. Here *LCT(5)-129* approaches the beach at Funafuti Atoll, transporting US Army Air Corps personnel on 11 November 1943. Note the early warning radar installations in the background.

Above: Troops of 2/165th Infantry, 27th Division assaulted Yellow Beach Two, Butaritari, Makin Atoll, on 20 November.

In April 1944, the US Fleet published *Amphibious Operations*. It said of 'Galvanic':

'Although operations for the capture of atolls have long been studied by the U. S. Navy and Marine Corps, this is the first operation in which we have engaged in atoll warfare. There are many points of difference between this and amphibious assault against an enemy occupying large land masses. ...

Our lack of anything like adequate information of the atolls and the enemy situation in the GILBERTS was, after considerable effort, considerably rectified through:
(a) The employment of aircraft for taking large numbers of vertical and oblique photographs of land areas, beaches, lagoons, reefs, channels and defense installations.
(b) The employment of the NAUTILUS (Submarine) on a special mission to obtain horizontal panoramic photographs of the atolls to observe enemy activities; and to obtain data as to surf, tidal, wind and current conditions.
(c) The assembly of about 15 British who had lived in the islands, or had been shipmasters operating small steamers and schooners among them.

... Attack on an atoll resembles in many respects the assault of a fort or fortified locality with, of course, the added complication of having to initiate the assault with the ship to shore movement. The successful assault of such a position requires:
(1) Early detailed information of the exact location, type, strength and character of the defenses.
(2) Early distribution of the above information to all echelons for the preparation of detailed plans.
(3) Training of all echelons down to the smallest units in the details they are to execute in the assault. Replicas and dummies of hostile defenses should be constructed for the training of small assault units.
(4) Protracted and intensive preparation fires by all possible supporting weapons with a view toward maximum destruction of enemy installations, guns, obstacles, communications and supplies.
(5) Adequate cover and protection for the assaulting troops to insure they arrive within assaulting distance of the defenses.
(6) Once the position is broken into, the timely arrival of supports and reserves must be insured for the reduction of the garrison.'

Left: Aerial photograph of the south side of the Tarawa Atoll, taken on 9 September 1943, from an altitude of 12,000ft. Betio Island is in the foreground, with Bairiki and Eita Islands beyond.

Below Left: Northwestern end of Betio Island, Tarawa, on 22 November 1943, with Red 1 Beach at left and Green Beach in centre and right. Several LVTs and a Japanese landing craft are on the beach. Several coast defense guns are also visible.

Right: Marine dead on one of the Betio Island landing beaches. Other marines are resting in the background, two of them on a broken-down M4.

Below Right: Seabees repairing the Betio Island airfield with bulldozers, as the battle for the Island continues at its extremities.

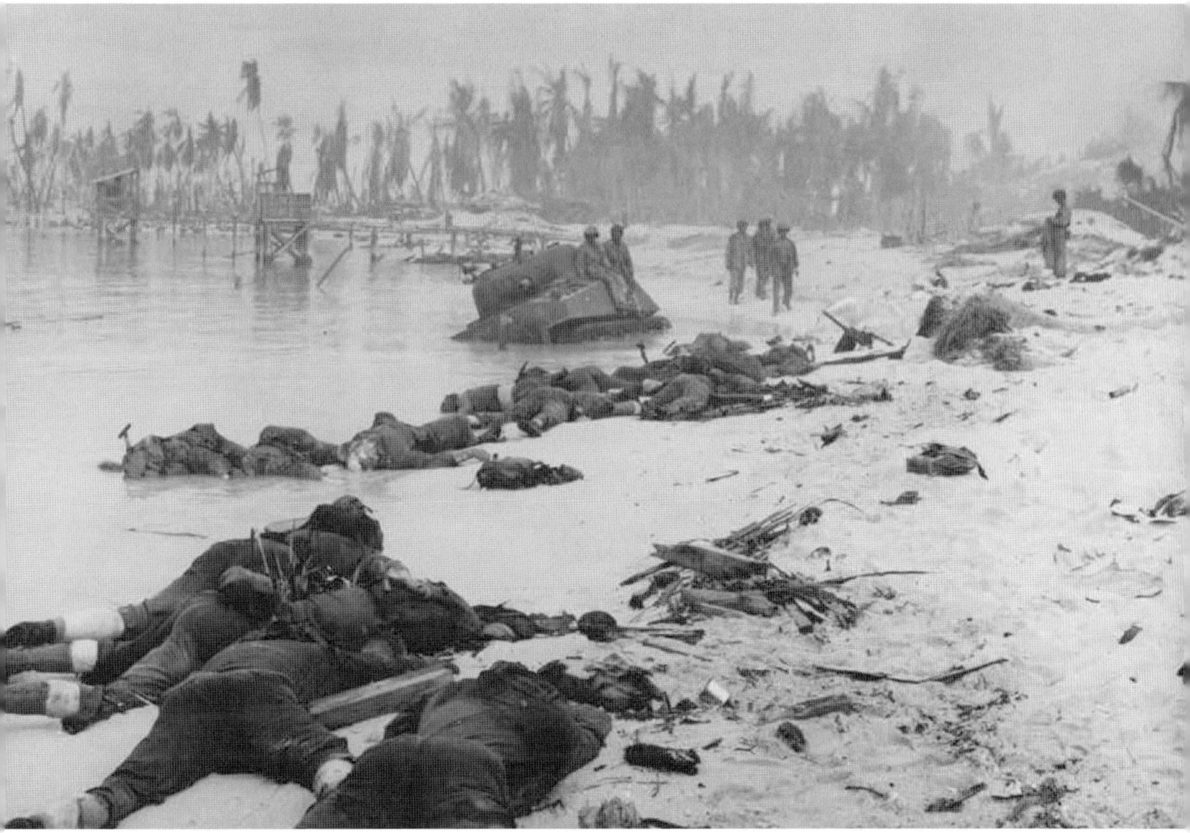

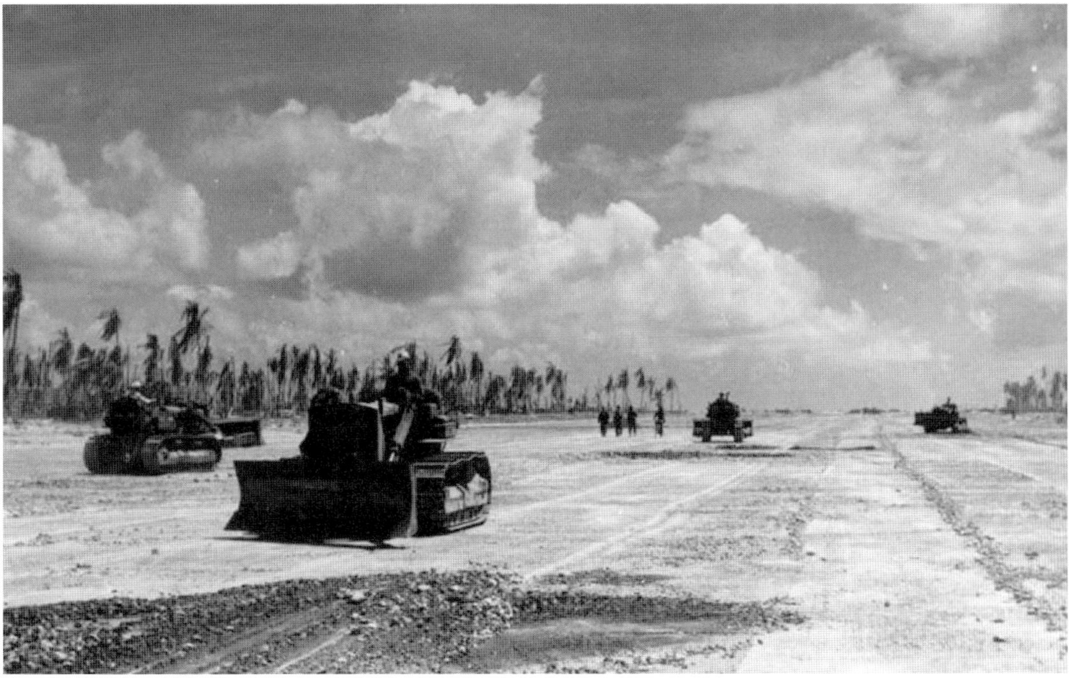

Kerch-Eltigen Operation (SOV)
November 1943 Crimea

Following Operation *Trappenjagd* (p. 63) in 1942, during which 160,000 Soviet soldiers were killed or captured and about 140,000 others were evacuated, a second attempt to recapture Kerch and the Crimea took place in November 1943. Landing at two locations on the eastern coast, the Soviet Kerch–Eltigen Operation marked the beginning of the new offensive.

The assault was undertaken by the 18th and 56th Armies of the 4th Ukrainian Front, supported by the Black Sea Fleet and the Azov Flotilla.

Despite bad weather, using fishing trawlers and other improvised boats as landing craft, the 18th Army's 318th Rifle Division and the 386th Naval Infantry Battalion were landed at Eltigen on 1 November and managed to secure a small beachhead against the Romanian defenders. Following this on 3 November 4,400 men of the Soviet 56th Army landed at Yenikale and established a firm beachhead despite opposition from the German V *Armeekorps* and Romanian 3rd Mountain Division. Continuing to reinforce, by 11 November the Soviets had landed some 27,700. Back at Eltigen, even though reinforced by the 117th Guards Rifle Regiment, the beachhead was contained and cut off by Axis naval and ground forces and continuously attacked by the Luftwaffe.

Above: Aerial photograph of Kerch.

Above and Centre Right: Russian troops land on the peninsula.

Below Right: Ruins of Feodosia destroyed by the German air force.

Finally, on 6–7 December Romanian mountain troops with artillery support collapsed the beachhead, killing 1,200 and taking 1,600 prisoners. Almost 1,000 Soviet troops managed to break out in an attempt to reach the other landing site at Yenikale, but were trapped on Mt Mithridates and defeated.

The Soviets continued to reinforce Yenikale and by 4 December had landed 75,000 men, 600 heavy guns, 128 tanks, 187 mortars and tons of ammunition. They then pushed inland some six miles, reaching the outskirts of Kerch. They were contained by the Germans but the reinforcements continued to flow in. By the time the offensive to retake the Crimea started on 8 April 1944, the Soviets had 470,000 men at their disposal. Kerch was liberated on 11 April. It take another six months before the entire Crimea was liberated in May 1944.

113

Operation Dexterity (Allies) December 1943 Bismarck Archipelago

Operation Dexterity was part of Operation Cartwheel, which was designed to surround and isolate the major Japanese harbour, airfield and fortress base at Rabaul on the northeastern end of New Britain. It also linked in closely with two other operations: 'Chronicle' on the islands of Kiriwina and Woodlark (25–30 June) and 'Postern' on the Huon Peninsula started by American landings at Lae on 3 September 1943.

'Dexterity' began on 15 December with Operation Director, the assault on the tip of the Arawe peninsula of the Island of New Britain. At the same time a company-size blocking raid took place in the rear of the Japanese positions to prevent their retreat. Unfortunately, this unit was spotted and machine gunned by the Japanese while still in their rubber dinghies. The main landing was undertaken by the 112th Cavalry and became a confused melee when successive waves became separated, but in the end superior US firepower succeeded in forcing a Japanese retreat.

The US now controlled the Arawe Peninsula, but a stalemate developed that was only broken when the Americans landed a Marine Corps tank company and additional infantry to reinforce the 112th Cavalry. With the protection and firepower of the tanks the Americans drove the Japanese from their trenches on 16 January.

'Director' had distracted the Japanese; Operation Backhander saw American landings at Cape Gloucester further to the west on 26 December. The 1st Marine Division seized the airfield without any real problems, although Japanese aircraft did manage to sink a destroyer and damage some support ships. The Japanese then kept their forces concentrated around Rabaul waiting for a ground assault which never came, while the Allies ignored the contained fortress and the troops trapped inside just as they did on the Atlantic coast of France after the Normandy landings.

The final element of Operation Dexterity was the amphibious landings made at Saidor (Operation Michaelmas) this stopped the Japanese retreating from attacks by the Australian Army advancing from Finschhafen, as part of the Huon Peninsula campaign.

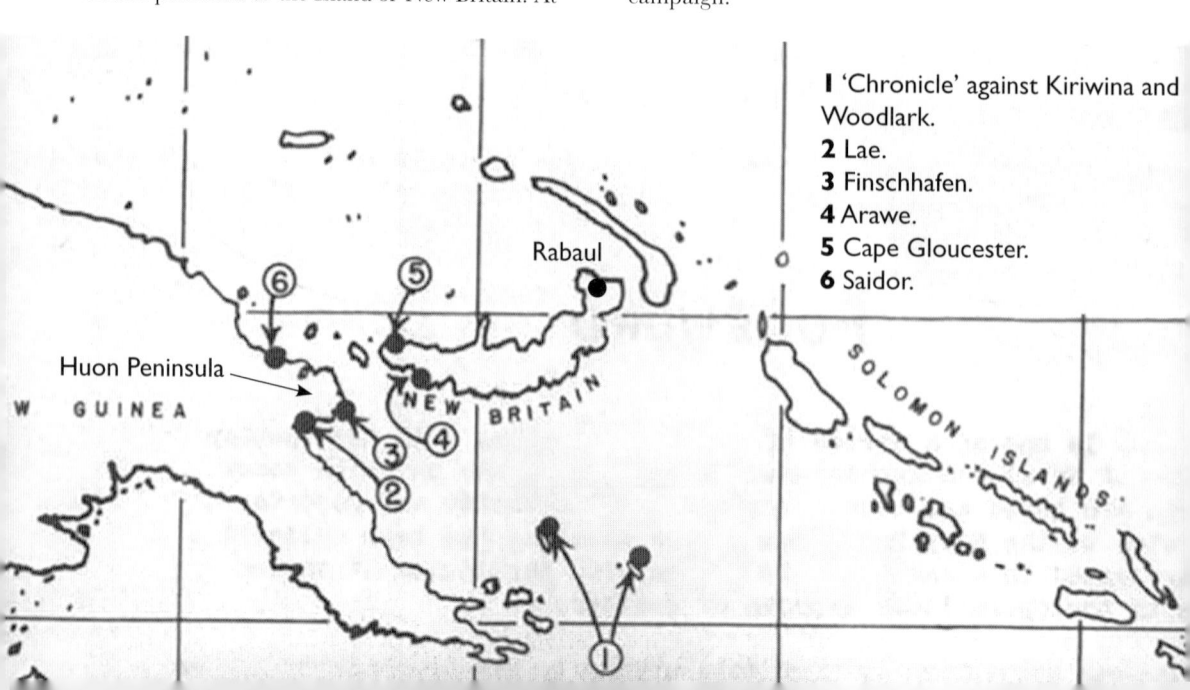

1 'Chronicle' against Kiriwina and Woodlark.
2 Lae.
3 Finschhafen.
4 Arawe.
5 Cape Gloucester.
6 Saidor.

Opposite, Above: Cape Gloucester invasion. Marines board USS *LCI-340* on 24 December 1943 at Oro Bay, New Guinea. On the 26th, they landed at Cape Gloucester on New Britain Island. Note the sniper's rifle (scope-equipped M1903 Springfield) at left.

Above: Marines push a jeep ashore from USS *LST-202* and *LST-204* (in the background) at Cape Gloucester, New Britain, around 26 December 1943.

Below: Marines wade ashore from a coast guard-manned LST, beached at Cape Gloucester. Note the nickname 'The Ace in the Hole' on the gunshield of 105mm gun being towed ashore by a bulldozer.

Operation Shingle (Allies) 22 January 1944 Anzio

The objective of Operation Shingle was to land a force behind the Gustav Line, compelling a German retreat from Monte Cassino and thereby to open up a route to Rome—and hoping to trap the Germans as they retreated. The west coast resort town of Anzio 30 miles south of the capital was the chosen target. The 3rd (US) Infantry Division, three battalions of Rangers and an airborne battalion supported by armour landed south of the port, and British 1st Infantry Division and commandos of 2nd Special Service Brigade also with armoured support landed to the north.

Both landings went well and were virtually unopposed. By the end of the day, 36,000 troops and 3,200 vehicles had been unloaded and a three-mile deep beachhead created. Had the invaders maintained their momentum perhaps the objectives would have been met. Instead, the force commander US Major General Lucas dug in and in doing so handed the advantage to the very able German commander GFM Albert Kesselring.

By 25 January 40,000 German troops had surrounded the Allied beachhead. By the 29th Allied forces totalled 69,000 men, 500 guns and 208 tanks while the defenders had risen to 71,500. There then followed a grim four-month struggle, that would produce 70,000 casualties and cost the lives of 12,000 men (7,000 Allies 5,000 German), before an Allied breakout was finally achieved and the Germans forced to retreat from the Gothic defence line.

Even then the Anzio troops moved towards Rome rather than attempting to trap the retreating Germans who were able to make their way back to prepared defence lines. Fifth Army commander Mark Clark went for glory and condemned the Italian campaign to another attritional year.

Opposite: Anzio—aerial photography of the port and quay.

Above Right: USS *LCI(L)-235* off the Salerno beachhead, photographed from the British minesweeper HMS *Circe*. *LCI(L)-235* took part in the landings on Sicily, Salerno, Anzio and the south of France—Operation Dragoon.

Centre Right: Troops and equipment come ashore on the Fifth (US) Army beachhead, 22 January 1944. USS *LCI-20* is burning at left, after having being hit by a German bomb. With her are (l–r): HMSs *LCI-274*, USS *LCI-39* and *LCI-260*. At right, beyond the DUKW, are USSs *LCI-36* (or *LCI-38*) and *LCI-44*.

Below: Destroyers laying smoke off Anzio.

Operation Flintlock (US) 31 January–23 February 1944 Kwajalein, Marshall Islands

The invasion of the Marshall islands would provide important airbases for future operations in the Marianas. As with Operation Galvanic, Fifth Fleet commander Vice Admiral Raymond A. Spruance, USN, was in overall command, with Rear Admiral Richmond K. Turner, USN, commanding the Joint Expeditionary Force and Major General Holland M. Smith, USMC, V Amphibious Corps. The first atoll attacked was Kwajalein. There were three landing forces: Northern Attack Force (Rear Admiral Richard L. Connolly, USN) against Roi-Namur Island; Southern (Turner) on Kwajalein; and the Majuro Attack Group (Rear Admiral Harry W. Hill, USN), although the latter were happy to find the Japanese had left in November 1942.

The atolls fell by 7 February. There were only around 250 Japanese survivors of around 8,000 garrisoning the atoll; their beach-line defence proving ineffective. After this, the Japanese changed tactics and defend in depth leading to much more costly battles. The relative ease of the American victory was continued on Ebeye Island (3–4 February), Engebi (18–19 February), Eniwetok (19–21 February) and Parry (22–23 February).

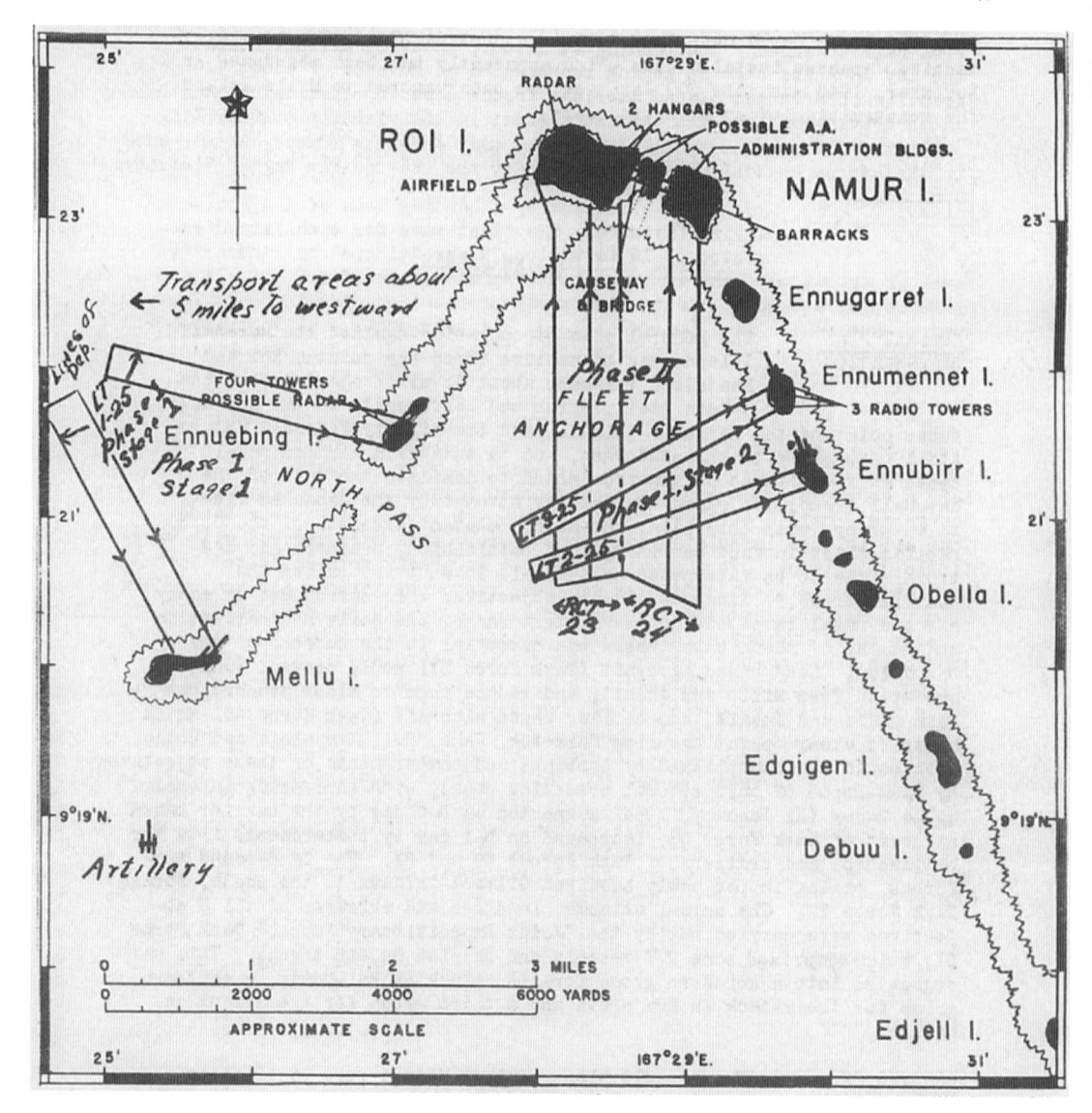

Above: Kwajalein Island, at the southern end of Kwajalein Atoll, under bombardment as landing craft approach its western end, 1 February 1944.

Below: Marines advancing under fire, near beach "red two" of Roi Island, Kwajalein Atoll, on 1 February 1944, the day of the initial assaults. Note smoking concrete bunker in background.

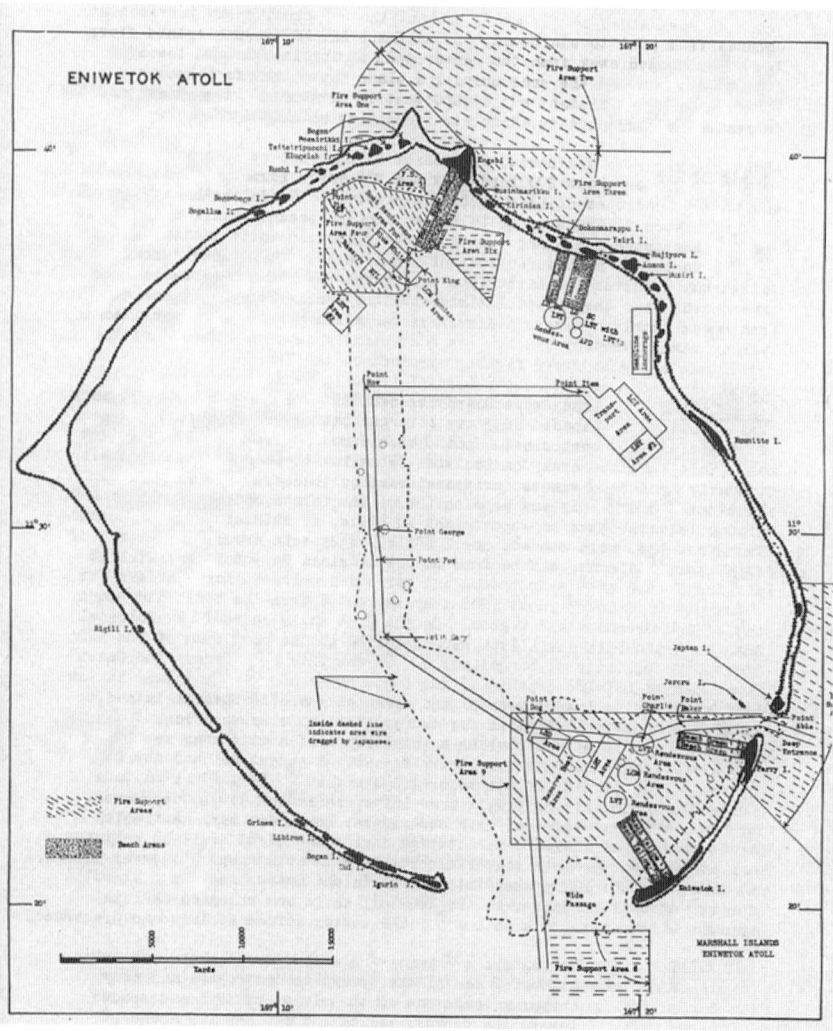

Above: Parry Island, Eniwetok Atoll, under bombardment on 21 February 1944, the day prior to landings. Eniwetok is in the upper distance, with amphibious shipping nearby.

Left: Eniwetok Atoll. Parry and Eniwetok are at bottom right.

Opposite, Above: Marines and Coast Guardsmen proudly display a Japanese flag, picked up by one of them during the capture of Engebi Island, Eniwetok Atoll, 19 February 1944.

Opposite, Below Left: USS *LST-39*.

Opposite, Below Right: Map showing the landings on Nissan Island, one of the Green islands.

Operation Squarepeg (NZ) 15-20 February 1944 Green Islands, New Guinea (today, Papua New Guinea)

Undertaken by 3rd New Zealand Division, again as part of operations against Rabaul, the Japanese defenders were few in number but received air support from Rabaul. The New Zealanders, supported by Valentine tanks, quickly took the islands and allowed the Seabees of 22nd Naval Construction Regiment to construct an airstrip by 6 March.

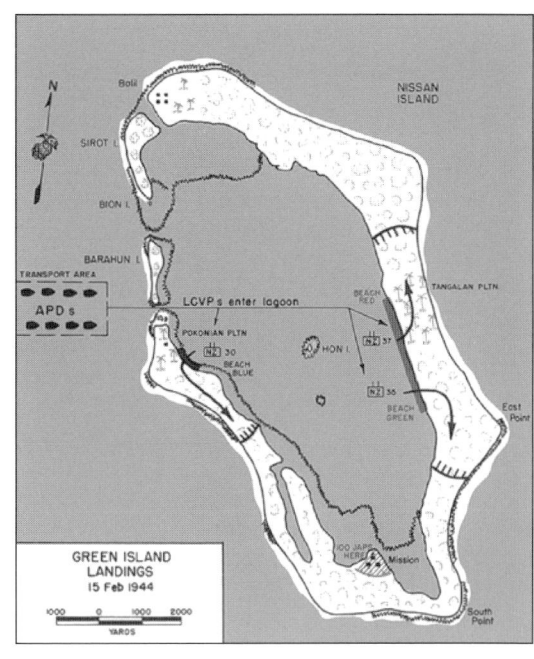

New Guinea Campaign (US) February 1944–August 1945

After the successful capture of the Solomon Islands and Bismarck Archipelago, 1944 saw northern areas again under scrutiny: first the Admiralty Islands in February, then Emirou Island (March) followed by attacks on the northern coast of New Guinea itself (Aitape and Hollandia in April; Wakde Island in May), before the western extremities were invaded from May: Biak Island (May), Noemfoor Island (July), Sansapor (July) and Morotai Island (September).

The attack on the Admiralty Islands (Operation Brewer) was launched on 29 February and by 18 May had succeeded. This was the final part of Operation Cartwheel, MacArthur's plan to surround and negate the major Japanese base at Rabaul. Initially, the landings at Los Negros close to Momote airstrip were a reconnaissance in force by a squadron of 1st Cavalry Division, but bravery, air superiority and a strong naval presence meant that the small foothold became a launching pad to take first the island and then the outlying islands.

The Americans lost 326 DIA and 1,190 WIA; the Japanese 3,280 KIA. More important than the body count, however, was the strategic importance of the islands.

Operation Reckless (US) 22 April 1944 Hollandia, New Guinea

Operation Reckless included two amphibious landings on the Island of Hollandia, which took place 22–27 April 1944 with the aim of taking the three airfields that the Japanese had constructed there. The naval forces gathered included USN, RN and RAN vessels; air cover was provided by the fast carriers of Task Force 58 and the ground troops were the US 24th and 41st Infantry Divisions. The Japanese had some 11,000 men on the island, although the majority of them were not combat troops but support staff for the airbases that had already been under sustained air attack. (Between 30 March and 3 April over 300 Japanese aircraft were destroyed, with 100 lost on 30 March alone.)

Following a naval barrage and with air support the 24th and 41st Divisions landings went in at 07:00 at Humboldt Bay and 07:45 at Tanahmerah Bay. Both met only slight resistance as the Japanese had mostly withdrawn rather than fight the landings on the beaches. The Tanahmerah Bay suffered delays due to the muddy conditions rather than enemy opposition. Japanese forces suffered at least 3,300 killed (primarily through bombardment and air attack) and over 600 were taken prisoner.

Left: Troops in a coast guard-manned LCM approach the New Guinea coast at Aitape, 22 April 1944. The men in the foreground are possibly Australians, although Australian 6th Division didn't take over the Aitape area until October 1944.

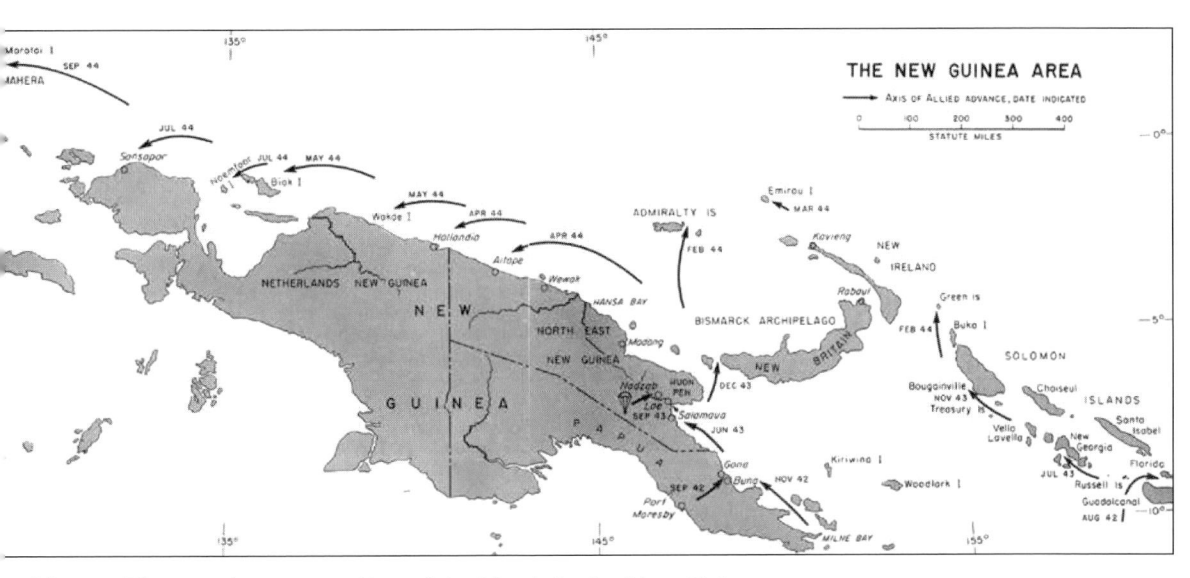

Above: The step-by-step retaking of the islands in the New Guinea area.

Below: LVTs head for the invasion beaches at Humboldt Bay, New Guinea, as cruisers bombard in the background, 22 April 1944. The ship firing tracer shells in the right centre is USS *Boise*. Just ahead of her is USS *Phoenix*.

Bottom: LSTs unloading on Beach Red Two, Tanahmerah Bay, 22 April 1944. *LST-22* is in the centre, with *LST-18* next to the right. Note smoke and propeller wash from one LST at left as she backs clear of the beach.

Operation Straight Line (US) 17-21 May 1944 Wakde Islands, Dutch New Guinea (today, Indonesia)

Having taken Hollandia, MacArthur moved on the north coast of Western New Guinea, choosing to attack the Wakde Islands, where there was a better potential airfield than Sarmi on the mainland. First, three battalions of 163rd Infantry Regiment were landed on the mainland around Arara. While they established their position, the smaller of Wakde's two islands, Insoemanai was occupied by a force that included a company of the 641st Tank Destroyer Battalion. Once the 163rd had established their position on the mainland, the next day the 1st Battalion attacked Wakde's larger island, Insoemoar, helped by the two tanks that reached the island. The fighting lasted three days, during which construction troops from 836th Engineer Aviation Battalion began work to repair and extend the airfield and having to fight off the Japanese as they did so. On the 18th, the Kumamba Islands were also occupied. They would be used for search radars to give the new base early warning of air attack. Taking Wakde saw 40 Americans killed and 107 wounded. The Japanese lost 759 killed. After the islands fell, the fighting on the mainland continued and US troops advanced towards Sarmi.

Operation Hurricane (US) 27 May-17 August 1944 Biak Island, Schouten Islands (today, Indonesia)

The next island to fall was Biak with its three airfields at Mokmer, Sorido and Borokoe that would put American bombers within 800 miles of the Philippines—due to be assaulted in October 1944. Another example of gritty Japanese defence to the last man, the battle for Biak cost 460 Americans their lives and over 2,400 wounded. There were also 7,234 non-battle casualties—around 1,000 as a result of scrub typhus, a horrible mite-borne illness.

The Japanese troop strength had been underestimated at 4,400, but it was much larger and was reinforced during the battle. Codenamed 'KON', three operations managed to get 1,200 men from 2nd Amphibious Brigade onto the island. The defenders did not contest the landings but lured the US forces—the landings were made by 41st Infantry Division; subsequently 24th Infantry was introduced—into an inland killing area enmeshed by strongpoints based on the numerous caves on the island. As well as the deaths of the Japanese land forces—between 4,500 and 6,000, many in suicidal charges—they also lost numbers of aircraft while supporting attempts to reinforce the garrison.

An LCVP headed for the beach in the Tor River area, near Arara, New Guinea, 17–18 May 1944. A destroyer is bombarding in the background.

Above: Biak Island during the Allied landings with a burning Japanese dump on beach.

Below: The assault force consisted of five destroyer transports (APD), eight LSTs eight LCTs and fifteen LCIs. Several Australian vessels including the cruisers HMAS *Australia* and *Shropshire* and the destroyer *Warramunga* were included in this task force. This photograph is taken from an RAN ship. Note the Polsten 20mm cannon.

Above: Sherman tanks and a wrecker unloaded from USS *LST-67* and USS *LST-66* on Noemfoor Island. Note the Sherman dozer.

Below: Convoy en route for the invasion of Cape Sansapor, New Guinea.

Opposite, Left and Right: To reach their APDs, troops embarked on LCP(R) landing craft, prior to boarding for the Sansapor Invasion. The APD here (Left) is USS *Ward* and photos were taken at Maffin Bay, New Guinea, near Wakde Island.

Operation Cyclone (US) 2 July–31 August 1944 Noemfoor Island, Dutch New Guinea (today Indonesia)

By 30 June the battle of Biak was almost over and preparations for the assault on nearby Noemfoor Island started with an aerial bombardment. The Japanese garrison—some 2,000, fewer than expected—was under the command of Colonel Shimizu who worked out both where the American landings would happen and when. However, after a large naval bombardment—the largest in the Southwest Pacific area to date—as at Biak, the initial landing was largely unopposed and the 158th RCT landed with only three Americans killed on the first day. There were plenty of well-constructed defensive positions, but the bombardment had stunned the Japanese. Concerned that the Japanese resistance would be stern elsewhere, the 503rd PIR was sent to the island, but the low-level drop of the 1st and 3rd Battalions led to too many non-battle casualties and 2nd Battalion was ferried by LCI. The Japanese continued fighting piecemeal over two months but the Allies secured the airfields on the island and by 31 August, 1,730 Japanese were dead for a loss of 66 KIA or MIA and 343 WIA. The island was used to support the fighting around Sansapor and on Morotai, and B-24s flying from the field bombed Balikpapan in Borneo.

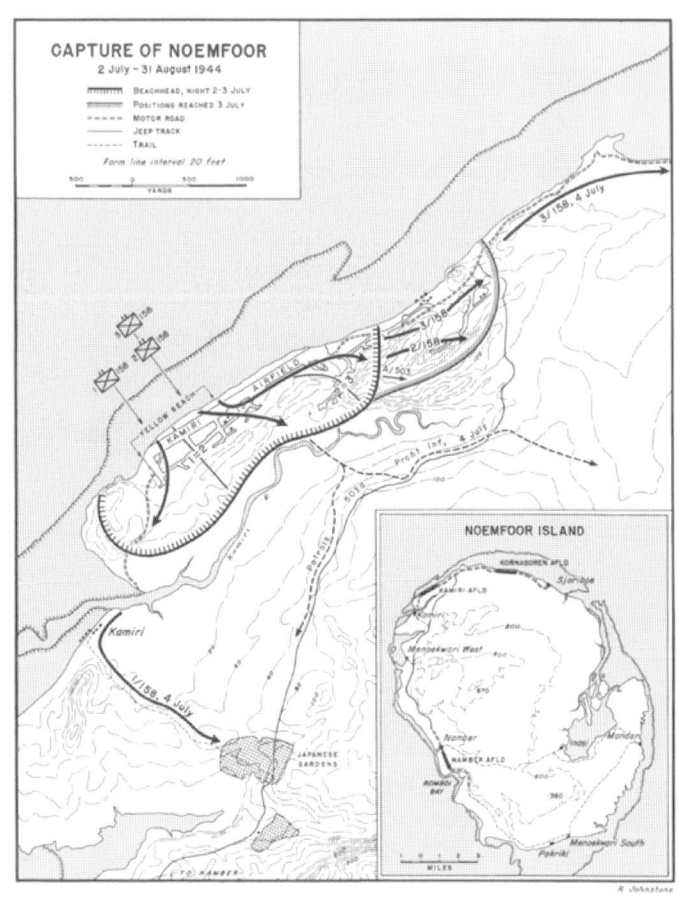

Operations Typhoon and Globetrotter (US) 30 July–31 August 1944 Sansapor, Dutch New Guinea (today Indonesia)

The westernmost end of New Guinea, the Vogelkop peninsula was invaded by US 6th Infantry Division on 30 July; a day later, Sansapor. The landings were unopposed but the Japanese sent 35th Division to confront the invaders. They arrived on 16 August and the fighting raged for two weeks until the Japanese gave up.

Operation Neptune (Allies) 6 June 1944 Normandy, France

The largest and most famous amphibious assault in history to date, part of overall Operation Overlord, 'Neptune' did not go completely to plan, yet was awesome in its reach and scope, as its statistics reveal. Preceded by 1,200-plane airborne assault, the 06:30 amphibious attack involved over 5,000 vessels. It landed 160,000 American, British and Canadian troops on the first day on five beaches (codenamed Gold, Juno, Sword, Omaha and Utah) along a 50-mile stretch of France's Normandy coast. By 11 June the beaches had been fully secured and over 326,000 troops, more than 50,000 vehicles and some 100,000 tons of equipment had been landed.

It involved intricate deception operations to hide the landing zones and new technologies and inventions to overcome problems and obstacles, including a fuel pipeline PLUTO (Pipeline Under the Ocean), two artificial ports made from giant concrete caissons—the Mulberry harbours—and Hobart's Funnies: specialised vehicles that were designed and produced to overcome obstacles. The Sherman Duplex Drive was an amphibious swimming tank that was used on all five beaches, whereas the Sherman Crab was a mine flail. The Churchill was also fitted with either an anti-mine flail, a flamethrower (the 'Crocodile') or as an AVRE with a mine plough, a bunker-busting spigot mortar, fascines, a bobbin carpet layer (for tanks to drive over soft sand) or a bridgelayer (ARK, Armoured Ramp Carrier).

None of the mission objectives were achieved on the first day, but the Allies persevered. When a German counterattack on 8 August failed and resulted in more than 50,000 German troops being encircled near the town of Falaise, the battle had been won. The Allies broke out of Normandy on 15 August, after landing nearly two million men in total. The cost of the campaign was high for both sides, the Allies suffering more than 226,386 casualties (72,911 killed/missing and 153,475 wounded), while German losses included over 240,000 casualties and 200,000 captured. Between 13,000 and 20,000 French civilians also died and many more were wounded.

Above: Over 700 British LCT Mks were built in Britain. This one, *LCT-1047* is seen off Normandy.

Below: The British and Canadian beaches had many strongpoints that held up the assault and, ultimately, the advance to Caen. This shows the beach opposite Strongpoint 'Cod'—*Stützpunkt 20 La Breche,* with a 7.5cm PaK 40, two 5cm KwK L/60 PaKs, a 3.7cm gun, many machine guns and two 8.14cm mortars—surrounded by a minefield and masses of barbed wire, it survived until 10:00 on D-Day before being taken by men of the 1st South Lancs and 2nd East Yorks.

The naval involvement throughout the battle of Normandy was vital—and not just for supplies and other logistical requirements. From the start, naval gunfire changed the outcome of many of the land battles: it was the fire of British and American destroyers off Omaha Beach that provided the crucial support necessary for the success of those landings on the heavily defended beach. And then there were the shore batteries. Vice Admiral Morton L. Deyo, USN said of the 21 batteries on the Cotentin: 'There were 3 batteries of 170mm, totalling 12 guns. These were of long range and could command all water areas and approaches to the beaches. Three batteries of 155-mm, totalling 18 guns of 25,000 yards range, covered the approaches including most of the transport area. Twelve batteries of 155, 150 and 105-mms, totalling 36 howitzers of 13,000 yards range, could reach the boat lanes and bombardment ships. Five or six more 155s, whose effectiveness was in some doubt, brought the total to about 75 guns.'

The heavy ships of the bombardment groups for Utah Beach were made up of: USS *Tuscaloosa* (flagship), USS *Nevada* (battleship, pictured **Above** on 6 June), USS *Quincy* (heavy cruiser), HMS *Erebus* (monitor), HMS *Hawkins* (heavy cruiser), HMS *Black Prince* (light cruiser), HMS *Enterprise* (light cruiser) and HNLMS *Soemba*. Deyo commented: 'Of these, the venerable *Nevada* was by far the most powerful with her ten 14" guns, sixteen 5" and up-to-date fire control equipment. Her lack of speed was no handicap in this assignment. *Quincy* was next, a new ship with nine 8", twelve 5" and everything modern. *Tuscaloosa*, a useful cruiser of nine 8", eight 5", eleven years old, and not the latest equipment. Of the British cruisers the *Hawkins* fitted with seven 7.5" and nine 4" guns but she was old. The others were smaller gunned ships. *Black Prince* was new but only eight 5.25" guns; *Enterprise* 6" but already due for decommissioning. *Erebus* boasted two 15" guns. She too was ancient and her accuracy of fire was questionable. *Soemba* was 19 years old, a gunboat with three 5.9" guns.'

As well attacking the batteries the groups gave 'a 40-minute "beach drenching" ... typical of up-to-date amphibious assaults.' But the battle wasn't one-sided, as Deyo noted: '*Corry*, under concentrated fire is hit. Compelled then to move, bad fortune slid her across a mine waiting just beneath an engine room. ... Her plight is seen and quickly an avenging concentration from *Tuscaloosa*, *Nevada*, *Quincy*, *Hobson* and *Fitch* smother the three offending batteries which proved to total six 155s and eight 105s together with numerous 88s and 75s. ... *Fitch*, coming quickly to the rescue, happily recovers most of the crew.'

Left: USSs *LST-55* and *LST-61* unloading cargo on Omaha Beach.

Below Left: Among the thousands of merchant vessels that took part in the invasion of France were a number from smaller countries such as Norway. This 14 June photo was taken from the mast of the Skudesnes boat *Vestmannrød* during the crossing to France. It shows Royal Engineers resting on deck while enjoying the sun over the Channel.

Above Right: Follow-up troops land on Omaha Beach from an LCVP. Ahead, a DUKW ferries stores as troops and vehicles make their way off the beach.

Below Right: Many different types of vessel make up an invasion fleet. This is HM Landing Barge Kitchen 6. Once a Thames lighter, it had the capacity to provide 1,600 hot meals and 800 cold meals a day and with a storage capacity to feed 900 men for a week. LBK 6 stood off Sword Beach as part of the 35th Supply and Repair Flotilla. They were manned by an officer and 22 crew and gave off a delightful smell of baking bread. The queue has insulated containers ready to be filled.

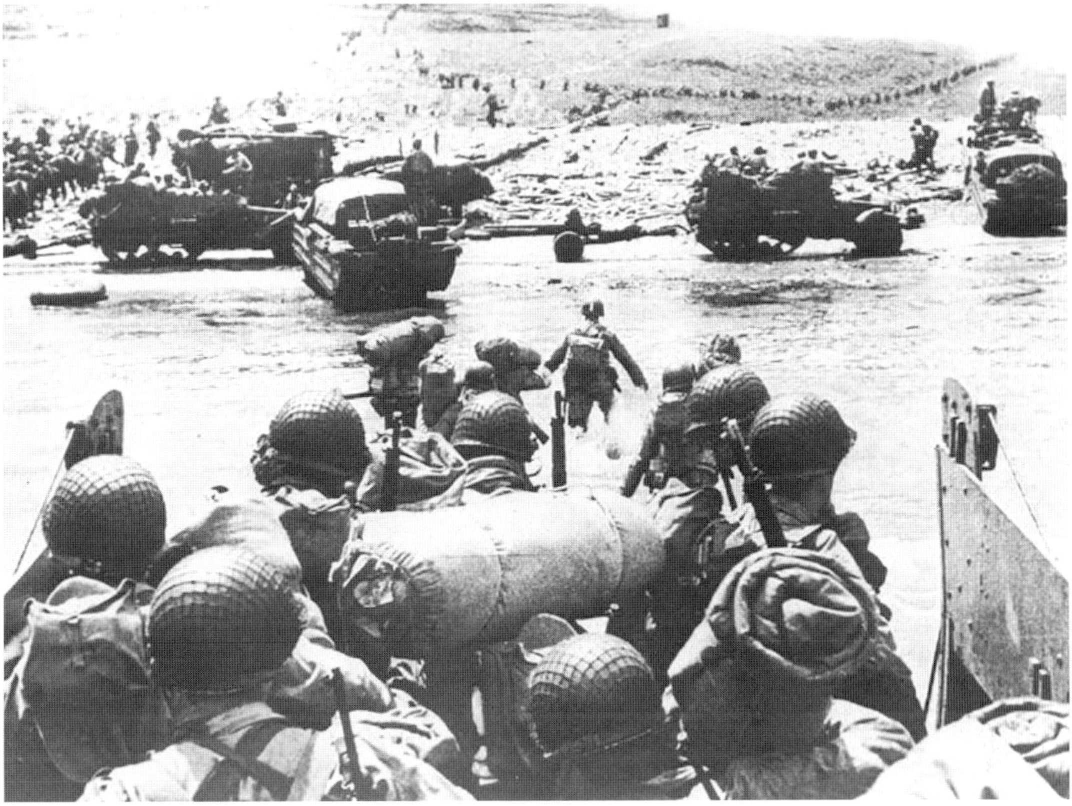

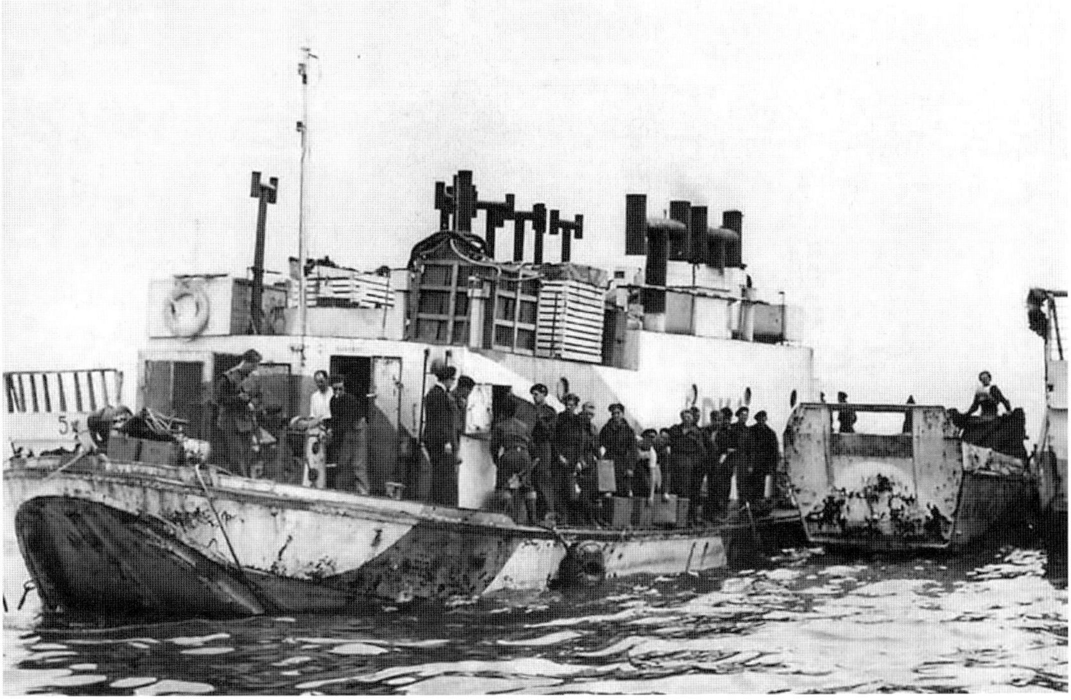

Operation Forager (US) 15 June 1944 Saipan, Mariana Islands

Operation Forager, the campaign to take the Mariana and Palau Islands (see p. 147), was launched by an attack on Saipan whose airfield would allow the USAAF to target the Japanese mainland, which was within reach of US B-29 Superfortresses flying from the island.

An invasion force of 56 attack transports, 84 landing craft and over 127,000 troops, protected by the US Navy's Task Force 58 equipped with 15 carriers, 7 battleships, 11 cruisers, 86 destroyers and over 900 aircraft took on the 30,000+ troops of 31st Japanese Army, concealed in bunkers, air-raid shelters and pillboxes with artillery and armour support.

Surrounded by reefs and with few potential landing sites, Saipan is dominated by Mount Tapotchau in its centre and the mountains running north to Mount Marpi. It took US forces over a month of hard fighting to subjugate what was a comparatively small island but one difficult terrain—cliffs, jungle, swamps and mountains. The Japanese troops for the most part survived the initial heavy bombing and naval bombardments and put down a maelstrom of fire onto the beaches and landing craft, ensuring heavy US casualties. Nevertheless, by nightfall on 15 June some 20,000 marines had been landed.

The Japanese then tried to resupply and to attack the task force with their own surface fleet. In the ensuing battle of the Philippines Sea the Japanese naval and air forces were comprehensively defeated.

With all hope now gone the Japanese—both military and civilian—chose to die, either in combat with suicidal Banzai charges or by leaping off cliffs or blowing themselves up. By the end of the month-long battle, the Americans had suffered 3,000 killed and 10,000 wounded, while 29,000 Japanese troops and 22,000 civilians had died.

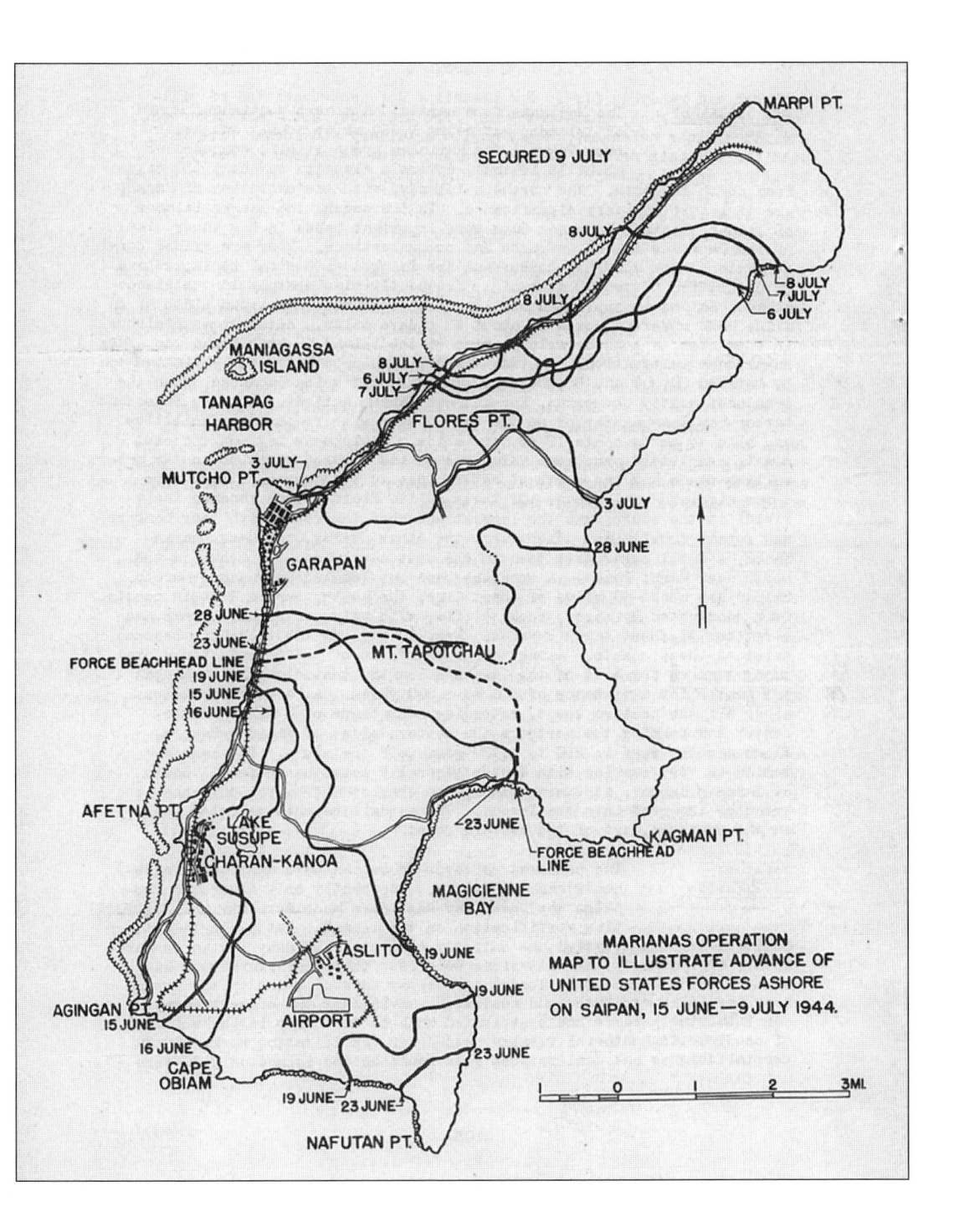

Left: Naval gunfire helped the marines to expand the bridgehead. The fighting was hard and it took three weeks before Japanese resistance was finally quashed. The civilian population suffered greatly during the Japanese occupation and the battle. They were interned in Camp Susupe, and the Japanese separated.

Above: Ships of the US Fifth Fleet (Admiral Raymond Spruance) at a Marshalls' anchorage, shortly before departure for the Marianas, 10 June 1944. By this time, the Fifth Fleet was the largest combat fleet in the world, with 535 warships. Of these, 59 troopships and 64 LSTs would land three divisions on Saipan, 2,400 miles from the base at Guadalcanal. Vice Admiral Richmond Kelly Turner was the amphibious and attack forces commander.

Below: *LCI(G)-725* and *LCI(G)-726* fire on the beach while landing craft form up in the background, during the initial assault, 15 June. Both ships started life as 'LCI(L)-351' class but became landing craft infantry (guns) on 15 June 1944. Their armament was improved to two single 40mm guns, four single 20mm guns, six .50cal machine guns and ten Mk 7 rocket launchers which fired 12 4.5-inch rockets.

Above: Marine LVTs head for the shore as part of the first wave of landings on Saipan. H-hour was at 08:40. Fifty-six of these vehicles attacked eight beaches in lines of four. There was a fringing reef roughly 1,500 yards offshore of the chosen landing sites. The LVTs could negotiate the reef, but the rest could not and were forced to turn back and find a passageway. The LVT armour wasn't heavy enough to withstand artillery—sometimes even the coral reefs punctured it—and they often added steel boilerplate to the bows and even carried wooden plugs to plug holes en route. Archaeological work on an LVT(A)-4 found in the lagoon 'possessed many field expedient armor modifications. Both the upper and lower bow had been reinforced with 3/8 inch boilerplate. A 0.30-caliber machine gun was added to the cabin at the radio operator's seat. A steel shield had been welded around the commander's turret and a pintle machine gun mount was added to the port side of the turret.' (W. Shawn Arnold)

Below: Marines of the first invasion wave hug the beach and prepare to move inland on 15 June. Note burning LVT in the background. All the assault regiments took heavy casualties from the constant shelling that was zeroed in by spotters on the high ground inland.

Operation Brassard (FRE) 17-19 June 1944 Elba, Italy

When Italy surrendered on 8 September 1943, the Italians on Elba tried to resist a German takeover. The Germans were too capable, however, and the day after the Luftwaffe bombed Portoferraio, killing 116 civilians, the Italian troops surrendered to *Fallschirmjäger* who had been sent to bolster the German garrison.

Ten months later, as the Allies prepared to assault the south of France, the French retook Elba, assisted by British commandos. The latter lost 38 men when demolition charges on the mole next to flak ship *Köln*, which they had just taken, exploded killing commandos and PoWs alike.

In total, the French lost 252 KIA and 635 WIA, the Germans 500 KIA and around 2,000 PoWs, although 400 *Fallschirmjäger* were evacuated. While postwar commentators have doubted the need to capture Elba, it blooded the French forces in Europe and removed any possibility of German artillery using the island.

Opposite, Above and Below: Men of 1./*Panzergrenadier-Regiment* 200 boarded at Livorno and landed in Portoferraio to reinforce the island.

Above: USS *LCI(L)-39*, *-44*, *-48* and *-69* load men of the French 13ème Régiment de Tirailleurs, 9ème Division d'Infanterie Coloniale at Porto Vecchio, Corsica on 16 June. Note the censor has blotted out the mast-top radars.

Below: A smokescreen being laid on Golfo di Campo Bay. **A** is the harbour and village of Marina di Campo nestling behind the promontory. Beach **1** is Kodak Red, **2** Kodak Amber and **3**, just off photo, is Kodak Green. Tenacious defence—and well sited defensive gun positions including Strongpoint Danzig (**B**)—saw the attack on Kodak Red aborted until later that afternoon once the defences had been cleared.

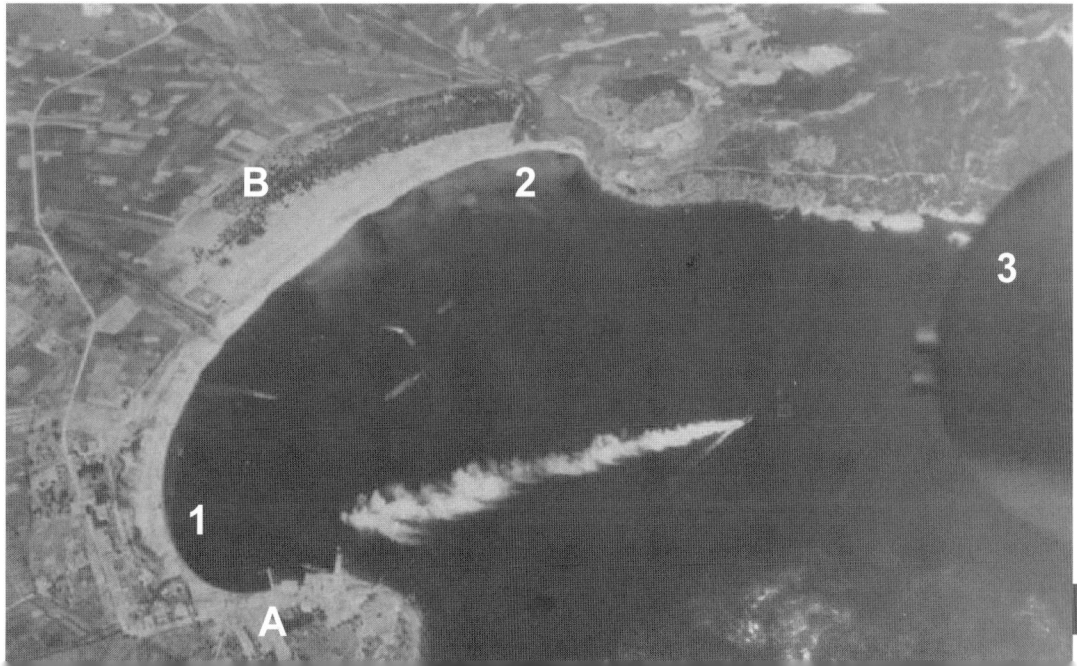

Operation Stevedore (US) 21 July 1944 Guam, Mariana Islands

1,500 miles south of Japan, Guam is the largest island of the Marianas (32 miles long and 4 to 12 miles wide) and a US possession since 1898. It had been captured by the Japanese in December 1941 and was retaken in Operation Stevedore in late July and early August 1944.

Two landings were carried out on either side of the Orote Peninsula on the west coast by the 60,000 strong III Amphibious Corps (consisting of both Marine and Army units), supported by over 270 ships. Both landings were strenuously opposed and Japanese artillery sank 30 LVTs and inflicted heavy casualties on the landing troops.

It took a week of hard fighting before the two beachheads were linked, in the face of continuous Japanese counterattacks, made mostly at night. As usual, the Japanese defenders (22,500 men of 29th Infantry Division supported by 40 tanks and artillery) fought almost to the last man from their network of pillboxes, bunkers, caves and shelters, and retreated to the interior and towards the hilly north end of the island as the US forces advanced. It took another two weeks until Guam was secured.

US casualties amounted to 1,700 dead and 6,000 wounded, while the Japanese deaths totalled over 18,000. Some small units of Japanese continued to fight in guerrilla mode after the official end of hostilities. One veteran finally emerged from the jungle over 25 years later in 1972!

Below: LVTs and other landing craft go ashore on the Northern invasion beaches, 25 July 1944, a few days after the initial landings.

Opposite, Below: The 14-inch guns of USS *New Mexico* opening fire on Guam during the pre-invasion bombardment.

MARIANAS OPERATION

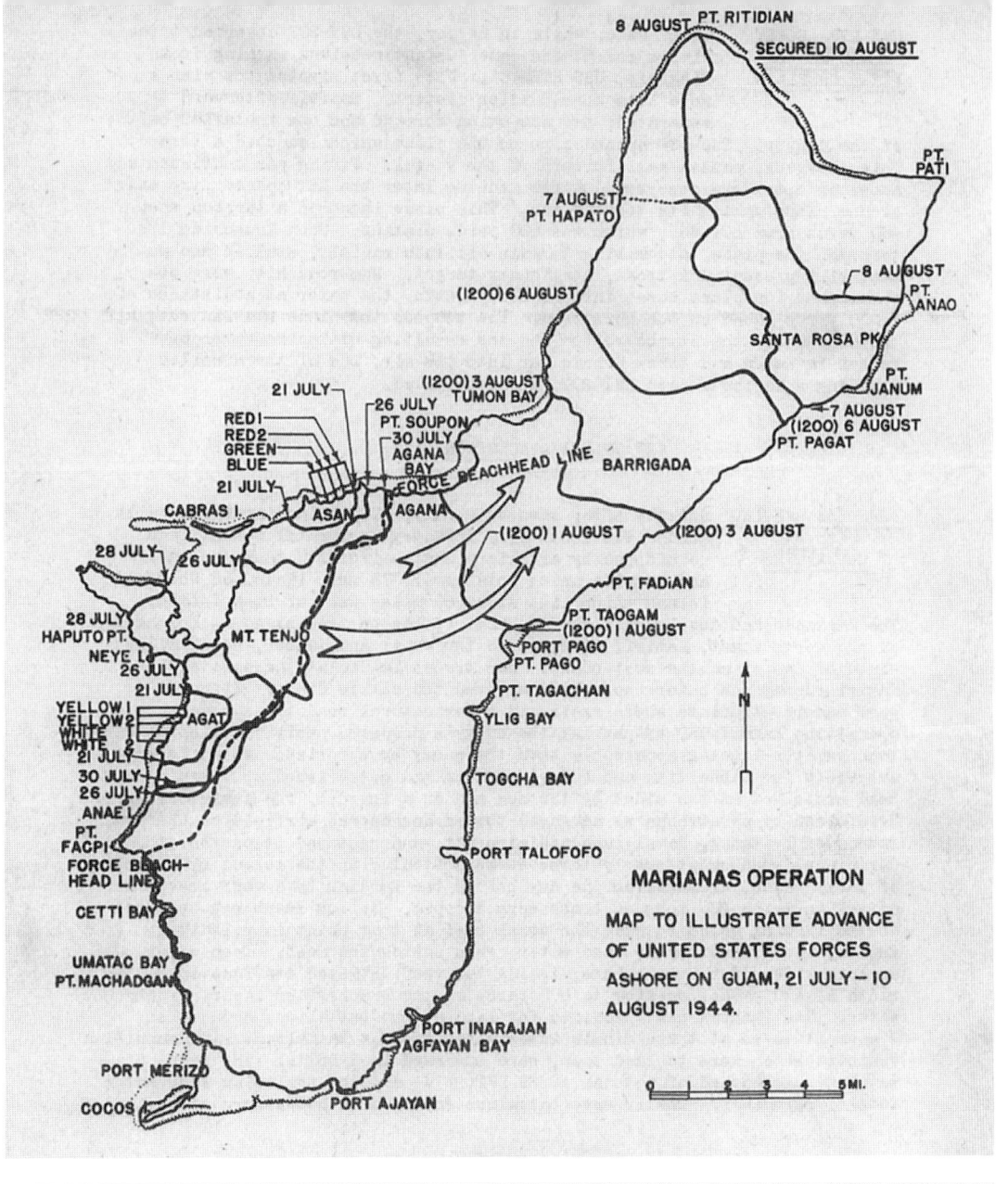

MAP TO ILLUSTRATE ADVANCE OF UNITED STATES FORCES ASHORE ON GUAM, 21 JULY – 10 AUGUST 1944.

Operation Granite II (US) 24 July 1944 Tinian, Mariana Islands

Tinian is one of the Mariana Islands, very flat, about 10.5 miles long and with a surface area of about 50 square miles. The assault forces were the same as used in the conquest of Saipan and the island was softened up with preliminary bombardments and air raids, although the shore batteries managed to repeatedly hit and damage a battleship (USS *Colorado*) and a destroyer (USS *Norman Scott*). On 24 July 15,600 men of the 2nd and 4th Marine Divisions landed on two beaches on the north coast while a diversionary feint towards the main town succeeded in diverting the defenders. The landings were a textbook success, as within 20 minutes three marine battalions were ashore backed up by bulldozers and then tanks, and the island was secured after nine days of fighting.

They were opposed by troops from the Japanese 50th Infantry Regiment with a company of light tanks and other small units totalling about 6,200 men. The Japanese fought with the same stubborn resistance as on Saipan, retreating during the day and attacking at night, and on July 31 the last elements were wiped out in a suicide charge. 13,000 Japanese civilians were then interned; 4,000 had died by suicide or had been killed in the fighting. The Americans lost almost 400 KIA and 1,800+ wounded. 15,000 combat engineers, the Seabees, then turned the island into the busiest airfield of the war, building six runways for USAAF B-29 Superfortresses to conduct raids on mainland Japan—firebombing Tokyo and dropping the world's first atomic bombs on Hiroshima and Nagasaki.

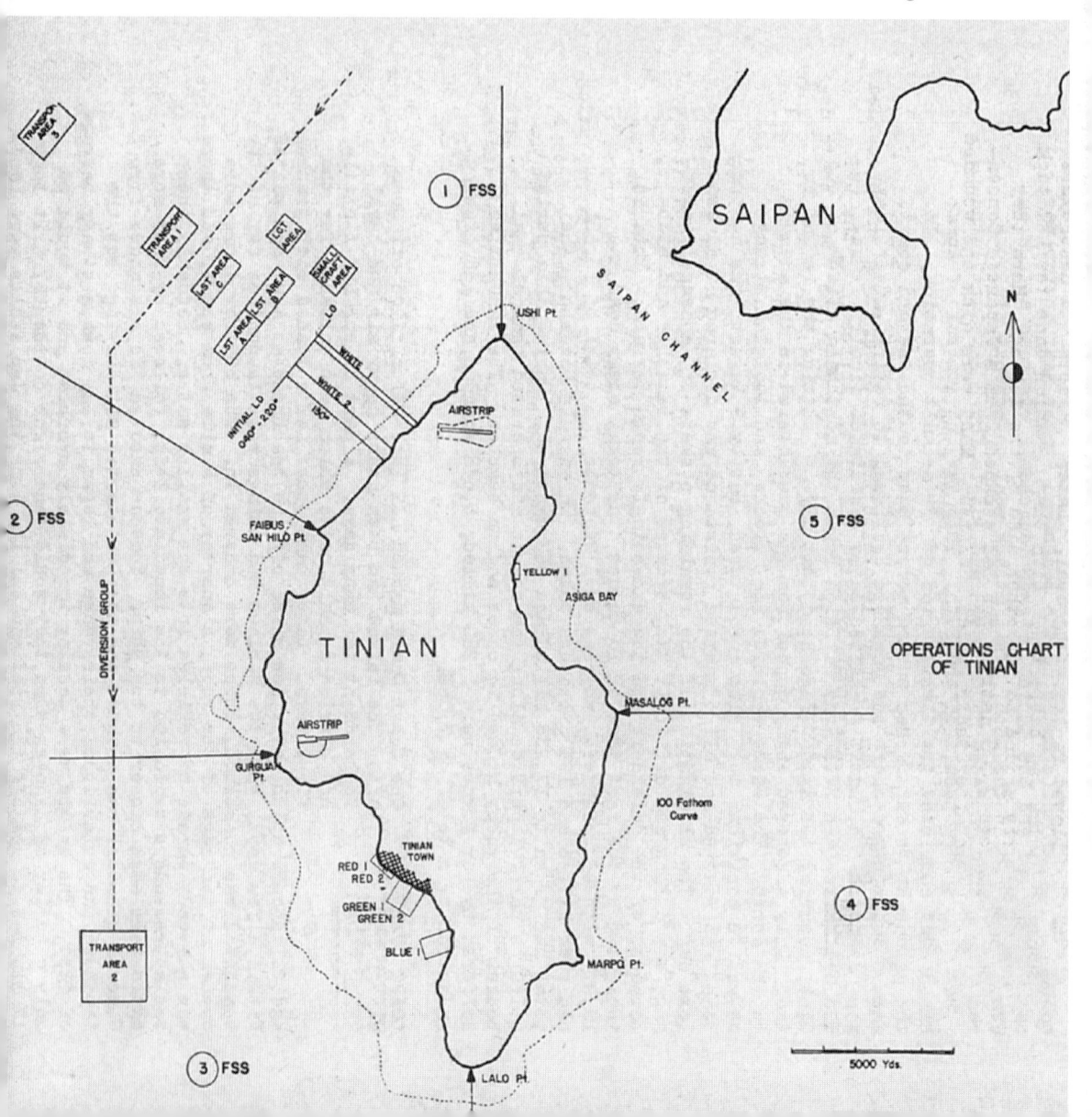

Marines load supplies aboard LSTs in preparation for the assault on Tinian, July 1944. There's a lot of artillery ammunition on view. American excellence at solving logistic problems in the Pacific war was a major factor in their success.

Operation Dragoon (Allies) 15 August 1944 French Riviera

Pressurised by Stalin, Roosevelt acceded to the plan to attack the south of France—much against Churchill's better judgement. He'd have preferred the effort in Italy to allow Allied forces to fight their way into Eastern Europe before the Soviets. Unfortunately, the Americans questioned British intentions and Italy was relegated to a sideshow.

In fact, the landings went like clockwork. On 15 August Operation Dragoon unleashed 900 Allied warships transporting four separate attack forces (two American and two French) and over 1,370 ship-borne assault landing craft to land at three main beaches (Alpha, Delta and Camel) after intense air and sea bombardments and preliminary commando raids. The US VI Corps, (3rd, 36th and 45th Inf Divs) landed first, followed by several divisions of the French Army B. All the landings were successful except for one sector of Camel beach, which was defended by several coastal guns and flak batteries—so it was simply skirted.

The defenders, Army Group G, had been weakened by the removal of some of its best troops to other fronts, replaced by *Ostbataillonen* with obsolete equipment and hindered heavily by French Resistance (FFI) sabotage, uprisings and incessant Allied air attacks. They were soon defeated, their counterattacks broken up and they were compelled to retreat north through the Rhône valley.

The speed of the Allied breakout and pursuit took the Germans by surprise, cutting off elements that were forced to surrender, however after an inconclusive battle at Montélimar the Germans manage to complete the withdrawal of most of their forces. Meanwhile, the French element of the invasion force had managed to capture the ports of Marseilles and Toulon, for the most part intact. This proved a major plus point for the Allies and alleviated their chronic supply issues as men and matériel flowed through the ports once they were cleared.

Below: LSTs loading for the invasion, at Bagnoli, Italy, 8 August 1944. They include *LST-76*, *LST-286* and *LST-174* among others. Note the LCS(S)(2) on bow davits of *LST-286* and LCVPs carried by other LSTs.

Opposite Below: The 45th US Infantry Division landed its 157th and 180th RCTs at Sainte-Maxime. This was its fourth amphibious assault—the others being Sicily, Salerno and Anzio. Here, German prisoners are marched to the boats for evacuation.

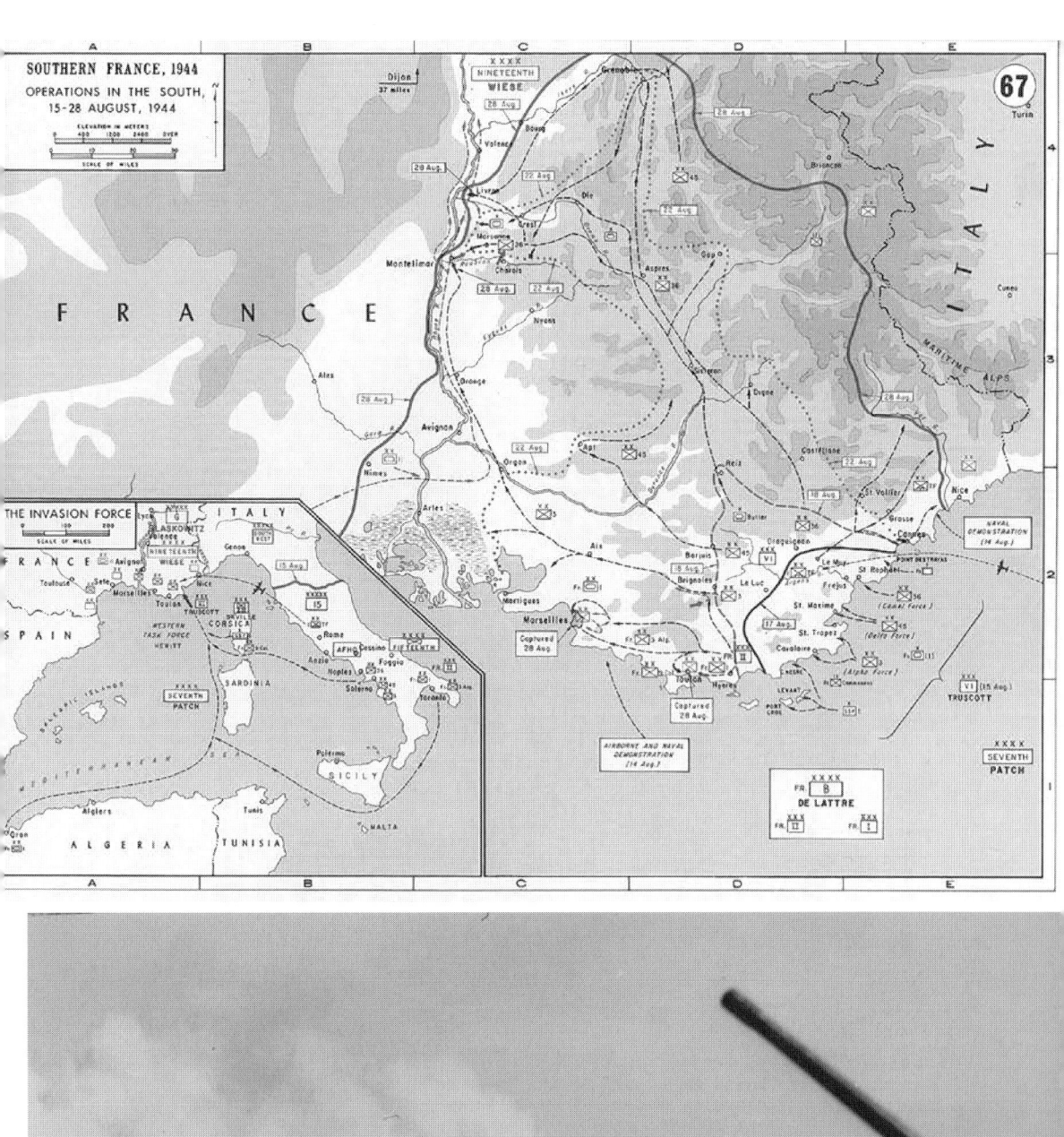

SOUTHERN FRANCE, 1944
OPERATIONS IN THE SOUTH, 15-28 AUGUST, 1944

Operation *Tanne Ost* (GER) (14-15 September 1944) Suursaari Island, Finland

This was an unsuccessful German attempt to seize the strategic island of Suursaari which controlled the eastern end of the Gulf of Finland from the Finns following their armistice negotiations with the Soviets. A first assault group of 1,400 mixed army and navy troops was transported in various minesweeper (*Minensuch-Flottille*) and landing craft (*Landungs-Flottille*) ships with *Schnellboot* escorts. As they went into land they met a heavier opposing Finnish force than expected which held up any advance although they did achieve a bridgehead. The Soviets also bombed the German ships and later the whole battlefield including the Finnish positions.

Having lost communications with the first wave of landed troops, the German commander (Capt Karl-Conrad Mecke) cancelled the second wave and abandoned the mission, leaving 150 men dead and over 1,200 with no recourse other than to surrender.

German naval losses included three landing craft, three patrol boats, one minesweeper and one tug, while the Finns lost 100 men killed or wounded and two patrol boats.

Below: Control of Suursaari was a strategic imperative for Germany as the war in the east went badly against them.

Bottom: This 88mm didn't even get off the landing craft.

Opposite: Views of the landing area after the fighting. Due to the air threat, the Germans did not dare to send the cruiser *Prinz Eugen* to support the landing forces.

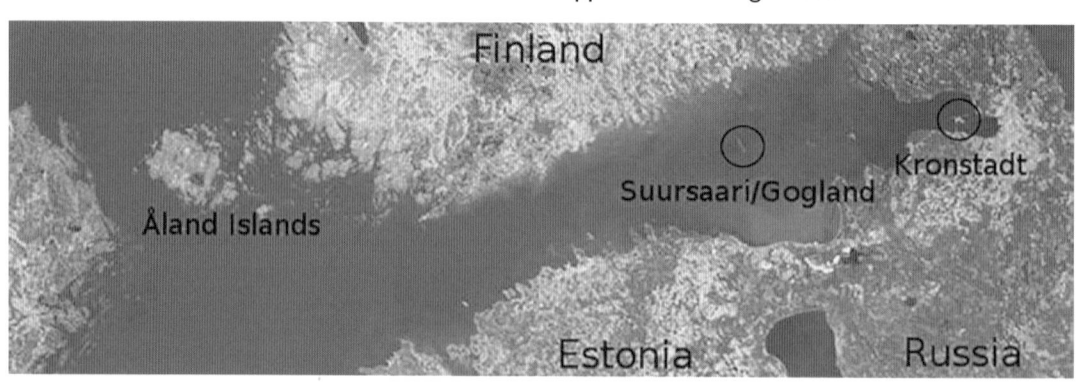

145

Operation Tradewind (US) 15 September 1944–August 1945 Morotai, Molucca Islands

On the approaches to the Philippines from New Guinea, and well placed for airstrips (the Japanese had built nine of them), Morotai was surprisingly weakly defended by around 500 Japanese when 31st Infantry Division landed from 15 September. The island was secured by 4 October. Units from Morotai were sent to take other small islands, such as Pegun and Bras in the Mapia Islands. The island was developed as a base area with fuel storage depots and a PT boat base as well as the airfields. Between September and November the Japanese pumped troops towards the island and while American PT boats destroyed a number, enough got through to ensure that US forces were fighting until mid-January and in patrolling until the end of the war.

Left: LVT(A)-1 amphibious vehicles leave the ramp of their LST, on D-day.

Below: Troops wade ashore from five LCIs on Red Beach.

Operation Stalemate II (US) 15 September 1944 Peleliu, Palau Islands

Part of the much larger Operation Forager offensive (see p. 132), Operation Stalemate II's purpose was to protect MacArthur's flank by capturing the Palau Islands which boasted two airfields, two seaplane bases, a submarine base and fleet anchorages. Originally planned as a two-corps attack, this changed as MacArthur's operations in the Philippines were accelerated (see p. 152) and the task fell to 1st Marine and 81st Infantry Divisions.

The small coral island of Peleliu was attacked first on 15 September, followed by Anguar (on the 17th) and Ngesebus (which fell to 5th Marines who attacked on 28 September). Taking Angaur and Peleliu isolated the largest islands, Babelthuap and Koror whose garrisons were over 25,000, and allowed them to be bypassed.

The assault on Peleliu was undertaken by almost 50,000 men, primarily from 1st Marine Division, with some other small supporting units. They were opposed by about 11,000 Japanese of 14th Infantry Division, 49th Mixed Brigade, 45th Guard Force and 46th Base Force, along with some 20 tanks.

The commander of the 1st Marine Division (Maj Gen Rupertus) had made the fateful claim that the island would fall in a few days—in fact, it took over two months of ferocious combat that would yield the highest American casualty rate (almost 2,000 killed and 10,000 wounded) of any Pacific amphibious operation. Once again the outnumbered Japanese had prepared elaborate defences to thwart the Americans and resist their huge pre-landing bombardments—and once again they fought to the last man.

On the 15th, 81st Infantry Division made a feint attack on Babelthuap which convinced the Japanese commander he would be attacked and so he didn't send reinforcements to the other islands. Landing on Peleliu simultaneously on five beaches, the Americans were held up by lethal crossfire that destroyed over 60 LVTs and DUKWs. By the end of the first day, they held their landing beaches, but little else. However, the next day they pushed on and 5th Marines took the airfield, destroying a Japanese armoured and infantry force sent to counterattack. The airfield was immediately put to use. However the inland ridges and Umurbrogol mountain proved even more dangerous and fatal than the landings.

The campaign in the Palaus was controversial: could the islands have been bypassed completely? The high casualty rate on Peleliu obviously added to these issues and postwar caused huge debate in the United States.

Below: A Vought OS2U Kingfisher—a catapult-launched observation floatplane—flies over invasion shipping as the first landing waves head for Angaur Island, whose eastern tip is at right. The LVTs in left centre are heading for Red Beach while battleships and cruisers are still bombarding the island. The assault was by 81st Infantry Division and Angaur fell in a four-day campaign, 17–20 September 1944, leaving 321st Infantry to mop up. Casualties were 264 dead and 1,354 wounded; the Japanese lost 1,350 dead and 50 captured. The 81st Division was also tasked with taking Ulithi and Yap Islands (between the Palaus and Guam). The former fell with no opposition; the latter with a large garrison was bypassed.

LINE OF ADVANCE ASHORE

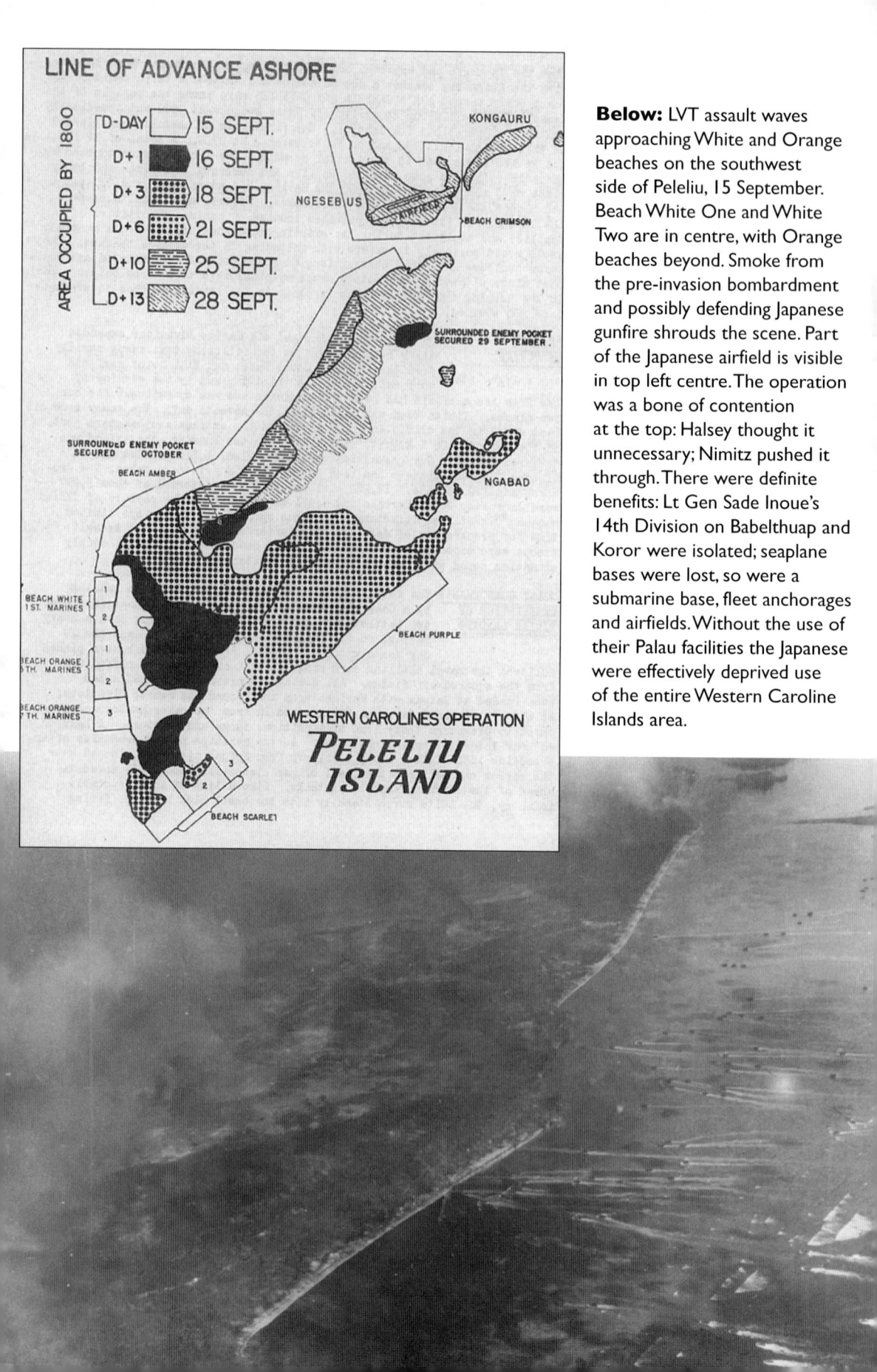

AREA OCCUPIED BY 1800

- D-DAY — 15 SEPT.
- D+1 — 16 SEPT.
- D+3 — 18 SEPT.
- D+6 — 21 SEPT.
- D+10 — 25 SEPT.
- D+13 — 28 SEPT.

KONGAURU

NGESEBUS

BEACH CRIMSON

SURROUNDED ENEMY POCKET SECURED 29 SEPTEMBER

SURROUNDED ENEMY POCKET SECURED OCTOBER

BEACH AMBER

NGABAD

BEACH WHITE 1ST. MARINES — 1, 2
BEACH ORANGE 5TH. MARINES — 1, 2
BEACH ORANGE 7TH. MARINES — 3

BEACH PURPLE

WESTERN CAROLINES OPERATION

PELELIU ISLAND

BEACH SCARLET

Below: LVT assault waves approaching White and Orange beaches on the southwest side of Peleliu, 15 September. Beach White One and White Two are in centre, with Orange beaches beyond. Smoke from the pre-invasion bombardment and possibly defending Japanese gunfire shrouds the scene. Part of the Japanese airfield is visible in top left centre. The operation was a bone of contention at the top: Halsey thought it unnecessary; Nimitz pushed it through. There were definite benefits: Lt Gen Sade Inoue's 14th Division on Babelthuap and Koror were isolated; seaplane bases were lost, so were a submarine base, fleet anchorages and airfields. Without the use of their Palau facilities the Japanese were effectively deprived use of the entire Western Caroline Islands area.

D-day on Peleliu; LVT(A)-4 protects marines on Orange Beaches.

Operation Mercerised (BR) 9-12 October 1944 Sarandë, Albania, and Corfu, Greece

For the attack on Sarandë, No 2 Cdo was reinforced with No 40 (RM) Cdo and the 25pdr guns of the 111th Field Regiment, RA. The attack was launched early on 9 October when the weather broke. After a half-hour bombardment, the attack went in. It was still dark, flares and incendiaries lighting the ground. The attack led to the capture of the port, in the process taking prisoner what was left of the garrison—some 600 Germans; the number of prisoners taken by the British and Albanians in this area later rose to about 1,000. The two commando units suffered 81 casualties after withstanding a strong counterattack.

Later that day, towards evening, Corfu's garrison commander and four boatloads of troops arrived on the beach at Sarandë and were captured. The British then dropped leaflets on Corfu advising the Germans to surrender. On 12 October white flags were seen and two days later No 40 Cdo crossed the channel to Corfu to take the surrender of a few German stragglers—the bulk of the garrison had been evacuated through Greece while Sarandë was under attack.

Time and Date	Location of Landing	Unit	Size of Landing Force	Size of Support Force	Other Support Activities	Nature of Opposition	Actions Ashore	Enemy Response	Outcome
1. 23:30 9 Oct–00:50 10 Oct	Maativuono Bay	1st, 2nd and 3rd Bns, 63rd Naval Inf Bde	2,750–3,000 in three waves	Mixture of 30 torpedo cutters and subchasers	Demonstration landing at Motovskii Bay; smoke screen; shore battery fire support	Illumination by searchlight; shore batteries; no enemy troops at water's edge	Attacked inland into flank and rear of German defenders	Heavy combat	Linked up with 12th Naval Inf Bde on 10 Oct; linked up with 14th Army on 13 Oct
2. 23:00–24:00 12 Oct	Liinakhamari Harbour	Composite	660 in three waves	Mixture of 14 torpedo cutters and subchasers	Smoke screen; shore battery fire support; Krestovyi raid	Heavy shore battery; piers in harbour mined; enemy garrison	Seized port and settlement; attacked Petsamo from north	Heavy combat	Controlled port by late 13 Oct; attacked southward to envelop Petsamo
3. 06:50–07:30 18 Oct	Suola-Vuono, Ares-Vuono	4th Bn, 12th Naval Inf Bde	485 in two groups	6 subchasers	Close air support when ashore	None at landing site; small garrisons of coastal installations	Attacked west to Norwegian border, defeating light opposition	Light to moderate opposition	Reached Norwegian border by late 19 Oct; linked up with ground forces of 368th Rifle Div
4. 06:00–06:30 23 Oct	Kobbholm Fjord	3rd Bn, 12th Naval Inf Bde; 125th Naval Inf Regt	625 in two groups	10 light craft	Close air support when ashore	None at landing site	Advanced on two separate axes, cleared coast of 75mm anti-aircraft and artillery batteries	Light opposition	Cleared zone; no significant impact
5. 04:55–05:50 25 Oct	Holmenger Fjord	2rd and 3rd Bns, 63rd Naval Inf Bde	835 in three waves	Mixture of 15 torpedo cutters and subchasers	3 cutters in overwatch	None at landing site	Advanced on two axes, clearing coastal installations	Light opposition	Reached Kirkenes vicinity on 27 Oct; little impact on outcome

Kirkenes (SOV) 9–25 October 1944

Forces of the Russian Northern Fleet conducted five separate amphibious landings in support of the Soviet ground offensive (as shown in the map **Right**). The Soviets were inexperienced at this sort of venture and the landings were less slickly organised than those of the Allies—the darkness also adding difficulties.

The initial landing was the largest, with a feint against Motovskii Bay by two destroyer escorts firing on the German shore installations and troops going ashore to distract the Germans. It didn't work but there were no troops on the beaches to oppose them—just as well as the unloading was slow compared to the Allies, because the Russian soldiers used planks over the bows to leave the boats.

The second landing, at Liinakhamari, included hydrographic preparation and training special units. The naval infantry captured the port and north of Petsamo.

The third landing was at Suola-Vuono and Ares-Vuono and embarked from Petsamo three days after it fell. The 368th Rifle Division, part of the force, captured the hydroelectric station at Kobbholm Fjord, which supplied electricity to the port of Kirkenes.30

The fourth landing also left from Petsamo and reached Kobbholm Fjord unopposed.

The fifth and final landing saw two battalions of the 63rd Naval Infantry Brigade leave Pummanki for Holmenger Fjord on 25 October, the same day the army attacked Kirkenes from east and south. They chased the retreating Germans away and took Kirkenes by midday 25 October.

Operation Crofter Finnmark (SOV/NOR) 5 November 1944–26 April 1945

In late October Force 138—a party of around 250 Norwegians, most from *Bergkompani* 2 (2nd Mountain Company)—embarked on 'County' class cruiser HMS *Berwick* for Murmansk. They arrived on 6 November and were then transported first to Liinakhamari by ship and then by lorry to Finnmark for 10 November. Under Colonel Arne Dagfin Dahl whose HQ was at Bjørnevatn, they were joined by local volunteers, police trained in Sweden flown in by US transport aircraft and more troops from Britain. By 26 April 1945 Finnmark was cleared of Germans.

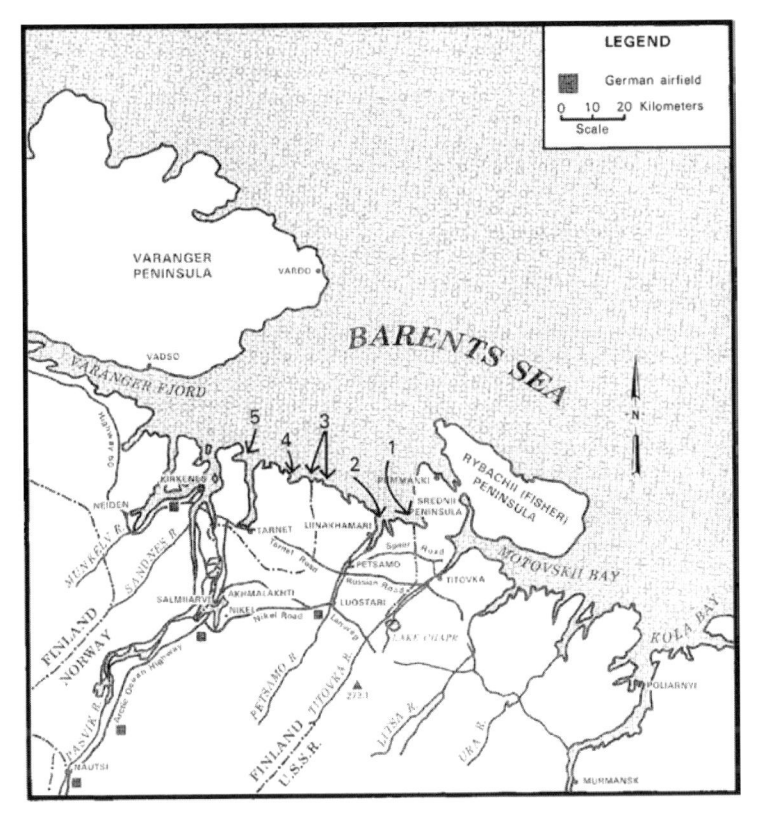

Left: The five Soviet landings as part of the Kirkenes operation. See table on opposite page for details.

Below: Norwegian soldiers on board a British cruiser en route to northern Norway to take up the fight against the Germans together with the Russian Arctic Army. The photo was taken the moment some of the soldiers were made aware of what the task was about. London, 5 November 1944

Operation King II (US) 20 October 1944 Leyte, Philippine Islands

There was much debate about the necessity to attack the Philippines. Two different war strategies boiled down to Admiral King arguing for an attack on Formosa with the Philippines bypassed, and General MacArthur arguing for an attack on the Philippines themselves. MacArthur won. The Joint Chiefs agreed with Admiral Halsey suggestion that Leyte should be attacked first but disagreed that the Palau Islands should be bypassed. Instead, they agreed a reduced Operation Stalemate II, which meant that a two-corps force would be reduced to two divisions (see p. 147).

The ensuing Philippines campaign of 1944–45 witnessed some of the key battles of the war in the Pacific, including the Battle of Leyte Gulf—the largest naval battle of the war and perhaps of all time—and the savage land battle for the island of Leyte itself, the largest amphibious operation in the Pacific.

About 110 miles long and 15–50 miles wide, the interior of Leyte is dominated by a heavily forested north–south mountain range that separates the two main valleys, or coastal plains—the larger Leyte Valley and the smaller and wilder Omroc Valley. On 20 October 1944, after a two-day naval bombardment by the US 7th Fleet, the US Sixth Army landed 175,000 men on the northeastern coast.

X Corps covered a four-mile front between Tacloban airfield and the Palo River; XXIV Corps a three-mile front between San José and the Daguitan River. The landings were mostly uncontested and the Allies soon established viable beachheads downloading heavy vehicles, artillery, ammunition and supplies.

Opposing them were 20,000 Japanese troops of 16th Division, who retreated inland, even as the Japanese Navy launched a three-fleet operation (*Sho-Go* or Victory Operation) to drive the US from the Philippines. This led to the battle of Leyte Gulf and the near total destruction of Japanese naval power. In desperation they took to using kamikaze attacks against US ships and they also managed to reinforce Leyte with a further 35,000 troops along with fresh supplies and ammunition, despite enduring heavy losses. There followed another bitter and bloody battle in the mountains on its western side in heavy monsoon rains. The US forces suffered more than 15,500 casualties, with almost 3,500 killed, while Japanese lost at least 49,000 men.

Opposite: MacArthur returns to the Philippines, as promised, wading ashore in 24th Division's sector on 20 October. His Philippine plans were codenamed 'Musketeer' the landings on Leyte, Luzon and Mindanao 'King', 'Mike' and 'Victor'.

Below: First, minesweeping operations cleared the way; next, Rangers took three islands and set up navigation lights for the convoys. Then the landings went in. They were virtually unopposed and cost 49 KIA, 192 WIA and 6 MIA. The campaign, however, was hard fought and bloody.

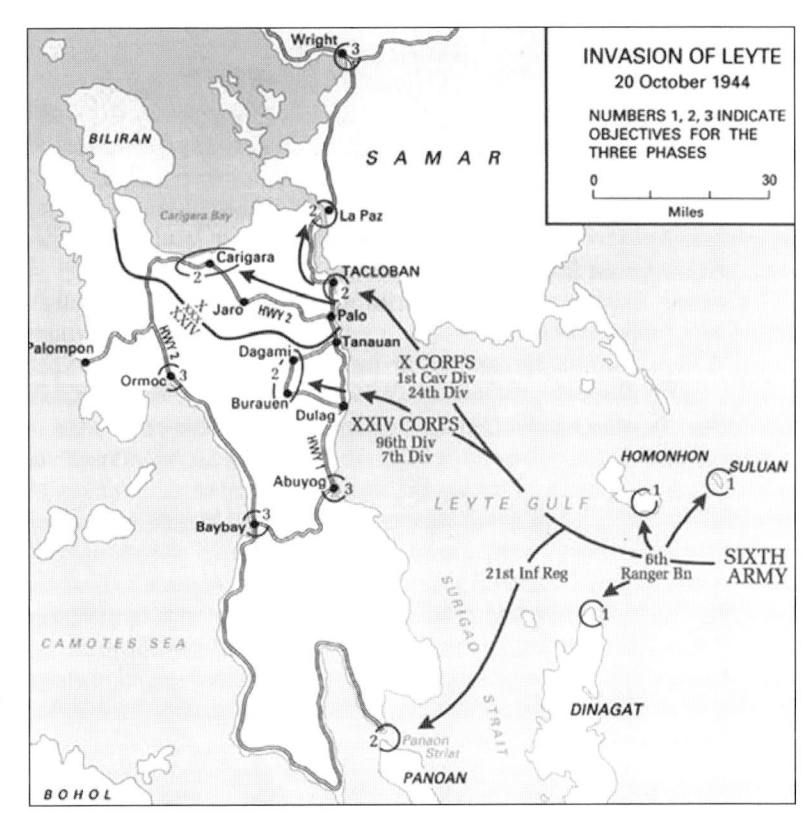

Above: This remarkable photograph shows 20 LSTs on Cataisan Point, near Tacloban City, Leyte in late October or early November 1944. Note large number of vehicles parked on and near the airfield.

Below: USS *Abner Read* sinking in Leyte Gulf on 1 November 1944 after being hit by a Aichi D3A kamikaze. A second Japanese suicide plane (circled) is attempting to crash on USS *Claxton*. It was shot down short of its target.

Operations Vitality II and Infatuate (UK/CAN) 2 November 1944 South Beveland/Walcheren Island, the Netherlands

The Allies needed the Scheldt clear so they could use the port of Antwerp. The Germans had kept the Breskens Pocket open south of the Scheldt while they ferried Fifteenth Army across (see p. 187). The Canadians cleared the pocket by Operation Switchback. The second part of the clearance plan was to attack through South Beveland towards Walcheren (Operation Vitality I). When this attack bogged down—held up by flooded terrain, minefields and the Beveland canal—Operation Vitality II was launched, a flanking amphibious assault across the Scheldt from Terneuzen.

The 21st Army Group report explains: '176 LVTs [44 LVT-2s; 132 LVT-4s] were used for the initial assault and follow up, 80 under command 5 Assault Regiment, RE, and 96 under command 11 RTks. In addition, 25 LCAs were available and 27 Terrapins were used in the buildup and maintenance programme.' The assault took place on 26 October as British 156th Infantry Brigade attacked two beaches. The operation was successful and soon the Canadians were advancing on Walcheren.

Operation Infatuate was a daring, two-pronged Allied assault on the heavily defended island of Walcheren at the mouth of the River Scheldt. It was carried out primarily by Anglo-Canadian forces (4th Special Service Brigade, 52nd Infantry Division, 2nd Can Infantry Division), but French, Belgian and Norwegian commando units also took part. The controversial RAF bombing of Walcheren in October had breached the dykes around the island and turned it into a massive lagoon (see overleaf), rimmed by long stretches of intact dykes which bristled with German guns (although half the concrete casemates, those in the interior, had been flooded), manned by 12,000 troops of the 70th Division.

Following a preliminary naval bombardment Nos 41, 48 (RM) and 10 (Inter-Allied) Cdos landed in 104 LVTs and 80 M29Cs on two beaches to the north and south of the breach in the sea dyke. Accompanying them were men from 59 GHQ Troops, RE for mine-clearing, work in the beach area and destruction of gun emplacements. Additionally, 79th Armoured Division supplied 10 flails, 2 Sherman gun tanks, 8 AVREs and 4 bulldozers, organised into four teams each in an LCT.

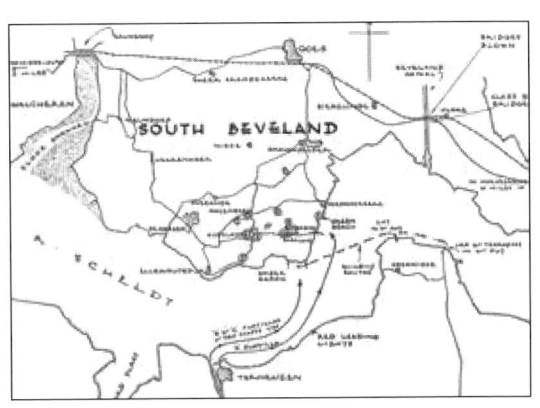

Most of the LCTs carrying the troops beached successfully (although three were subsequently lost). The 79th Armoured's LCTs were badly hit, one to the extent that it returned to Ostend without unloading its damaged contents. Of the others, 4 AVREs, 3 flails and a bulldozer were bogged down immediately and the other three flails drowned as the tide rose.

To support the landings, two dozen armed landing craft deliberately engaged the German gun batteries to divert their fire from the assaulting troops, losing 20 craft and sustaining over 370 casualties. The 21st Army Group report notes that the losses after the first four hours were: 4 LCG, 2 LCF, 3 LCS(L), 1 LCT and 1 LCI(S) by gunfire after unloading, and 3 LCT on mines, two after unloading, and one before beaching.

'*Had* [the enemy] *paid more attention to the* [troop-carrying vessels], *it is doubtful whether the assault would have succeeded. ... The success of the landing at Westkapelle was largely due to the determintion of the Support Squadron to ensure that the Commandos should arrive safely on the beach, and receive the maximum support. The Squadron put up a magnificent fight against formidable defences, and suffered severely, but they drew to themselves the fire of the enemy batteries and thus enabled the troop-carrying craft to go in with relatively few casualties.*'

Resolutely, the Allied commandos fought their way through Westkapelle in the face of fierce resistance. 41 Cdo advanced north along the dunes of the narrow unflooded coastal strip and secured Domburg by dusk, while 48 Cdo advanced southeast along the dunes toward Zoutelande.

By nightfall, 4th Brigade had secured a six-mile beachhead. Next morning, on 2 November, 48 Cdo captured Zoutelande, taking 150 prisoners, and 47 Cdo fought its way forward to the final German emplacements, which fell the next day.

No 4 Cdo and a Dutch section of 10 (IA) Cdo assaulted Flushing (Vlissingen) from Breskens on 1 November, using 20 LCAs; 155th Infantry Brigade followed up in another 20. Hard street fighting saw the town fall after three days. Finally, on 4 November, Nos 47 and 4 Cdo linked up to advance northwest along the dunes from Flushing.

The 21st Army Group report says:

'LVTs (BUFFALOES) over flooded and waterlogged country performed better than any other vehicle available, except M29Cs. They can master a mud-covered beach, provided the mud is NOT too deep or a layer of sand surface exists. Thick belts of wire and quantities of fallen telegraph wire proved an obstacle. They are mechanically reliable and will perform well, provided they are properly maintained, regularly overhauled and the crews are NOT worked to exhaustion. They present a small, though noisy, target when swimming, but are conspicuous and vulnerable on land.

'M29Cs (WEASELS). Low freeboard and lack of steerage way when swimming make thir employment in anything but calm, still water extremely hazardous. 50% of casualties were due to vehicles drowning. Their performance in mud, swamp and sand was good. Steep banks, ditches or runnels of 6ft width or more, are impassable as the bow of model M29C protrudes in front of the tracks and digs itself into the far bank of the obstacle. They are halted by wire obstacles.'

Above: The dyke at Westkapelle was breached by the RAF on 3 October 1944.

Below: No 41 (RM) Cdo LVTs and Weasels disembark from an LCT at Westkapelle.

3 Cdo Bde goes ashore at Kangaw.

Operations Talon (Akyab), Pungent (Myebon), Matador (Ramree) Sankey (Cheduba) and Kangaw) (BR) 3-22 January 1945 Arakan, Burma (today, Myanmar

The Arakan had been in Japanese hands since early 1942 despite a British attack later that year. In 1944 the Allies tried again as XV Indian Corps attacked towards Akyab Island, at the end of the Mayu Peninsula and the mouth of the Kaladan River. The airfield there would help support the troops in Central Burma. Two West African divisions (the 81st and 82nd) attacked down the river while 3 Commando Brigade made an amphibious landing on 3 January only to find the Japanese had slipped away.

The next landing was at Myebon, which had been reconnoitred by a COPP team who had found underwater obstacles. On the night of 11/12 January, the COPP went in again, this time to lay delayed-action charges to cut a lane through the obstacles. As No 42 Cdo approached on the morning of the 12th the charges went off, the lane was cleared and the attack went in. Over the next two days 6,635 personnel and 41 vehicles were landed and the commandos (Nos 1, 5, 42 and 44) and a brigade of 25th Division cleared the peninsula to ensure that the Japanese from the interior couldn't escape by sea.

Operation Matador saw 26th Indian Division assault Ramree Island on the 21st, with a bombardment force that included battleship HMS *Queen Elizabeth*. The airfield and main port, Kyaukpyu, fell by 7 February. During the fighting, commandos landed on Cheduba on 26 January and found it deserted. With the rivers and coast captured, the remaining Japanese escape route was the Myobaung to Tamandu road—which the attack on Kangaw should cut.

Again reconnoitred by the COPP, 3 Commando Brigade's assault went in on 22 January. By D+2 they had taken Hill 170, the most prominent feature near the landing area, and village of Kangaw. The Japanese 54th Division counterattack led to the hardest fighting of the campaign. They were cleared from the hill and the Allies moved forward to the next hill, codenamed 'Pinner', where there was hand-to-hand fighting as the Japanese attacked relentlessly. The commandos and Indian troops—25th Division—with the assistance of two Shermans of 19th Lancers managed to turn the tide of the battle and take the village of Kangaw. Japanese casualties were as many as 2,000—340 or more dead on Hill 170; the commandos lost 45 DIA and 90 WIA. Japanese Twenty-Eighth Army was forced to withdraw from the Arakan or face annihilation.

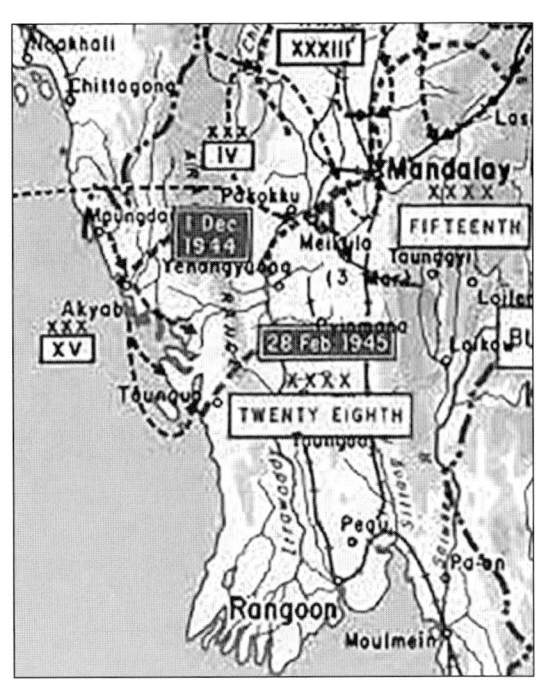

Operation Mike I (US) 9 January–15 August 1945 Luzon, Philippine Islands

The fighting in the Philippines was bloody and protracted with substantial casualties on both sides: 8,000 Americans died, nearly 30,000 were wounded; civilian deaths were around 150,000, many of them murdered by the Japanese; at least 200,000 Japanese soldiers died, many from disease or starvation.

First, US forces attacked Leyte in October 1944 (see p. 152). Then, in December, Mindoro Island was assaulted and fell. Next, in January 1945, the landings were made on Luzon's Lingayen Gulf. On 9 January 1945 there were further operations, codenamed 'Victor', on Panay, Cebu and Negros (I and II), Mindanao (V), Palawan, (III) and the Sulu archipelago (IV).

The assault on Luzon started with a bombardment by 70 battleships and cruisers. Of the vessels involved in the operation, 24 were sunk—including escort carrier *Ommaney Bay* and 67 damaged by kamikaze aircraft. Two army corps from US Sixth Army (Lt Gen Walter Krueger), were opposed by Japanese Fourteenth Area Army. The assault was by four divisions, 6th and 43rd (I Army Corps) and 37th and 40th (XIV).

On 26 January another major landing took place on Luzon, southwest of Manila: the city took a month to clear and was devastated in the process. At least 100,000 civilians died during the fighting—some used as human shields, many murdered by the Japanese, many others killed by US artillery.

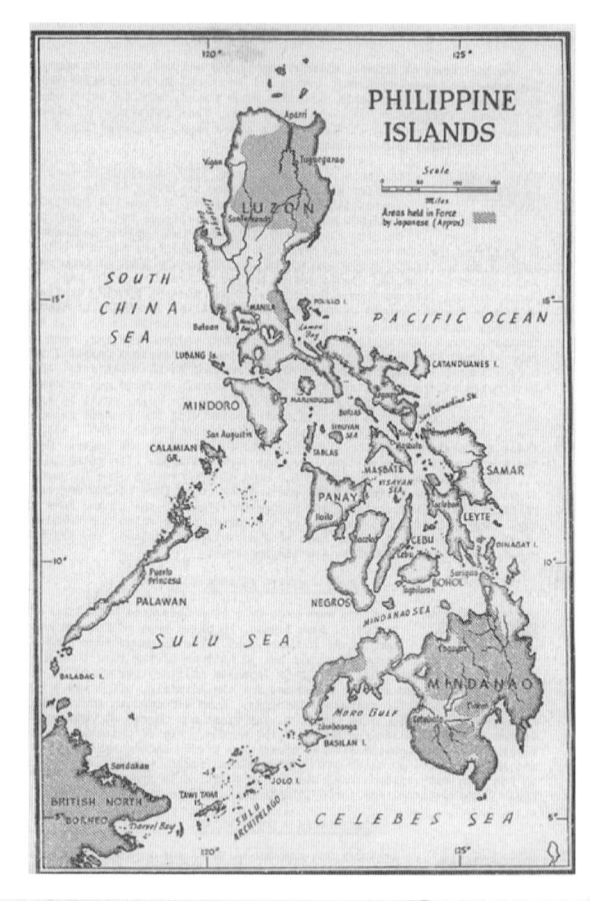

Right and Below
Right: USS *Louisville*, a 'Northampton' class cruiser, about to be hit by a kamikaze in Lingayen Gulf, on 6 January 1945, and then the explosion. The aircraft was a Mitsubishi Ki-51. 43 men were killed including Rear Admiral Theodore E. Chandler, commander of Cruiser Division 4 who was injured helping sailors manhandle fire hoses. This was *Louisville's* third kamikaze strike: the first, at Leyte, was only shrapnel which killed one person; the second, on 5 January, also killed one man.

158

Top: Anti-aircraft fire from the US Navy task force in Lingayen Gulf, as seen from USS *Boise* on 10 January 1945.

Above and Below: The landings on Lingayen beach on 9 January were virtually unopposed and assault troops advanced rapidly inland. 7th Amphibious Force landed I Corps on the northern beaches; and 3rd Amphibious Force landed XIV Corps on the southern beaches.

Above: Downed Japanese Aichi E13A1 Jake and the American landing ship *LST-806* on Palawan near Puerto Princesa. Operation Victor III saw the Palawan Islands cleared 28 February–22 April 1945. Of 2,000 Japanese defenders, 900 were KIA, 200 WIA; US casualties were 12 KIA.

Below and Opposite: LCIs and smaller LCMs unload men and equipment of 2/34th Regiment (24th Infantry Division). The recapture of Corregidor took place between 2 and 26 February 1945. It opened with 503rd PRCT making an extremely risky drop from low altitude into high winds onto Topside, the island's highest point (see map). The subsequent amphibious landing saw little initial resistance. Here, LCIs and smaller LCMs can be seen on the beach. A tank is visible forward of the centre LCM. In the end, 503rd PRCT suffered 169 dead and 531 wounded. The 34th Infantry Regiment had 38 killed and 153 wounded. Of the 6,700 Japanese on the island only 50 survived. Another 19 were taken prisoner and 20 Japanese holdouts surfaced after the war on 1 January 1946.

Opposite, Above: USS *LCS-8* stands off Corregidor to provide fire support. Above, USAAF C-47 planes drop 503rd PRCT on the island fortress, 16 February 1945.

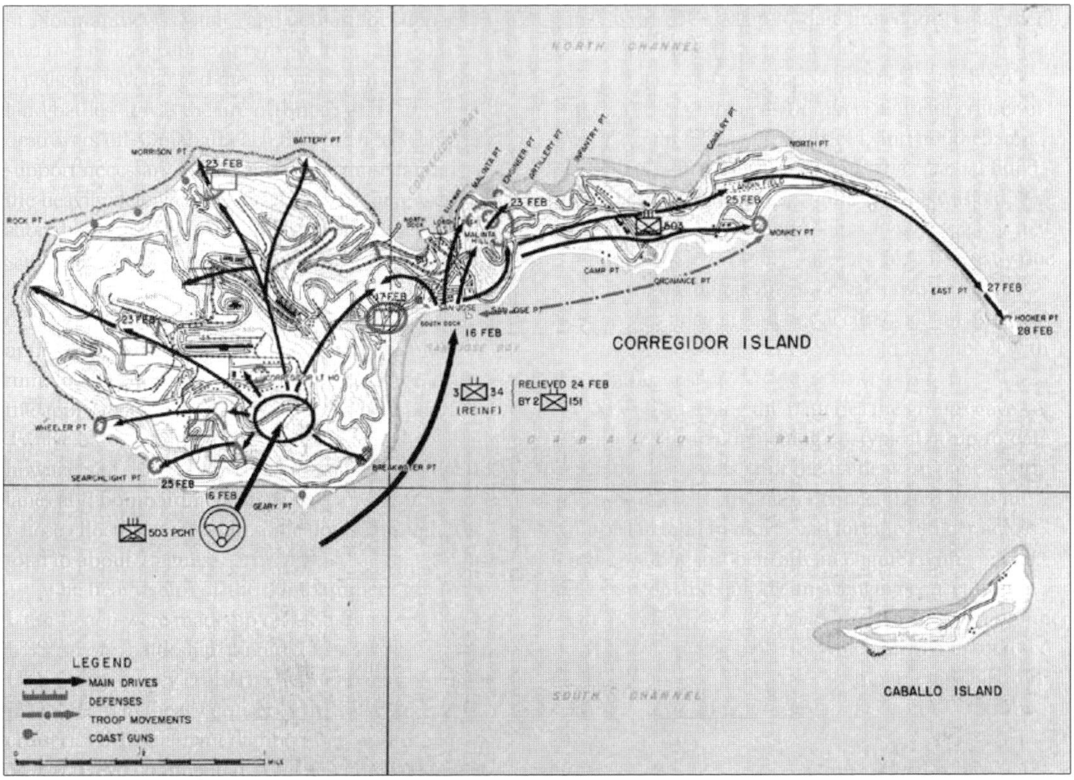
NORTH CHANNEL
MORRISON PT
BATTERY PT
ROCK PT
23 FEB
23 FEB
23 FEB
MALINTA PT
ENGINEER PT
ARTILLERY PT
INFANTRY PT
CAVALRY PT
NORTH PT
25 FEB
503
MONKEY PT
MALINTA HILL
CAMP PT
ORDNANCE PT
SAN JOSE PT
SAN JOSE
SOUTH DOCK
17 FEB
16 FEB
EAST PT
27 FEB
HOOKER PT
28 FEB
CORREGIDOR ISLAND
3 34 (REINF)
RELIEVED 24 FEB BY 2 151
WHEELER PT
SEARCHLIGHT PT
25 FEB
BREAKWATER PT
16 FEB
GEARY PT
503 PCHT
LEGEND
MAIN DRIVES
DEFENSES
TROOP MOVEMENTS
COAST GUNS
SOUTH CHANNEL
CABALLO ISLAND

Operation Detachment (US) 19 February 1945 Iwo Jima, Volcano Islands, Japan

Iwo Jima is the last island before the Japanese home islands, flat apart from Mt Suribachi on its southern tip and about eight square miles in area. Knowing the propensity for the Japanese no-surrender defence, the US pummelled the island with a three-day bombardment and air attack. What they didn't know (but could have guessed) is that the Japanese had created a dense, deep, tunnel-linked bunker and pillbox defence-in-depth system that mostly survived the US bombardment. Beach defences were minimal as the plan was to draw American troops inland and inflict the highest casualty rate they possibly could, so hidden artillery, mortar positions and land mines were placed all over the island.

Transported and protected by a huge carrier fleet (Task Force 58), some 70,000 US marines and several thousand Seabees (Naval Construction Battalions) landed on Iwo Jima at 09:00 on 19 February, far outnumbering the Japanese troops on the island. However, once again the Americans underestimated the sheer tenacity of the Japanese. The battle that they expected to last a few days took five weeks and cost 25,000 casualties, including nearly 7,000 deaths. Additionally, the beaches that had been thought convenient were found to be bordered by a slope of thick soft volcanic ash. Moving inland was difficult and the crowded troops were bombarded by inland artillery.

The defenders fought virtually to the last man, using ambushes, night attacks and reoccupying taken positions. After the south part of the island had fallen, the northern part still held eight infantry battalions, a tank regiment, two artillery and three heavy mortar battalions, 5,000 gunners and some naval infantry, all of whom continued to fight on and had to be methodically hunted down and killed. In the end only some 200 survived out of the garrison of 21,000.

Below: Mt Suribachi towers 554ft over the Iwo Jima beaches seen top right.

Opposite: 10th Amphibious Tractor Battalion reported: 'the weather was clear, sea calm and the tentative H-hour of 09:00 was confirmed. By 07:35 two columns of LSTs arrived in the LST area and took positions as planned. Waves were formed and dispatched according to orders without difficulty. Sporadic light automatic gun fire was received from the beach at about 08:00 while LVT waves were forming. As the waves approached to within 600 yards from the beach ineffective light mortar and artillery fire was received. The 6th wave received the heaviest volume of fire. ... In the assault, LVT(2)s carried 18–20 troops, and LVT(4)s carried 28-30 troops.'

IWO JIMA

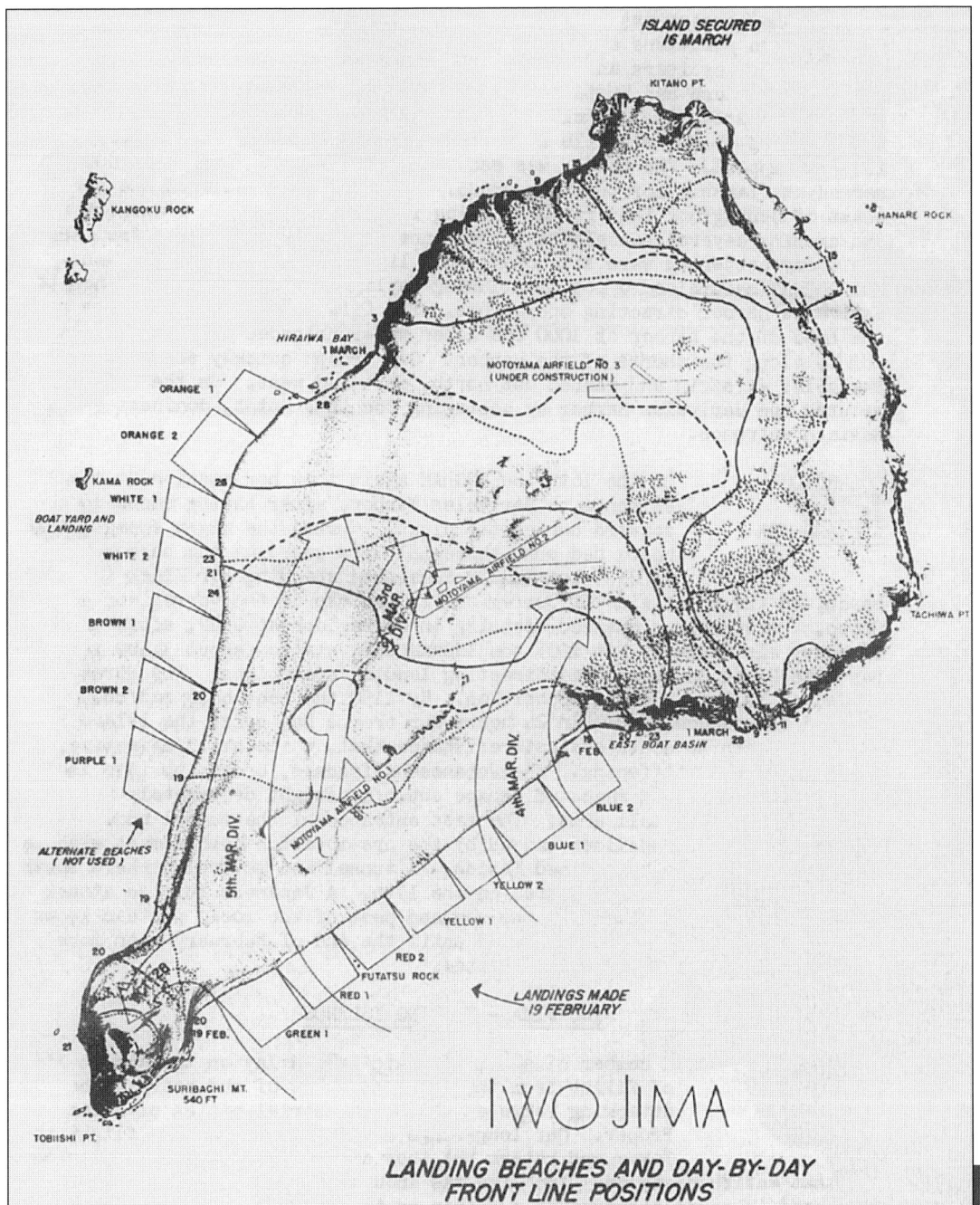

LANDING BEACHES AND DAY-BY-DAY FRONT LINE POSITIONS

PREPARATION OF LVTs FOR COMBAT

On 1 April 1945 the CO of 10th Amphibious Tractor Battalion produced a *Special Action Report, Iwo Jima Campaign*. It shows the types of modifications in the field that took place as a result of performance in action.

'(a) The conversion of the original LVT(4) machine shop into a command LVT. This command LVT had 3 TCS radios installed, special additional batteries, a battery charger, a switchboard and other communication equipment so that it could be used as a message center and command post afloat or ashore.

'(b) The conversion of 2 cargo LVT(4)s (one for each task company) into maintenance units. Each LVT was equipped with a folding boom and chain hoists, blocks and tackle, electric welding and oxy-acetylene cutting equipment.

'(c) The modification of the transmission oil pressure valve, by cutting 3 turns of wire from the tension spring thus permitting freer movement of oil from the transmission to the oil coolers.

'(d) The modification of the ramps of LVT(4)s, by cutting off approximately 4in of the reinforcing tubing along the top edge of the ramp. This reduced the chances of damage to the ramp and the possibilities of forcing the ramp open when coming alongside a ship.

'(e) The cutting of vision slits for the driver in the cab. One slit was cut for forward vision and one was cut for side vision, each 5in wide by 1in high. This was necessitated by the fogging of periscope globes and periscopes due to the heat and steam from the transmission.

'(f) Cutting 0.5in from the inside end of each grouser to reduce overhanging lips. This cut down on grouser wear by reducing "tearing" action; in cases of torn grousers the danger of ripping the hull was reduced.

'(g) Cutting lubricating holes in the control channel housing to permit greasing of controls, connections, and guides without removal of the whole panel.

'(h) Changing engine and transmission oil from mineral to detergent.

'(i) Welding windows over vision slits cut (see (e) above).

'(j) Removing periscopes and covers and welding plates over openings.

'(k) Welding steps on the sides of LVT(4)s.

'(l) Modifying and welding M48 Machine Gun Mounts to LVTs.

'(m) Installing 1 rifle rack in each cab for an M1 rifle, to increase fire power of crew (armed with pistols) in event LVT had to be abandoned near enemy.

'(n) Placing baffles on bow to reduce shipping of water into cargo compartment.

'(o) Installing canvas curtains over rear cab entrance to reduce shipping of water into cab.

'(p) Installing gas decontamination apparatus.

'(q) Installing brackets, forward, on each LVT designed to secure 2 ladders to be used by infantry in debarking from LVT on to a ledge if terrain required this procedure.

'(r) Realigning 25 return idlers.

'(s) Replacing towing shackles with hooks to expedite handling of tow cable connections.

'(t) Extending the turning handle of the cuno filter through top of engine compartment so that the filter could be turned without danger of burns from exhaust pipes.

'(u) Removing armor plate brackets which interferred with the adjustment of track tension and welding armor plate to hull.

'(v) Installing machine gun shields.

'(w) Camouflage painting all LVTs.

'(x) Marking all LVTs according to 4th Mar Div directive.

'(y) Running all LVTs 20 hours to permit proper mechanical adjustments and discovery and remedy of minor defects.'

Opposite: LVTs head towards the beaches on 19 February 1945.

This page: Offloading on the steep beach. The report said: 'The surf was moderate and the beach was steep. However it was unnecessary to use the scaling ladders provided. ...All LVTs retracted under their own power, except two, which broke down after leaving and were towed out to a maintenance LST. The retraction was orderly and according to plan. The LVTs reported to assigned ships and took on loads of supplies.'

Operation Plunder (Allies) 23-27 March 1945 River Rhine Crossing

Montgomery's set-piece crossing of the Rhine, Operation Plunder was one of several Allied assaults across the river, the last major obstacle before Germany itself. Its focus was on a 20-mile stretch of the river between Rees and Wesel and its massive size and meticulous planning ensured its success. A preliminary 4,000-gun bombardment combined with incessant intensive air attacks from over 2,000 fighters and bombers helped break German resistance.

With the Canadian First army on its left flank, British Second Army crossed opposite Rees and the 1st Commando Brigade crossed just to the north of Wesel. US Ninth Army crossed further to the south on the right flank. Over a million men, tanks and other heavy equipment from 21st Army Group were transported using four regiments equipped with Buffalo LVTs.

They were opposed by 70,000 men from Army Group H's 1st *Fallschirmjäger-Armee*, supported by about 70 tanks of 116th Panzer Division. Preceded by four days of continuous smoke screening, on the night on 23 March the LVTs and DUKWs began transporting British and US troops across the river under heavy fire from the enemy bank. The British attack at Rees was the most heavily opposed, as the Germans were strongest there. The US assault faced less opposition and a bridge was built within five hours.

In the early hours of the 24th, Operation Varsity, the largest airborne operation of the war, was carried out in support of 'Plunder' by the American 17th Airborne and the British 6th Airborne Divisions using thousands of transports and gliders to deliver over 22,000 airborne infantry including 14,000 paratroopers immediately behind the enemy lines. The overwhelming firepower and numbers of the Allied forces soon told and the German 1st *Fallschirmjäger-Armee* was forced into a strategic retreat beyond the Dortmund-Ems Canal and into the Teutoburg Forest, leaving a gap between it and the German Fifteenth *Armee* in the Ruhr—US Ninth and First Armies advanced and encircled the Ruhr.

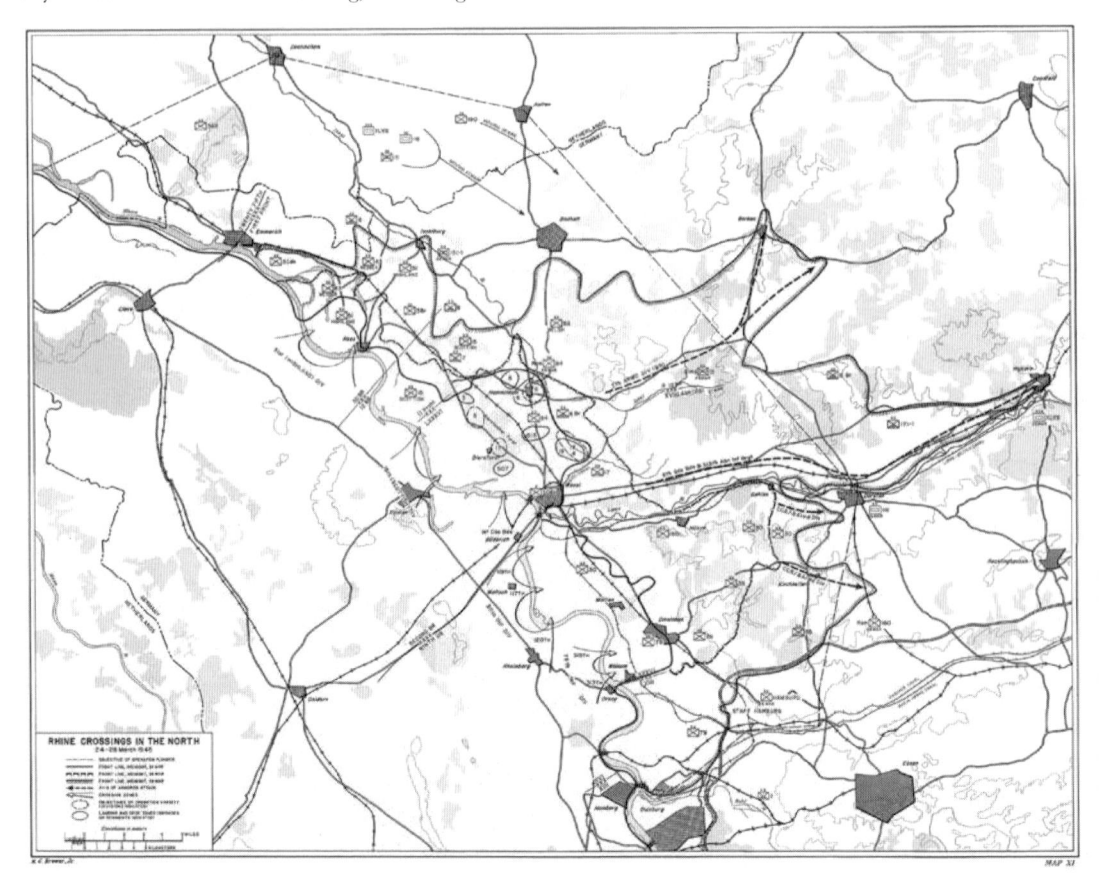

Above: LVTs were used extensively in Europe in the latter parts of the war—particularly in the fighting around the Scheldt and Rhineland. The British called them Buffaloes and 200 had been delivered by the end of 1943. By the time of the Rhine crossing 600 were available. Here, infantrymen of the North Shore Regiment board an LVT near Nijmegen, 8 February 1945. These vehicles proved a godsend, particularly along the areas of the Rhine that had been deliberately flooded.

Right: Men and vehicles of the 80th Infantry Division, Third US Army, unload from a landing craft after crossing the Rhine River, Germany, 29 March 1945.

Above: LVT-4s carry troops of 7th Infantry Division for the Purple and Orange beaches, just before H-hour. In the background, USS *Tennessee* fires her 5-inch secondary battery. The landings were unopposed and American casualties were 55 killed and 104 wounded on the first day.

Below: On 9 June, as part of cleaning up operations, 2nd Marine Division's 8th Regiment landed on Aguni Shima, an island west of Okinawa.

Bottom: The flag of the 77th Infantry Division flies on the pinnacle of Mount Gusuku, Ie Island, at 10:25 on 21 April 1945.

Operation Iceberg (US) 1 April–22 June 1945 Okinawa, Japan

The battle for the island of Okinawa was the last major battle of World War II and one of its fiercest and bloodiest. Okinawa's almost 500 square miles of rugged hills and dense jungle made it the perfect location for a final stand by the Imperial Japanese Army in an attempt to protect the motherland from the relentless US advance. Of course the IJA inevitably failed in their task, but the next three months saw the destruction of multiple ships, aircraft and tanks, along with the deaths of perhaps 300,000 people.

Fearing a desperate fight to establish a beachhead the Americans began with a massive bombardment—expending 1,500 16-inch rounds, 4,600 14-inch rounds, 750 12-inch rounds, 5,800 8-inch rounds, 7,200 6-inch rounds, was well as over 50,000 5-inch rounds, and prodigious amounts of aerial bombs, rockets and napalm—before landing over 180,000 Army and Marine Corps troops.

The Japanese commander, Lt Gen Mitsuru Ushijima, had worked out where the landings were likely to take place and ensured there were few troops there—and so the rain of steel was mainly wasted. The landings were unopposed and both Kadena and Yontan airfields swiftly taken. The defending Japanese (130,000 men, 70,000 of the 32nd Army, 10,000 naval troops plus 40,000 conscripted Okinawans) were waiting, hidden away in the most inaccessible and rugged parts of the island, primarily in the southern Shuri area and the Motobu Peninsula in the north, where they had prepared defences in depth.

There then followed another uncompromisingly ferocious struggle against a fanatical enemy, the jungle terrain and torrential rains.

Both sides suffered extensive casualties—the Americans had over 75,000 including 20,000 killed, while about 110,000 Japanese soldiers lost their lives and between 40,000 and 150,000 Okinawans were also killed. The US Fifth Fleet endured incessant kamikaze attacks that accounted for 36 ships sunk and 368 damaged, with 5,000 men killed and a further 5,000 wounded. The Japanese lost their super battleship *Yamato*, 15 other surface vessels and over 1,500 aircraft.

The ferocity of this battle at the end of the island-hopping campaign contributed greatly to President Truman's decision to use the newly invented nuclear weapons to force the surrender of the Japanese rather than expend countless more American lives subduing the Japanese home islands.

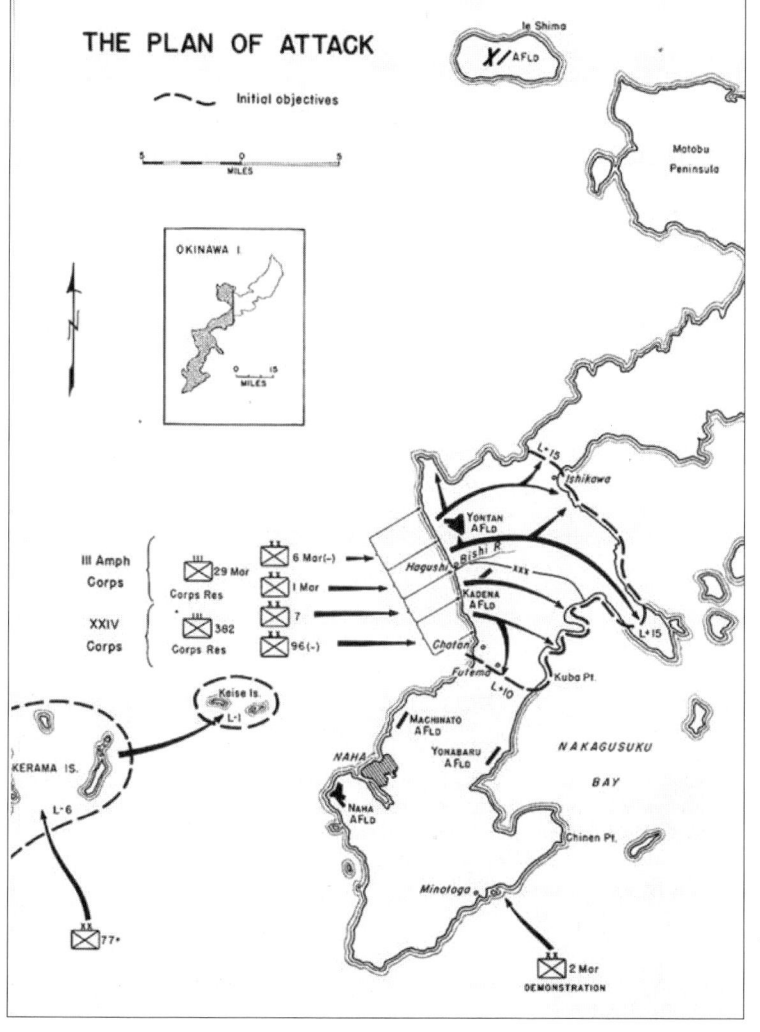

Above Left: Marines climb down a debarkation ladder from a Coast Guard-manned assault transport, to board an LCVP to take part in the initial attack on Okinawa, 1 April 1945.

Above Right: Conditions on the island took a marked turn for the worse at the end of May when the monsoon rains hit.

Below: Photographed off the invasion beaches during the bombardment, in foreground are *LCS-16*, *LCS-15* and *LCS-14*. USS *West Virginia* is beyond them, at left. Firing in right distance is USS *Idaho*.

Opposite: Unloading a landing craft of troops and vehicles of the 15th Indian Corps at Elephant Point, south of Rangoon at the beginning of operation 'Dracula', 2 May 1945.

Operation Dracula (UK) 1 May 1945 Rangoon, Burma (today, Myanmar)

Given its critical strategic importance, an amphibious assault on Burma's capital Rangoon was first considered in July 1944 by the British South East Asia Command, to cut the Japanese lines of supply and communication and force their withdrawal from Burma. However, the wherewithal required to accomplish it was not available to run concurrent with the Normandy landings, which were under way at that time. It was, therefore, postponed for almost a year before being put into action as Operation Dracula on 1 May 1945. By April that year units of the British Fourteenth Army had advanced to within 50 miles of Rangoon before being held by the Japanese at Pegu, thus triggering 'Dracula'. A Gurkha parachute battalion was dropped near Elephant Point at the mouth of the River Rangoon and fought a brief but fierce action to take the coastal gun batteries protecting the city. Once they had secured these objectives, minesweepers were brought in to clear the river, followed by the landing of elements of the Indian 26th Division on 2 May. They encountered no further resistance and it was then realised that the Japanese had already evacuated the city.

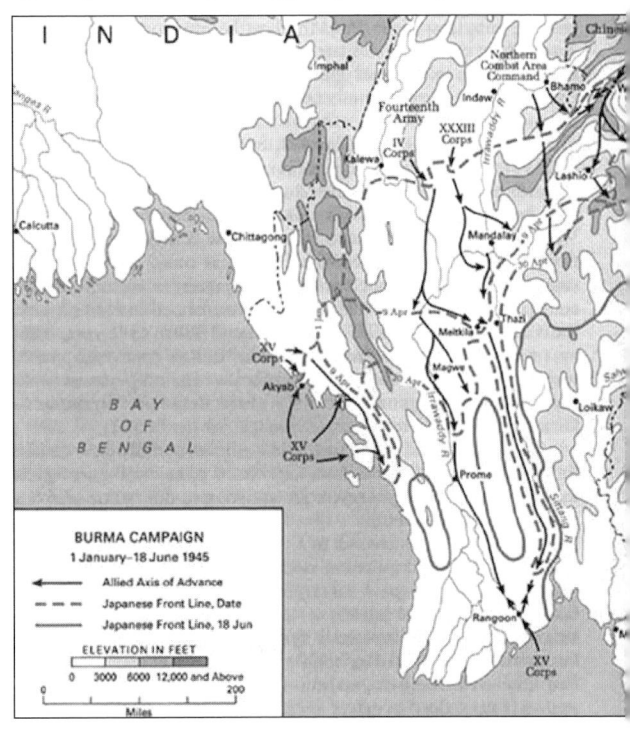

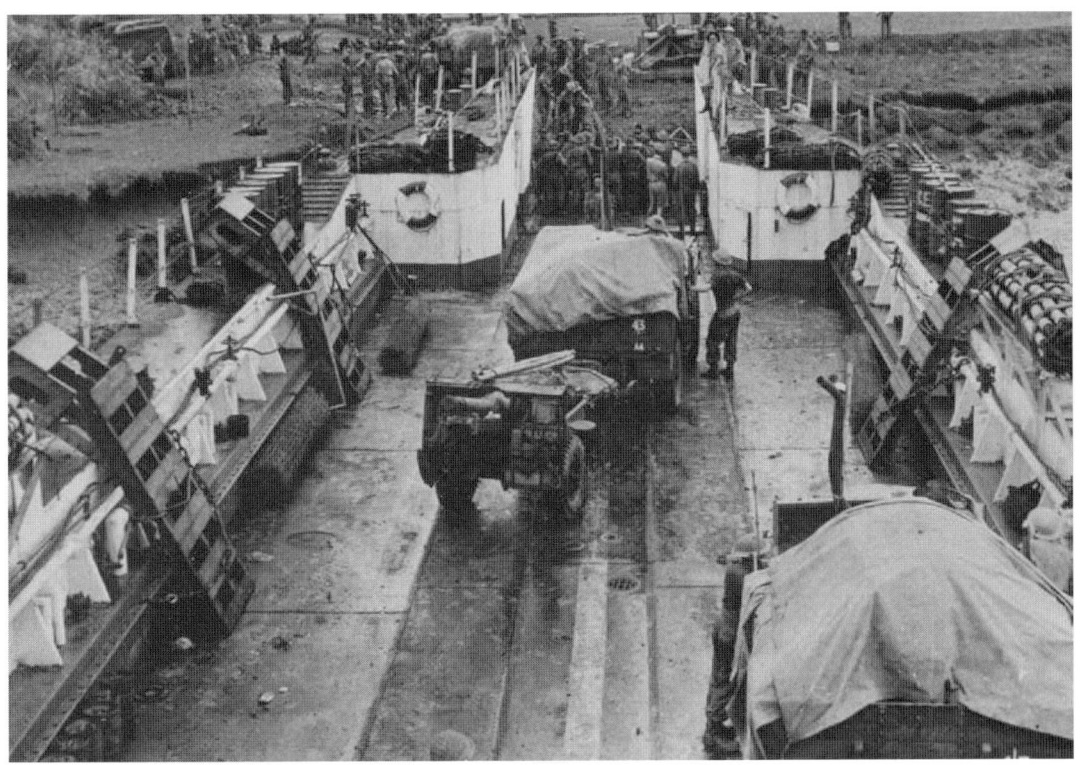

Above and Below: The Gurkha airborne assault had cleared the guns from Elephant Point allowing 26th Indian Division to follow the minesweepers into Rangoon.

Maoka Landing (SOV) 19-22 August 1945 Maoka, South Sakhalin Island, Japan (today Kholmsk, Russia)

Russia finally declared war on Japan on 9 August 1945, after Germany's defeat. Almost immediately, they invaded Manchukuo (Manchuria). This was followed on 18 August by several Soviet amphibious landings—three in northern Korea, one in the Chishima Islands and one on South Sakhalin following the deadlock between Soviet forces (Sixteenth Army) attacking from the north of the island and South Sakhalin's Japanese defenders (elements of the 88th Division).

After a successful landing at Port Toro on the 16th, some 3,500 Soviet troops including a battalion of marines and the 113th Rifle Brigade landed in Port Maoka in heavy fog on the 19th, to be met with fierce Japanese resistance. The Soviets responded with an intense naval bombardment of the city, causing approximately 1,000 civilian deaths. Maoka fell on 22 August. On 25 August, a further 1,600 Soviet troops landed in Otomari, where the Japanese garrison of 3,400 surrendered. Later the same day the remnants of the Japanese 88th Division surrendered to the Soviet Sixteenth Army, with the city of Toyohara being captured without further fighting, thus bringing to an end the successful Russian invasion of Sakhalin. In all over 18,000 Japanese were captured, many being sent to labour camps in Siberia, while some 100,000 Japanese civilians fled the Soviet occupation of the island and returned to Japan.

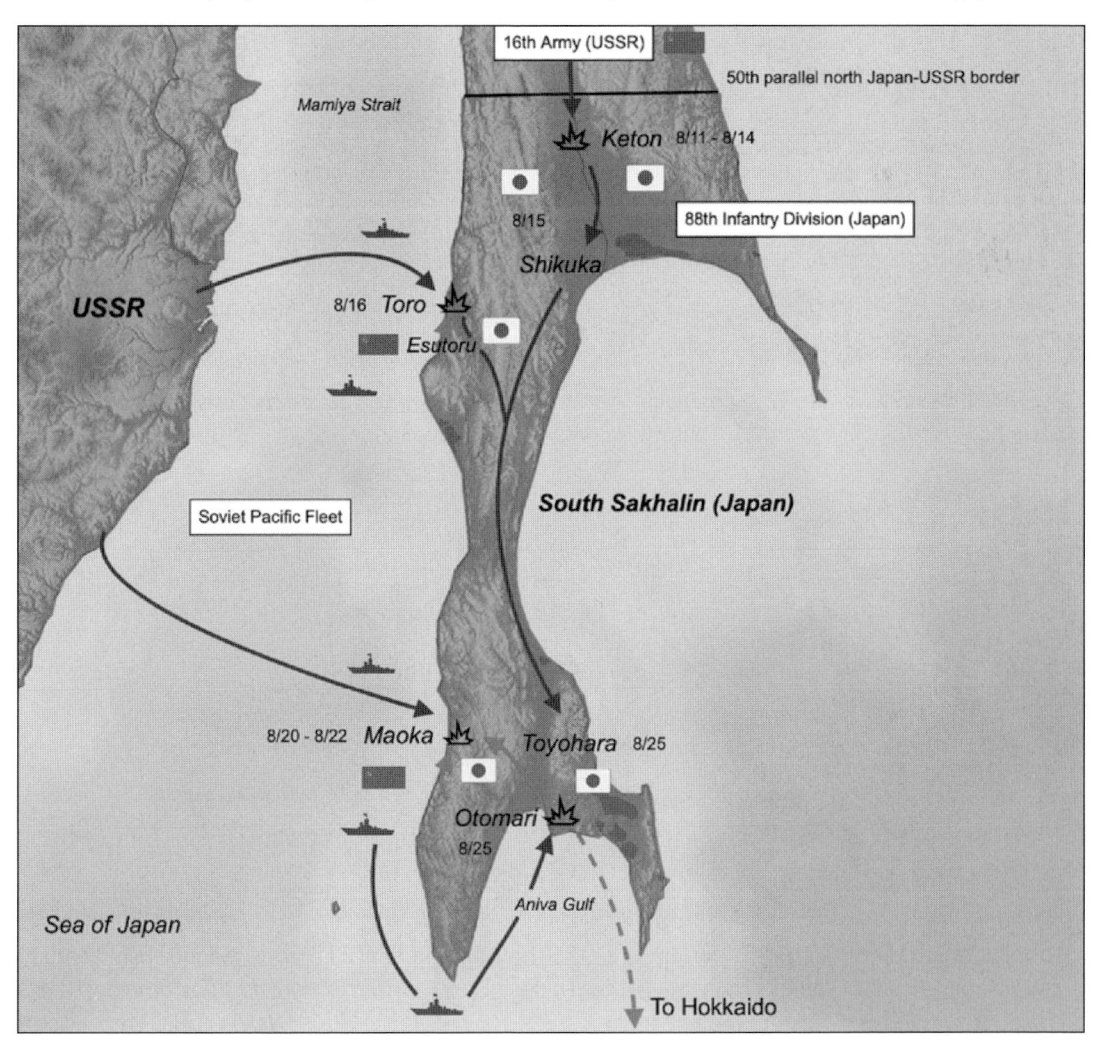

The Great Escape!
The evacuation from Dunkirk let the British Army survive to fight another day, provided a huge psychological boost to a beleaguered nation and cemented Winston Churchill's place in history. Operation Dynamo was organised by Admiral Bertram Ramsey, who went on to provide the naval planning for Operation Neptune.

3 Evacuations

World War II was notable for some huge evacuations of armies and civilians. For the British, probably the most important were Operation Dynamo and the less well-known 'Cycle' and 'Aerial' that together saved sufficient numbers of servicemen to allow Britain to defend itself against the rampant German Army. Without these men—experienced soldiers who needed no basic training—it is doubtful that even Winston Churchill would have been able to stop the British parliament suing for peace.

The British became all too familiar with evacuations in the first years of the war as first France, then Greece, then Crete forced them to save men. The losses of materiel meant that they needed ever more help from American Lend-Lease and Canadian factories.

The Germans didn't need to worry about evacuations until the tide turned in 1942, and then Hitler's regular exhortations to 'fight to the last man' meant that German Sixth Army remained bottled up in Stalingrad; and 250,000 men were captured in Tunisia as the Germans reinforced an untenable position rather than evacuate. In Sicily and then later on the Seine and the Scheldt, German ability to organise well in a crisis saw many men rescued to fight again from seemingly impossible positions.

The Soviets, too, tended to hold positions till the last man, but at Odessa in 1941, sense prevailed and the evacuation took place allowing the garrison to move to Sevastopol—where they were encircled and fought to the last. Out of the frying pan and into the fire indeed!

In the Pacific, the distances meant that evacuation opportunities were limited. The British were unable to save many of the soldiers in Malaya and Singapore; many men from the Commonwealth forces and Americans entered captivity as the Japanese advanced so quickly. For the US Army, the capture by the Japanese of the Philippines in 1941 saw 100,000 US and Filipino soldiers enter captivity. But again, when the tide turned, the Japanese proved more likely to accept the idea of fighting to the last man—and then committing suicide rather than enter captivity. There are a few instances where they evacuated their soldiers—such as Kiska and Guadalcanal—but the attrition of the merchant marine by submarine and air attack reduced their ability to move troops.

Perhaps the most remarkable evacuation of the war was that of the Germans soldiers and civilians from the Baltic states and Pomerania, Operation *Hannibal*, that saw 2.5 million escape west in spite of the huge losses to Russian submarines.

Operation Alphabet (UK/FR) 4-8 June 1940 Norway

Operation Alphabet was the Royal Navy's evacuation of some 25,500 British, French and Polish troops from the Narvik area of Norway over the course of four days in June 1940. Despite defeat of the *Kriegsmarine* and the final success of the Allied effort in taking Narvik on 28 May, the German victories in France and the Low Countries swiftly and drastically changed the situation so that the Allied evacuation of Norway then became paramount. Thus by 2 June the aircraft carriers HMSs *Ark Royal* and *Glorious* arrived off the coast of Norway along with 15 troop transports to join the fleet that had already established dominance.

Over each of the next five nights some 5,000 men were embarked upon the ships by a flotilla of varied small craft from many different points in the Norwegian fjords, under the protection of the carrier aircraft. The first convoy of half a dozen transports then departed on 4 June, protected only by the cruiser HMS *Vindictive*, reaching Scapa Flow on 8 June without mishap. On 7 June the second troop transport convoy consisting of seven ships set off, escorted by two light cruisers, seven destroyers and 10 armed trawlers and they too reached the Clyde without loss, confirming 'Alphabet's success. The only compensation for the Germans, who had missed their opportunity to attack the transports, was the sinking of the *Glorious* and her escorting destroyers HMSs *Acasta* and *Ardent* by the battleships *Scharnhorst* and *Gneisenau*. However, in the two main Narvik sea battles with the Royal Navy the *Kriegsmarine* had lost 10 destroyers and for the rest of the war they suffered from a shortage of escorts for their capital ships.

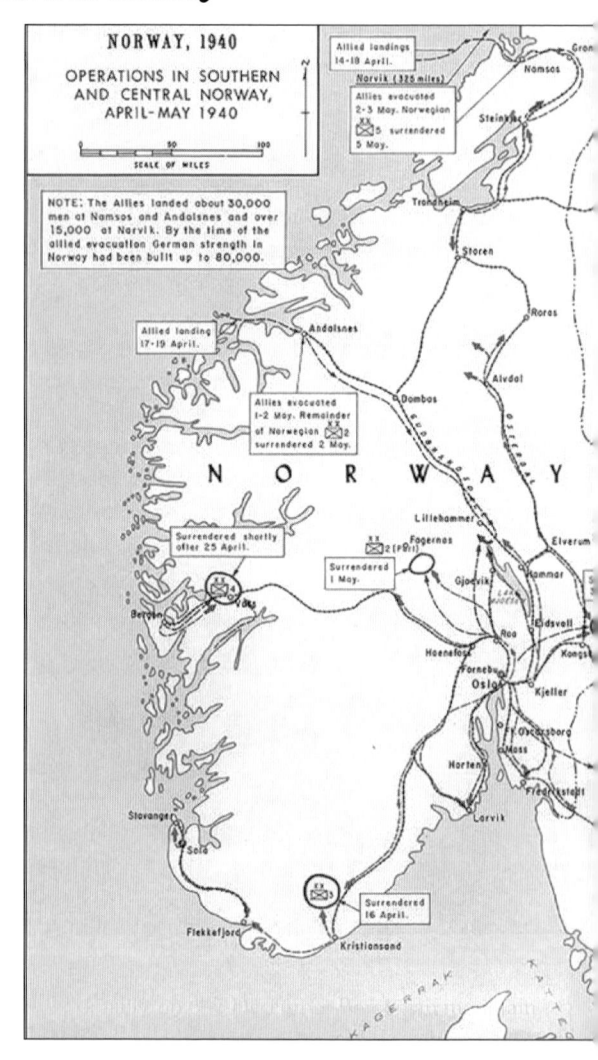

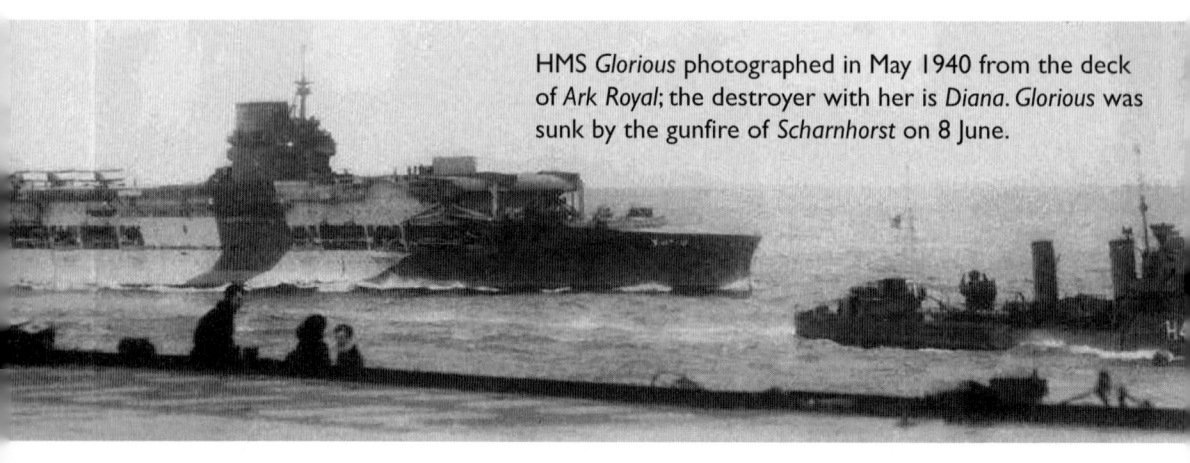

HMS *Glorious* photographed in May 1940 from the deck of *Ark Royal*; the destroyer with her is *Diana*. *Glorious* was sunk by the gunfire of *Scharnhorst* on 8 June.

Operation Dynamo (UK/FRA) 26 May–4 June 1940 Evacuation of Dunkirk, France

The successful evacuation carried out by the Royal Navy of primarily British but also French and Belgian troops from the beaches and harbour of Dunkirk was a critical factor in the survival of Britain in 1940.

Such a worst case scenario had been considered by the British for some time, given the increasingly catastrophic situation that was swiftly developing for the Allied defence of the Low Countries. The Admiralty put out a nationwide appeal and began collecting together an extraordinary flotilla of civilian small boats that would pay a critical part in the rescue of the troops.

Masterminded by Vice Admiral Dover, Bertram Ramsey, once Operation Dynamo was put into action its commander, Capt William Tennant, was on the ground making decisions that were critical for the mission's success. With much of the port infrastructure of Dunkirk destroyed by German air attack, the primary route of evacuation he chose was the eastern breakwater of the harbour entrance. 1,400 yards long and surmounted by a wooden boardwalk, it was wide enough for a column of troops four abreast to traverse and some 200,000 men were able to use it to board the rescue ships.

The remaining Allied forces had to be taken directly off the beaches of Dunkirk, making the evacuation slower and more difficult. This is where the small civilian boats were so useful. In the end about 198,000 British troops were taken away, as well as 140,000 Allied troops, mainly French, though almost all heavy equipment was left behind.

The success of Dynamo depended upon the air cover provided by RAF, the incredible effort of the RN and its civilian flotilla and the calm and discipline displayed by the troops on the ground. However, German actions also helped. Hitler was over-cautious, hardly believing the success enjoyed by his Panzers; additionally, there was some anxiety after the British tank counterattack at Arras and the Luftwaffe failed in its promise to prevent the evacuation.

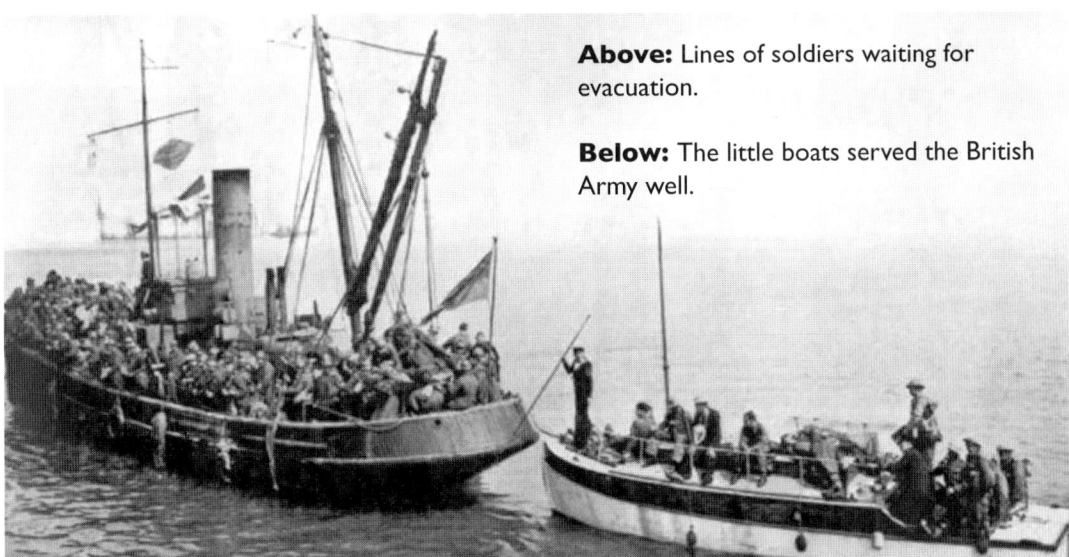

Above: Lines of soldiers waiting for evacuation.

Below: The little boats served the British Army well.

Operations Cycle and Aerial (UK) June 1940 Evacuation from Le Havre and west coast of France

Most people think that Dunkirk was the final evacuation of Allied troops to Britain from the continent following the fall of France, in fact a further 200,000+ troops were rescued by the Royal Navy from almost a dozen ports after the completion of Operation Dynamo, although not all these attempts enjoyed the same level of success.

On 5 June the Germans had launched *Fall Rot* (Case Red), their offensive to complete the defeat of France and destroy any Allied forces still at large in the country. Breaching the line on the Somme forced the British 1st Armoured and the 51st (Highland) Infantry Divisions, fighting alongside French units, to fall back towards the coast.

In response, the British Operation Cycle from 10 to 13 June was an attempt to evacuate the troops from Le Havre in Upper Normandy. Almost a dozen destroyers and a fleet of transports were sent to the port, where 11,000 men were evacuated, with one troopship (the *Bruges*) sunk by German bombing.

The rest of the Allied forces were then cut off from the port by German ground troops. It was hoped that the bulk could be evacuated from St Valery-en-Caux, but the Panzers were too quick. Another 3,000 were rescued from Veules-les-Roses but in the end the rest of the Allied troops, including 6,000 men from the Highland Division, were forced to surrender.

Next came Operation Aerial, an audacious plan by the Royal Navy to work its way down the coast supported by a fleet of merchant navy ships, picking up both Allied soldiers and British civilians from various ports ahead of the oncoming German advance. It was a resounding success and another 180,000+ people were picked up from Cherbourg, St Malo, Brest, St Nazaire, La Pallice and other Atlantic and Mediterranean ports between 14 and 25 June. Combined with 'Dynamo', Operations Aerial and Cycle enabled over half a million Allied soldiers to be successfully evacuated from the continent between late May and late June.

Below: Operation Dynamo wasn't the only evacuation of British and French soldiers in this period: between 15 and 25 June, 191,870 British, Polish and Czech troops were evacuated from the French ports shown below as part of Operations Cycle and Aerial.

1. Dunkirk
2. St Valery-en-Caux/Veules-les-Roses
3. Le Havre
4. Cherbourg
5. St. Malo
6. Brest
7. St. Nazaire. It was off this port that SS *Lancastria* was bombed and sunk with the loss of at least 4,000 lives (some estimate 7,000) although there were 2,477 survivors.
8. Nantes
9. La Pallice
10. Le Verdon
11. Bordeaux
12. Bayonne
13. St. Jean-de-Luz

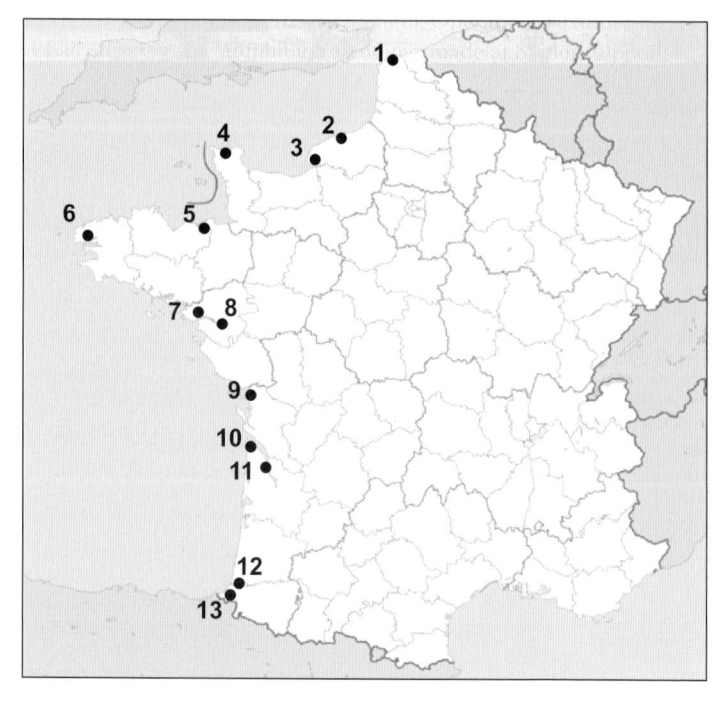

Operation Demon (Allies)
24 April–1 May 1941 Evacuation of Greece

Operation Demon saw over 50,000 troops of the British Expeditionary Force to Greece evacuated from the mainland by a flotilla of 30 warships from the Royal and the Australian navies (including six cruisers, twenty destroyers and four escort ships) along with nine troopships, including three of Dutch origin, all of which were all sunk.

The Germans enjoyed air and ground superiority throughout the Greek campaign, with the Luftwaffe scoring some impressive successes against Allied shipping. On 7 April an attack on the Athens port of Piraeus blew up a British ammunition carrier, the *Clan Fraser*, whose destruction took another 13 ships with her as well as entirely destroying the harbour facilities. This forced the British to depend thereafter on various much smaller harbours, such as Rafina and Porto Raffi east of Piraeus, Megra west of Athens and Nauplia (Nafplio), Monemvasia and Kalamata in the Peloponnese—and to restrict movements as much as possible to the hours of darkness.

Despite these conditions and the loss of ships Operation Demon succeeded in evacuating over 50,000 troops, although they were forced to leave behind all their heavy equipment and weapons. The Dutch troopship SS *Slamat* was lost on 27 April off the coast of the Peloponnese, along with its two escort RN destroyers (HMSs *Diamond* and *Wryneck*) due to intense attacks by Luftwaffe Junkers Ju87 dive bombers, killing almost 1,000 men. Many other RN and RAN ships were also badly damaged and more troopships sunk.

Most of the troops were taken to Crete, but others went to Egypt.

Above: Out of the frying pan into the fire—most of the evacuees were taken from Greece to Crete.

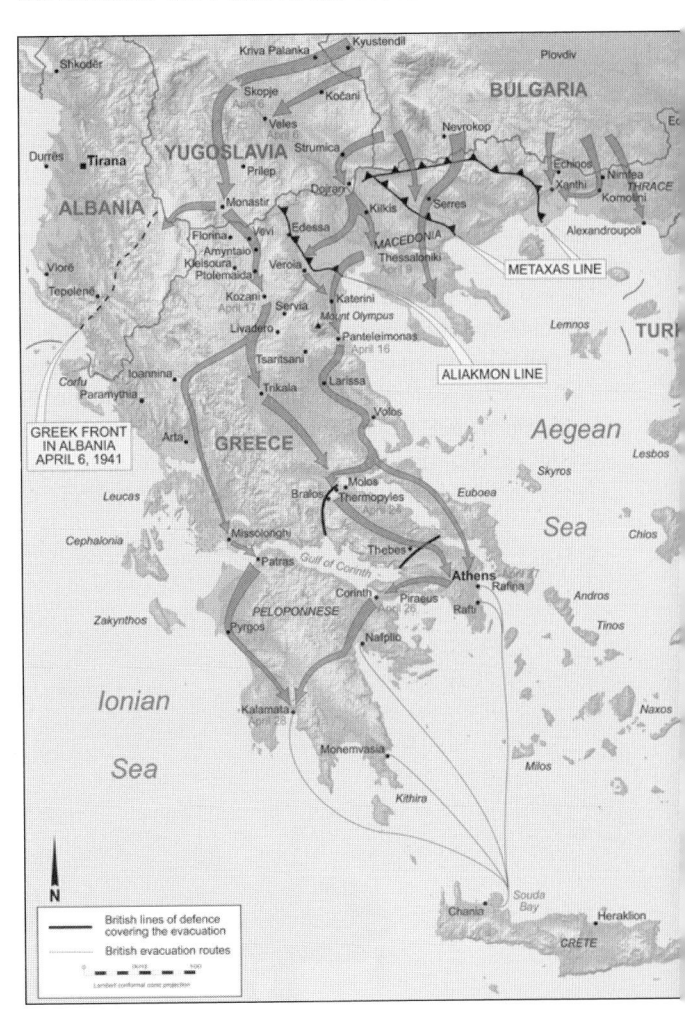

TRANSPORTATION OF THE ARMY TO GREECE

(From supplement to the *London Gazette*, 19 May 1948 https://www.ibiblio.org/hyperwar/UN/UK/LondonGazette/38293.pdf)

'Submitted to the Lords Commissioners of the Admiralty on the 11 December 1941, by Admiral Sir Andrew B. Cunningham, G.C.B., D.S.O., C-i-C, Mediterranean Station.

'OPERATION "LUSTRE".
The operation moved to Greece some 58,000 troops with their mechanical transport, full equipment and stores between 4 March and 24 April when the evacuation started.

'The passage from Egyptian ports to Piraeus, virtually the only port of the country, led past the enemy bases in the Dodecanese from which his air and sea forces were in a good position to operate against our lines of communication. Cover had also to be provided against interference from enemy surface forces from Italy. In consequence it was desirable to move as many personnel as possible in warships whose high speed would take them quickly through the danger zone. ...

'This policy proved successful and during the whole period of this complicated operation no men or equipment were lost at sea except for a few casualties from bomb splinters in one merchant ship. The losses sustained were either in ships proceeding in the convoys but not connected with "Lustre" or in ships returning empty (see list at right).

'During the greater part of the move a proportion of the Battle Fleet was kept at sea to the westward of Crete to provide heavy cover for our forces. In addition, Operation M.C.9, running a Malta convoy, was carried out between 19th and 24th March whilst "Lustre" still proceeded.

'CASUALTIES TO SHIPPING DURING "LUSTRE".
21 March: Danish oiler MARIE MAERSK, in Convoy A.N.21, hit and set on fire. Crew taken off by H.M.A.S. WATERHEN who towed the ship to Suda Bay.
22 March: Convoy A.S.21 attacked by HE.111s S.E. of Gavdo. Greek NICHOLAS EMBIRICOS and SOLHEIM both badly damaged; former sank later and SOLHEIM abandoned.
31 March: H.M.S. BONAVENTURE, escorting Convoy G.A.8, was hit amidships by two torpedoes at 0830 and sank almost immediately.
2nd April: Convoy A.S.23 attacked by six JU.88 D/B [dive bombers]. KOULANDIS XENOS and HOMEFIELD hit and abandoned. S.S. TETI, who had apparently been near missed, reported that she was leaking badly and proceeded to an anchorage near Lissmoss.
2nd April: Convoy A.N.F.24 attacked by H.L.B. [high level bombers]. S.S. DEVIS hit in No 6 hold and fire started, 7 men being killed and 14 injured.
3rd April: Convoy A.N.F.24 attacked by D/B. NORTHERN PRINCE (carrying important stores for Greece from U.K.) was hit and set on fire—later blew up and sank.
17 April: Convoy A.N.27 attacked by H.L.B . and T/B [torpedo bombers]. Oiler BRITISH SCIENCE torpedoed and speed reduced to 6 knots. Proceeded for Suda Bay. Torpedoed again at 1530/18 and caught fire. Ship abandoned and later sank.
21 April: Convoy A.S.26 attacked by D/B. BRITISH LORD hit and later, taken in tow by AUCKLAND.'

EVACUATION OF THE ARMY FROM GREECE

'Submitted 7 July 1941, by Admiral Sir Andrew B. Cunningham, G.C.B., D.S.O., Commander-in-Chief, Mediterranean Station.

'OPERATION "DEMON".
The attached reports on the evacuation of Imperial troops from Greece between 24 and 29 April.

'The operations were conducted by the Vice Admiral, Light Forces [Vice Adm H.D. Pridham-Wippell, C.B., C.V.O.], who met the needs of a confused and constantly changing military situation in a masterly manner. In this he was substantially assisted by the untiring efforts of Rear Admiral H.T. Baillie-Grohman, C.B., D.S.O., O.B.E., who was in charge of arrangements ashore in Greece.

'The conduct of the naval forces involved including the special landing craft was, with few exceptions, beyond praise. Officers and men went for many days almost without rest under conditions of great discomfort with their ships crowded with troops under constant air attack. They were materially helped in their task by the admirable discipline and spirit among the troops they embarked.

'A notable feature of the operation was the gallant and enterprising performance of the merchant seamen in the troopships who had to take their ships into unlighted and difficult anchorages, in many cases without adequate charts. A high proportion of Dutch ships were included and were particularly noticeable for their efficient and seamanlike performance.

'It was most fortunate that the Glen ships [merchant ships converted to "Infantry Assault Ships", subsequently known as "Landing Ships, Infantry", for use in Combined Operations] with their landing craft were present in the Mediterranean. These ships, although playing their role in the reverse of that for which they were intended, proved invaluable and made it possible to embark more troops than would otherwise have been the case.

'The operation was a most anxious one; performed with no cover from enemy surface interference. The need for destroyers for the evacuation precluded the provision of screens to enable the sorely needed battleship cover. Had our enemy shown more enterprise the results might have been very different.

'**Report of Office of Flag Officer Attached Middle East, General Headquarters, Middle East. [Rear Admiral H.T. Baillie-Grohman]**
'The numbers of the beach parties allocated to the operation proved to be sufficient and their composition well balanced. The information brought in by beach reconnaissance parties, together with that supplied by Capt. Razikostikas, Hydrographer of the Greek Navy, proved, in the event, to be accurate arid was invaluable

to the conduct of the evacuation. This officer was most helpful and obliging, and the Greek Admiralty at all times most helpful.

'The operation was to a great extent rendered possible by the employment of considerable numbers of our own landing craft. Of the total approximate number of 47,000 embarked, only 14,000 were taken from recognised wharves or piers, the rest being taken from open beaches in landing craft and ships' boats. The max loads which it was found practicable to lift in the various types of landing craft were: L.C.T. 900; L.C.A. 60–70; L.C.M. 150.

'**Thursday, 17 April:** Combined naval and military parties reconnoitred all suitable beaches and landing places in Euboea, the Gulf of Corinth, the south and east coast between Khalkis and the Corinth Canal, and the south and east coasts of the Morea between the Corinth Canal and Kalamata.

'**Friday, 18 April:** Owing to the exploding of an ammunition ship in the harbour a few nights previously, after an air raid, twelve merchant ships in Piraeus harbour were lost and great damage was done to the facilities, tugs and small craft were destroyed; the telephone system was out of action and only five berths of twelve were available. In addition there were some twenty or more merchant ships, mostly Greek, gathered round Phaleron Bay, Salamis Bay, Piraeus and off Eleusis, who could not obtain water or coal. Some ten of these would have to sail not later than Saturday night, 19 April, otherwise they would run short of fuel.

'Two considerations pointed to an early withdrawal: the enemy's superiority in the air; and the fact that if our forces remained in Greece we would undoubtedly be confronted, at an early date, with the problem of feeding two million people.

'**Sunday, 20 April:** Most of the beach reconnaissance parties returned and an outline plan was drawn up in collaboration with the Army and R.A.F. The plan was of necessity only rough, as it was impossible at this time, to arrive at reliable figures, or predict the sequence of events.

'**Monday, 21 April:** [Because of the surrender of the Greek Army in the Epirus] General Wilson decided that evacuation must begin at the earliest possible moment ...

'**Tuesday, 22 April:** ... likely to be the night of 24/25 April.

A fresh outline programme was then made out and signalled ... [it] was subsequently altered due to the unexpectedly rapid advance of the German forces, to embark the rearguard from the Megara area, and that it would be necessary to withdraw these troops across the Corinth Canal and embark them from positions in the Morea. ... this plan had again to be altered owing to the attack on the Corinth Canal by German parachute troops at daylight on Saturday, 26th April.

'On 21st and 22nd April there were heavy massed air attacks on shipping and 23 vessels including two hospital ships and the Greek destroyer HYDRA were reported sunk in local waters on these two days. This did not promise well for the evacuation. After consultation with Air Vice Marshal d'Albiac, and considering both the naval and air aspects, I decided that the best time for transports to arrive at the beaches was one hour after dark, and to leave at 0300. This would prevent enemy reconnaissance aircraft from spotting the exact beaches being used, and so bombing them by the light of flares, while the transports should still be able to find the beaches. The early return from the beaches would give some chance of the ships clearing the coast without being spotted, and would give them more time to reach the area within support of the fighters from Crete by daylight or as soon as possible afterwards. There would be no such support from Greece whatsoever from 24th April onwards. I decided to accept the disadvantage of reducing the time the ships were at the beaches in order to give this possible extra security, and as events turned out it appears this was justified. The only transport to leave really late, the SLAMAT, was bombed and sunk and was the only ship to become a total loss after loading. Moreover, no beaches were bombed during embarkation.

'**Wednesday, 23 April:** L.C.T. arrived at their beaches as follows: L.C.T.1 and 19 at Megara, L.C.T.6 at Nauplion, and L.C.T.5 at Lavrion. All except L.C.T.6 were lost in this operation.

Evacuation of the British colony, and certain numbers of troops, was proceeding irregularly in Greek steamers, sailing after dark, mostly for Crete. It was usually with the utmost difficulty that these ships could be found, fuelled and watered The majority of them were very slow, and nearly all unescorted.

'**Thursday, 24 April. D1 Day:** Embarkation from the area east of Athens and Nauplia on the night 24th/25th was satisfactory, 10,200 personnel being embarked. Unfortunately, at Nauplia, ULSTER PRINCE grounded across the fairway, thus denying the use of the wharves to destroyers on succeeding nights. ULSTER PRINCE'S quota of troops taken off by PHOEBE. This embarkation was greatly assisted by ten caiques under the command of Lieut. Commander Carr, R.N.R., and again on the night 26th/27th.

'H.M. King George and some members of the Greek Government left Athens for Crete in a flying boat. This was not announced until some days later.

'A large Greek yacht, the HELLAS, arrived unexpectedly in Piraeus harbour, reporting that she could steam 18 knots and take 1,000 passengers. She was instructed to sail after dark, loading to take place as late as possible. About 500 of the British community (mostly Maltese and Cypriots) decided to leave in this ship and walking cases from an Australian hospital were sent on board. About 1900 the HELLAS was dive bombed in the harbour and hit by two bombs, which set fire to the ship and jetty alongside. Colonel Renton, who was on board at the time, considers that four to five hundred people must have lost their lives and he believes the only gangway to the shore was destroyed. There were no hoses working on board at all and none from the jetty until nearly an hour afterwards.

'**Friday, 25 April. D2 Day:** At 1930 the Joint Planning Staff and I left Athens bound for the new H.Q. with General Wilson at Myli, in the Morea. This change in H.Q. was made at the last possible moment to maintain the advantage of good W/T communications at Athens as long as possible. ... During this day, ULSTER

PRINCE, on shore at Nauplia, was heavily bombed and became a total loss.

'On this night (25th/26th April), 5,700 troops were embarked from the Megara area (P beach) in spite of the losses of the transport S.S. PENNLAND on the way north, and of one of the two L.C.T. which had arrived in this area. Seven caiques under the command of Commander Michell assisted. It is believed that about 500, many of them wounded, were left on shore after waiting four days near the beach. This was due to the facts that they were to be embarked last, and that the L.C.T. fouled her propeller with a wire on her last trip (the other engine already being out of action). It is not yet known whether the wounded were taken off from another beach, and to what extent the caiques were able to assist.

'Saturday, 26 April. D3 Day: At 0530 we arrived at the new H.Q. near Myli. These were established in an olive grove in order to obtain cover from enemy dive bombers. This was very necessary, as for some days the enemy had had complete air superiority, and I believe I am correct in saying that after 23rd April not one British plane left the ground in Greece (mainland) in support of our troops or ships. This is of course in no way whatever intended as a criticism of the R.A.F., whose pilots, hopelessly outnumbered fought most gallantly to the end, but it is intended to emphasise our complete inferiority in the air at this time. ...

'At 0900 news was received that the Corinth Canal, together with the road and rail bridge, had been attacked and was probably held by German parachute troops, following on an intense aerial bombardment. This necessitated a further alteration of plan, as it was then evident that the only place from which the rearguard could be withdrawn with reasonable safety was from the embarkation points in the area to the east of Athens. A fresh plan was made and signalled, and this was adhered to for the remainder of the evacuation.

'At sunset we abandoned our H.Q. and the whole party proceeded to Myli pier. On arrival at the pier it was found that the flying boat had arrived, but there was no sign of the destroyer.

The more important passengers were embarked in the flying-boat.

'General Wilson suggested that I should leave with him that night, but I decided to remain until the N.Z. Brigade under General Freyberg had been evacuated, and to proceed to their beaches at Monemvasia myself, taking with me my signal staff, W/T set, beachmasters, etc.

'It appeared to me at the time that if the L.C.T. failed to arrive, this might be a difficult operation and lengthy, and I preferred to be on the spot myself.

'The enemy air superiority made it necessary for us to get to Monemvasia, 56 miles distant, before daylight. As an alternative method of proceeding, in the event of a destroyer not being available, the Crown Prince of Greece's motor yacht had been placed at my disposal, with Lieut. Harrison, R.N.R. in command, but this yacht had been bombed and put out of action during the course of the afternoon. The only other alternative was a caique chartered by Colonel Smith-Dorrien, and, in the absence of the destroyer, we proceeded to board her—later the destroyer HAVOCK arrived and took us off the caique, and enabled us to reach Monemvasia before daylight.

'Sunday, 27 April. Near Monemvasia: Off Monemvasia we unexpectedly came up with ten L.C.A. belonging to GLENEARN who had been bombed on Saturday. We landed in these and lay in a small bay four miles north of Monemvasia, scattering the L.C.A. amongst the beaches about half a mile apart. It was most fortunate that these were not spotted by enemy aircraft which were constantly overhead for the next two days.

'Heavy bombing was heard to the northward during the morning, which later proved to have been the attack on the Dutch transport SLAMAT which resulted in her loss, together with that of the destroyers DIAMOND and WRYNECK.

'In the forenoon, Commander James, the Principal Beachmaster at Monemvasia, and other officers, reconnoitred the beaches in preparation for the coming night's embarkation. ... Brigadier Galloway, also got into touch with General Freyberg and found the retirement on Monemvasia was going according to plan. After dark I sent three L.C.A. further north to increase their dispersion.

'Communication from Monemvasia was not perfect throughout, as even after all the spares carried with the W/T set had been used, one of the remaining transmitting valves was found to be soft and lost its emission as soon as it heated up. Despite this handicap, all messages vital to the operation were cleared and similar messages from V.A.L.F. and Suda were received.

'Embarkations.

On the night 26th/27th April, a total of approximately 18,000 troops were evacuated, and all areas were used except the Megara area. Owing to a heavy ground swell off Raphena (C beach) difficulty was experienced in transferring troops from landing craft alongside the GLENGYLE. The Commanding Officer therefore issued instructions that the last landing craft were to be clear of the beach by 0215, in order that craft could be hoisted in time for GLENGYLE to sail at 0300. About 700 men were left ashore and were brought off the next night.

'The numbers embarked from Nauplia were greatly reduced owing to the stranding of ULSTER PRINCE preventing the use of wharves by destroyers, and also to the non-arrival of GLENEARN landing craft, due to the ship having been disabled by bombing attack on 26th April. The numbers actually embarked from this area (Beaches S and T) were approximately 5,500 instead of the 8,000 planned.

'On the night 27th/28th April, approximately 4,700 embarked from the area to the east of Athens. This party included the rearguard formed, by the 4th N.Z. Brigade, whom ... had been intended in the first instance to embark from Megara, and subsequently from the Peloponnese. The latter project had to be abandoned when the Corinth Canal was seized by the enemy.

'Monday, 28 April: Reconnaissance aircraft were over the beach on which we were established early, followed by dive bombers who made a series of heavy attacks on some craft about three-quarters of a mile distant immediately the other side of the hill behind our beach and invisible to us. It subsequently turned out that the object of their attack was L.C.T. 5 from Nauplia, which had left that beach on Sunday morning, laid up for the day and proceeded to Monemvasia on Sunday night, arriving at daylight Monday, with 600 Australians on board. The Australians had been landed at Monemvasia at dawn and took cover with the N.Z. Division, but the L.C.T. was seen, and bombed shortly afterwards. The L.C.T., though she replied vigorously at first, was soon on fire, and there was a constant series of ammunition explosions from her during the day. … There were no casualties.

The above incident left the L.C.A. as practically the only means for embarking the N.Z. Division this night, and it was most fortunate they were not seen and bombed, also that the C.O. GLENEARN had the foresight to send them to Monemvasia, as they could not have made Nauplia in time, after this ship had been bombed.

'After dark, I proceeded with all L.C.A. to the embarkation point at Monemvasia, where I met General Freyberg in his H.Q. near the beach at 2130. … At 2230 no ships had arrived, so I despatched Lieut.-Cdr. Robertson in a L.C.A. to endeavour to get in touch beyond Monemvasia Island which hid the beaches from seaward. He soon contacted the destroyers, which were actually on their way in, and I proceeded on board GRIFFIN and led her close to the North Jetty, leaving Lieut.-Cdr. Robertson in the ISIS to go to the South Jetty.

'The embarkation which took place mainly from the causeway connecting the Island to the mainland, began at 2350 and was completed by 0300/29, 3,800 men being embarked. General Freyberg and I saw the beaches cleared and went on board AJAX at 0300/29. Two caiques were employed on this night under the command of Lieut. Cumberlege, R.N.R., and Lieut.-Cdr. Hook, R.N. (Retd.) and did excellent work.

'The whole embarkation was remarkably well carried out from five different points. The Army organisation in rear of the beaches and the discipline of the troops were magnificent; especially considering that they had been fighting a rearguard action for some weeks, from Salonika almost to Cape Matapan. AJAX and destroyers all closed well in to the jetties, and the organisation for embarking the troops in the ships was excellent. The fact that we had at this time collected extra signalmen and so had good communication with the ships, much accelerated the whole operation. The young officers in the L.C.A. handled their craft very well.

'I had arranged with the Commanding Officers of AJAX and GRIFFIN to place charges in the L.C.A. so as to destroy them before departure. The charges were placed in each craft, and the C.O. AJAX gave the order for their destruction. However, at this time, fires on shore caused by burning M.T. lit up the ships in the bay, and the C.O. AJAX decided he could not wait to complete the destruction. The lights on shore had been bright for some time, and with the danger of submarines I considered he was correct to leave at once. One submarine had been depth charged on the way to the beaches. One or two L.C.A. were destroyed by the destroyer HOTSPUR, but four or five were left afloat.

During the same night it had been intended to embark approximately 8,000 personnel from Kalamata. This operation was, however, frustrated, as on the arrival of the ships off the entrance to the harbour, it was reported that [it] was in the possession of the enemy, and … had been mined. Some of our troops were collected in an area to the south-east of the harbour, but in view of the close proximity of the enemy and the absence of landing craft (which had not been provided as it had been intended to use the wharves in the harbour) it was not possible to embark more than a very few of these troops. Ships withdrew at about 0230/29, leaving a total of approximately 4,000 British and 2,000 Palestinian and Cypriot troops, together with 1,500 Jugoslav refugees, on shore. [In fact the British had driven the Germans out of the town but had no signalmen or equipment to let the ships know.]

'**Tuesday, 29 April:** I arrived at Suda Bay in AJAX at 0800 and reported with General Freyberg to General Sir Maitland Wilson at his H.Q. This night destroyers were sent to Kalamata with the object of bringing off any troops that could be embarked from the beaches in the vicinity, but this only resulted in about 120 officers and men being recovered.

'**Wednesday, 30th April:** At 0430 I left for Alexandria in a flying boat. On this night, destroyers were again sent to the Kalamata area, approximately 136 officers and men being recovered. Two destroyers were also sent to Milos, and succeeded in evacuating 650 troops, of whom, approximately 400 were Palestinians.'

ADDENDUM TO VICE ADMIRAL, LIGHT FORCES' REPORT DATED 5TH MAY, 1941.

Night	Kalamata	Monemvasia	Tolon and Nauplia	Raphina and Raphtis	Megara	Kithera	Milo
24th/25th			6,685	5,700			
25th/26th					5,900		
26th/27th	8,650		4,527	8,223			
27th/28th				4,640			
28th/29th	332	4,320				760	
29th/30th	33						
30th/1st	202						700
Totals	9,217	4,320	11,212	18,563	5,900	760	700

Total embarked 50,672
Lost in SLAMAT 500
Nett Total 50,172

Evacuation of Crete (UK) 28 May–1 June 1941

The Battle of Crete was fought from 20 May to 1 June 1941. It saw the first large-scale use of German paratroops, although their high casualty rate (4,000 dead, 2,640 wounded and 370 aircraft destroyed) meant they were never used for a mass airdrop attack again, but as infantry instead.

For the Allies, despite having access to decoded Enigma transcriptions and inflicting heavy casualties on the Germans, the defence of Crete was a disaster. On the island itself 4,000 men were killed, 1,900 wounded and 17,000 captured, while at sea the Royal Navy suffered the costliest naval campaign of the entire war, with nine warships sunk and eighteen damaged.

Once the Germans managed to hold onto the airfield at Maleme the airbridge then created enabled them to land more and more troops with which to maintain the momentum of their attack.

When the tide of the battle had turned the Allies were faced with the evacuation of their forces by sea to Egypt. This began with 6,000 troops embarked at Sfakia on the night of 28/29 May. They suffered many casualties from intense Luftwaffe attacks on the journey. 4,000 men were also withdrawn from Heraklion on the same night. The following night (30/31) 1,500 soldiers were evacuated by four destroyers and night after (31 May/1 June) another 4,000 men were embarked. In total almost 18,600 men of the 32,000 British, Australian and New Zealand troops on the island were saved. Most of the remaining troops were forced to surrender, along with thousands of Greek soldiers still on the island when it came under full German control on 1 June. A few hundred British and Dominion troops remained, who fought on with the Cretan partisans and continued to harass the Germans from the mountains.

Australian and New Zealand nurses in Crete. They had been evacuated there after Greece fell and were subsequently evacuated from Crete too.

Evacuation of Odessa (SOV) 14–15 October 1941

Odessa in Ukraine was attacked very soon after the Axis powers invaded the Soviet Union. However, it didn't fall as quickly as other locations and—with the Russian Black Sea fleet resupplying them from the sea—the first two attacks by the Romanian Fourth Army petered out. By early October the position had got worse as the Romanians and part of the German Eleventh Army attacked. Pushed back, with casualties mounting, the Stavka decided to pull out of the city and use its troops elsewhere. Accordingly the Black Sea Fleet evacuated 121,000 troops and civilians, 1,000 trucks and 20,000 tons of ammunition to Sevastopol, where soon they would be besieged again.

The total number of people evacuated varies greatly among the sources. On top of the garrison taken to Sevastopol some put the additional figure as high as 230,000 making 350,000 in total.

By the evening of 15 October the evacuation was complete and the following day Romanian troops entered the city. It would not be liberated until the Third Ukrainian Front recaptured the city on 10 April 1944.

Operation *Ke* (Jap) 14 January–7 February 1943 Evacuation of Guadalcanal

In the latter years of World War II, as the Allies leapfrogged from island to island, the Japanese Army was not known for its evacuation of troops but for dogged resistance to the last man and the bitter end. Suicide of large numbers of men, murder of the civilian workforce and the occasional refusnik who fought lone wars into the late 1940s and 1950s were more usual. However, on a few occasions in 1943, evacuation did take place, most notably at Guadalcanal in February 1943 and on Kiska in the Aleutians in July.

At Kiska, Rear Admiral Kimura Masatomi was able to beat the American blockade (the US forces had taken Attu in May 1943 (see p. 98) and evacuate 5,193 men on cruisers *Abukuma* (1,212) and *Kiso* (1,189), and destroyers *Yūgumo* (479 men), *Kazagumo* (478 men), *Usugumo* (478 men), *Asagumo* (476 men), *Akigumo* (463 men) and *Hibiki* (418 men).

On Guadalcanal, the Japanese had taken a pounding. The sizeable 30,000-strong force had been reduced to some 14,000 in battle and through natural causes—starvation and disease. Rather than allow these men to succumb to attrition, the Japanese decided to evacuate them.

The Japanese were nowhere near as good at logistics as the Allies—compounded in later years by the predation on their convoys by Allied submarines, particularly after the US solved the issue of defective torpedoes that so badly affected submarine actions in the first two years of war. The Japanese merchant marine lost 2,000,000 tons of shipping in 1943, and that doubled in 1944; troopships also suffered (as, unfortunately, did ships carrying PoWs or civilian labourers).

Operation *Ke* started on 14 January 1943 when a rearguard of fresh troops—the Yano Battalion—was landed. The Americans expected a major assault to take Henderson Field, instead the Japanese retreated westward on the nights of 1, 4 and 7 February when destroyers took off the troops. They evacuated 10,652 men, of whom 600 died and 3,000 more required extensive hospital care. It was only on 9 February that the Allies realised they were gone.

Operation *Lehrgang* (GER) 11–17 August 1943 Evacuation of Sicily

Operation *Lehrgang* (course) was the evacuation of German forces from the island of Sicily to the Italian mainland carried out over six days, following the Allied invasion of 9 July.

Although Operation Husky had been a overall success, it also shone a spotlight on the imperfections of the Allies, who were not only learning the art of combined-arms amphibious warfare, but also how to share command and cooperate together despite having very different military cultures. There had been no master plan for the operation, so it was unsurprising that the actions of the two Allied armies were not properly co-ordinated. The result of this was that the Axis forces were able to do what they hadn't done in Tunisia: to escape to fight again.

Helped by the terrain, the Germans gave a masterclass in fighting withdrawal and the Italians, brilliantly led by the charismatic General Guzzoni, also acquitted themselves well. Interestingly, both Axis forces conducted their own evacuations separately and mainly from different ports. '*Lehrgang*' was planned and executed by the district commandant of the Messina Straits, Oberst Ernst Baade, and Kapitän Gustav von Liebenstein of the *Kriegsmarine*. The assembled ad hoc fleet used ten ferries, seven barges and over 100 smaller boats and sailed from a dozen separate evacuation points. The week before '*Lehrgang*' was spent evolving and refining the process with the evacuation of some 12,000 men, 4,500 vehicles and 5,000 tons of supplies. By the time the main operation began the straits were protected by two Flak brigades and hundreds of artillery pieces, all of which put up such a rate of fire that Allied pilots found low-level attack impossible and no large Allied warships would approach the straits. What the air raids did achieve was a constant tweaking of the numbers of ships used, their routes and their time of operation.

In the end switching primarily to daytime evacuation, some 40,000 German troops, 5,000 wounded and a high proportion of their heavy equipment and weapons including AFVs, artillery, ammunition and fuel were rescued. The Italians also evacuated over 60,000 men, as well as 250 vehicles and some 40 artillery pieces, their main vessel being the 932-ton train ferry, the *Villa* that could carry 3,000 men at a time. When *Villa* caught fire on 12 August, it was out of commission for 48 hours and motor rafts were used to transport 20,000 men at the rate of 1,000 a trip.

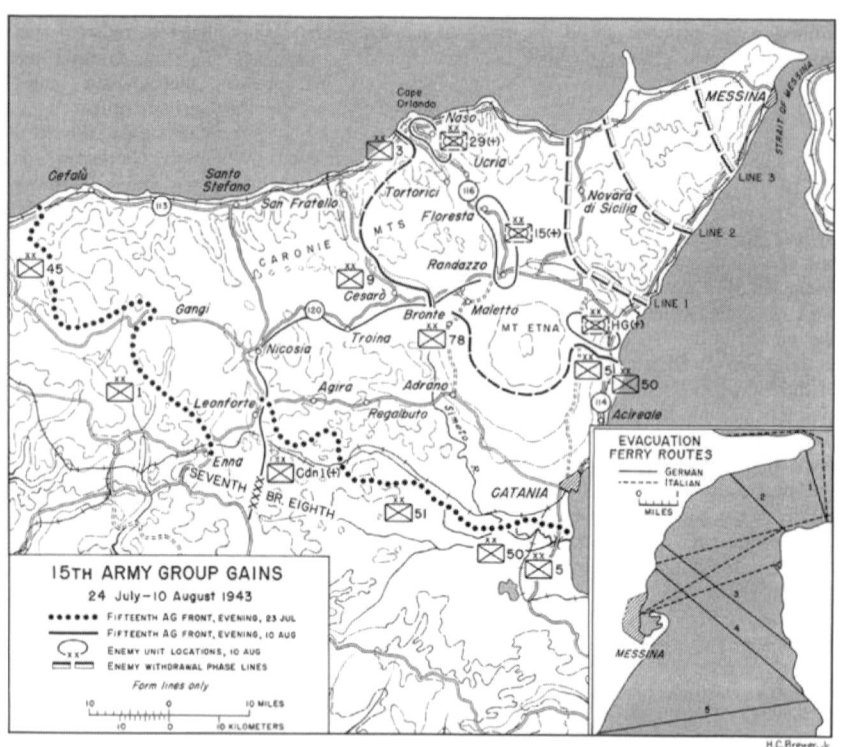

Left: The Germans proved adept at saving lost causes as the tide of war turned against them.

Below: Saving the heavy weapons—especially the 88s—was of prime importance to 'Lehrgang'.

Bottom: The German Siebel ferries could carry heavy loads. They evacuated just about everything from Sicily.

Evacuation of Fifteenth *Armee* over the Westerscheldt (GER) 7-21 September 1944

The loss of the battle of Normandy had forced the German army to retreat back through France. Many of them were trapped around Falaise; for most of the others, the first major obstacle was the River Seine, which the Germans scrambled across effectively. Jean Paul Pallud's estimate of German losses at the Seine were 5–10,000 vehicles and 60 tanks; some 225,000 men and 39,000 motor vehicles made it across.

All this left German Fifteenth *Armee*, stationed around the Pas de Calais in anticipation of an Allied invasion that never came, between a rock and a hard place: the Canadians were advancing up the coastline and the British reached Antwerp on 4 September and now had sufficient forces to block any breakout to the northeast towards Brussels.

Pushed towards the Scheldt estuary, the Germans set up a defensive position—the Breskens Pocket—and organised a mass evacuation of Fifteenth *Armee* over the Scheldt to Walcheren (from Breskens) and South Beveland (from Terneuzen) where they would be able to escape to Germany through the Netherlands. They would also be able to protect the Scheldt from being cleared—Hitler ordered fortresses to be established: Scheldt Süd and Walcheren to prevent the Allies from using the port of Antwerp.

The evacuation started on 7 September, but by the 13th the Canadians were knocking on the door, the Algonquin Regiment having gained a slender foothold across the parallel canals at Moerkerke. The Germans threw everything at the bridgehead and First Canadian Army had nothing more to support the Algonquins: II Canadian Corps was stretched and I British Corps was too far south. The chance evaporated and by 21 September the Germans had ferried across the Scheldt (Pallud 2007 figures) 86,100 men, 616 artillery pieces, 6,200 vehicles and 6,200 horses and 6,500 bicycles.

They had done so in spite of Allied air superiority with only a small number of vessels. Men of Fifteenth *Armee* would prove a thorn in the Allies' side immediately, their presence on the road between Eindhoven and Nijmegen being crucial.

Below: With Walcheren and South Beveland in German hands, Fifteenth *Armee* was transported from the Terneuzen in the Breskens Pocket. Over 86,000 men survived to fight the Allies during the last months of the war and made a major contribution to the attacks on the flanks of Operation Market Garden and cutting the road link between Eindhoven and Nijmegen on a number of occasions.

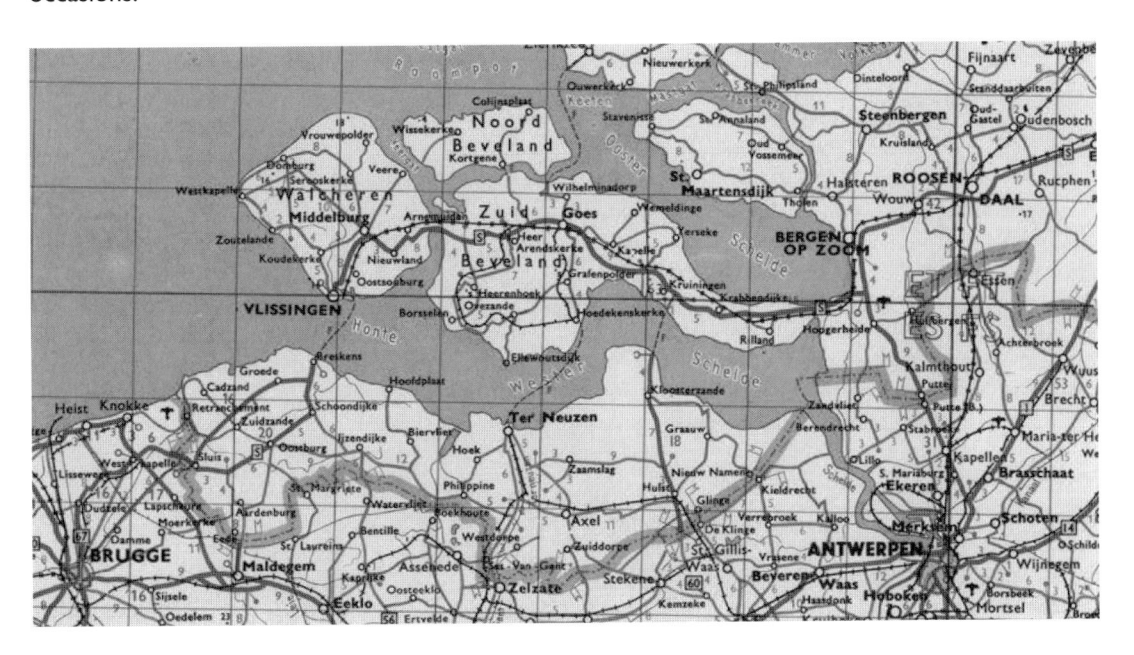

Operation Hannibal (GER) 13 January–8 May 1945 Evacuation of Königsberg/Baltic States

After the collapse of the Eastern Front following the start of the Soviet East Prussian and Vistula offensives in early January 1945, the Nazis launched what would turn out to be the largest evacuation by sea in history under the codename Operation Hannibal, lasting from mid-January 1945 until the end of the war in early May. As the Soviets swept into Germany they bypassed many pockets of determined resistance. By March they had reached the Oder and the Baltic coast, cutting off hundreds of thousands of German soldiers and civilians in East Prussia, the Courland Peninsula and around Danzig.

Wanting to rescue these fighters, Admiral Dönitz ordered Rear Admiral Konrad Engelhardt, head of the *Kriegsmarine*'s Transport Service, to begin the *Rettungsaktion* (evacuation operation) to ferry primarily troops but also civilian refugees to the west. At his disposal Engelhardt had 13 large liners, two dozen freighters and hundreds of smaller merchant vessels, barges and fishing boats. He also had access to the remaining *Kriegsmarine* warships, including the heavy cruisers *Prinz Eugen* and *Admiral Hipper*, the pocket battleships *Admiral Scheer* and *Lützow*, a handful of destroyers and large torpedo boats, several flotillas of minesweepers and countless smaller auxiliaries and patrol boats. In all, more than 1,000 ships of all kinds were used to evacuate over two million people across the Baltic Sea to Germany and German-occupied Denmark over the next 15 weeks.

At least 250 of them were sunk, causing the deaths of at least 33,000 people, the greatest single loss being the liner *Wilhelm Gustloff*, torpedoed by a Russian submarine on 30 January with almost 10,000 dead—the largest maritime disaster on record. Some ships made multiple crossings to and from Gdynia to Kiel, evacuating many thousands of refugees and wounded soldiers. On becoming Reich President on 1 May Dönitz at first planned to continue the war and issued a new priority to concentrate on combat capable troops, but by 6 May he no longer had any options. However, right up till 8 May Germans were still being evacuated in a frantic attempt to escape capture by the Soviets.

Below: Taken from a German propaganda magazine, this graphic view of a sinking merchant ship highlights the dangers from Russian submarines to the evacuation. The loss of the *Wilhelm Gustloff*, the *Steuben* (10 February, over 4,000 dead) and the *Goya* (16 April, 6,000–7,000 dead) to submarines were three of the greatest maritime tragedies ever. There was a further tragedy in Lübeck bay on 3 May when three ships, including the *Cap Arcona*, were sunk by RAF Typhoons under the misapprehension that they contained Nazi officials fleeing to Norway to continue the war. In fact, they contained concentration camp victims: 7,000–8,0000 died as a result.

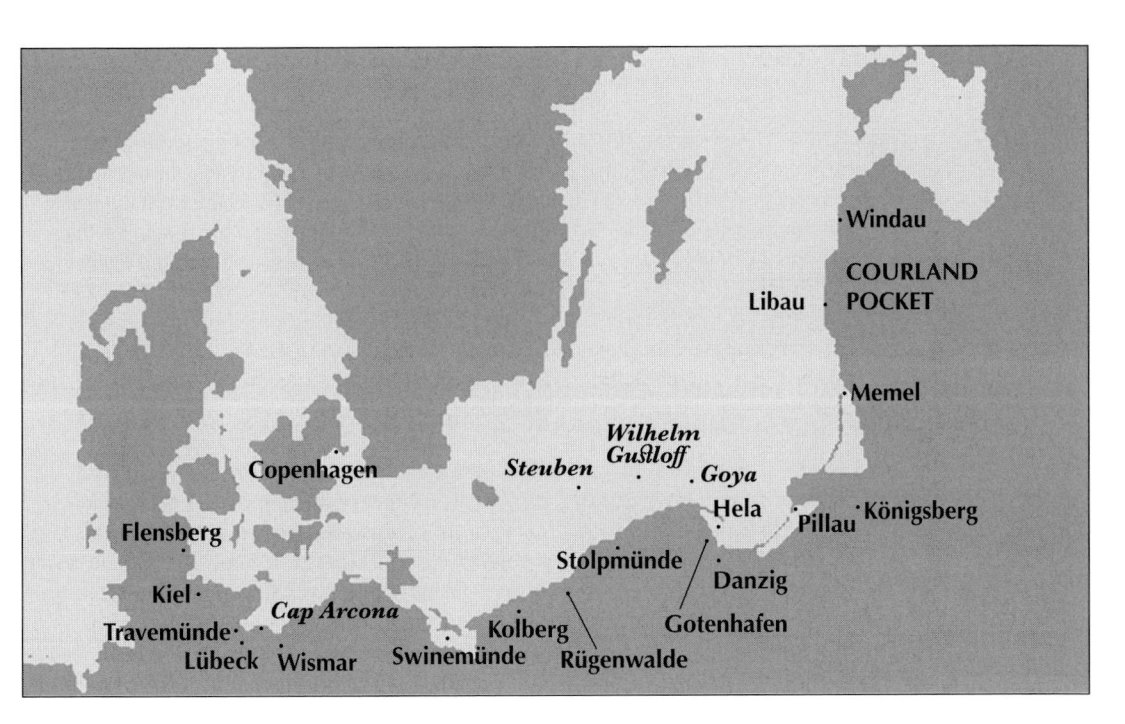

Above: The main ports involved in the evacuation and the location of the sinking of *Wilhelm Gustloff*, *Steuben*, *Goya* and *Cap Arcona*. The sinking of the first three ships accounted for most of the deaths that occurred during 'Hannibal'. The Courland Pocket remained in German hands at the end of the war; the other Pomeranian and Baltic ports fell between March and April—Memel fell to the Soviets on 28 January, Königsberg on 9 April, Pillau on 25 April, Gotenhafen on 28 March, Danzig on 30 March, Stolpmünde on 8 March, Kolberg on 18 March. Hela held out till 14 May.

Below: *Wilhelm Gustloff* (white hull, one funnel) and *Cap Arcona* in Hamburg harbour before the war.

4 What Might Have Been

The nature of warfare means that there are frequent operations that are planned but never fulfilled: adverse weather, military reverses, the exigencies of other theatres or battles—there are many reasons why this would be the case. There are too many of these cancelled operations to allow a book like this to be in any way comprehensive, but three of the most intriguing are dealt with below: Operation *Seelöwe* (Sealion), the projected invasion of Britain; Operation *Herkules* (Hercules), the joint Italian/German invasion of the strategically important island of Malta, linchpin of Britain's defence of the Mediterranean; and Operation Downfall, the invasion of Japan, whose anticipated casualty levels made every American pleased to hear of the use of nuclear weapons—something little understood three quarters of a century later.

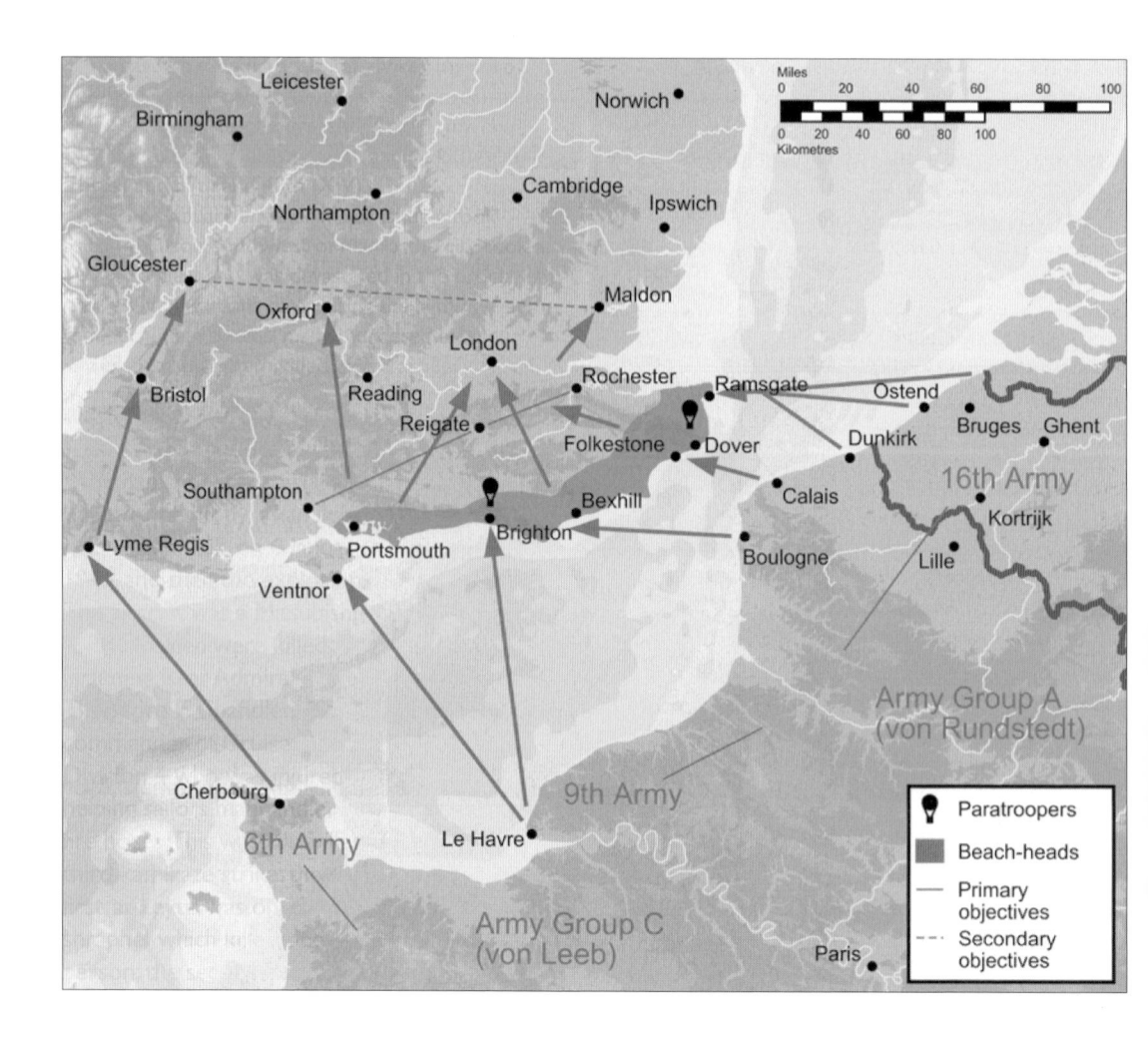

Operation *Seelöwe* (GER) 1940 Invasion of Britain

One of the great 'what ifs' of World War II, Operation *Seelöwe* (Sealion) could have changed the course of the war. If Britain had been invaded and fallen to the Germans, the Nazis would have reigned supreme in Europe. They could have better executed their attack against the Soviet Union with more forces at their disposal. There would have been no bombing of German industry from British airfields, no 1944 cross-Channel attack and no British manufacturing.

On 16 July 1940 Hitler issued *Führer* Directive No 16, ordering preparations for the invasion. German plans were well advanced by September 1940 when Hitler postponed it, concerned that the Luftwaffe hadn't destroyed the RAF—as was evidenced by the successful British bombing of the invasion fleet in September 1940—that the power of Royal Navy would prove decisive and because he was unsure of an amphibious operation of a size not seen before in modern warfare. This was in spite of the fact that new techniques—submersible tanks, landing craft with ramps, sea-going Herbert and Siebel ferries, heavy auxiliary gunboats—had been developed and a huge armada of some 4,000 vessels prepared. This work involved conversion of river barges, routing huge numbers of vessels to the Channel ports—usually by inland waterways—and procuring sufficient personnel to man them: the *Kriegsmarine* estimated on 6 August that it would need some 14,700 personnel. In fact, more were recruited.

The *Kriegsmarine*'s plan was to protect the invasion by threats of landings elsewhere—the east and northeast of England and the south of Ireland—large amounts of coastal artillery, with heavyweight batteries between Calais and Boulogne (Oldenburg, Prinz Heinrich, *Großer Kurfürst*, Siegfried, Friedrich August, Hamburg and Yorck), and large numbers of mines. Of course, they also needed large numbers of minesweepers to sweep channels through the British minefields.

The German army had outlined a plan that would see landings on the English coast from Eastbourne to Folkestone by two armies: Ninth and Sixteenth—the first wave would have been nine divisions in total—plus 7. *Flieger-Division* and, possibly, what remained of 22. *Luftlande-Division* which had sustained heavy losses in the Netherlands. They would be supported by three *Luftflotten*: *Luftflotte* 3 supporting Ninth *Armee*, *Luftflotte* 2 the Sixteenth and *Luftflotte* 5 was aimed at the British naval assets.

Would it have worked? No one knows, but momentum was on the German side and they had shown—and would show on into 1941 and 1942—the ability to pull off remarkable victories with surprisingly small forces—one need look no further than Rommel's victories in the desert. Nevertheless, in any analysis of the outcome, it's hard to forget the strength of the Royal Navy and Royal Air Force.

Below: RAF recce photo showing invasion barges in Boulogne habour.

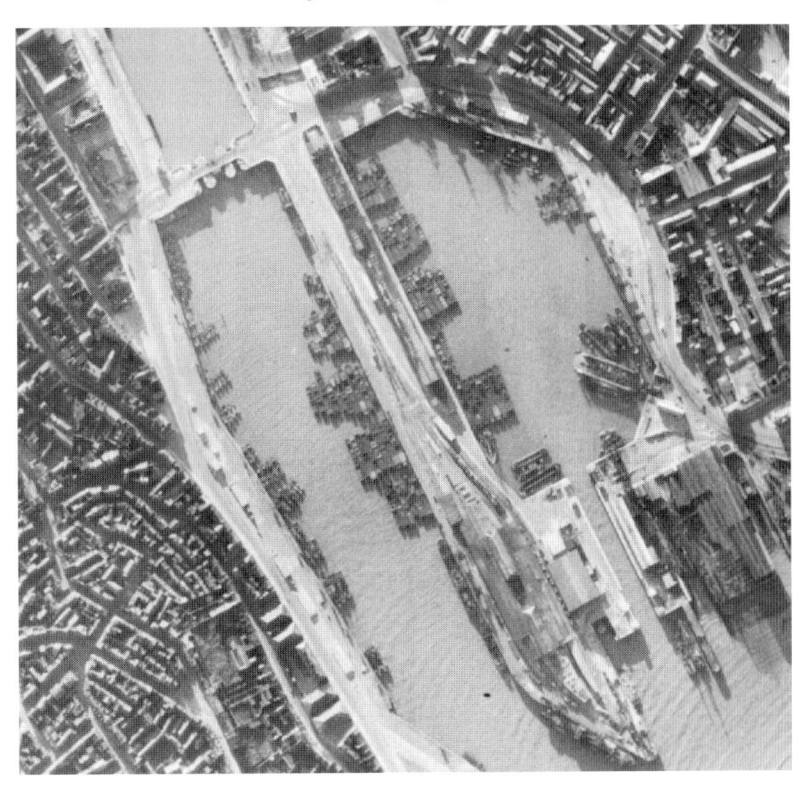

Directive No 16 Preparations for the invasion of England

(From supplement to the London Gazette, 19 May 1948 https://www.ibiblio.org/hyperwar/UN/UK/LondonGazette/38293.pdf)

'Since England, in spite of her hopeless military situation, shows no signs of being ready to come to an understanding, I have decided to prepare to invade and, if necessary, to carry this out.

'The aim of this operation will be to eliminate England as a base for the prosecution of the war against Germany and, if necessary, to occupy it completely.

I therefore order as follows:

'1. The landing will be carried out as a surprise crossing on a wide front from about Ramsgate to the area west of the Isle of Wight. Units of the Luftwaffe will act as artillery, and units of the Navy as engineers.

'The possible advantages of limited operations before the general crossing (e.g. the occupation of the Isle of Wight or of the county of Cornwall) are to be considered from the point of view of each branch of the Armed Forces and the results reported to me. I reserve the decision to myself.

'Preparations for the entire operation must be completed by the middle of August.

'2. These preparations must also create such conditions as will make a landing in England possible, viz:
(a) The English Air Force must be so reduced morally and physically that it is unable to deliver any significant attack against the German crossing.
(b) Mine-free channels must be cleared.
(c) The Straits of Dover must be closely sealed off with minefields on both flanks; also the Western entrance to the Channel approximately on the line Alderney–Portland.
(d) Strong forces of coastal artillery must command and protect the forward coastal area.
(e) It is desirable that the English Navy be tied down shortly before the crossing, both in the North Sea and in the Mediterranean (by the Italians). For this purpose we must attempt even now to damage English home-based naval forces by air and torpedo attack as far as possible.

'3. Command organisation and preparations.
Under my overriding command and according to my general instructions, the Commanders-in-Chief will command the branches of the Armed Forces for which they are responsible.

'From 1 August the operations staffs of Commander-in-Chief Army, Commander-in-Chief Navy and Commander-in-Chief Air Force are to be located at a distance of not more than 50km from my Headquarters (Ziegenberg).

'It seems to me useful that the inner operations staffs of Commander-in-Chief Army and Commander-in-Chief Navy should be placed together at Giessen.

'Commander-in-Chief Army will detail one Army Group to carry out the invasion.

'The invasion will bear the cover name 'Seelöwe [Sea-Lion]'.

'In the preparation and execution of this operation the following tasks are allotted to each Service:

'(a) Army:
The Army will draw up the operational and crossing plans for all formations of the first wave of the invasion. The anti-aircraft artillery which is to cross with the first wave will remain subordinate to the Army (to individual crossing units) until it is possible to allocate its responsibilities between the support and protection of troops on the ground, the protection of disembarkation points and the protection of the airfields which are to be occupied.

'The Army will, moreover, lay down the methods by which the invasion is to be carried out and the individual forces to be employed, and will determine points of embarkation and disembarkation in conjunction with the Navy.

'(b) Navy:
The Navy will procure the means for invasion and will take them, in accordance with the wishes of the Army, but with due regard to navigational considerations, to the various embarkation points. Use will be made, as far as possible, of the shipping of defeated enemy countries.

'The Navy will furnish each embarkation point with the staff necessary to give nautical advice, with escort vessels and guards. In conjunction with air forces assigned for protection, it will defend the crossing of the Channel on both flanks. Further orders will lay down the chain of command during the crossing. It is also the task of the Navy to co-ordinate the setting up of coastal artillery—ie all artillery, both naval and military, intended to engage targets at sea—and generally to direct its fire. The largest possible number of extra-heavy guns will be brought into position as soon as possible in order to cover the crossing and to shield the flanks against enemy action at sea. For this purpose railway guns will also be used (reinforced by all available captured weapons) and will be sited on railway turntables. Those batteries intended only to deal with targets on the English mainland (K5 and K12) will not be included. Apart from this the existing extra-heavy platform-gun batteries are to be enclosed in concrete opposite the Straits of Dover in such a manner that they can withstand the heaviest air attacks and will permanently, in all conditions, command the Straits of Dover within the limits of their range. The technical work will be the responsibility of the Organization Todt.

'(c) The task of the Air Force will be:
    'To prevent interference by the enemy Air Force.
    'To destroy coastal fortresses which might operate against our disembarkation points, to break the first resistance of enemy land forces and to disperse reserves on their way to the front. In carrying out this task the closest liaison is necessary between individual Air Force units and the Army invasion forces.
    'Also, to destroy important transport highways by which enemy reserves might be brought up and to attack approaching enemy naval forces as far as possible from our disembarkation points. I request that suggestions be made to me regarding the employment of parachute and airborne troops. In this connection it should be considered, in conjunction with the Army, whether it would be useful at the beginning to hold parachute and airborne troops in readiness as a reserve, to be thrown in quickly in case of need.

'4. Preparations to ensure the necessary communications between France and the English mainland will be handled by the Chief, Armed Forces Signals.

'The use of the remaining 80km of the East Prussia cable is to be examined in co-operation with the Navy.

'5. I request Commanders-in-Chief to submit to me as soon as possible—
(a) The plans of the Navy and Air Force to establish the necessary conditions for crossing the Channel (see paragraph 2).
(b) Details of the building of coastal batteries (Navy).
(c) A general survey of the shipping required and the methods by which it is proposed to prepare and procure it. Should civil authorities be involved? (Navy).
(d) The organisation of Air Defence in the assembly areas for invasion troops and ships (Air Force).
(e) The crossing and operation plan of the Army, the composition and equipment of the first wave of invasion.
(f) The organisation and plans of the Navy and Air Force for the execution of the actual crossing, for its protection and for the support of the landing.
(g) Proposals for the use of parachute and airborne troops and also for the organisation and command of antiaircraft artillery as soon as sufficient English territory has been captured.
(h) Proposal for the location of Naval and Air Headquarters.
(i) Views of the Navy and Air Force whether limited operations are regarded as useful before a general landing and, if so, of what kind.
(k) Proposal from Army and Navy regarding command during the crossing.

Signed: ADOLF HITLER'

Operation *Herkules* (GER) 1942 Invasion of Malta

Strategically, the fall of Crete should have been followed by an assault on Malta, the base from where the British were able to disrupt Axis resupply of their forces in North Africa. However, German eyes were on Russia and it wasn't until spring 1942 that planning got underway in earnest. Codenamed '*Herkules*' by the OKW, the operation was promoted by the *Kriegsmarine* as well—for example in a meeting between Admiral Raeder and Hitler on 12 April. Raeder also recommended that Hitler pressurise the Japanese to launch an offensive in the western part of the Indian Ocean and the Persian Gulf to split British forces. Hitler was never completely convinced, but he allowed planning to continue. At the end of April, Mussolini met Hitler at Berchtesgaden and set up a timetable that would see Rommel begin an offensive in May, take Tobruk and then stop on the Egyptian frontier (by mid-June). At that point, the Luftwaffe would switch to attacking Malta before an invasion, which would take place around 17 July. After Malta fell, the Luftwaffe would return to Rommel's aid.

'*Herkules*' would have been a joint Italian/German operation with five main phases as illustrated. The troops allocated were:

By Air: 30,000 men
- German XI. *Fliegerkorps* (7. *Flieger-Division*, plus three *Fallschirmjäger* Regiments)
- Italian 1st *Folgore* Parachute and 80th *La Spezia* Air Landing Divisions.

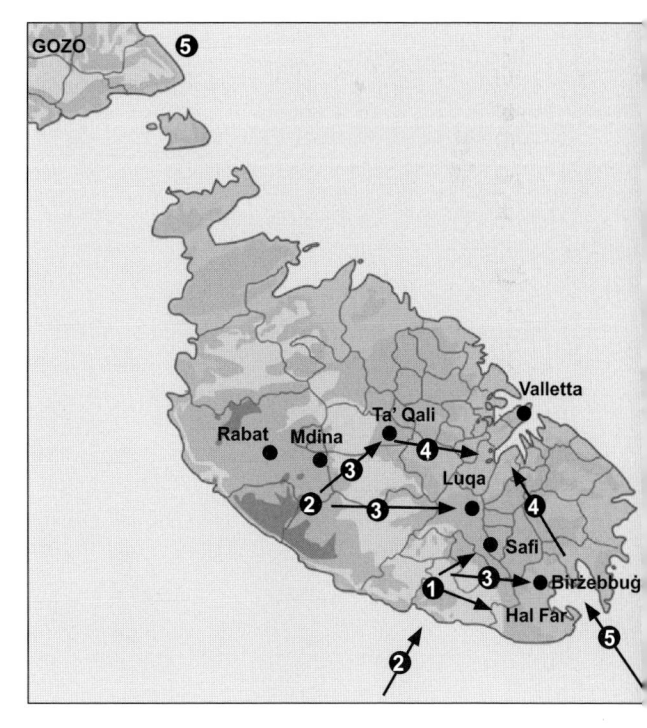

1. First airborne landing and attack on airfields at Ta' Qali, Safi and Hal Far.
2. Second airborne landing and seaborne landings.
3. Breakout.
4. Capture of Valletta.
5. Landing of additional troops.

Continued on p. 194.

By Sea: Total 70,000 men
First wave:
- Italian XXX Army Corps (1st *Superga*, 4th *Livorno* and 20th *Fruili* Infantry Divisions
- Italian 10th Armoured Brigade
- Italian *San Marco* Naval and *Camicie Nere da Sbarco* Infantry Brigades.

Second wave:
- Italian XVI Army Corps with the 26th *Assietta* and 54th *Napoli* Infantry Divisions

In reserve: German mountain division if necessary

Air forces:
- 500 Ju52 and 12 Me323 transport aircraft
- 300 DFS-230 and 200 Go242 gliders
- 216 fighters to escort and 200 other aircraft to support the operation.
- The Italians allocated 222 fighters and 470 mixed bombers, torpedo-bombers and other assault aircraft.

Maritime forces:
These and the support of the landings were primarily Italian: merchant vessels, landing craft (*motozattere*) and floating barges protected by five battleships, four heavy cruisers, twenty-one destroyers and fourteen submarines along with motor torpedo boats and minesweepers.

One difficulty—as it would be for the Allies when they started their great seaborne invasions—was the availability and construction of ferries and landing craft to be able to carry the personnel required.

Hitler's true feelings became known to Student in June when he cast doubt on the Italian navy's staying power. Hitler felt that once the Royal Navy got stuck in, the Italians would cut and run leaving the German troops on the island to themselves.

And so it never happened.

Operation Downfall (Olympic and Coronet) (Allies) 1946 Invasion of Japan

The American campaign in the Pacific against Japan had been inexorable, and during the fighting, the science of amphibious warfare and combined operations was hammered out on the beaches of numerous islands. The cost in casualties and equipment was profound—victory on Okinawa, for

Below: Operation Olympic possible invasion beaches on Kyoto.

Below: US assessment of Japanese defenders on Kyoto.

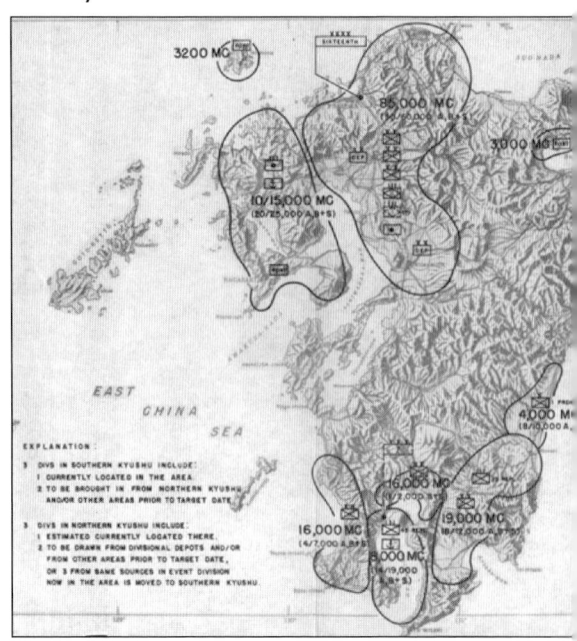

example, was achieved after 82 days of fighting and saw some 20,000 Americans, 110,000 Japanese and Okinawan conscripts and more than 100,000 Okinawan civilians die. An important part of the Japanese defence here was the use of kamikaze aircraft and boats: more than 1,500 damaged or destroyed around 150 ships causing around 4,000 US Navy deaths.

It was with this in mind that the plans for the invasion of Japan were drawn up. There would be two assaults: Operation Olympic (later changed to 'Majestic'), planned for 1 November 1945, would attack southern Kyoto with between 14 and 17 divisions; Operation Coronet was planned to land 25 divisions on Honshu's Kanto Plain near Tokyo on 1 March 1946, with a further 20 US and 5 Commonwealth divisions as the follow-up force.

Japanese defensive plans were based around a propaganda campaign, 'The Glorious Death of One Hundred Million', and planned to make the cost of victory so high the Allies would agree to an armistice. Unsurprisingly perhaps, the Americans opted to drop nuclear bombs to show the Japanese government an alternative that didn't risk hundreds of thousands of Allied soldiers' lives.

And then, of course, there were the Soviet plans, so often forgotten in light of the events at Hiroshima and Nagasaki. The Soviet declaration of war on 8 August, the invasion of Manchukuo and the swift Soviet victories threatened Japan's complete annihilation. Some suggest it was this and not the nuclear bombs that prompted Japan's surrender. Either way, Operation Downfall was relegated to the history books on 15 August 1945 when the emperor announced the country's unconditional surrender. The Allied occupation of Japan began on 28 August.

Right: A Japanese aircraft shot down over escort carrier USS *Kitkun Bay*.

Above: A comrade tightens the *hachimaki* for a Japanese kamikaze pilot.

Below: Japanese Type D (Koryu) midget submarines at Kure Naval Base.

'DOWNFALL'
Strategic Plan for Operations in the Japanese Archipelago

'MISSION
a. This Plan ... covers operations of United States Army and Naval Forces in the PACIFIC to force the unconditional surrender of JAPAN by invasion of the Japanese Archipelago.
b. The following over-all objective for the operations is assigned by the Joint Chiefs of Staff:

"To force the unconditional surrender of JAPAN by:
(1) Lowering Japanese ability and will to resist by establishing sea and air blockades, conducting intensive air bombardments and destroying Japanese air and naval strength.
(2) Invading and seizing objectives in the industrial heart of JAPAN."

'ASSUMPTIONS.
'a. Hostile.
(1) That the Japanese will continue the war to the utmost extent of their capabilities and will prepare to defend the main islands of JAPAN with every means available to them. That operations in this area will be opposed not only by the available organized military forces of the Empire, but also by a fanatically hostile population.
(2) That approximately three (3) hostile divisions will be disposed in Southern KYUSHU and an additional three (3) in Northern KYUSHU at initiation of the OLYMPIC operation.
(3) That total hostile forces committed against KYUSHU operations will not exceed eight (8) to ten (10) divisions and that this level will be speedily attained.
(4) That approximately twenty-one (21) hostile divisions, including depot divisions, will be on HONSHU at initiation of that operation and that fourteen (14) of these divisions may be employed in the KANTO PLAIN area.
(5) That the enemy may withdraw his land-based air forces to the Asiatic Mainland for protection from our neutralizing attacks. That under such circumstances he can possibly amass from 2,000 to 2,500 planes in that area by exercise of rigid economy, and that this force can operate against KYUSHU landing by staging through homeland fields.
(6) That the attrition caused by our continued land-based and carrier-based air preparation and support, and by our destruction of aircraft manufacturing and maintenance facilities, will reduce the hostile capability for air action against our landings to suicide attacks of uncertain proportions at an early phase of the operations.
(7) That hostile fleet elements will be forced to withdraw to the YELLOW SEA or Western SEA OF JAPAN. That the enemy will maintain the capability of a suicide attack against KYUSHU landings with the approximate strength of a typical carrier task group. That his remaining submarines and large numbers of small suicide craft will oppose our landings and that mines will be used in large numbers.
(8) That hostile sea communications across the JAPAN SEA, while relatively unimpaired prior to KYUSHU landings, will be progressively and rapidly restricted to complete interdiction by the time air is operating from HONSHU.
(9) That during continuation of Russian neutrality, the production capacity of hostile industries and raw material sources in MANCHURIA, North CHINA and KOREA will remain relatively unimpaired.
(10) That hostile logistic position will permit determined defense in areas of projected operations by hostile ground forces enumerated in (3) and (4) above.

'b. Own Forces.
(1) That the entire resources available to the Commander-in-Chief, United States Army Forces in the Pacific and the Commander-in-Chief, United States Pacific Fleet will be available for the support of these operations.
(2) That there will be no effective redeployment of major ground combat units from EUROPE in time for commitment prior to early 1946.
(3) That entry of RUSSIA into the war against JAPAN at some stage of the operations may be expected.
(4) That United States Forces will be established on the line BONINS-Northern RYUKYUS at initiation of the operations.
(5) That at initiation of the operations, land-based air forces will have attained offensive air superiority over Southern KYUSHU. That strategic land and carrier-based air forces will have effectively crippled the hostile aircraft and electronics industries and reduced capacity of rail lines in Southern HONSHU, SHIKOKU and KYUSHU to an extent providing little capacity beyond tactical needs.
(6) That at initiation of the operations the United States Pacific Fleet will dominate waters east of the main islands of JAPAN, and the EAST CHINA SEA and as far north as Southern KYUSHU. That forward naval bases will be functioning in the PHILIPPINES, RYUKYUS and MARIANAS.

'OPERATIONS.
'a. Concept.
This plan of campaign visualizes attainment of the assigned objectives by two (2) successive operations, the first to advance our land-based air forces into Southern KYUSHU to support the second, a knock-out blow to the enemy's heart in the TOKYO area. The operations are continued and extended until such time as organized resistance in the Japanese Archipelago ceases.

'Concept of the OLYMPIC operation visualizes entry into Southern KYUSHU by major joint overseas landing operations after intensive air preparation. Preparatory air operations include assaults by Carrier Task Groups and prolonged action by land-based elements operating in force from the RYUKYUS and MARIANAS. Initial assaults seize and develop the KAGOSHIMA WAN and ARIAKI WAN as ports of entry. The area is occupied as far north as the general line TSUNO-SENDAI to block mountain defiles and prevent hostile interference with our operations.

'These operations are expected to require fourteen (14) to seventeen (17) divisions with appropriate supporting troops, drawn from forces available in the PACIFIC with minimum use of redeployed elements. Forty (40) land-based air groups and naval elements for blockade and direct support are established for support of the CORONET operation.

'Concept of the CORONET operation visualizes a major joint assault supported by the massed air and naval power in the PACIFIC, to destroy hostile forces and seize the TOKYO-YOKOHAMA area.

'Initial operations establish local air support and drive into the KANTO PLAIN from outlying beaches, while defenses of the approaches to the TOKYO WAN and Northern SAGAMI BAY are reduced by intensive naval and air action. Forces are built up by subsequent landings, and operations are continued to the occupation of the TOKYO–YOKOHAMA Area and the KANTO PLAIN.

'These operations are expected to require initially twenty-five (25) divisions with appropriate supporting troops, drawn from PACIFIC resources remaining after OLYMPIC, augmented by redeployment. Land-based air elements and naval forces are established as required to support operations in central and northern JAPAN to conclusion, and to operate against the Asiatic Mainland as necessary. Logistic facilities are established in the TOKYO WAN to support consolidation of central and northern JAPAN.

'It is estimated that the maximum air garrison will not exceed fifty (50) groups, which figure is subject to revision as the situation develops.

Occupation of the KANTO PLAIN is followed by such ope'rations from the OLYMPIC and CORONET areas as may be necessary to terminate organized resistance in the Japanese Archipelago.

'If required by the situation prior to CORONET, intermediate operations are conducted to establish advance fighter elements in Southern SHIKOKU or Southeast HONSHU to cover our advance.

'In event forces allocated OLYMPIC operation are insufficient to accomplish tasks assigned, build-up in OLYMPIC area from elements earmarked for CORONET is continued at the rate of three (3) divisions per month beginning about (X plus 30) with supporting troops as required by the situation. The CORONET operation is adjusted accordingly.

'In event forces allocated CORONET operation are insufficient to successfully perform tasks assigned, build-up from the War Department Strategic Reserve is continued direct to the objective area at a rate of four (4) divisions and appropriate supporting troops per month beginning about (Y plus 90) to a strength required by the situation.

'The United States Pacific Fleet conducts the amphibious phases of the operations, supports ground action after landing and covers the operation by naval and air action against hostile supporting air, naval and land forces.

'The Twentieth Air Force, initially employed on strategic targets in coordination with long-range land-based and carrier-based air action, tactically supports as necessary the amphibious and ground phases of the respective assaults.

'The Commanding General, CHINA Theater cooperates by conduct of diversionary and containing operations within the limits of his capabilities.

'Should RUSSIA enter the war prior to completion of the CORONET assault phase, diversions from forces herein allocated may be directed by the Joint Chiefs of Staff in order to establish and maintain a sea route to Eastern SIBERIA. In this event, the operations outlined above are conducted with minimum alteration, such adjustments being made in timing as may be required to procure essential replacements for the forces committed.'

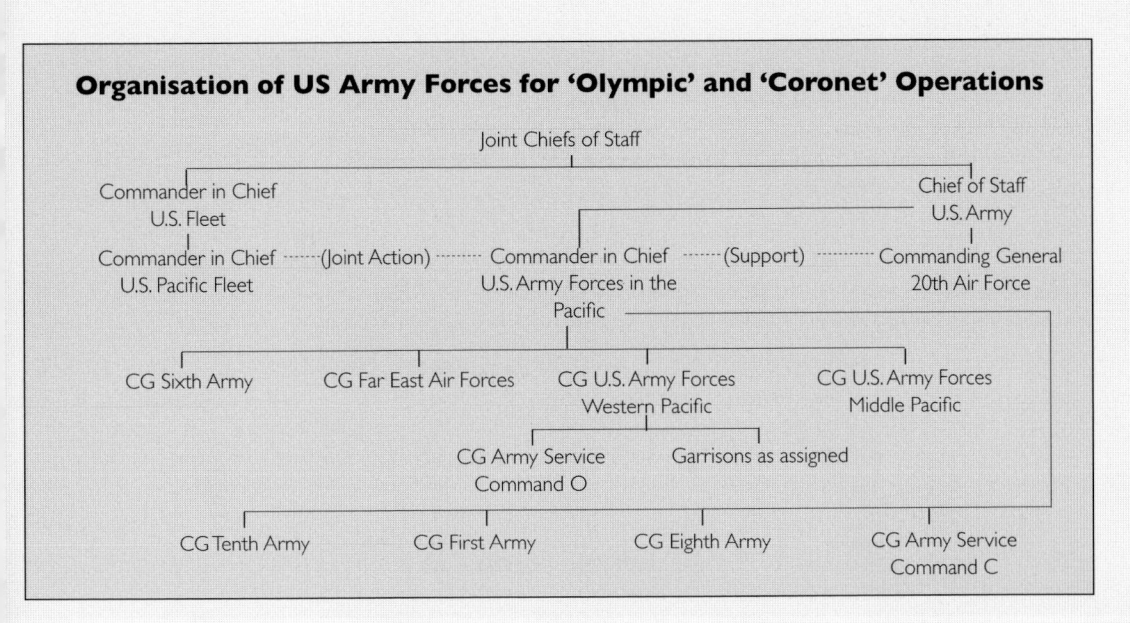

Organisation of US Army Forces for 'Olympic' and 'Coronet' Operations

```
                              Joint Chiefs of Staff
                                       |
    Commander in Chief                                              Chief of Staff
       U.S. Fleet                                                     U.S. Army
            |                                                             |
    Commander in Chief ····(Joint Action)···· Commander in Chief ····(Support)···· Commanding General
     U.S. Pacific Fleet                        U.S. Army Forces in the               20th Air Force
                                                       Pacific
                                                          |
     ┌──────────────────┬──────────────────┬──────────────────┐
  CG Sixth Army    CG Far East Air Forces   CG U.S. Army Forces    CG U.S. Army Forces
                                              Western Pacific        Middle Pacific
                                                    |
                                        ┌───────────┴───────────┐
                                 CG Army Service          Garrisons as assigned
                                    Command O
                                        |
                    ┌───────────────┬───────────────┬───────────────┐
              CG Tenth Army    CG First Army    CG Eighth Army    CG Army Service
                                                                      Command C
```

Appendices

1 Landing craft

Landing troops on hostile shores wasn't a new phenomenon, but World War II—as in so many fields of warfare—saw a thorough development of the machinery by which this could be accomplished successfully. The Japanese were ahead of the game with their 'Daihatsu' class and a range of other designs that were used to great effect in their 1941–42 conquests. The Soviets had a design based on a grain carrier, the 'Elpidifor' class, and the 'Russud' motor lighters. The Germans had improvised a range of craft for Operation *Seelöwe*, and had pushed the development of what became the *Marinefährprahm* (see pp. 212–213), but their methods were never put to the test in an all-out invasion. It was the British and, latterly, the Americans, who took the idea and ran with it.

Gallipoli had spurred the British to design the X-lighter or 'Beetle' which could carry 500 men, had a spoon-shaped bow to allow for shelving beaches, and a drop-down ramp. Over 200 were built (including some without engines) and four survived to be used in the Dunkirk evacuation. During the 1920s, J. Samuel White of Cowes built nine motor landing craft with a bow ramp and the capability of carrying 10 tons. They were used in the Norwegian campaign (see p. 59) alongside infantry-carrying LCAs

Right: The Japanese had developed a range of landing craft in the 1930s and led the world at the start of the war. The September 1944 *Intelligence Bulletin* (Vol III No 1) identified 'Japanese Landing Craft Most Frequently Encountered':

'The Type "A," a large barge with a landing ramp in its bow, is the Japanese landing craft most commonly used. It is known as a Daihatsu, This barge is intended for personnel, light artillery, and small vehicles. The hull is of steel, partly sheathed in wood. There is a raised deck aft, to accommodate the control personnel, the antiaircraft machine guns (usually of rifle caliber), and the stern anchor and winch. The winch is used to pull the craft off the beach after it has been grounded. Some Daihatsu have an armor shield to protect the control personnel. During landing operations, units which are to go ashore with infantry howitzers or antitank guns may mount these weapons in the bows of Daihatsu, to fire directly forward. Recently constructed Daihatsu are likely to be at least 10 feet longer than the hitherto standard 49-foot type.

'To land personnel, the Japanese may use a craft (Type "B") resembling an ordinary lifeboat. This type is quite seaworthy, and can effect landings under conditions more adverse than those the low-sided craft can cope with. The Type "B" is 30 feet long, and can carry about 40 men. At least some landing craft of Type "B" have an armor shield in the bow. This is intended to protect one of the light machine guns of the infantry unit on board.

'A fast diesel-powered armored craft with two gun turrets is in use as a patrol boat. More recent versions may mount dual 12.7-mm antiaircraft machine guns forward. The craft of this general type shown **[Right]** mounts machine guns of rifle caliber; it is armored, and can do 25 knots.

'Type "D," another barge for personnel and freight, is a more seaworthy craft than the Daihatsu. Type "D" usually has a flared clipper bow and a slightly raised deck aft. Evidently an older type, this barge may or may not be equipped with engines.

'Recently a Daihatsu with a square bow and stern (Type "H") has been used extensively. Its high poop and high gunwales make it a seagoing vessel, and suitable for supplying isolated garrisons. Like the original Daihatsu, it has a bow ramp, which can be lowered.'

Type "A" Landing Barge (*Daihatsu*)

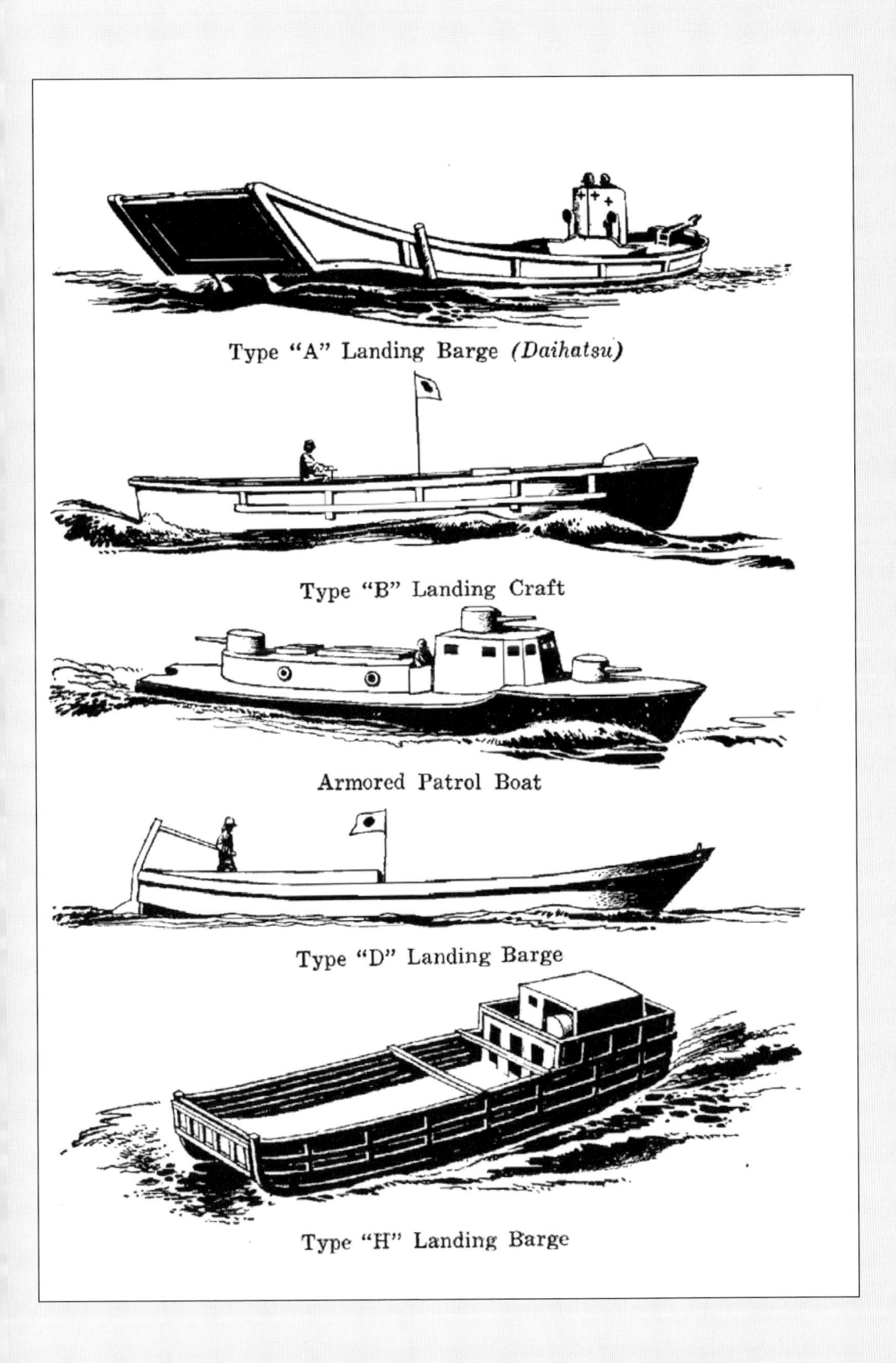

Type "B" Landing Craft

Armored Patrol Boat

Type "D" Landing Barge

Type "H" Landing Barge

Above and Below: 36ft Higgins Eureka landing boat during a demonstration near New Orleans, about May 1941. This would form the basis of the ubiquitous LCVP, originally called the LCP(R) as seen below—but Higgins would have to study the ramps on the Japanese *Daihatsu* craft to make the landing craft that was so important to the Allied war effort.

Opposite, Left: RN Beach Commandos from the 529th Flotilla inside an LCA during a May 1944 exercise. The major disadvantage with this craft was that there was no ramp to allow dismounting.

Opposite, Right: *LST-350* en route to North Africa, 15 April 1943. The photograph shows clearly the relative sizes of LST, the LCT carried as deck cargo and the LCPR and small patrol boat carried inside the LCT.

(landing craft assault) designed to carry 36 troops with a crew of four. The British saw the need for other bespoke landing craft—initially, the landing craft infantry and landing craft tank—but didn't have the production manufacturing capabilities to build everything they wanted and so passed the ideas over to the United States, who ran with them, improving the designs as they progressed. The LCIs and LCTs spawned the LST, the first of which were built to a British requirement by converting other vessels. Following these conversions, the UK and the US again collaborated with a joint design. The Americans went on to build 1,000 of them.

The LST proved to be one of the most successful of all amphibious warfare ship designs. It was the work of John C. Niedermair, who used the specifications provided by the British: that the vessel be able to manage an open ocean voyage, have a speed of ten knots, carry 40 ton tanks and conduct operations to a beach with a 1:150 slope. Niedermair's design—sketched out after only a few hours—had a flat-bottomed hull to reduce the draft and ballast tanks that would be filled for the deeper draft required for open ocean transits and then pumped out to achieve the required draft for beaching. Brilliantly conceived, the LST ended up being 328ft long and 50ft wide with five decks, the third of which, the tank deck, had the capacity for 20 M4s or 39 M3/M5 light tanks, or 17 LVTs (see p. 21 for an example of LVT loadings).

The flat bottom may not have helped their seaworthiness, but the design was easy to build: the first 30 were built and delivered in 10 months at the Bethlehem Steele yards in Baltimore. By the end of the war, an LST was taking only two months to build. Used for the first time during Operation Husky, they became so important to Allied amphibious warfare requirements that the date of D-Day itself was predicated on the time needed to build enough of them.

Many versions of the LCT and LST were produced—from rocket-carrier to hospital ship—but the other significant developments for amphibious warfare were two amphibians: the LVT and DUKW. These transformed the logistics of ferrying men and materiel to shore from larger vessels when no port facilities were available.

Above: British *LCA-1377* carries American troops during preparations for the Normandy invasion. Letters PB on the boat's side indicate that it is assigned to Landing Ship Infantry HMS *Prince Baudouin*.

Below Left: Australian infantry train to descend to assault boats by netting.

Below Right: US marines in an LCA on the way to disembark in Oran during Operation Torch.

Opposite, Above: A Coast Guard-manned LST launches an LVT-4 amphibious tractor in the initial assault wave bound for Okinawa, 1 April 1945.

Opposite, Centre: A DUKW off Noemfoor Island in July 1944 approaches the ramp of USS *LST-204*. Only the smaller vessels could approach the island's shallow water reefs.

Opposite, Below: LCVPs by a floating pier at Eniwetok, probably in early July 1944.

203

USS *LST-202* and USS *LST-204* (background) beached at Cape Gloucester, New Britain, while off loading tanks and other equipment, 27 December 1943.

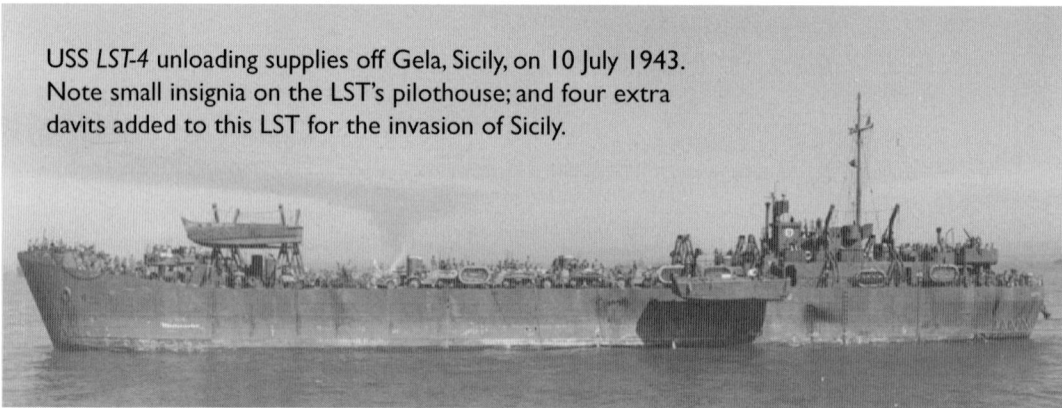

USS *LST-4* unloading supplies off Gela, Sicily, on 10 July 1943. Note small insignia on the LST's pilothouse; and four extra davits added to this LST for the invasion of Sicily.

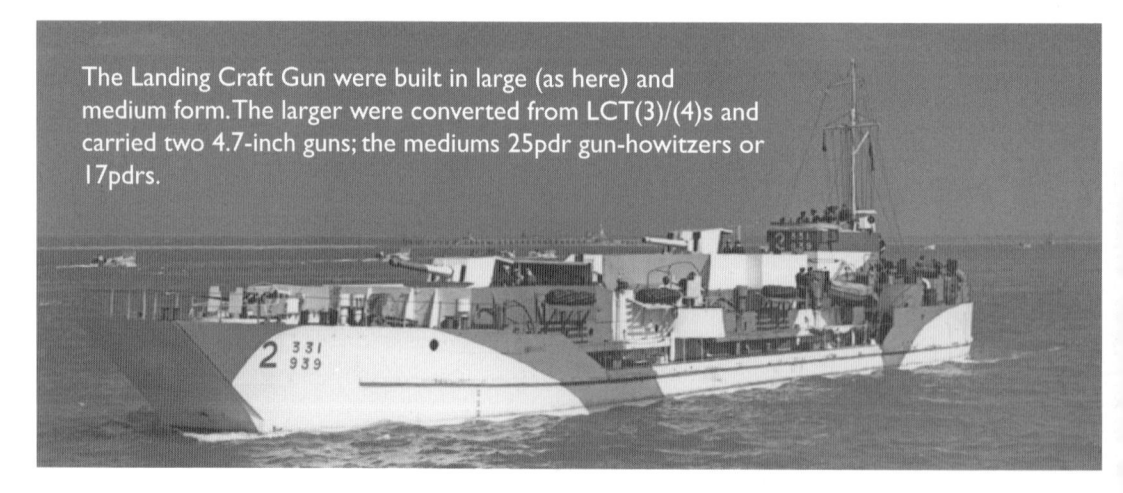

The Landing Craft Gun were built in large (as here) and medium form. The larger were converted from LCT(3)/(4)s and carried two 4.7-inch guns; the mediums 25pdr gun-howitzers or 17pdrs.

LCT (2)/(£)/(4) were converted into Landing Craft Flak with various combinations of AA weapons. This is *LCF(3) 4* armed with eight single Pom-Poms plus four 20 mm guns.

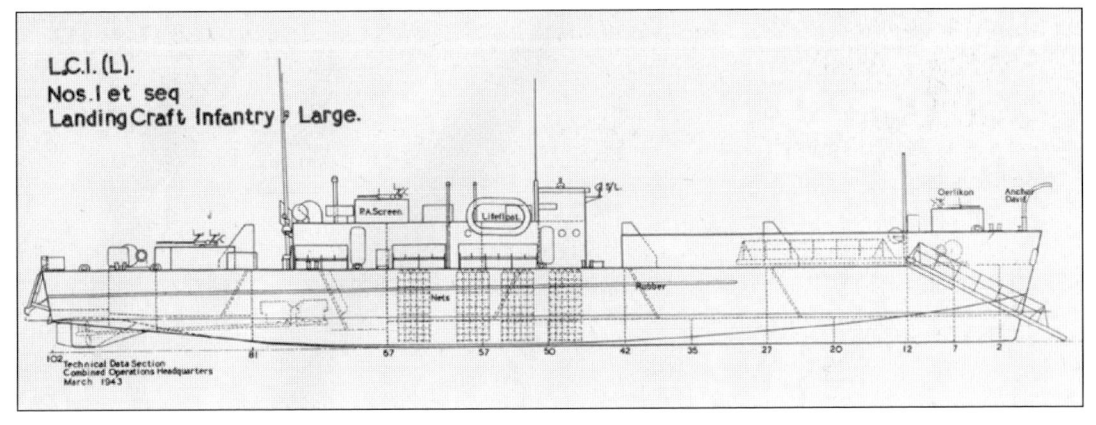

Above and Top: The LCI(L) had ramps at the front for troops to dismount. HMCS *LCI(L)-299* of the 2nd Canadian LCI Flotilla photographed around midday on 6 June as the Stormont, Dundas and Glengarry Highlanders, part of the reserve 9th Inf Bde, came ashore on Nan White Sector of Juno Beach, Bernières-Sur-Mer. As the LCI(L)s approached the beach, the troops moved to the stern allowing the bows to rise and thus ram and ride over obstacles.

Opposite, Left: Okinawa, 13 April 1945—LCTs unload at Yellow Beach, Okinawa. L–R: USSs *LCT-1415*, *LCT-1175*, *LCT-1265* and *LCT-1049*. USSs *LSM-220*, *LST-1000* and *LCT-418* are standing off the beach. In the middle distance in the centre USSs *LSM-84* and *SC-1281* are just visible.

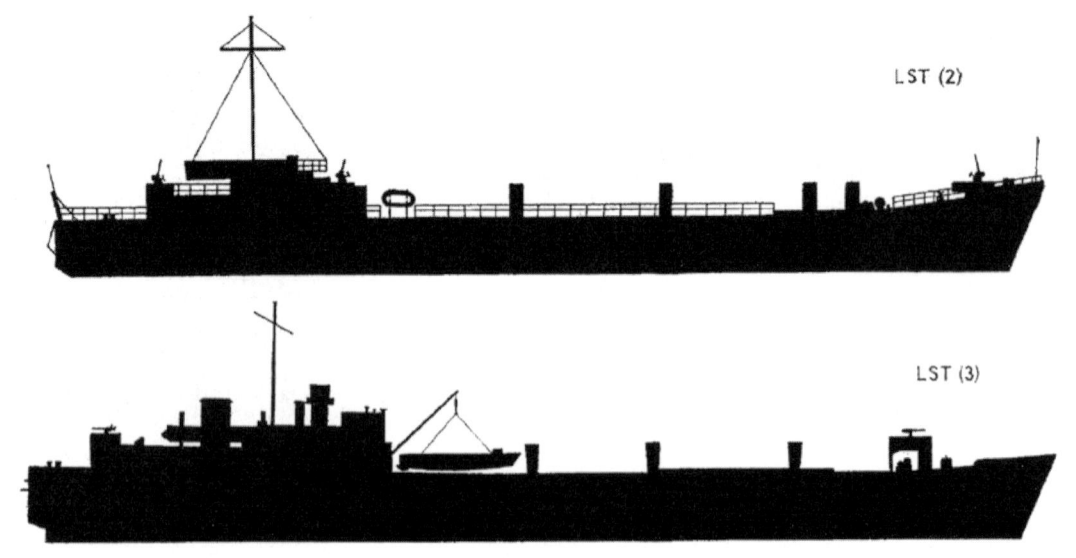

LST (2)

LST (3)

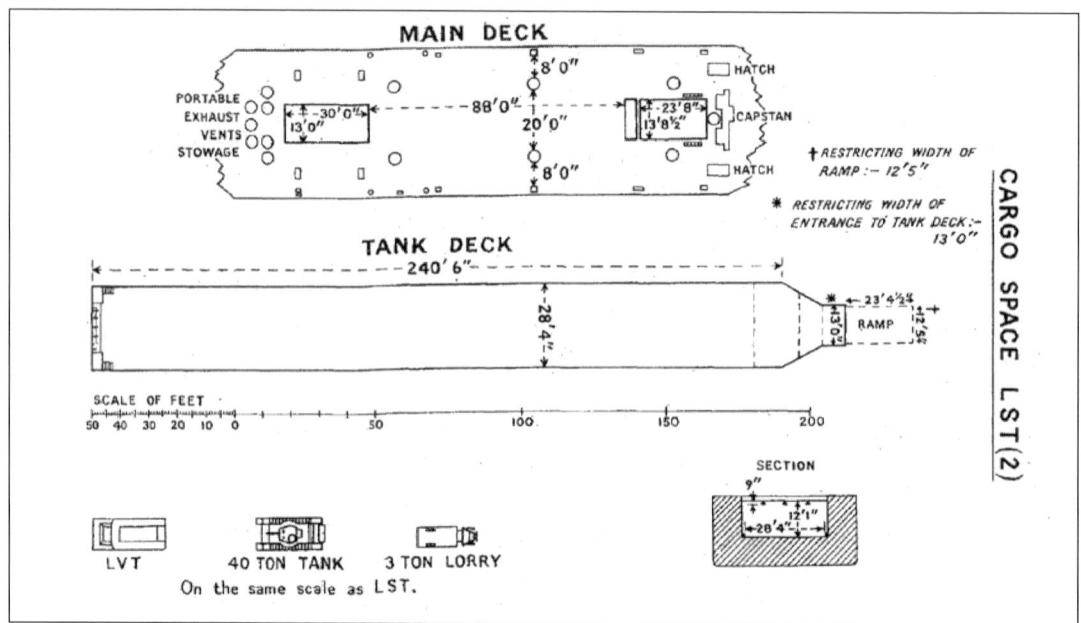

CARGO SPACE LST(2)

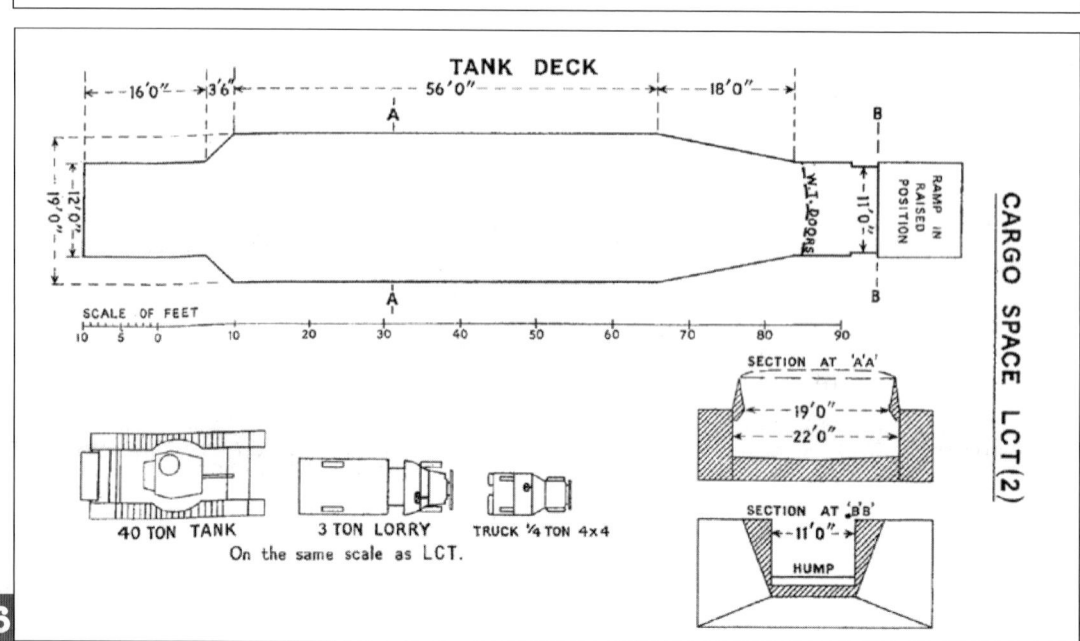

MAIN DECK

PORTABLE EXHAUST VENTS STOWAGE

30'0"
13'0"
88'0"
8'0"
20'0"
8'0"
23'8"
13'8½"
HATCH
CAPSTAN
HATCH

† RESTRICTING WIDTH OF RAMP :- 12'5"

* RESTRICTING WIDTH OF ENTRANCE TO TANK DECK :- 13'0"

TANK DECK
240'6"
28'4½"
23'4½"
13'0"
12'5"
RAMP

SCALE OF FEET
50 40 30 20 10 0   50   100   150   200

SECTION
9"
12'1"
28'4"

LVT   40 TON TANK   3 TON LORRY
On the same scale as LST.

CARGO SPACE LCT(2)

TANK DECK
16'0" 3'6" 56'0" 18'0"
19'0"
12'0"
A
A
B
B
W.T. DOORS
11'0"
RAMP IN RAISED POSITION

SCALE OF FEET
10 5 0   10   20   30   40   50   60   70   80   90

SECTION AT 'AA'
19'0"
22'0"

40 TON TANK   3 TON LORRY   TRUCK ¼ TON 4x4
On the same scale as LCT.

SECTION AT 'BB'
11'0"
HUMP

206

Sherman tanks of A Squadron, Nottinghamshire Yeomanry (Sherwood Rangers), 8th Armoured Brigade, come ashore from *LCT(4)-1076* on Jig sector of Gold Beach, 6 June 1944. On the right, a bulldozer helps clear a path off the beach. *1076* foundered and sank on 5 August 1944. The LCT(4)s could carry nine 30-tonne tanks. 864 were built, of which 39 were lost.

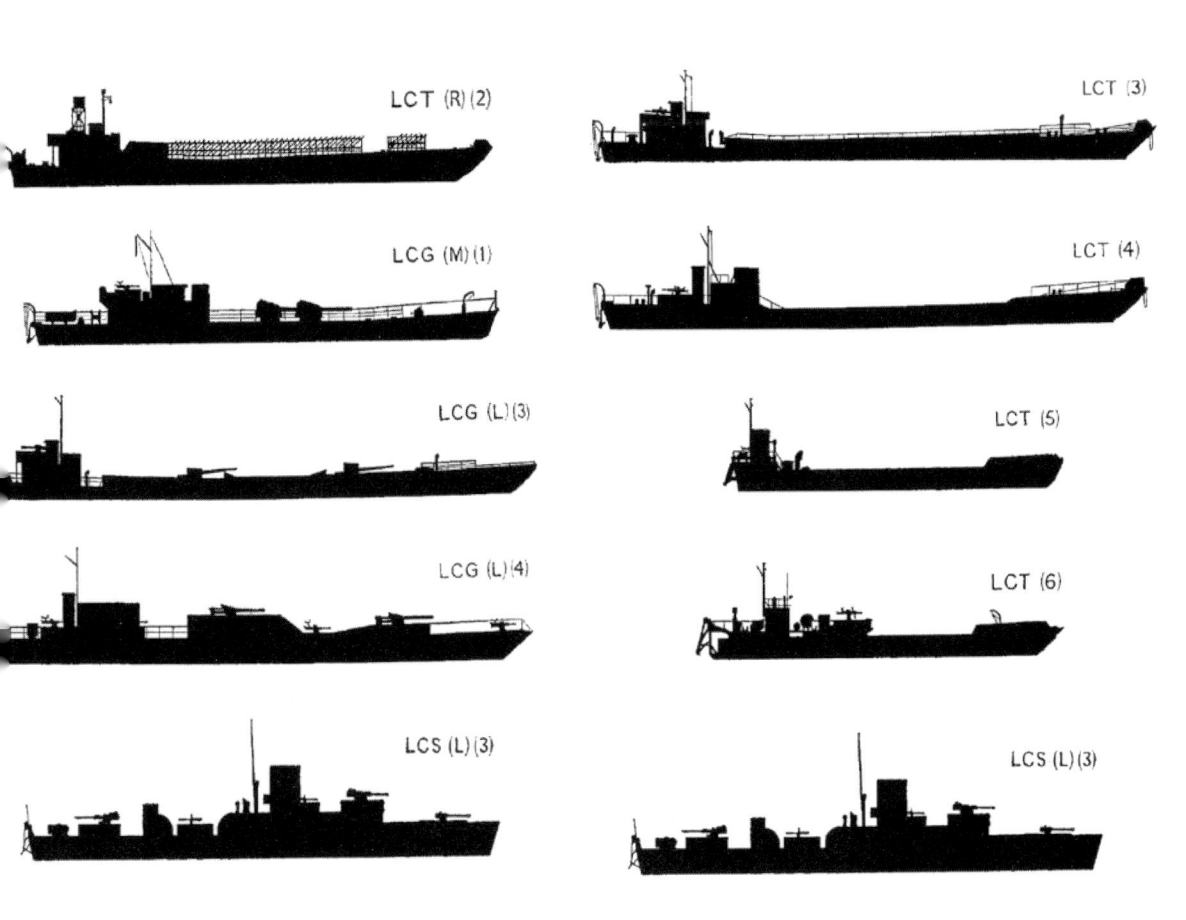

LCT (R) (2)

LCT (3)

LCG (M) (1)

LCT (4)

LCG (L) (3)

LCT (5)

LCG (L) (4)

LCT (6)

LCS (L) (3)

LCS (L) (3)

LANDING SHIPS

Title	Short Title	Crew	Troops	Tanks	Trucks	DUKWs	LVTs
Landing ship, carrier (derrick hoisting)	LSC						
Landing ship, dock	LSD	141	244		46	41	44 (92 LVT/108 DUKW with two temporary decks)
Landing ship, emergency repair	LSE						
Landing ship, emergency repair landing craft)	LSE(LC)						
Landing ship, emergency repair (landing ship)	LSE(LS)						
Landing ship, fighter direction	LSF						
Landing ship, gantry	LSG	92	266				
Landing ship, headquarters (command)	LSH(C)						
Landing ship, headquarters (large)	LSH(L)						
Landing ship, headquarters (small)	LSH(S)						
Landing ship, infantry (large)	LSI(L)						
Landing ship, infantry (medium)	LSI(M)						
Landing ship, infantry (small)	LSI(S)						
Landing ship, infantry (hand hoisting)	LSI(H)						
Landing ship, medium	LSM						
Landing ship, personnel	LSP						
Landing ship, tank	LST (2)	69	177	18 Churchills, 20 Shermans, 52 3-tonners, 22 DUKW, 36 LVTs			
	LST (3)	129	168	18 Churchills, 20 Shermans, 52 3-tonners, 22 DUKW, 36 LVTs			

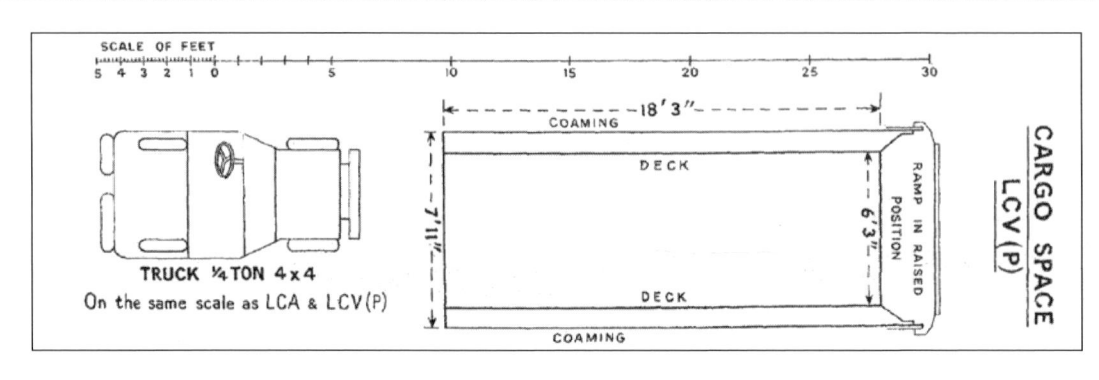

TRUCK ¼ TON 4x4
On the same scale as LCA & LCV(P)

CARGO SPACE LCV(P)

LANDING CRAFT

Title	Short Title	Crew	Troops	Tanks/Rockets
Landing craft, administration	LCQ			
Landing craft, flak	LCF	68 (3), 76 (4)		8 x 20mm cannon or 4 x 2pdr Pom-Pom
Landing craft, gun (large)	LCG(L)	45 (3/4) 2 x 4.7 QF/BL and 2 x Oerlikon (3); 2 x 4.7 BL and 7 x Oerlikon (4)		
Landing craft, gun (medium)	LCG(M)	31 (1) 2 x 17pdr, 2 x 25pdr, 2 x twin Oerlikon		
Landing craft, gun (tower)	LCG(T)			
Landing craft, headquarters	LCH	c. 35 (converted from LCI(L) 1–350)		
Landing craft, infantry (large)	LCI(L)	19 (1–350), 29 (350 on)	200 (1–350 + 46 seated on upper deck), 186 (351 on in bunks)	
Landing craft, infantry (small)	LCI(S)	17	102 (on seats)	
Landing craft, support (large) mks II and III	LCS(L) (2) and (3)			
Landing craft, support (rocket)	LCS(R)			
Landing craft, tank	LCT (3)	12		5 x Churchill, 8 x Sherman, 10 x 3-tonners
	LCT (4)	12		6 x Churchill, 9 x Sherman, 12 x 3-tonners
	LCT (5)	12		4 x Churchill, 5 x Sherman, 9 x 3-tonners
	LCT (8)	?		? x Churchill, ? x Sherman, ? x 3-tonners
Landing craft, tank (armoured)	LCT(A)			To provide fire support for D-Day, two Centaur tanks (w/o engines) on board. Montgomery insisted they be able to drive. Only 20 of 80 landed in the first hour—and only 28 over the rest of the day.
Landing craft, tank (emergency repair)	LCT(E)			
Landing craft, tank (rocket)	LCT(R) (2)	17+1 r/t mechanic in every 2 craft		792 5in rockets or 1,000 RP-3 rockets, first used during Operation Husky
	LCT(R) (3)	17+1 r/t mechanic in every 2 craft		1,044 5in rockets

Title	Short Title	Crew	Troops/Notes
Landing craft, assault	LCA	4	35
Landing craft, assault (hedgerow)	LCA(HR)		Armed with 4 × 6 Spigot mortars
Landing craft, assault (obstruction clearance)	LCA(OC)		
Landing craft, control	LCC		Equipped with radar to find safe routes to the beaches
Landing craft, emergency repair	LCE		
Landing craft, mechanized	LCM	6	60
Landing craft, navigation	LCN	9	
Landing craft, personnel (large)—the US Higgins boat.	LCP(L)	3	Loaded by scramble net from larger ships. Before the ramped version, infantry (25 carried by RN version/36 by US) had to jump off the bow.
Landing craft, personnel (medium)	LCP(M)		
Landing craft, personnel (nested)	LCP(N)		
Landing craft, personnel (ramped)	LCP(R)		
Landing craft, personnel (small)	LCP(S)		
Landing craft, rubber	LCR		
Landing craft, support (large)	LCS(L)	13 (1), 25 (2)	1 x 2pdr, 1 x twin .5 MG, 1 x 4in smoke (1), 1 x 6pdr, 2 Oerlikon, 1 x 4in smoke (12)
Landing craft, support (medium)	LCS(M)	11	2 x .5 MG, 1 x 4in smoke
Landing craft, support (small)	LCS(S)		
Landing craft, vehicle	LCV		
Landing craft, vehicle (personnel)	LCV(P)	3	25

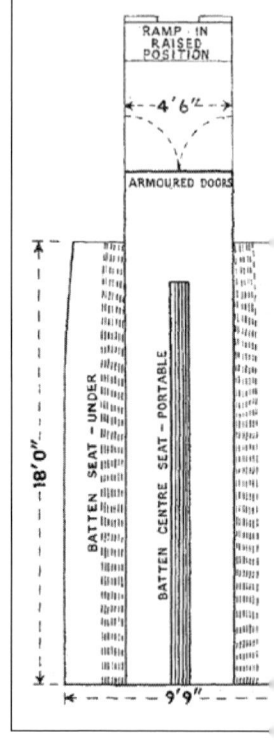

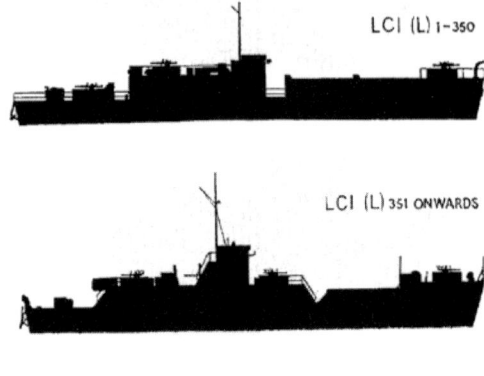

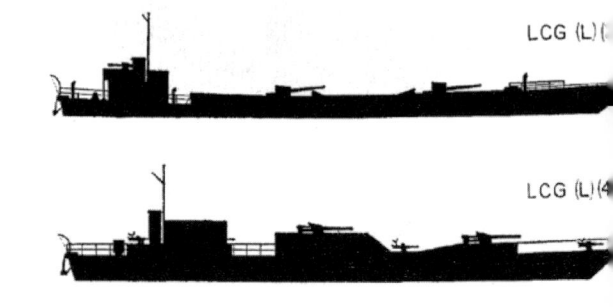

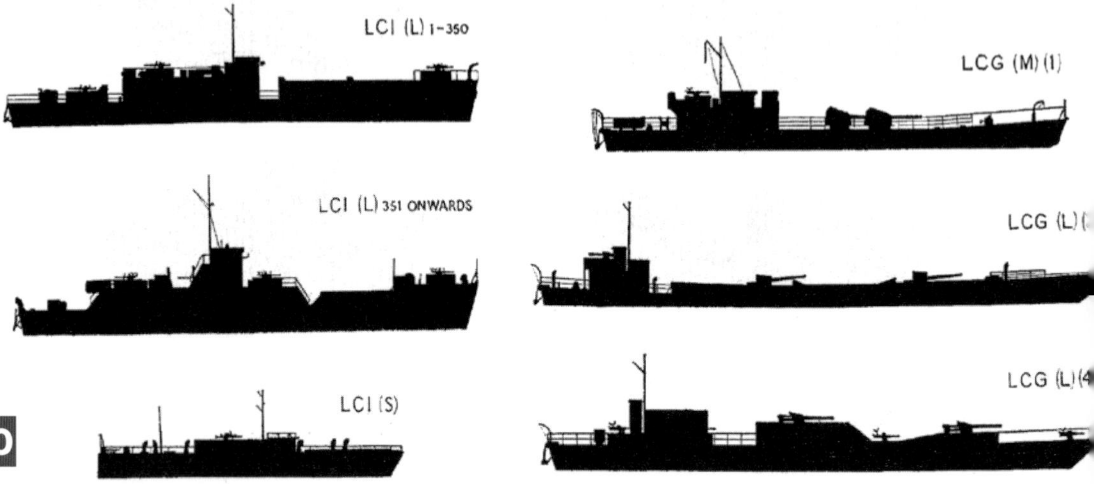

TROOPS SPACE LCA

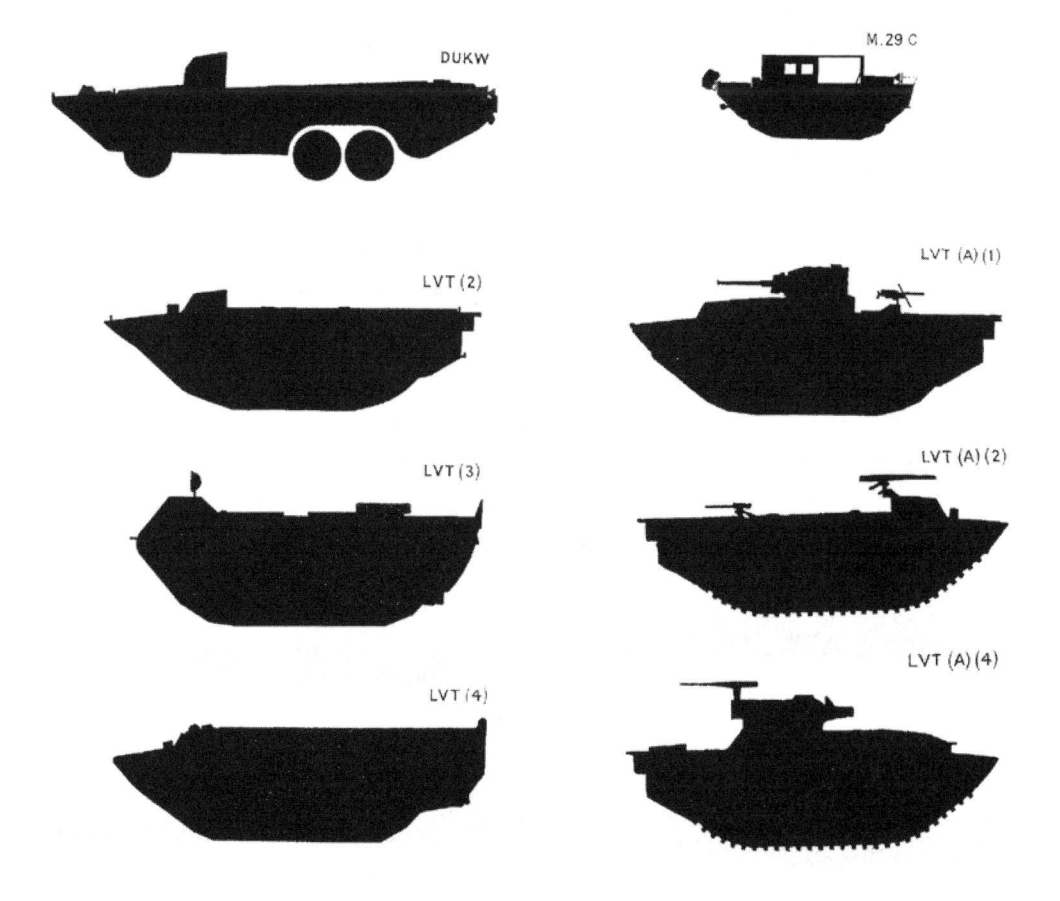

The LCN, landing craft, navigation, was used by the Royal Marines and Special Boat Service for surveying landing sites.

DUKW

M.29 C

LVT (2)

LVT (A) (1)

LVT (3)

LVT (A) (2)

LVT (4)

LVT (A) (4)

SCALE OF FEET
10 9 8 7 6 5 4 3 2 1 0   10   20

While gathering together barges and lighters for the invasion of Britain, the Germans experimented with ramp modifications to barges and ferries made up of heavy bridge pontoons powered by BMW 6U aero engines. This led on to the production of Siebel ferries which were originally airscrew-powered, although later versions used more conventional waterscrews and three Deutz truck engines.

In February 1941 a building programmestarted for the *Marinefährprahm*, a landing craft with a ramp. 700 were built during the war and they were used as transports and modified as minelayers and gunboats. There were several types (A–D), and they were used from Operation Barbarossa onwards in every war theatre and could transport even the heavy Tiger tanks. MFPs were used extensively during 1943 to ferry Seventeenth *Armee* troops back to the Crimea from the Kuban bridgehead. In all 239,669 soldiers, 16,311 wounded, 27,456 civilians and 115,477 tons of military equipment (primarily ammunition), 21,230 vehicles, 74 tanks, 1,815 guns and 74,657 horses.

The Italians built a total of 95 *motozattere*—versions of the MFP—under licence. The first batch, 65 MFP-As built mainly around Palermo in summer 1942, would have been used in Operation *Herkules*, the invasion of Malta (see pp. 193–194). They had Italian engines and weapons. In September 1942 another 40 were ordered with improvements; upgunned they acted as effective gunboats—it was Italian *motozattere* gunboats that dispersed British MTBs during Operation Agreement (see p. 47). Further orders of a version of the MFP-D didn't take place after the Italian surrender.

Above: A Siebel ferry of *Einsatzstab Fähre Ost* in Finland. This one is set up as a Flak ship.

Below: Soviet marines of the Red Army Navy on board a captured German Siebel ferry on Lake Ladoga.

Battle raft *M32* as seen from the deck of another ferry on Lake Ladoga, 18 August 1944.

MFP F-935 on the Adriatic in summer 1944.

Above: An up-armoured F-Lighter (British term for a MFP) in the Mediterranean. It has twin-barrelled 20mm guns amidships and a larger calibre gun astern. Built at the Porte de Bouc shipyard near Marseilles in 1944, it could carry three medium tanks, or 200 men or 140 tons of cargo.

Below: German landing barges unload troops at Cape Kazantip in the Sea of Azov. September 1942.

2 Resupply

Logistics is a key element in all warfare, but in amphibious landings—particularly those far from the central supply points—what was carried, when it was dispensed and who organised the operation was of vital importance. Logistics in the Pacific war were always an issue. The Allied supply chain was crucial to success and their opponents showed exactly what happened when it went wrong. Poorly supplied, their resupply operations bedevilled by Allied intervention by air, sea and submarine, Japanese troops often starved in the field for want of the basic requirements. The Japanese soldier had a reputation for being able to survive on a pocketful of rice. In truth, this was because that's all he could get.

FM31-5 *Landing Operations on Hostile Shores* had this to say about logistic considerations in small island or atoll operations:

'(1) In the assault phase, the amount of supply landed is held to actual requirements because of lack of dispersal areas and slowness in unloading. The latter results from the passage of amphibian vehicles over reefs and the movement of boat traffic through narrow boat lanes.

'(2) Supply points usually are established in close proximity to the landing beach and remain there throughout the operation. Reliance must be placed on amphibian trucks (DUKW) for movement.

'(3) The flow of supply to the beach must be controlled rigidly by the shore party commander to insure timely replenishment of specific items. Regulation is effected by the use of a floating pool of landing boats and amphibian tractors or trucks lying off a control boat. Each craft or vehicle exhibits a distinctive flag to indicate the nature of its load. A representative of the combat team or landing team supply section is stationed in the control boat with a list showing the type of ammunition or other supplies in each boat so that he may insure prompt dispatch of the desired item to the beach. When directed by the shore party commander, the beachmaster calls in the desired class of supply.

'(4) If supplies must be landed in amphibian vehicles during the early phase of a landing, they will consist chiefly of loose cargo rather than pallets.

'(5) Natural sources for fresh water may be lacking.

'(6) Atoll warfare calls for a specific type of combat loading which will permit maximum flexibility in debarkation priorities to meet emergencies, owing to the difficulties of building up balanced supply levels on the beach. This need is met by very light loading, and balanced supply in each hold, so far as permitted by naval safety regulations.'

Opposite: A busy scene in the Marshall Islands. As ammunition and fuel are unloaded, automotive repairs are carried out to jeeps and a DUKW.

Left: Flat freight cars of the US Army Transportation Corps roll onto a French railroad from a Coast guard-manned LST whose tank deck is equipped with tracks. Rail transport was rebuilt as soon as possible after the Normandy invasion to assist Allied logistics.

In the Mediterranean, there were fewer supply issues for the Allies. The distances from ports or beachheads were never big enough to lead to significant problems. The real trouble in northwest Europe came after the amphibious stage had finished—particularly after the Mulberry harbour off Omaha beach was wrecked in a storm. The battle of Normandy won, Allied success meant the armies outstripped their supply lines. Aircraft were used but lacked the capacity and it wasn't until the ports of Marseilles and then Antwerp were developed that the logistical crisis was averted. A DUKW could carry 25 soldiers or 5,000lb of equipment. Example aircraft loads in pounds given in the Combined Operations staff notebook were:

Type	Free drop	Air landing	Para containers CLE Mk III	Para drop panniers	Remarks
Dakota C47	5,500	–	–	–	Same weight by air landing
Dakota C47	–	–	–	16	Panniers packed to 350lb (or 6 CLE+10 panniers)
Halifax II, III, V	–	–	15	2	Panniers and containers packed 350lb
Halifax II	–	3,000	–	–	15 panniers and 3 containers max
Halifax III	–	6,000	–	–	
Halifax V	–	3,500	–	–	
Lancaster I, II, III	–	–	14	–	Containers packed to 350lb gross
Lancaster III	6,250	–	–	–	Stores in SBC and resting on bomb doors
Lancaster III	–	5,304	–	–	Packed in 22 panniers and 6 containers max
Stirling I, III, IV	–	–	24	4	Panniers and containers packed to 350lb gross
Stirling I, III, IV	–	5,000	–	–	Packed in 19 panniers and 3 containers max
Halifax A/B conversion	–	–	12,000	–	"C" conversion 10,000
Halifax "B" conversion	–	12,000	–	–	
Stirling conversion	–	9,500	–	–	
Liberator B24	–	–	12	2	Panniers and containers packed to 350lb gross
Commando C46	–	10,000	–	–	

Material and Logistics: Planning, Preparation, and Training Period
Edited excerpts from Vice Adm H.K. Hewitt's Action Report on Operation Husky

'The ['Husky'] amphibious assaults were uniformly successful. The only serious threat was an enemy counter-attack on D+1 against the 1st Infantry Division when a German tank force drove across the Gela plain to within one thousand yards of the DIME beaches. The destruction of this armored force by naval gunfire delivered by US cruisers and destroyers, and the recovery of the situation through naval support, was one of the most noteworthy events of the operations. The continued employment of naval gunfire against enemy positions on the north coast during the reduction of the island phase of the campaign, the unique employment of landing craft in providing a service of supply of food, fuel and munitions to our front line troops on the north coast, and the skillful execution of flanking amphibious landings on the north coast contributed to a marked degree in the rapid defeat of the enemy.

'1. Commencing 21 February, 1943, after a detailed survey of available sites, Amphibious Training and Repair Bases were established as follows: Port Lyautey, French Morocco; Nemours, Beni-Saf, Arzew, Mostaganem, Tenes and Cherchell, Algeria. Beni-Saf was designated as the main repair base for PCs, SCs, and YMSs. The base at Port Lyautey was abandoned as soon as facilities inside the Mediterranean were sufficiently equipped to handle the additional craft. Repair facilities at the Naval Operating Base, Oran, Algeria, augmented by the facilities of the USS DELTA in March, were utilized to the fullest extent.

'2. Large quantities of spare parts and equipment consigned to this theater were loaded in merchant ships and in both United States and British LSTs whose destinations were not in conformance with that of the cargo. The result was serious delay and enormous trans-shipment to effect proper delivery. LCT(5)s were largely used in transferring material. While this was most satisfactory and expeditious, it did resultin loss of time and training and increased the maintenance problem of LCT(5)s considerably.

'3. During the latter part of April, LCT(5)s were again diverted from training to provide valuable assistance to the US Army in landing operations in the Tunisian campaign.

'4. Early in May, the advance party of Commander Landing Craft and Bases, Northwest African Waters, entered Tunisia and established Advanced Amphibious Training Bases at Bizerta and La Goulette. LSTs, LCI(L)s and LCT(5)s were used to transfer personnel and material from Algerian Bases to the new Tunisian Bases. These craft were based from then on at Bizerta and La Goulette. The USS ACHELOUS (ARL1) arrived at Bizerta on 4 June and the USS DELTA on 24 June. One Advanced Base Mobile Repair Unit was retained at Arzew and the other which arrived immediately prior to the operation was based at Bizerta. PT Base No. 12 was also located at Bizerta.

'5. The USS VULCAN was based at Algiers, Algeria, from 2 July primarily as repair ship for cruisers and destroyers temporarily assigned to the EIGHTH Fleet.

'6. Thirteen (13) 250 ton and six (6) 350 ton pontoon dry-docks were received and were allotted to the United States and British forces as operational requirements of landing craft and small ships required. All of these, however, were not assembled prior to the operation due to late arrival in the theater. The 250-ton dry-docks were used for LCT(5)s and PTs. The 350-ton dry-docks were used for LCI(L)s and SCs, although not entirely satisfactory for the former due to the discrepancy in length. One 100-ton pontoon dry-dock was assembled at PT Base No. 12 at Bizerta for PTs and ARBs.

'7. Detailed plans for the establishment of Advanced Bases in Sicily and studies of harbors and existing petroleum installations were made to determine the requirements for specialized equipment to supplement the standard functional components of Lions and Cubs which had been set up.

'8. Constant and harmonious planning was carried out with representative of the British Navy and the US Army on the innumerable and detailed logistic problems which arose.

'9. The following brief outline of fueling arrangements is indicative of the magnitude of the operation:
(a) Seven (7) fleet tankers (AO) (78,000 tons of fuel oil) were required to fuel the larger ships. of the Western Naval Task Force upon their arrival in the Mediterranean.
(b) Small diesel powered ships and all landing craft were normally fueled at Bizerta and La Goulette:
(c) It was estimated that 212,000 tons of fuel oil and 60,000 tons of diesel oil might be required for the period D-day to D+21. Actually on D-day, shore stocks alone approximated these figures and in addition, large and small tankers were strategically placed to provide expeditious alongside fueling at ports near the theater of operations. An additional large reserve was maintained at Casablanca, French Morocco.

'10. Fresh, refrigerated and dry provisions were obtained from the US Army in accordance with existing instructions. It was necessary, however, to augment these by provisions loaded in the USS TARAZED which arrived late in June.

'11. Clothing and small stores, particularly items required for survivors, were stocked at Oran, Bizerta and La Goulette. In addition each APA, XAP and AKA had been directed to provide additional stocks of these items prior to departure from the United States.

'12. It is of interest to note that a total of 601 ships and landing craft and 1,124 ship-borne landing craft were assigned to the Western Naval Task Force. These figures include 32 Liberty Ships and 96 LCM(3)s carried by them which arrived off the Southern beaches between D+1 and D+8.

'UNLOADING TRANSPORTS

'1. On approaching the beach loaded, report to the control boat. If not ordered in to the beach immediately, back out and stay clear of the beach approaches. Help avoid congestion. The enemy hopes you will cause it.

'2. When ordered in to the beach go in promptly and retract promptly when unloaded.

'3. Don't leave your boat no matter how tempting the souvenier hunting becomes ashore. You may be blown up by a booby-trap and you will add to the confusion which always exIsts during the first five days of any operation.

'4. Make your boat crew a team. Your boat will be your bunk mess hall, head and recreation center for at least the first three days of an operation. All hands should be interchangeable so that one in four can rest whenever possible.

'5. If your boat broaches, don't give up. Your boat is badly needed for the success and safety of human lives and material. Help yourself and help the salvage boat.

Know the procedure for accepting and using the aid of the salvage boat. If you have to lie off the beach in a loaded condition for long hours (and you will) remember the beachmaster is having one hell of a job and wants you unloaded as much as you want it.

'6. You are a part of the Combat Force and before we get to Tokyo, a member of a boat crew will be as respected as a paratrooper for daring and endurance.

'7. In the confusion of battle don't spread rumors and report only facts that exist,

'8. Don't be discouraged by the mistakes of others. The tide of battle might be swayed because you stayed on the job and did it right. The Jap has a reputation for dying because he loses. Most of us will live in winning.

3 Waterproofing

The problem with amphibious landings is that any equipment landed by its own means has to be waterproofed. Tanks, AFVs and personnel carriers, trucks, jeeps: everything will succumb to flooding or have its performance reduced. Flooded engines may hold up egress of shiploads of crucial material, so this was a subject that wasn't taken lightly by the Allies. The table on pp. 214–215 gives an idea of the actions taken to waterproof vehicles and then, just as critical, to remove the waterproofing once landed to stop overheating.

Tanks and armoured vehicles were of particular importance, as their involvement during the battle for the beachhead was often crucial. There were three areas of development: true submersible tanks (which the Germans favoured); amphibious tanks using flotation devices (such as the DD Shermans); and tanks equipped with wading facilities—such as the ducts illustrated opposite. All hatches and openings were sealed with black waterproofing resin.

Right: An 18th Panzer Division PzKpfw III Ausf J medium tank negotiating a river crossing—probably the River Bug in June 1941. The Germans worked hard on creating submersible tanks for the invasion of Britain.

Below: Tigers had the capability to travel underwater to a depth of around 15ft after half an hour's preparation. The snorkel could fit onto the commander's cupola or rear decking.

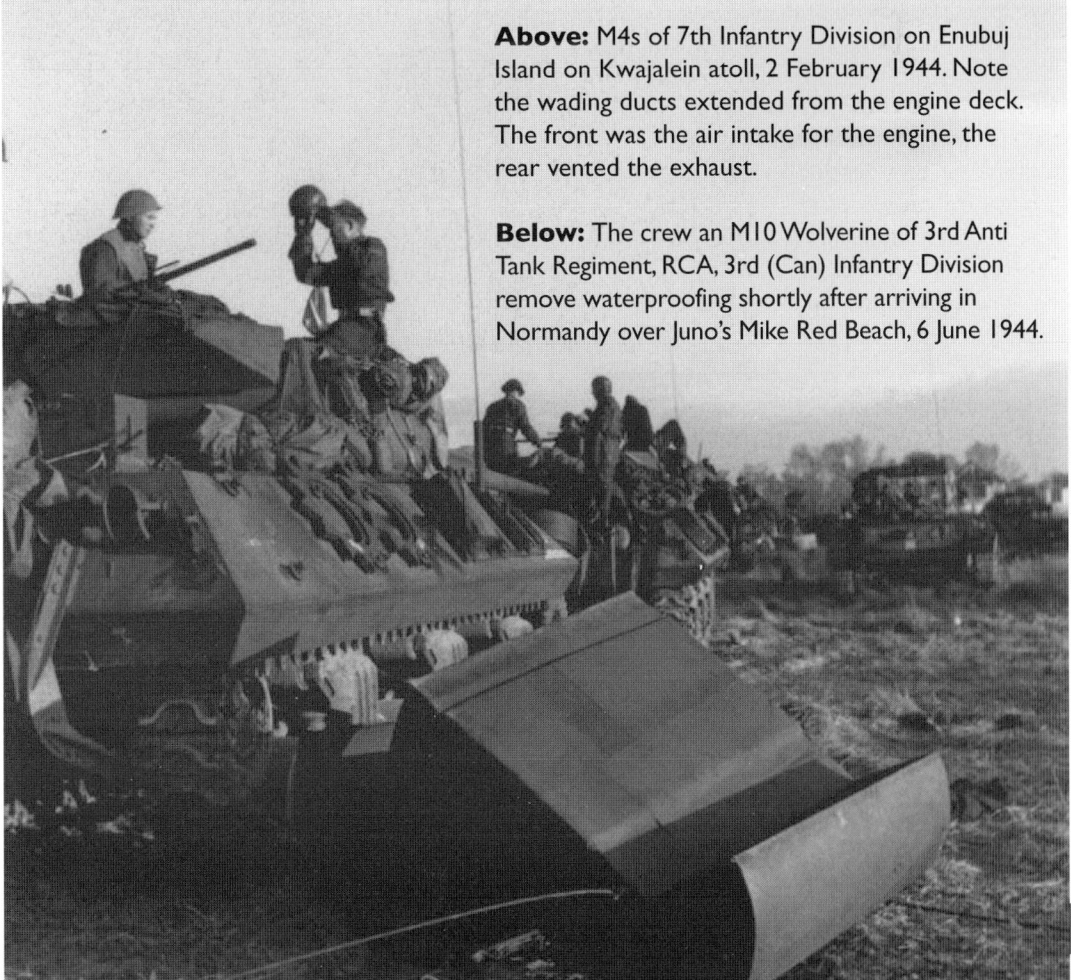

Above: M4s of 7th Infantry Division on Enubuj Island on Kwajalein atoll, 2 February 1944. Note the wading ducts extended from the engine deck. The front was the air intake for the engine, the rear vented the exhaust.

Below: The crew an M10 Wolverine of 3rd Anti Tank Regiment, RCA, 3rd (Can) Infantry Division remove waterproofing shortly after arriving in Normandy over Juno's Mike Red Beach, 6 June 1944.

Type of vehicles	Stage	Description	Max subsequent distance	Time taken	Where done	By whom
B vehicles for all formations	Before embarkation A	Major preparation	200 miles	3 days	Concentration area	Unit drivers under formation REME supervision except RASC units under their own technical supervision
	Before embarkation B(i)	Semi-final preparation	20 miles	6 hours	Marshalling area	Unit drivers under static REME supervision
	Before embarkation B(ii)	Fitting of waterproof ground sheet, sealing engine and distributor breathers	1–2 miles	15 mins	Vicinity of point of embarkation	Unit drivers under static REME supervision
	After crossing C	Preliminary de-waterproofing	200 miles	–	Beach transit area	Unit drivers. Max distance from beach to Stage C is 2 miles, but groundsheets will be removed immediately on landing.
	D	Final de-waterproofing: general inspection and complete lubrication	–	–	As soon as conditions permit	Unit drivers and formation REME
A vehicles (heavy). Tanks and SPs for all formations	Preliminary work	Fitting weldware	No restriction	–	By REME or manufacturers before issue	
	Before embarkation 1	Maintenance and inspection. Sealing hull, turret etc., fitting hardware, cowls, etc, greasing internal parts and testing in fresh water pit etc	100 miles	70–84 daylight working hours	Concentration area	Crews, fitters and electricians
	Before embarkation 2	Final adjustments, fitting extensions to air intake and exhaust etc	20 miles	6–8 hours	Marshalling area	Crews, and for some vehicles, fitters and electricians
	During voyage 3	General attention to details (vide Wading Instruction Book)	–	–	On craft	Crews

	4, 5 & 6	In accordance with Instruction Book		off—as tactical situation demands	—beach transit area or where possible (Does not affect performance.)	
A vehicles (light). Carriers, armoured cars, scout cars for all formations	Before embarkation 1	Inspection and maintenance, cleaning waterproofing engine, sealing hull etc. Testing in fresh-water pit.	150 miles	49–70 daylight working hours	Concentration area	Crew, fitters and electricians
	Before embarkation 2(a)	Semi-final preparation eg stowage bins, sealing visors, lamps, etc	20 miles	4 hours	Marshalling area	Crew, and for some vehicles, fitters and electricians
	Before embarkation 2(b)	Final preparations, sealing breathers, etc	½ mile	15 minutes	Vicinity of point of embarkation or on craft	Crew
	During voyage 3	General attention to details (vide Wading Instruction Book)	—	According to duration of voyage	On craft	Crew
	After landing 4, 5 & 6	Removal of stage 2 (vide Wading Instruction Book)	No restriction	Beach transit area	As soon as conditions permit	Crew

MARKING OF VEHICLES TO SHOW COMPLETION OF WATERPROOFING STAGES

Colour	Meaning	Where affixed	By whom affixed
Blue	That STAGE A has been carried out	Unit lines or concentration area	Formation REME or RASC officer or NCO supervising unit waterproofing
Yellow	That STAGE A has been checked and STAGE B(i) carried out by the unit	Marshalling area	Static REME officer or NCO checking unit waterproofing
Red	That STAGE B(ii) has been carried out by the unit and that vehicle has been passed for embarkation	Port of embarkation	Static REME officer or NCO checking unit waterproofing
White	That the vehicle cannot be waterproofed	Unit lines or concentration area	Formation REME or RASC officer or NCO supervising unit waterproofing

Above: The Soviets also examined using flotation screens on tanks. These are T-37A amphibious tanks travelling across a river in the 1930s.

Below: Universal carriers of 1st Dorsetshire Regiment, 231st Brigade, 50th Division wade ashore from landing craft on Gold Beach, 6 June. Note the built up sides—a set of steel panels with locking stakes—to allow deep wading.

Above: The original work on the Nichlas Strassler's invention—the Duplex Drive and flotation screens for tanks—was on the Tetrach in 1941. 625 Valentines were converted and some from B Wing of 79th Armoured Division are seen at the Saltwater Training Wing, Stokes Bay, Hampshire.

Below: These British Shermans of 44th Royal Tank Regiment have their flotation screens down having crossed the Rhine. They are moving inland to support 15th (Scottish) Division. Note the propeller at A.

4 Medical

Beachhead medics filled a crucial position between treatment and evacuation to better medical facilities on ships (hospital or other). The table opposite gives an idea of the numbers of wounded the various landing craft could manage. Source is the *Combined Operations Notebook* of 1945.

Above Left: A US Navy corpsman (left) dresses a back wound on Iwo Jima.

Centre Left: US Navy doctors and corpsmen tend to wounded marines at a first aid station on 20 February 1945. Navy medical personnel began landing on the island on D-day, 19 February, only 30 minutes after the initial landings of the 4th and 5th Marine Divisions. When the men of Medical Battalion, Co A, landed near Green Beach on 28 February, they set up a 110-bed hospital facility. It was finished within 8-hours of their arrival. Evacuating the wounded as the stretcher teams were constantly attacked by Japanese snipers.

Below Left: This LVT was used by the RCAMC to transport the wounded during the Battle of the Scheldt.

Type	Stretcher	Total No of stretcher and walking wounded	Remarks
AKA	15	65	
APA	150	475	
LSI(L)	150	475	
LST(2)	144 In an emergency up to 130 additional stretcher cases can be embarked which, together with 165 walking wounded gives a casualty lift of 439. The numbers embarked, however, must depend on climatic conditions and on the length of the voyage. If serious cases requiring nursing are carried, then the stretcher cases should not exceed 50.	244	All British LST for the Far East are equipped for carrying casualties for periods up to 36 hours. A LST can be speedily adapted for casualty carrying, particularly for a short sea voyage when the demands for surgical procedure and nursing do not require the use of a hospital ship.
LCT(2)	60	110	
LCT(3)	80	140	
LCT(4)	100	150	
LCT(5)	50	80	
LCI(L)		100	
LCI(S)		70	
LCA	6	21	
LCM	12	42	If fitted with wooden frame, will take 21 stretchers
LCP(L)	4	8	Canopy off when using six stretchers
LCP(R)	6	11	
LCP(S)	6	13	Angle iron runners are fitted port and starboard. A small piece is cut from the coaming each side to permit the carriage of stretchers with extension bars
LCV(P)	6	18	
LVT(2)	13	13	Cross beams are necessary for the stowage of this number of stretchers
LVT(3)	3		Absence of springing makes it unsuitable as a casualty carrier
LVT(4)	3		Absence of springing makes it unsuitable as a casualty carrier
M29C2	2	2 or 3	Can take either 2 stretcher or 3 walking wounded
DUKW	7	14	
Terrapin	3	3	Absence of springing makes it unsuitable as a casualty carrier

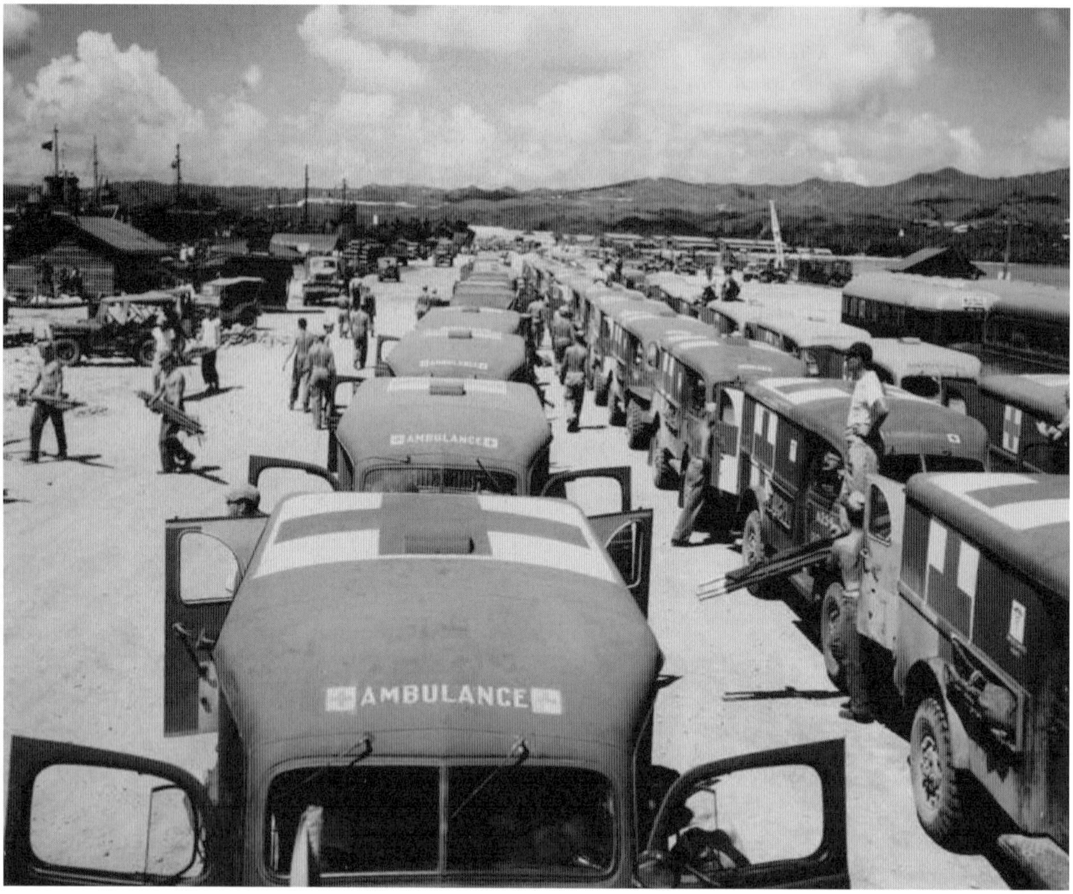
AMBULANCE
AMBULANCE
AMBULANCE

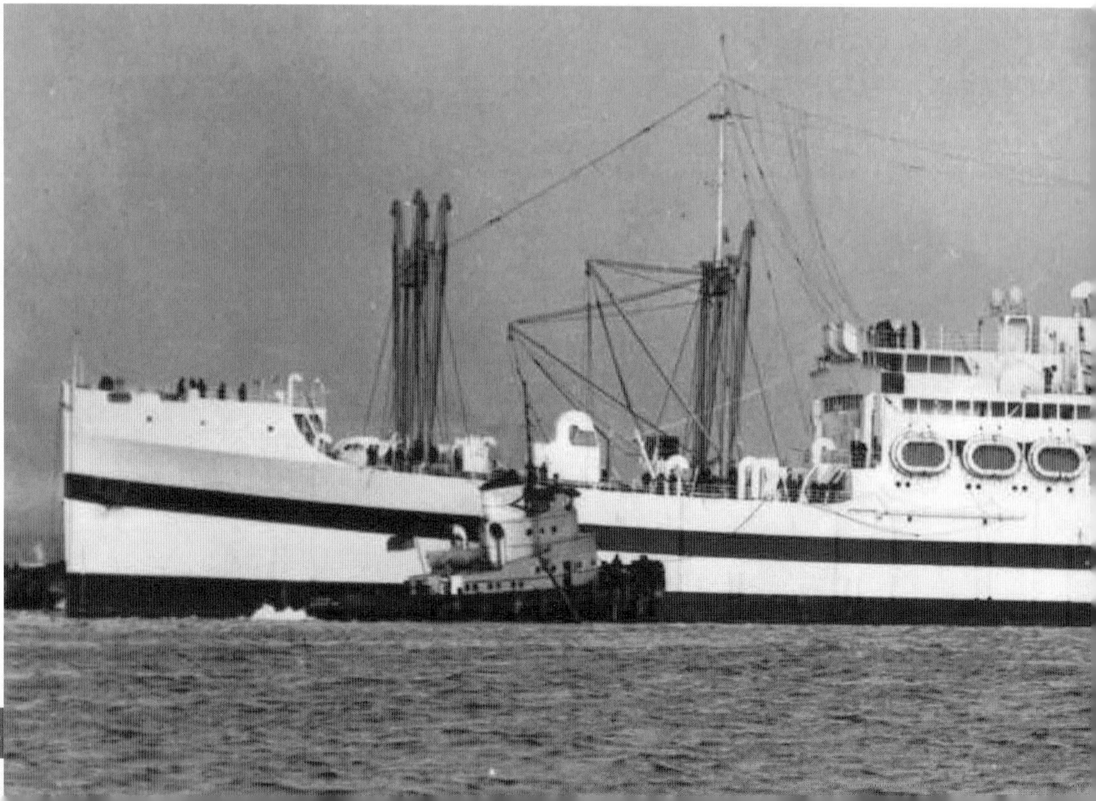

Left: Military ambulances lined up on shore at Guam, awaiting the arrival of US Navy Hospital Ship USS *Solace* with casualties from Okinawa, 4 June 1945.

Above Right: As soon as possible army hospitals are set up on hostile shores. This one is 79th General Hospital at Bayeux, 20 June 1944. Royal Army Medical Corps nurses and women of the Queen Alexandra's Imperial Military Nursing Service (QAIMNS) carry a wounded soldier out of the operating tent.

Right: Wounded Canadian soldiers awaiting transfer to a Casualty Clearing Station on D-Day, Courseulles-sur-Mer.

Below: Hospital ship USS *Refuge* at Baltimore, Maryland, March 1944.

5 Intelligence

REQUIREMENTS
(Edited excerpts from FM 5-31 Landing Operations on Hostile Shores *November 1944)*

'For joint planning, the landing force commander must have certain intelligence as a basis on which to determine the practicability of various landing places and to understand pertinent naval portions of the estimate. Various items of such intelligence are needed in detail by army commanders, to include the lowest echelon. This is this list of requirements that was provided by clandestine operations, often provided by brave men who went into hostile environments under the enemy's noses.

'Beaches.
  (a) Exact location.
  (b) Landmarks in the vicinity visible from seaward (detailed information).
  (c) Length of any portion with clear approaches.
  (d) Gradient of underwater approach as it affects beaching of landing ships and craft. (Includes area especially to line four feet below low water; including fifteen-foot line if practicable. Cross sections are valuable. Location of bars is especially important to avoid unloading of landing craft at points separated from the true beach by depths of water unsatisfactory for personnel or vehicles.)
  (e) Tides (complete statistics; horizontal movement of water line).
  (f) Nature of bottom immediately off the beach (mud, sand, shingle, shell, smooth rock, jagged rock).
  (g) Reefs, shoals, rocks, and other hazards to landing ships and craft.
  (h) Currents, especially near shore.
  (i) Physical consistency (mud, sand, shingle, or rock; difficulty of crossing for foot troops and for tracked and wheeled vehicles).
  (j) Width.
  (k) Terrain immediately behind beaches (dunes, swamp, jungle, cliffs, towns).
  (l) Exits (roads, paths, or cross-country; for men and tracked and wheeled vehicles).
  (m) Landmarks for night movement away from beaches (hedges, walls, streams, fences).
  (n) Nearest cover for artillery positions and supply points.

'(3) Shore lines other than beaches (dimensions, gradient, and physical consistency). Information generally desired is same as in (2).

'(4) Surf conditions.
  (a) Severity of surf (expressed in height and frequency).
  (b) Distance from beach to outmost breakers.
  (c) Number, width, and location of lanes of unbroken water through the surf area.'

COMBINED OPERATIONS PILOTAGE PARTIES

The landings at Dieppe in 1942 had been a disaster: 12 of the 27 Churchill tanks that landed couldn't cope with shingle. It became clear that planners needed to know much more about the beaches on which they intended to land, the geology, the currents, how the beaches shelved—and of course the enemy's fortifications and defences. Photo-reconnaissance and intelligence operations helped, but information from the locations themselves was essential. The answer for the British was the men of the COPP.

The unit was set up as a result of the efforts of Lt Cdr Nigel Clogstoun Willmott, RN. It was based in a depot at the Hayling Island Sailing Club on Sandy Point. Around 10 COPPs were formed between 1943 and 1945 and their complement never rose above 200 men.

Their mission divided into work before and during the operation. Delivered to the area they needed to survey, often by submarine, the teams would use two-man canoes to get close to the beaches before swimming in and surveying the area. They'd identify the shelving, take soil samples, and check on defences at sea and on the beach. On the day of the invasion they would help signal the landing parties into the correct channels. On D-Day they did this from midget submarines.

COPP 1 surveyed the Normandy beaches in 1943; the Operation Dragoon beaches in 1944; and then saw action in the Far East in the Arakan.
COPP 2 also surveyed Normandy coasts in 1943 and then Sicily, Salerno before assisting raiding parties in the Mediterranean (including Elba and Lake Comacchio before Operation Roast), Aegean and Adriatic Seas.
COPP 3 was at Sicily before Operation Husky in 1943 then the Arakan (Akyab Island) followed by Thailand and Malaya.
COPP 4 saw action at Sicily, Italy and in the Arakan.
COPP 5 was at Sicily and Salerno in 1943. They recced the Rhine crossings at Wesel.
COPP 6 worked at Sicily, Italy, Normandy and then the Mediterranean.
COPP 7 were off Burma in 1943, the Far East in 1944. In 1945 they were in Europe, surveying the River Elbe crossing.
COPP 8 operated in the Arakan.
COPP 9 was off Normandy in 1943, then the Mediterranean and the Arakan.
COPP 10 Italy, Yugoslavia, Dalmatia and Greece.
Middle East COPP teams surveyed beaches on Sicily, and at Salerno and Anzio.

Naval Underwater Demolition Teams (UDTs)
Edited excerpts from Observers' and 96th Infantry Reports on the Okinawa Operation, 3 March–9 April 1945.

'**Mission.** The teams were to reconnoiter the approaches to all assigned beaches, remove natural and man-made obstacles and antiboat mines to facilitate the landing of troops and materiel. Specifically, they were given 8 distinct tasks:
1. Reef Conditions: Data, such as the distance of the reef from the beach, depth in feet from the reef to the beach, condition of the reef itself and 10 other vital characteristics were to be obtained.
2. Man-made Obstacles: The type, size, location, number of rows, spacing, intervals, and any evidence of mining were to be reported.
3. Natural Obstacles: All data possible was to be secured regarding these obstacles.
4. Estimates as to the time and ability to remove obstacles were to be submitted.
5. Surf conditions were to be reported.
6. Onshore beach conditions were to be reported.
7. A data chart covering the above was to be completed and submitted.
8. Any other information of value was to be reported.

'**Organization.** A UDT consists of around 7 officers and 65–70 enlisted men. It is designed in general to take care of one beach. The men are all volunteers, expert swimmers, show an aptitude for demolition work and have a working knowledge of landing craft characteristics. They must be able to make accurate charts, obtain correct required data for the charts, and estimate the suitability of the beach for various types of landing.

'**Employment.** A minimum of one pair of swimmers were assigned for every 100 yards of beach with a minimum of two pairs for any one beach. For each beach an additional pair of swimmers were to reconnoiter the edge of the reef, working parallel to the beach. Swimmers were to carry two-hour delay mine exploders to destroy any mines found. Units were embarked in APDs. LCPRs were to be used for the work parties. Each LCPR had 1 officer in charge, an SCR-610 radio and operator, visual signalling apparatus and signalman, and the usual standard boat equipment.

'At R hour the landing craft were to reach the line of destroyers, headed for the beach for the reconnaissance or demolition operations. At P hour the landing craft were to proceed in to pick up swimmers. At K hour the fuzes were to be pulled in the demolition operations. At X hour the landing craft were to be on the destroyer line on their way out from the shore. The above schedule was to be a daily, rigid affair.

'**Results.** UDTs did their work for the 77th Division landings on the Kerama Retto and on L-4 commenced reconnaissance of the Okinawa beaches. From L-3 to L-1 demolitions work was executed. On L Day the demolition personnel reported to the control parties to assist the leading waves of troops to the correct beaches. After L Day all the necessary demolition work was done. Posts which were placed in the reef by the Japs and which had attached demolition charges set to go off when landing craft hit them were successfully removed.'

The 96th Infantry report said:

'It was considered that the enemy would avail himself of all defensive weapons and obstacles to combat our landing. Such obstacles were expected in the form of anti-boat anti-tank, anti-personnel and the inert type mines, dragon teeth, horned scullies and barbed wire. These were expected in density along the reef that in itself proved to be a formidable obstacle.

'Removal of underwater obstacles is a responsibility of the navy and the standard underwater demolition teams were provided as is the practice in amphibious operations. These teams are charged with the clearance of mines submerged close to the beach and take no part in the clearing of the naval mines which are placed only where there is sufficient depth of water for the passage of ships of deep draft.

'The clearing of beach underwater obstacles was to start on L-3 but was delayed as mine sweepers had not completed the task of sweeping the channel. The underwater demolition teams started operation on L-2. The teams made the voyage to that target area in APDs (auxilliary personnel, destroyer) and transferred there into small boats (LCPRs) which took them near the reef. They then swam to the reef reconnoitered and destroyed by demolition charges such obstacles as located. They had a dual role of reconnaissance of reef and beach as well as removal of obstacles. No man made obstacles were located on the 96th Division beaches, however, 'information gathered was of great value. Seven officers from each division accompanied the underwater demolition teams. Each assault battalion, assault regiment, and the division provided one officer. These officers were returned to the ships in which their unit was embarked on the afternoon of L-I where their information was transmitted to the unit commander.

'No casualties were suffered by any underwater demolition teams attached to the 96th Division although their reconnaissance reached to the beach itself. The swimmers of underwater demolition teams were rendered almost invisible by painting their bodies with silver paint and wearing silver colored bathing suits [see photo **Below**].'

6 Beaches: control and construction

At first, attacking a beach looks to be about overwhelming enemy defences, countering their air and artillery assets and getting a foothold. Of course, it's not as simple as that. First, the beach has to be usable by ships, vehicles and a lot of men. Next, it has to have suitable exits. Obstacles have to be cleared—natural or placed by the enemy. The beach has to be suitably marked so that those arriving know where to go. There needs to be someone in charge who can control the beach, organise the removal of casualties and PoWs, and coordinate the arrival of men, equipment, vehicles and stores.

The intelligence and obstacle removal was handled, as shown in Appendix 5, by the COPPs and UDTs. The command and control function was handled by a beach party. In the case of the British, this was the RN Beach Commandos. The Americans (per *FM31-5 Landing Operations on Hostile Shores*) had shore groups and the Engineer Special Brigades.

RN Beach Commandos: The beach commander coordinated the flow of incoming and outgoing landing craft. RN Beach Commandos had to secure the chosen area in advance of the commander's landing. Each of the beach commando groups—denoted by letters rather than numbers, from A to W (the latter being all-Canadian)—numbered around 70 with 10 officers and 60 ratings, the officers including the principal beachmaster (usually a lieutenant commander), a deputy and three beachmasters. Each commando had an HQ and three units, one for each landing area. The beach commandos were responsible to the high-water mark of a beach; the army was responsible above that. As an example of how it worked on D-Day, on Juno Beach three RN Beach Commandos (P, S and U) were involved. The first personnel to arrive recce'd the beach, identified the locations for the beachmasters and assessed the physical nature of the beach. The advance party arrived at H+20 and began to relay information back to the Deputy Senior Officer Assault Group—the Advanced Beach Signal stations should have been working by H+30. Those on Mike Green and Nan Green were, and Nan White just a little later. That on Nan Red was not ready until H+120. The main party arrived and surveyed the beach to choose where the LSTs would come in—all the while assisting with unloading and making good the beach. After the fighting had died down, they cleared the beach obstacles.

US Shore Party: 'This term applies to the composite group of military and naval personnel designed to organize and control beach activities in support of one BLT. It is formed by an engineer shore company from the shore battalion, a naval platoon (beach party) and one communication team from a joint assault signal company. The joint shore party is commanded by the engineer company commander, who exercises control of the beach party through the naval beachmaster. It normally is attached to the landing team until beach operation responsibilities are taken over by higher authority. A shore party may be increased by attachment of other service units available within the shore group. Duties are: (1) Engineer combat group or engineer shore regiment: To unload vehicles and supplies, conduct reconnaissance for roads and supply points, establish and operate initial supply points, provide close defense for beach areas, decontaminate gassed areas (in absence of chemical companies), control beach traffic, stragglers, and prisoners of war (in absence of military police companies), and perform all engineering work on landing beaches, such as clearance of mines and obstacles, construction of beach roads, improvement of beach exits, and operation of equipment to facilitate unloading. (2) Joint assault signal company: To provide communication sections for each shore party; to establish and operate all special amphibious shore communication in the landing assault. (3) Naval beach parties: To perform naval functions on the landing beach, including control of boat traffic, salvage and repair of landing craft, and establishment and operation of initial beach medical installations for care and seaward evacuation of casualties.'

1. First Assault Wave

Two men from the Boat Control Section attached to the Shore Company land and set up range markers—on the centre line of the beach—by which the coxswains in subsequent waves check their bearings. Then from the water's edge they signal these waves in. Shielded lights are used if the attack is in darkness.

2. Third Wave

The forward echelon of HQ Pl of the Shore Co lands. The Shore Co CP is located just off the beach. The Boat Control Sect (regulates boat as distinct from beach traffic) is located close to the CP but far enough away so a single bomb/shell cannot destroy both. From these posts, the recce necessary to organise the beach area is directed. The limits of the beach are marked by shielded lights or large coloured panels

3. Before the Fourth Wave

Suitable landing sites for vehicles are marked. Note the centre one here isn't a track yet. Coxswains in the next wave will bring heavy vehicles to the nearest of these three because they are either free of obstacles or soon to be.

4. Later

By now the Demolition Sect has removed obstacles, and the Construction Sect has developed three roadways. The dump sites have been selected, located and marked. Shore engineers are ready to handle heavy vehicles, supplies and equipment as rapidly as they can come ashore. Beach markers indicating landing points for rations, water, ammunition and for gasoline and oil will be erected to meet the resupply plan. Suitable locations for the Medical Bn's clearing station, motor pool and PoWs have been chosen.

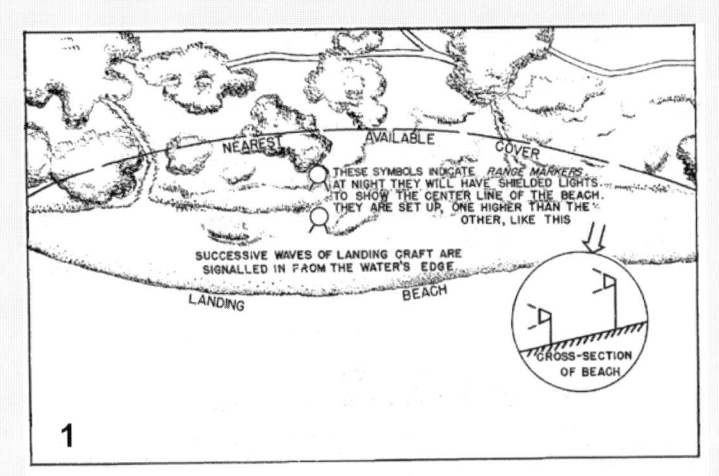

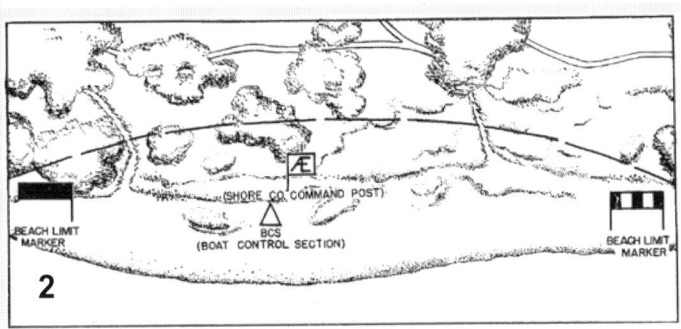

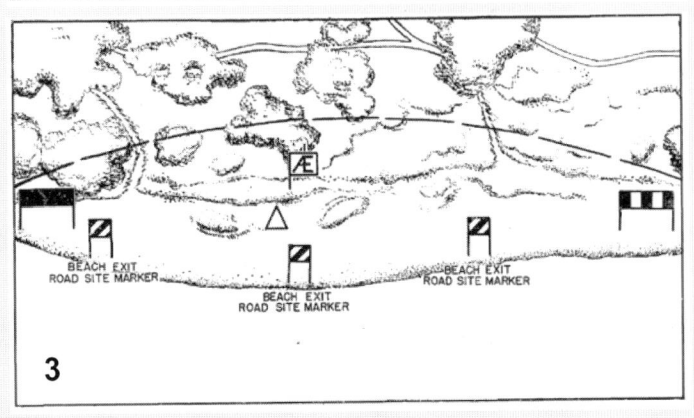

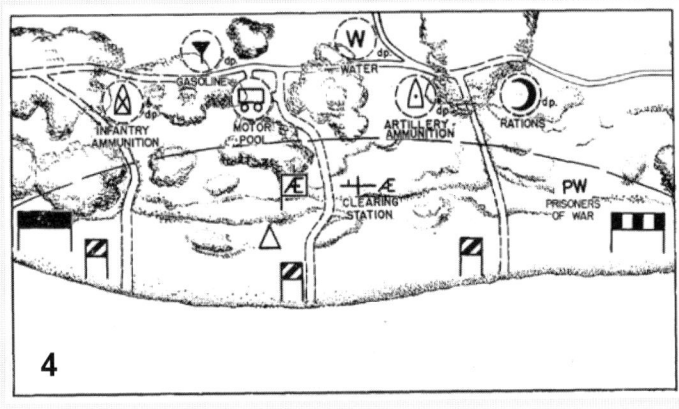

5

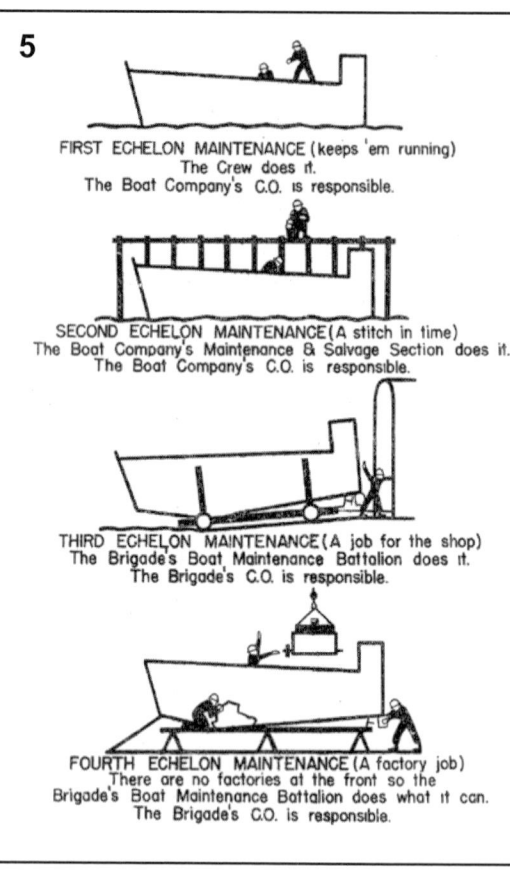

FIRST ECHELON MAINTENANCE (keeps 'em running)
The Crew does it.
The Boat Company's C.O. is responsible.

SECOND ECHELON MAINTENANCE (A stitch in time)
The Boat Company's Maintenance & Salvage Section does it.
The Boat Company's C.O. is responsible.

THIRD ECHELON MAINTENANCE (A job for the shop)
The Brigade's Boat Maintenance Battalion does it.
The Brigade's C.O. is responsible.

FOURTH ECHELON MAINTENANCE (A factory job)
There are no factories at the front so the
Brigade's Boat Maintenance Battalion does what it can.
The Brigade's C.O. is responsible.

1 and 2. The Normandy landings were unique as the Allies brought harbours with them. Each had a 'Gooseberry'—a line of ships sunk to create a breakwater—and the floating Mulberry Harbour. This one is at Arromanches. They were protected by Flak towers (**2**).

3. American soldiers construct ramps to the Mulberry harbour off Omaha Beach.

4. Aerial view of the Gooseberry off Omaha Beach.

5. The four echelons of maintenance for US Engineer Amphibian Troops.

Lessons from Operation Husky

(Edited excerpts from Hewitt report—Points were numbered 1–179; see also pp. 94 95.)

'SHORE PARTY:

106. Training of the Shore Party should include full-scale landing of infantry divisions with supplies and equipment by day and night, practical training in all types of boats and landing craft, and in working cargo on board ship and as winchmen.
107. The Shore Party organization requires immediate reorganization to provide adequate labor troops to unload boats on the assault beaches until the combat-loaded transports have landed artillery, anti-tank weapons, and ammunition replacements.
108. The Shore Party should develop, prior to the assault, detailed plans for the organization and location of beach dumps. Vehicles should be earmarked for beach to dump traffic and these trucks should not be diverted from such employment without the approval of the Shore Party Commander.
109. When assault beaches are backed by extensive dunes without road exits, the Road Construction units of the Shore Engineers must be greatly augmented.
110. The Shore Party Commander must be fully conversant with the unloading plans and his organization must allow for some flexibility in the landing of army stores and equipment at other than planned beaches.
111. The Engineer Shore Regiment should not be withdrawn from the beaches to inland combat positions unless the Commanding General is prepared to accept a complete break-down in his supply system.
112. There is a need for air-raid sirens or warning devices on beaches where large numbers of craft and personnel are employed.
113. More guns of large calibre should be assigned to AA beach defense which should be centrally-controlled on each division beach.
114. Slit trenches and foxholes should be promptly dug on beaches near boat landing points.
115. Mobile firefighting trucks should be part of the Shore Party equipment; fires in beach dumps caused by enemy strafing produce serious losses of maintenance stores unless extinguished by fire fighting equipment.
116. Stores must be segregated in dumps; the piling of ammunition, food, gasoline, and mis-cellaneous stores in one vast mass presents a target to enemy aircraft.
117. Beaches must be kept clear of stores by movement to beach dumps behind the dune line.
118. Greater attention must be given to the prompt erection of beach markers; the marking of safe landing points for DUKWs is important.
119. Prompt clearance and sign-posting of paths through minefields is essential prior to the arrival of DUKWs and motor transport on the beaches.
120. Until the transports are unloaded, DUKWs should not be diverted to the interior beyond the dune dumps; DUKWs may be used advantageously to unload LSTs and merchant ships.
121. Closer coordination and more positivel and-line communications should exist between Army and Navy Medical groups on shore; casualties should not be brought to exposed beaches until boats are available to evacuate them at once.
122. Military Police must keep idlers off unloading beaches or impress them into labor of unloading boats at the shore line. Troops, upon landing, must be directed to properly marked staging areas and not be allowed to loiter on beaches. Military Police must be particularly active at night to prevent unauthorized absence from beaches by Shore Party personnel.'

'BEACH PARTY:

123. Beach Battalions should receive intensive shipboard training of all ratings along pre determined lines.
124. Shore training of Beach Battalions should include basic field training of the soldier, overhead firing and battle courses. Joint training with the Shore Party Engineers should include defensive tactics of the rifle squad and platoon, the detection, removal and destruction of enemy mines and booby traps, removal of wire and beach obstacles, swimming and life saving.
125. The plans of Naval Task Force Commanders should provide in detail for the hydrographic surveys to be conducted at first light off assault beaches, and for the utilization of this information by the Beachmaster.
127. The plans of Naval Task Force Commanders should provide in detail for the boat salvage organization off assault beaches.
128. The Beachmaster should be fully conversant with the attack plans and the unloading plans showing Army priority of items.
129. Beachmaster should be officers of adequate rank, experiences and personality.
130. Personnel of the Navy Beach Battalions should be garbed in a distinctive uniform, and helmets should be marked so as they may be identified on the beaches.
131. Except in an emergency, personnel of Naval Beach Parties should not be diverted from their assigned tasks.
132. Navy Beach Battalions should be provided with adequate motor transport to enable the organization to function on beaches of a wide frontage. They should have as organic equipment 12 jeeps and 10 2/112 ton trucks with 1-ton trailers.
133. Each infantry division beach should be provided with a "Jaheemey" with a bulldozer as a prime mover. The "Jaheemey" must be completely rigged prior to being landed on the beach.
134. Naval Combat Demolitions Units should be utilized in amphibious operations to assist in the removal of underwater obstacles at assault beaches and later assist Beachmasters in salvage, marking of channels, and other offshore work.
135. Beach Parties required to remain ashore for protracted periods should have as additional equipment such items as tentage, bedding rolls, field kitchens, water-making apparatus, etc. Cooks should be included in the complement. Special items as mosquito bars, insect repellents, flea powder, etc., should be provided.
136. Beach Parties should be relieved at the earliest opportunity by Advance Base organiza-tions; Beach Parties normally should withdraw from the assault area with the combat-loaded transports or as soon thereafter as the military maintenance situation permits.'

Above: Seabees installing a floating fuel pipeline off White Beach, Tinian, 25 October 1944.

Below: Men of the 302nd CBs repair a pontoon causeway that broached at Tinian's White Beach during a storm.

Opposite, Above: Canadian 3rd Division Beach Group (note anchor insignia) about to disembark from HMCS *Prince David*, on D-Day.

Opposite, Centre: Mobile construction battalion working day and night during the campaign on Los Negros.

Opposite, Below: Seabees laying steel mats during the construction of a new bomber airfield on Bougainville, 15-19 December 1943.

German beach organisation

Peter Schenk's excellent book on Operation Sealion outlines the German approach to beach organisation:

'beach parties were divided up into units each of which consisted of two officers (a harbour captain and a director of shipping), eight naval NCOs and 32 crew. Fourteen of these units were formed ... they were to lend technical assistance and advice to army and engineering troops in unloading and constructing landing bridges ... Every naval amphibious unit had ... lanterns to mark the landing zones so they could be seen at night.'

Signals

Successful amphibian operations are dependent on successful control. Successful control can be achieved only through good communications. In amphibian operations, boat-to-boat, boat-to-shore and inter-shore communications are involved in addition to normal signal functions. The Signal Company will use: radio (boat control afloat is primarily radio); wire; visual signals (pyrotechnics—flares, rockets; lights—blinker signal lights, flashlights; flags—semaphore flags; panels—2ft × 12ft framed cloth or canvas panels); sound signals (boat whistle or siren; percussion signal sounds); and pigeons.

Vital for every aspect of beach control, the table on p. 229 gives an idea of the sort of equipment required in the early stages of an operation. This comes from the *Combined Operations Notebook* of 1945. (Note, Bmr = Beachmaster; PBmr = Principal beachmaster.)

235

A crowded beach at Courseulles-sur-Mer on 6 June 1944. Engineers are working hard with matting and wood to provide a firm base for tanks of the 1st Hussars.

ORGANISATION OF SIGNAL PARTIES LANDED EARLY IN THE ASSAULT

Serial	Name	Strength Offr-ORs	Main equipment	Lands	Function
RN					
1	Beach signal section RN	2-30	6-46 sets, 2-22 sets 1 Jeep, VS eqpt	With advance parties (6 each) with Bmrs. With main party (2 plus 18) with PBmr.	One section per beach sector includes: 1 advanced station per beach, 1 main station per sector, Provides RN shore-ship communications
2	FOB parties	1-3, 2 Jeeps	1-18 set, 1-22 set	With assault battalion HQ	Observation of naval bombardment
Army					
3	Assault signal sections Royal Signals*	3-48	15-46 sets 12-22 sets	Prior to brigade command on each sector	1 section per assault division subdivided into 3 parties (1 per assault brigade plus 1 in reserve) Sets up assault signal office on beach. For use of successive formation HQs on landing
4	Contact car (air)	1-4	1-TR 1143 1-No 22, 1-No 12	Ditto	1 CCA per brigade headquarters for direction of support aircraft
5	Air support signals unit tentacle	0-4	1-No 12	Ditto	1 tentacle per brigade headquarters to provide an independent signals network for transmission of air support messages
6	Beach brigade signal company (less beach group signal sections)	8-148	?	Approximately divisional level	To provide communications for the beach brigade to higher formations and laterally to adjacent beach brigades
7	Beach group signal sections	4-136	?	Approximately brigade level	To provide all communications within the beach group
RAF					
8	RAF beach signals section	1-10	Pack sets, eg Collins 18Q	Approximately divisional level	To provide communications between RAF beach squadrons and airfields or airstrips captured or constructed

* Special signal units eg contact car air and ASSU tentacles (for general direction of ground attack aircraft) and reconnaissance detachments are attached to assaulting brigades. In general, these land just after tactical brigade headquarters.

Abbreviations

APA	Auxiliary Personnel, Attack; US troopship
APD	US fast transports converted from destroyers and destroyer escorts (AP = transport, D = destroyer)
Bde	Brigade
BLT	Battalion landing team
Cdo	Commando unit; eg No 4 Cdo (army); 41 RM Cdo (navy)
CIGS	Chief of the Imperial General Staff
Cockle	British special forces' kayaks which came in various marks; designed by Fred Goatley. (See p. 48; also Folboat, below)
COPP	Combined Operations Pilotage Parties. See p. 228.
Co/Coy	Company (US/Brit)
CP	Command post
DBLE	Demi-Brigade de Légion Étrangère
DD	Duplex Drive; this powered amphibious tanks (from 1944 mainly Shermans)
EM	Enlisted man (US)
ETO	Eastern Theater of Operations (US)
Folboat	Folding kayak. Many made in Australia by Hoehn and Hedley and used in the Pacific (see p. 49). Not to be confused with Folbot, a company started in England which moved to the US in 1935 and also made folding kayaks
HMNLS	His Majesty's Ship (the Netherlands)
HMS/HMSs	Her Majesty's Ship(s) (UK)
KIA	Killed in action
LC/LS	Landing craft/ships: for full list see pp. 208–210
LCA	Landing craft, assault
LCI	Landing craft, infantry
LCT	Landing craft tank
LCVP	Landing craft, vehicle/personnel (the Higgins boat)
LST	Landing ship, tank
LVT/LVT(A)	Landing vehicle tracked (armoured) In various forms also called amtrak/Alligator/amtank/Buffalo
ME	Middle East as in Nos 50/52 (ME) Cdo
MFP	*Marinefährprahm*; German landing craft
MGB	Motor gun boats
MIA	Missing in action
ML	Motor launch
MNBDO	Mobile Naval Base Defence Organisation. Beach defence unit
MT	Motor transport
MTB	Motor torpedo boat
NEIA	Netherlands East Indies Army
OKW	*Oberkommando der Wehrmacht* (High Command of the German Armed Forces)
OR	Other rank (British and Commonwealth)
OSS	Office of Strategic Services; US Intelligence service
PIR	Parachute infantry regiment
Pl	Platoon
PoW	Prisoner of war
PRCT	Parachute RCT
PTO	Pacific Theater of Operations (US)
RAAF	Royal Australian Air Force
RAF	Royal Air Force (British)
RAMC	Royal Army Medical Corps (British)
RAN	Royal Australian Navy
RCAF	Royal Canadian Air Force
RCAMC	Royal Canadian Army Medical Corps
RCN	Royal Canadian Navy
RCT	Regiment combat team
RM	Royal Marines (British)
RMBPD	Royal Marines Boom Patrol Detachment; cover name for SBS-style unit. Became School of Combined Operations, Beach and Boat Section, postwar
RN	Royal Navy (British)
RNLN	Royal Dutch Navy
SBS	Special Boat Service. Originally the Folboat Troop, then the Special Boat Section. Primarily used (along with COPP) to recce beaches
Sect	Section
SOE	Special Operations Executive. British organisation involved in spying, clandestine operations and supporting resistance movements against the Nazis
SSRF	Small Scale Raiding Force
SW Pacific	The US divided the Pacific theatre into: Pacific Ocean Areas (Supreme Allied Commander was US Admiral Chester Nimitz); the SW Pacific (US General Douglas MacArthur)
UDT	Underwater demolition team (US). See also p. 223
USAAF	US Army Air Forces (became the US Air Force in 1947)
USMC	US Marine Corps
USN	US Navy
USS/USSs	US Ship(s)
WIA	Wounded in action
Z Special Unit	Special forces unit set up in Australia where it trained. Made a number of clandestine mission in the SW Pacific, in Borneo in particular (Operations Python, Agas, Semut, and various Platypus missions) See also pp. 49 and 53.

Acknowledgements and Credits

Acknowledgements

The text includes a number of directly quoted or edited excerpts from works which are identified in the text and covered in the Bibliography. Most of these documents came via the excellent online resources of the Ike Skelton Combined Arms Research Library (CARL) Digital Library. Please note that these excerpts are contemporary and produced based on intelligence available at the time: there will be some, understandable, inaccuracies. Thanks to Leo for introducing me to NARA and the staff in the library in College Park, MD.

Finally, thanks to Tara Moran of Pen & Sword for being such an understanding editor.

Photo credits

Battlefield Historian: 47A, 128, 131B, 205A, 207A, 219B, 222B, 223B, 227 (A&C), 232 (all), 236. *British Official:* 61A; via Martin Warren: 35 (both), 68B, 95 (both), 155 (both/The Clearing of the Scheldt Estuary), 174, 222A (via Martin Warren). *Bundesarchiv:* 12B (146-1970-074-34), 58T (1011-758-0056-35). *Combined Ops Landing Craft:* 205B, 207C, 206 (all), 207 (BL&R), 208, 210 (all), 211 (all). *HMSO:* 32, 36 (both), 37A, 38, 39 (all), 40 (all), 41A, 44, 45 (both), 60B, 61 (all), 72, 73 (all) G Forty collection: 25B, 60A, 62C, 63A, 66B, 78B, 80T, 113T&C, 172A, 177 (both), 188, 189 (via RCT), 191, 215A (Signal), 216BL&R (Barry Hook). *Library and Archives of Canada:* 167A, 201L, 235A. *LoC:* 8A. *NARA:* 2–3, 4–5, 6, 12A, 20, 25T/C, 26, 27, 29, 31, 41B, 42, 43B, 54, 67B, 74, 75B, 76, 82 (both), 83T, 87 (both), 90 (both), 91, 92T, 93 (both), 94 (both), 98 (both), 99 (all), 102, 104B, 105T&C, 106 (both), 107 (both), 108, 109, 110T, 111 (both), 114T, 115 (both), 117 (all), 119 (both), 120T, 121 (all), 122 123C&B, 125B, 127BL&BR, 129, 130T, 132, 134 (both), 135 (both), 137 (both), 138, 139B, 141, 142, 143B, 146 (both), 147, 148B, 149A, 152, 153B, 154A, 156A, 157A, 158C&B, 159 (all), 160 (both), 161A, 162, 163A, 164, 167B, 168A&C, 170AR, 171B, 172B, 195 (all), 200B, 201R, 202 (A&BR), 203 (all), 204 (T&C), 205B, 215, 219A, 223A, 224C, 226 (Both), 229, 234B, 235 (C&B), 238. *Narodowe Archiwum Cyfrowe (Polish Archives):* 59A, 62B, 63B, 64B, 100, 101 (both), 112, 113B, 136 (both), 186C. *Nationaal Archief:* 156A. *Naval History and Heritage Command:* 16, 42A, 68 (both), 69T, 110B, 114B (from Operations of the Seventh Amphibious Force), 154B, 168B, 170AR&B, 176B, 200A, 224A, 234A. *Perry-Castañeda Library:* 51, 53, 56, 78T, 88 (both), 149B, 187 *Riksarkivet:* 50 (RA/PA-1209/U/Uj/ L0205), 57B, 58B (RA/PA-1209/U/Uj/L0219b), 128T (RA/PA-1209/U/Uj/L0213), 130B (RA/PA-1209/U/Uk/0223), 151B (RA/PA-1209/U/Uj/L0214) *SA-Kuva (Finnish Archives):* 80B, 81 (both), 144B, 145 (both), 186B, 212A, 213A. *SArgus Newspaper Collection of Photographs, State Library of Victoria:* 10A, 10B, 11A, 11B, 125T, 126B, 179A, 184, 202BR, 214. *US Army:* 94 (both/Downfall–Olympic), 199 (Intelligence Bulletin Vol iii No 1), 213/232 (Engineer Amphibian Troops). *US Army/CMH:* 62A, 67A, 69C, 71, 75A, 92B, 123T, 127T, 151A, 153A, 161B, 166, 169, 171A, 186A. *US Coast Guard:* 119, 120B, 126T, 131T, 133, 139A, 140, 148A, 158A, 163B, 165. *US Navy:* 103 (Hewitt, Salerno), 104T (Hewitt, Salerno). *WikiCommons:* 8B (http://hdl.handle.net/10934/RM0001.COLLECT.340356); 9A (Anne S. K. Brown Military Collection); 9B (W. Simpson (drawing), E. Walker (lithograph)); 37B (Guycarmeli), 43A, 47B, 48A (RM Museum), 48B (Cobber17), 49A (Calistemon), 49B (AWM), 52 (Adrian Seligman), 57T&C (Bjoertvedt), 58C, 59B (United States Military Academy's Department of History), 65B (Автор: 177 - Собственная работа), 66A (Geographicus Rare Antique Maps), 70 (RAAF), 77T (SpoolWhippets), 77C&B (Anotherclown at English Wikipedia), 83B (United States Military Academy's Department of History), 89 (Oneam: changed to mono), 124, 143T (United States Military Academy's Department of History), 144A (NASA photo; Bobby D. Bryant text), 157B (United States Military Academy's Department of History), 173 (User1781982739981661?2), 176A (United States Military Academy's Department of History), 179 (Eric Gaba – Wikimedia Commons user: Sting), 190 (Wereon), 224 (Provincial Archives of Alberta). *Waralbum.ru:* 213C. *Ww2 Photo Archive:* 212B.

Bibliography

Documents

776 Amtank Bn Operation Report Ryukyu Campaign; July 1945.
AWM 54 Services Reconnaissance Dept Operation Opossum.
Combat Lessons, various.
Combined Operations Staff Notebook; 1945.
Details of Combined Operations Landing Craft and Barges; June 1944.
Details of Combined Operations Landing Craft and Barges Addendum No 1; August 1944.
'Die Schlagader des Brückenkopfes', *Die Wehrmacht*; 1943.
'Downfall' Strategic Plan for Operations in the Japanese Archipelago; 28 May 1945.
Engineer Amphibian Troops, 1943.
FM31-5 Landing Operations on Foreign Shores; War Department, 1944.
Hewitt, Vice Adm H.K.: *Action Report Western Naval Task Force The Salerno Landings.*
Hewitt, Vice Adm H.K.: *Action Report Western Naval Task Force The Sicilian Campaign.*
Intelligence Bulletin, various.
Observer's Report Okinawa Operation.
OKW Directives for the Invasion of UK Operation Seelöwe; retrieved from https://www.ibiblio.org/hyperwar/
Report of the Flintlock Operation; Commander Fifth Amphibious Force.
Report of Luzon Operation (Lingayen Gulf), Philippine Islands; Commander Third Amphibious Forge CTF 79.
Report on the Okinawa Operation; 1945.
Ship-to-Shore Movement General Instructions for Transports, Cargo Vessels, and Landing Craft; HQ of the Commander in Chief US Fleet, 1943.
Special Action Report, Iwo Jima Campaign; 1945.
Special Series 27 Soldier's Guide to the Japanese Army; Military Intelligence Division, 1944.
Staff Studies Operations 'Coronet' 1945.
Staff Studies Operations 'Olympic' 1945.
Supplement to The London Gazette, Friday 8th October 1948.
Tactics and Techniques Soviet Field Artillery in the Offensive; Military Intelligence Division, 1945.
The Clearing of the Scheldt Estuary; 21st Army Group
TM-E30-480 Handbook on Japanese Military Forces; WD, 1944.

Publications

Adcock, Al: *Warships 17: WWII US Landing Craft in Action*; Squadron/Signal Publications, Inc, 2003.
Amphibious Operations August–December 1943; April 1944.
Amphibious Operations January–March 1944; August 1944.
Amphibious Operations 27 March–21 June 1945; 1946.
American Faces in Action Series: Anzio Beachhead; Department of the Army, 1947.
Arnold, W. Shawn: 'Expedient Field Modifications of a WWII Amphibious Landing Craft in Saipan,' The MUA Collection, accessed June 16, 2022, http://www.themua.org/collections/items/show/1190.
Atwater, Charles B.: *Soviet Amphibious Operations in the Black Sea, 1941–1943*; https://www.globalsecurity.org/military/library/report/1995/ACB.htm
Beckman, Kyle B.: 'Personality and Strategy: How the Personalities of General MacArthur and Admiral King Shaped Allied Strategy in the Pacific in World War Two'; thesis Fort Leavenworth, 2002.
Combined Operations, 1940-1942; HMSO, 1943.
Cox, Samuel J.: *H-057-1: Operations Downfall and Ketsugo – November 1945*; Naval History and Heritage Command, 2021.
DeGroot, S.J.: 'Escape of the German Army Across the Westerscheldt', *Canadian Military History*, vol 6 Iss 1, 1997.
Department of the Army Pamphlet No 20-260: *The German Campaign in the Balkans (Spring 1941)*; Department of the Army, 1953.
Farr, Scott T.: 'The Historical Record, Strategic Decision Making, and Carrier Support to Operation Watchtower'; thesis, Fort Leavenworth, 1992.
Hodges, Lt Col Daniel C.: 'Operation Stalemate II'; Thesis, Fort Leavenworth, 2004.
Hoffman, Maj Jon T.: *From Makin to Bougainville Marine Raiders in the Pacific War*; USMC, 1995.
Japanese Monographs No 16 *Ambon and Timor Invasion Operations*; Military History Section, HQ Army Forces Far East, 1953.
Kavanaugh, Maj Stephen L.W.: 'Comparison of the invasion of Crete and the Proposed Invasion of Malta'; thesis, Fort Leavenworth, 2006.
Killeen, Maj Christopher J.: *Operation Cartwheel, 1943–1944: Integrated Force Projection to Overcome Limited Access*; thesis Fort Leavenworth, 2014.
Morgan, Lt Col Henry G, Jr: 'Planning the Defeat of Total War Strategy'; thesis Fort Leavenworth.
Rottmann, Gordon L.: *Battle Orders 12 US Special Warfare Units in the Pacific Theater Scouts, Raiders, Rangers and Reconnaissance Units*; Osprey Publishing, 2005.
Rottmann, Gordon L.: *Elite 117 US World War II Amphibious Tactics Army and Marine Corps Pacific Theater*; Osprey Publishing, 2004.
Kotzampopoulos, Theofanis-Marios: 'British-Greek Special Forces in the Aegean 1943-1945: A Case Study of "Hybrid" War in German-Occupied Maritime Greece; Lancaster University MA thesis, 2020.
Ladd, James D.: *By Sea By Land*; HarperCollins, 1998.
Ladd, James D.: *Commandos and Rangers of World War II*; Macdonald and Jane's, 1978.
Pallud, Jean Paul: *Rückmarsch! The German Retreat From Normandy Then and Now*; Battle of Britain International Ltd, 2006.
Pallud, Jean Paul: 'The Two Invasions of the Isle of Elba'; *After the Battle*; Battle of Britain International Ltd, 2016.
Petersen, Robert K.D.: 'The Real Enemy Scrub Typhus and the Invasion of Sansapor'; Downloaded from https://academic.oup.com/ae/article/55/2/91/2364768 on 12 May 2022.
Rein, Christopher M.: *Multi-Domain Battle in the Southwest Pacific Theater of World War II.*
Shenk, Peter: *Invasion of England 1940 The Planning of Operation Sealion*; Conway, 1990.
Special Series 29 *Japanese Defense Against Amphibious Operations*; 1945.
The Royal Marines The Admiralty Account of their Achievement 1939–43; HMSO, 1944.
Updegraph, Charles L, Jr: *Special Marine Corps Units of World War II*; USMC, 1972.
The Coast Guard at War VI The Pacific Landings; USCG, 1946.

Websites

www.history.navy.mil/our-collections/photography.html (the US Naval History and Heritage Command for their high quality histories and access to photographs)
www.combinedops.com (everything about British Combined Operations)
www.coppsurvey.uk (deails of the COPP)
www.navsource.org/archives/home.html (details of individual ships)

Index of Operations

Accolade, 51, 52, 100
Aerial, 175, 179
Agas, 237
Agreement, 33, 47, 212
AL, 71
Alphabet, 176
Anklet, 34
Anvil, 24
Appearance, 61
Archery, 34
Avalanche, 13, 24, 102–105

Backhander, 114
Baytown, 13, 102
Beowulf II, 64
Biting, 13, 34–35
Blau, 78
Blissful, 89
Blücher, 78–79
Bodyguard, 55
Brassard, 136–137
Brazil, 80–81
Brewer, 122

Cartwheel, 55, 89, 114
Chariot, 38–39
Cherryblossom, 106–107
Chronicle, 89, 114
Citronella, 50
Claymore, 34
Cleanslate, 91
Collar, 13
Copper, 53
Coronet, 194–197
Cottage, 96–97
Crofter, 150–151
Cycle, 175, 178
Cyclone, 126–127

D-Day, see Neptune
Darlington II, 51
Demon, 179–183
Detachment, 162–165
Detained, 51
Dexterity, 89, 114–115
Director, 114
Downfall, 194–197
Dracula, 171–172
Dragoon, 24, 54, 57, 142–143, 228
Dynamo, 175, 177, 178

Eisbär, 100
Endowment, 51
Evacuation of Crete, 184
Evacuation of Fifteenth Army, 187

Evacuation of Odessa, 184
Farrier, 51
Fetlock, 109
Flintlock, 118–120
Flounced, 51
Forager, 132–135, 147
Fork, 60
Fortitude, 55
Frankton, 33, 48, 52
Freischütz, 51

Galvanic, 108–111, 118
Gauntlet, 50
Globetrotter, 127
Goodtime, 89
Granite II, 140

Hannibal, 175, 188–189
Herkules, 190, 193–194
Hurricane, 124–125
Husky, 13, 24, 92–97, 209, 216–217, 228, 233

Iceberg, 14, 29, 168–170
Infatuate, 155–156
Ironclad, 72–73

Jaywick, 49
Jubilee, 44–47, 55

Ke, 185
Kerch-Feodosian Landing Operation, 65
Kerch–Eltigen Operation, 112–113
King II, 152–154
Kirkenes, 150–151

Landcrab, 98–99
Lehrgang, 185–187
Leopard, 101
Lustre, 179

Maoka Landing, 173
Marita, 62
Matador, 157
Maurice, 58–59
Menace, 62
Mercerised, 149
Merkur, 62–63
Michaelmas, 114
Mike I, 28–29, 158–163
Mincemeat, 55
Morsky, 88

Neptune (D-Day), 4, 24, 27, 32, 33, 55, 128–131, 144, 201, 209

Olympic, 194–197
Opossum, 53

Pastel, 55
Platypus, 237
Plunder, 166–167
Postern, 89, 114
Pungent, 157
Python, 237

R, 70
RE, 76–77
Reckless, 122–123
Rimau, 49
Roast, 53, 228
Rösselsprung, 51

Sankey, 157
Seelöwe, 81, 190, 191–193, 198, 212
Semut, 237
Shingle, 116–117
Shoot III, 51
Sickle, 58–59
Southern, 66
Squarepeg, 121
Stalemate II, 147–149
Stevedore, 138–139
Straight Line, 124
Stream Line Jane, 72
Sunbeam, 51–52

Talon, 157
Tanne Ost, 144–145
Tenement, 52
Toenails, 91, 92–93
Torch, 13, 24, 55, 84–89, 202
Tradewind, 146
Trappenjagd, 65
Typhoon, 127

Valentine, 60
Varsity, 166
Veritable, 24
Victor I–V, 158
Vitality II, 155–156

Watchtower, 41–42, 76–77
Weserübung Süd, 56
Weserübung, 56